THE GENERAL WAS A SPY

(Previously published as NETWORK)

Heinz Höhne was born in 1926 and brought up in Berlin; during the war he served in the German Army on the Eastern Front. In 1947 he became a reporter on a Munich newspaper and later joined *Der Spiegel*, becoming head of the foreign department in 1963; he is now serials editor of the paper. His published work includes a history of the SS, *The Order of the Death's Head* (Pan, 1972) and *Codeword Direktor* (Secker and Warburg, 1971), the story of the Communist spy ring Red Orchestra, which will be published by Pan Books in 1973.

Hermann Zolling was born in 1924; he was a paratrooper in the last war and spent some time as a prisoner in the United States. He worked for *Der Spiegel* as editor on secret service and espionage subjects. Hermann Zolling died in December 1971.

D1249000

Also available by Heinz Höhne in Pan Books

THE ORDER OF THE DEATH'S HEAD

HEINZ HÖHNE and
HERMANN ZOLLING

THE GENERAL WAS
A SPY

The truth about General Gehlen and his spy ring

(Previously published as NETWORK)

Translated from the German by
RICHARD BARRY

Introduction by
H. R. TREVOR-ROPER

UNABRIDGED

PAN BOOKS LTD : LONDON

First published in German under the title
PULLACH INTERN
First published in Great Britain 1972 as
NETWORK by Martin Secker & Warburg Ltd.
This edition published 1973 by Pan Books Ltd,
33 Tothill Street, London, SW1.

ISBN 0 330 23516 8

Made and printed in Great Britain by
Cox & Wyman Ltd, London, Reading and Fakenham

CONTENTS

LIST OF ILLUSTRATIONS

(between pages 158 and 159)

IN MEMORIAM

During work on the English edition of this book my colleague and collaborator Hermann Zolling died of a heart attack. It was his idea, using the Federal Intelligence Service as an example, to highlight the problems, opportunities and dangers which any secret service throws up in a modern society. We worked on this project together for two years of detailed and complex research, despite the fact that we sometimes differed both in temperament and in our views. I have known no other journalist who devoted himself to his task with more enthusiasm and devotion. To give one's all for a subject – that, in fact, became a sad reality for Hermann Zolling. This book is therefore dedicated to his memory.

Heinz Höhne

Throughout this translation references to General Gehlen's memoirs are exclusively to the original German edition.

INTRODUCTION

by
H. R. Trevor-Roper

REINHARD Gehlen, founder and head of the Bundesnachrichten-dienst or BND, the Federal Intelligence Service in the days of the cold war, has enjoyed a publicity remarkable for one who, ostensibly (not to say ostentatiously), has fled the limelight. For in the days of his power he always moved in the shadows. He invariably wore dark glasses and a low hat that concealed his face. He approached and left his office by the back door. He allowed false photographs of himself to circulate. And yet, in spite of all these precautions, he has evidently failed in his ambition of anonymity. In his account of his work, he dwells with apparent envy on the methods of the British secret service, whose reigning head is never known to the public or named in the Press. Could this, he asks, happen with us in Germany? Perhaps not, we may reply, if the head of the German secret service makes himself so conspicuous by his secretiveness; if he boasts of his contact with the media; if he seeks to use the press as an ally, or a weapon, in the internal politics of his department; if he allows his organization to be known by his name; and if, in the end, he publishes his memoirs.

Gehlen himself would say that this publicity has been forced upon him. It was Sefton Delmer's article in the *Daily Express* of March 17th, 1952, he says, which, by unleashing a 'flood of further publications', dragged him into the daylight. The public loves a spy-story; it also loves a mystery-man; and in a period of ideological war there are many who love to have someone to hate. Moreover, Gehlen himself has doubled the intensity of feeling about him by being active in two different, if over-lapping, ideological struggles. Once the hunt was up, he could be attacked alike from the West as an old Nazi, employing other old Nazis, and thereby discrediting the 'democratic' West German government, and from the East as an agent of American imperialism, using that government, and the old Nazis in it, to continue Hitler's aims. The former argument is implicit in the article by Sefton Delmer; the latter has been repeated, with fanatical iteration, in the copious writings of Gehlen's most persistent East German persecutor, Julius Mader. The climax of the publicity came when Hermann Zolling and Heinz Höhne published in the German periodical *Der Spiegel* a series of articles about Gehlen. It was those articles, Gehlen now says, which provoked him into writing, in his retirement, his own memoirs. It is those articles which have now been expanded into this book.

Gehlen is certainly a very controversial man; but he is also, it must be admitted, a remarkable man. Apart from anything else, he is remarkable for his power to survive. When his name first came to my notice during the war, he was head of Fremde Heere Ost (FHO), the section of the German General Staff which, through the Abwehr or secret service of the Armed Forces, collected military intelligence about the countries of Eastern Europe. He had held this position since the spring of 1942: the failure of the first offensive against Russia had been fatal to his predecessor, whose intelligence reports had been almost invariably wrong. Two years later it looked as if it would be Gehlen's turn to go. Hitler then decided that the whole Abwehr had failed. He dismissed its chief, Admiral Canaris, and ordered Himmler to create a new unified service under the control of the SS. In the following months, heads rolled throughout the old Abwehr and the SS took over the amputated fragments of its body. But Gehlen somehow survived. His own Eastern organization remained intact within the new system, and he himself became the trusted ally of the SS. This was the first of his survivals. It was a pattern that was to be repeated again and again.

It is true Gehlen was once dismissed; but that dismissal proved a great asset to him. It came three weeks before the end of the war, the outcome of one of Hitler's rages. It had no practical effect except to provide Gehlen with a small drop of anti-Nazi virtue, which he afterwards greatly increased and used to lubricate his next, and most difficult, act of survival: his transformation from Hitler's and Himmler's chief intelligence officer in the East into the Central European expert of the American CIA and, afterwards, the head of the secret service of the Federal Republic of Germany.

The key, of course, lay in the East. If Gehlen had been an intelligence officer on the Western front, we would probably never have heard of him again. But in the East it was different. Circumstances there were special. For when the halcyon days of the Grand Alliance ended and the Iron Curtain dropped, cutting off half of Germany and all of Eastern Europe, the Western Allies had almost no sources of intelligence behind it. During the war, inevitably, they had left military intelligence there, like military operations, to their Eastern ally. So, when the Eastern ally became, potentially, the Eastern enemy, they were at a great disadvantage. Their disadvantage was Gehlen's opportunity. The Germans alone had had an intelligence system which had worked continuously in the vast area now dominated by Russia. Gehlen had controlled that system. He had controlled and used it effectively. The very fact of his dismissal by Hitler was proof of his efficiency, for Hitler had resented the discouraging accuracy of his reports. And finally the very fact of German division strengthened his hand. For intelligence purposes, a divided country is a natural bridgehead. East Germany was a natural recruiting ground for West German agents, which only a system controlled by Germans could fully exploit. The formula could also, of course, be reversed: as Gehlen was to find.

With the visible imminence of the Cold War, the opportunity was clear, and Gehlen's tactical skill lay in his seizure of it. This book shows, in detail, how he seized it and how, through every crisis, he contrived to preserve his position: how he persuaded first the Americans, then the Federal Government of Dr Adenauer, that he alone could provide intelligence from the East; and to what extent he provided it. It also shows the price at which these Western governments bought that provision, and the internal manoeuvres by which Gehlen ensured the continuation, and expansion, of his personal power.

Part of the price was, of course, that Gehlen was, or had been, a Nazi and was believed to continue into the Adenauer era not only the methods but also the contacts which he had discovered and used when he had served Hitler. Naturally the Russians would seize on this fact, in order to exploit the doubts of Western moralists – although, being themselves realists, they do not apply this severe morality to their own political actions. Allen Dulles and Adenauer would no doubt have had an answer to this objection. Gehlen was certainly a Nazi in his mental structure, and it is clear from his memoirs that even today his only objection to Hitler is that he lost the war. However, most German professionals of his time had this mentality, and it could be argued that what was needed in 1946 was, above all, a professional. The British did not like Gehlen, and preferred to back a more virtuous *amateur*. The result was not a success. The ruthless Gehlen soon destroyed (with his own aid) the more sympathetic Otto John.

More serious was the objection that Gehlen recruited into his service other Nazis who perhaps, as they were less professional, were more objectionable than himself, and that, as it grew in power, the organization used Nazi methods to protect itself against internal enemies. One of the most interesting parts of his book describes how Gehlen, having at first kept his distance from the ex-SS men, gradually recovered confidence and brought them into his organization – and how, after the disastrous Felfe trial, he was obliged, in order to avoid damaging publicity, quickly to pay them off.

Why did Gehlen's power so grow? This book makes the answer quite clear. Whatever extensions he added to it, with his excursions into Asia, Africa, South America, and the Near East, the centre of Gehlen's system was always, after as during the war, espionage against Russia in Eastern Europe. He lived on the Cold War and on the favour of those American and German governments which believed in the primacy of the Cold War. This need not be held against him, or them. The Cold War was a historical fact, perhaps a historical necessity. If Western governments had not hardened their postures in the decade after the Second World War, Germany, and with it Western Europe, might well have been subverted and conquered by Stalin. This being so, no Western government is to be blamed for taking what may have been the only means of filling a vital gap. It is legitimate to use Beelzebub to drive out Satan. What can be deplored, and what those Germans who were determined to clear German politics of the Nazi taint did both deplore and oppose, was the large measure of irresponsible power which these governments, in their anxiety, allowed to Gehlen: a man whose philosophy – as shown by his own book – was narrow, whose past was tainted, and whose methods reflected that past. This book shows how Gehlen, by his personal courtship of Adenauer, gained a central position, responsible, through the State Secretary Hans Globke, to the Chancellor alone. Since Globke himself was widely distrusted for his past services to the Nazi Party, this made Gehlen's privileged and secret activities even more suspect.

However, the proof of the pudding is always in the eating. Ultimately, any secret service justifies itself by results. How well did Gehlen in fact serve his Western masters? How fully did he justify the huge budget which he obtained, the power and the privilege which he exercised? Gehlen himself, of course, makes large claims; but they are curiously vague and undocumented. Those who read his memoirs* will also find that they leave much out. There is, in that book, a curious lack of proportion. Two-thirds of it is spent in describing the author's history, and that of his organization, up to 1955 – ie, up to the year in which the Gehlen organization at last achieved its long-pursued aim and became the official secret service of the Federal Republic. The events of the next twelve years, the period when it acted as such, are squeezed into one chapter; and the rest of the book consists of not very profound general-

* All my comments on Gehlen's memoirs are based upon the German text, *Der Dienst* (von Hase & Koehler, Mainz & Wiesbaden 1971). H. R. T-R.

ities. Those who seek a reason for this falling-off in the memoirs will find it, amply documented, in Messrs Höhne and Zolling's book. The falling-off in the detail of the memoirs is directly related to the falling off of the efficiency of the BND.

There is a certain momentum in the history of secret services which, I believe, is accentuated by their secrecy and compounded by their privilege. Espionage is always at a disadvantage compared with counter-espionage, for the former depends on individual skill in hostile surroundings, while the latter operates on home ground, supported by the ample resources of the state. Successful espionage therefore requires continual regeneration: fresh thought, constant vigilance, continuous adaptation to changing circumstances. Only thus can it keep the advantage which it may have gained by initial enterprise. But the privileged secrecy of a secret service, which can protect its members from the strain, or the stimulus, of regular criticism, operates in the opposite direction. The chief of a secret service, who knows that he has this additional protection, is inevitably tempted to exploit it. He is the priest of a mystery, guarded by ritual formulae and sacred taboos, which it becomes second nature to invoke when success is lacking or small failures need to be attenuated or covered up. Only a great failure, which cannot be so concealed, can finally break through the protective wall which successive uncorrected small defects may already have silently rotted.

In its early days the Gehlen organization certainly enjoyed some successes, which are here recorded; but from 1958 the decline in its efficiency is clear. There was a series of small failures. Then, in 1962–3, came the great failures. First came the 'Spiegel affair' of 1962 – Gehlen's attempt, in an alliance of convenience with the periodical Der Spiegel, to ruin Adenauer's Defence Minister, Franz Josef Strauss. This led to a public scandal. Those who enlist the media in their private battles must expect publicity, and although Strauss was destroyed, so was the old alliance between Adenauer and Gehlen. Then, in 1963, came the trial of Heinz Felfe, which showed that Gehlen's whole organization in East Germany had been penetrated by the 'enemy'. Finally, in 1963, Adenauer retired and was replaced as Chancellor by the unsympathetic Ludwig Erhard, who loved neither Gehlen nor espionage. Erhard even evicted the BND's liaison staff from the Chancellery attics: he refused 'to live under the same roof with these people'. With the heart of his empire rotten and his external patron gone, Gehlen's days were numbered. He was allowed to serve out his time, but the legend had been destroyed and, after he had gone in 1968, a government inquiry revealed the nepotism, the scandal and the ineptitude that had thrived in a privileged private empire sustained and protected from criticism by the political conjuncture of the Cold War.

Such is the story told in this highly readable book, which rests on a fine combination of historical scholarship and journalistic resources. It is, I believe, objectively written, with fairness and political understanding. It is also, in some sense, a moral story, concerning the function, purpose and method of secret intelligence. But that moral I shall not try to draw. The authors have left it to the readers, after they have studied the evidence here fairly set out.

GLOSSARY

BfV	Bundesamt für Verfassungsschutz – Federal Internal Security Office. An organization set up in West Germany in 1950 under Dr Otto John to keep extremist tendencies, whether of the Right or the Left, under surveillance.
BND	Bundesnachrichtendienst – Federal Intelligence Service or West German Secret Service. The title of Gehlen's organization after its acceptance as a West German governmental agency.
BV	Bezirksvertretung – District Agency. A third-level office in Gehlen's organization, responsible to a GV (qv) and in charge of a number of UV (qv).
CIA	Central Intelligence Agency – the main United States intelligence organization formed after the war.
CIC	Counter-intelligence Corps – the counter-espionage organization of the US Army.
FHO	Fremde Heere Ost – Foreign Armies East. The section of the German army staff which dealt with intelligence on the Russian front and in Eastern Europe during the war. Commanded by Gehlen from April 1st, 1942.
GRU	Glavnoye Razvedyvatelnoye Upravlenie – Main Administration for Intelligence. The title of the Russian Army staff's secret service.
GV	Generalvertretung – General Agency. The senior-level office in Gehlen's organization below the Pullach headquarters. The main operational outstations.
KGB	Komitet Gossudarstvennoi Bezopasnosti – Committee for State Security – the Russian Secret Police.
KgU	Kampfgruppe gegen Unmenschlichkeit – 'Anti-inhumanity Combat Group'. A private organization formed in West Berlin after the war, exploited by the US intelligence organization.
MAD	Militärischer Abschirmdienst – Military Security Service. The counter-espionage organization of the Federal (West German) Armed Forces.
MfS	Ministerium für Staatssicherheit – the East German Ministry of State Security.
MGB	Ministerstvo Gossudarstvennoi Bezopasnosti – the Russian Ministry of State Security.

NOB   Nachrichtenoffizier Berlin – Intelligence Officer Berlin. A German intelligence agency set up during the First World War with the specific purpose of obtaining information on Russia.

NTS   A Russian émigré organization set up after the First World War.

OKW   Oberkommando der Wehrmacht – High Command of the Armed Forces. The supreme directing organization of the German armed forces under Hitler during the war.

OSS   Office of Strategic Services. A United States wartime organization formed for intelligence and sabotage purposes. After the war disbanded and absorbed into the CIA.

RSHA   Reichssicherheitshauptamt – Reich Central Security Department. The SS organization set up in 1939 under Himmler and Heydrich to deal with all security and police questions in Nazi Germany.

SD   Sicherheitsdienst – Security Service. The SS Security Service – subordinate to the RSHA.

SDECE   Service de Documentation Extérieure et de Contre-Espionage – the French post-war secret service.

SED   Sozialistische Einheitspartei Deutschlands – Socialist Unity Party. The communist-run government party in East Germany.

SSD   Staatssicherheitsdienst – the East German State Security Service.

UV   Untervertretung – Sub-Agency. The fourth-level office in Gehlen's organization. Responsible to a BV (qv) and in charge of a number of 'Filialen' (local branches), the actual directing offices for agents.

VfK   Verwaltung für Koordinierung – Administration for Coordination. The cover-name for the intelligence organization of the East German armed forces.

PROLOGUE

IT was a world-wide sensation; there was general suspense; fears of political revelations were in the air. On Sunday September 5th, 1971, the *New York Times* announced that Reinhard Gehlen, the former legendary German spy-king, had written his memoirs and that they would be published shortly. The world's secret-service men pricked up their ears, and everyone interested in politics, whether historians or not, waited impatiently for the views and revelations of one of the most mysterious figures of the last thirty years. Many politicians of the Social-Democrat/Liberal coalition in Bonn, tenaciously pursuing their Eastern policy, were agitated by the announcement of Gehlen's 'Now it can be told' book. Alongside Franz-Josef Strauss, Axel Springer and Baron Guttenberg, Reinhard Gehlen was one of the West German anti-communists *par excellence*. Would he try to mobilize the people, and therefore the 1973 electors, against the new policy?

Rumour ran rife. Gehlen, generally thought to be an almost omniscient expert in German and international politics, was about to 'spill the beans'. The great tight-lipped man would expose Social-Democrats like Gustav Heinemann and Egon Bahr as 'Trojan horses' of the Kremlin. Professor Horst Ehmke, Minister in the Federal Chancellery with overall authority over the BND (Bundesnachrichtendienst – Federal Intelligence Service), sent Gehlen a personal letter reminding him that even a retired head of the BND was still bound by the security regulations governing state or official secrets. In reply Gehlen assured him that he would not violate this official ban – nor did he.

The local representatives of the CIA, the American secret service, in Bonn and Munich went to their friends in the BND's headquarters at Pullach to ask what Gehlen had written and what attitude he had adopted in his book to the Eastern policy of the Bonn coalition. The men of the BND could only shrug their shoulders; even the headquarters staff under General (retd) Gerhard Wessel declared that they knew nothing of the precise contents of the memoirs. One BND official said of Gehlen: 'He sat beside Lake Starnberg and wrote and wrote and wrote.'

However, when the German newspaper *Die Welt* gave an expectant public the first extract from Gehlen's memoirs, *Der Dienst*, on September 11th, 1971, historians raised their eyebrows, experienced secret-service men shook their heads and senior politicians in Bonn turned, re-assured, to their routine business. There was widespread incredulity and scepticism. This could not be true: here was Reinhard Gehlen, until 1945 head of the German Wehrmacht's 'Foreign Armies East', after the end of the war head of the 'Gehlen Org' which spied in the East on behalf of the Americans, and from 1956 to 1968 President of the BND, the West German secret service, telling all he knew – and the most important piece of knowledge which a lifetime of secret service had given him was that Martin Bormann, Reichsleiter of the Nazi Party and Hitler's confidant, had been an agent of Stalin, that after the war Bormann had lived in the Soviet Union 'under perfect cover' and had died there in subsequent years. Gehlen's substantiation of this story is 'In the 1950s two reliable pieces of information made me certain . . .'

The editors of *Die Welt* (who had paid 450,000 marks for the serial rights) asked urgently for further facts to support this somewhat surprising theory about Bormann; they met with a cold refusal from the memoir-writer on Lake Starnberg. *Die Welt* had no alternative but to issue editorials playing down Gehlen's version of Bormann's whereabouts – 'Conclusive proof is lacking' – 'Too many questions about Bormann remained unanswered' – 'Innumerable hot trails'.

Horst von Glasenapp, a Frankfurt investigating judge who is still hoping to track Bormann down, immediately asked Gehlen to record his secret information on the Nazi leader, and the Federal government gave Gehlen permission to make a statement. In 1946 or 1947, Gehlen said, one of his contact men had seen the weekly newsreel in an East Berlin cinema; it included a sporting event in Moscow and during the film the camera had swung along the mass of spectators in the stadium. Gehlen's man had detected Bormann among the crowd. This was all Gehlen's statement to Glasenapp amounted to. Moreover, he was not prepared to make the statement (which ran to four foolscap pages) on oath.

Die Welt was embarrassed and the public disappointed by the later serialized extracts from the Gehlen memoirs. The 'Grand Old Man' of German espionage proved to be a somewhat unproductive source both for the historians and for the secret-service experts. In fact his material was so meagre that Dr Herbert Kremp, the editor of *Die Welt*, had to use his own editorial staff on time-wasting research. They had to fill the gaps and correct the historical inaccuracies left, deliberately or otherwise, by the man whose motto was 'Now it can be told'. The German illustrated newspaper *Die Stern* commented as follows on this attempt to give substance to Gehlen's book: '*Die Welt*'s team is making use of the *Spiegel* series "Pullach intern" [extracts from the present book] which contains severe criticism of the conduct of his office by the author of these memoirs.'

Die Stern's comment reveals the motive which led the hitherto taciturn Gehlen to commit his reminiscences to paper. In a series of fifteen issues appearing from spring to summer 1971 the German news magazine *Der Spiegel* had described the rise, the achievements, the weaknesses and the mismanagements of the spy-king Reinhard Gehlen; it had destroyed the mystic legend which he had so carefully preserved for decades. Upon Gehlen fell the ultimate responsibility for what millions could read in *Der Spiegel*: crisis had overtaken the BND, West Germany's espionage organization. Franz Josef Strauss, Chairman of the Christian Social Union, considered the BND 'practically incapable of functioning' and was unwilling 'any longer to be a spectator of this betrayal of secrecy'. Horst Ehmke, Minister in the Federal Chancellery, 'indignantly' rejected Strauss' statements as 'irresponsible'; the Chancellor intervened; Fritz Baier, a Christian Social deputy, called upon the Attorney-General to act. On everyone's lips was the question put by the Vienna newspaper, *Presse*: 'Is Bonn's intelligence service in ruins?'[1]

Many would have answered the question in the affirmative. The *Kölner Stadtanzeiger* reported: 'The crisis in the German secret service cannot be pushed under the rug by all the denials from Bonn or assurances from Ahlers, the government spokesman, that the Federal Government has full confidence in Wessel, the President of the BND; the *National-Zeitung* of Basle commented: 'Unless the government can remove the impression of laxity on the part of the BND, it will soon be able to save the money spent on this service'; the *Neue Bildpost* even stated: 'According to expert opinion, by surrendering its most important secrets the BND has become practically paralysed. Observers in Bonn say that the BND has collapsed.'[2]

Such forthright comments were the result of the extracts from the present book published in *Der Spiegel*. They had revealed a reduction in output which the BND leaders had been unable to make good ever since the organization had been toppled from its previous peak of efficiency by a series of catastrophes (construction of the Berlin Wall, the '*Spiegel* Affair' and the Felfe case) and by shortcomings at the higher levels. In fifteen issues of *Der Spiegel* the authors of the series had attempted to give chapter and verse for the reasons which made reform of the West German secret service a matter of urgency.[8]

The shrill reaction to these revelations, however, showed the continuing German inability to deal rationally with secret-service questions. The general public in West Germany is not mentally prepared to voice an opinion on intelligence matters. It is neither adequately informed nor has it the necessary understanding of the subject – and without that no country can cope with the age-old problem of 'democracy and secret service'.

The comments made illustrate the perplexity which overtakes the West German citizenry when confronted with a secret official machine such as the Federal Intelligence Service. Many are plagued by a feeling of impotence aptly summarized by the socialist Bundestag deputy Martin Hirsch in the phrase: 'If they tell us some tale, we cannot even recognize it as such.'[4] Torn between terror that the secret service might be a secret police in disguise and unthinking overestimation of the efficiency of secret-service activities, many West Germans feel that they are pursued by BND agents tapping their telephones and prying into their correspondence; they do not realize that the BND is only allowed to gather intelligence abroad. For many the letters BND have become synonymous with spying and intrigue.

Many would agree with Chancellor Erhard, who showed his aversion to all espionage services by expelling the BND liaison staff from the attics of the Chancellery with the words: 'I do not wish to sit under the same roof as these people.' Hardly anyone reflected, however, that Erhard was thereby giving proof of that naïve non-political mentality which had led Leo von Caprivi, the Reich Chancellor of 1890, to discourage all attempts to form a political secret service and leave the only existing secret service in the hands of the military. In Germany it has never been regarded as 'quite nice' to concern oneself with secret-service matters.

People preferred to leave the BND and secret-service questions in general to the sensational writers and the dramatizers of the cinema, the radio and television. Both the politicians and the historians gave the whole field of espionage a wide berth; no scientific treatise was available to tell the Germans of the strengths and weaknesses of this profession; the history of the German Secret Service was not regarded as a subject for historians. Only the official chroniclers of other interested secret services provided some details – and they were generally angled and embroidered.

Initially even the chiefs and masters of the BND were confused. Horst Ehmke thought that the BND worked 'in the twilight somewhere between the old "Eastern Intelligence Section" of the General Staff and

James Bond, 007'.[5] Before assuming office Dieter Blötz, Vice-President of the BND, turned to the enemy for enlightenment about the rudiments of secret-service work.

Finding that the West German bookshops had nothing to offer him about the work of the BND, Blötz took home with him an East German propaganda publication, Julius Mader's book *Nicht länger geheim* [No longer secret]. Blötz, the tyro, however, found this disquisition on 'Development, system and methods of the German imperialist secret service' by the official scribe of the East German Ministry of State Security to be as unrewarding as Ehmke had found *Die anonyme Macht* [The nameless power] by Gert Buchheit, a West German author with some secret-service background.[6]

The lack of published material on the subject of espionage has a simple historical explanation. For decades the German secret service had been a preserve of the military and they had effectively warned the Press against prying too closely into the espionage business. It was no accident that war censorship, as practised ever since 1870, had been invented by the Prussian/German secret service; in the First World War the Army Press Office, which was subordinate to the military secret service, had been responsible for censorship. After the liberal interlude of the Weimar period military censorship was again exerted in secret-service matters from 1933 onwards. At a meeting in the Reich War Ministry on January 11th, 1935, it was decided that: 'Publication in newspapers and periodicals of spy novels or reports is forbidden.'[7]

When the SS laid hands on the secret services, public interest in intelligence matters was totally stifled. All curiosity vanished in face of the nightmare of Gestapo and SD [Sicherheitsdienst – the SS Security Service]; espionage became a lethal field which no German would willingly enter. Even years later the effects of the Gestapo's reign of terror were such that both politicians and scholars put the secret services out of their minds as far as possible. For the majority of Germans espionage remained a dirty business, a stamping ground for shady characters.

Such an attitude, however, is a luxury which no present-day society can afford. Secret foreign intelligence has become an indispensable instrument of any national foreign policy, although admittedly it can also be the source of an increase in the influence exerted upon the top-level leadership of the State by authorities subject to no control. Nevertheless the secret service is among the few certain factors upon which the peace of our world depends. An inefficient secret service can carry a large share of responsibility for a political crisis of world proportions, because it has denied a government knowledge of the potential and intentions of foreign states, without which no successful foreign policy can be conducted. Professor Harry Howe Ransom, the American espionage theorist, has said: 'Accurate secret intelligence is a key to success, particularly in a period of complex tensions.'[8]

Applying this to Germany's situation, it means that the Federal Republic requires an efficient secret service if it is not to be exposed to unnecessary external dangers. So long as the Soviet Union, with its overpowering might, is located on German soil and so long as the inward-looking social system of the East is a source of potential danger, the Federal Intelligence Service must attempt to give Bonn forewarning of the intentions and relative strength of the communist camp. Observation of the Soviet railway network, an infallible indication of Russian troop movements, is as important in this sense as the registration of tiny changes in the climate of Moscow's policy towards Germany.

The existence of a secret service would, of course, be easier to defend, were it not for its potentiality of becoming a twin-headed monster. Being by definition a secret organization, it is prone to beget dark, barely fathomable, forces. Frequently the government itself does not know what it is doing in the secret-service field; the purpose and scope of secret-service activities are not discussed at cabinet meetings – for fear that someone might violate the security regulations. In such semi-darkness, however, individuals whose names the nation has never heard can exert an inordinate influence on government decisions with no controlling authority to stop them.

Is the Federal Intelligence Service so constituted that it can avoid these dangers? Is it in a position to do its job properly? The authors of this book have pursued these questions, the answers to which may assist in forming a judgement on the question of democracy and the security of the Federal Republic. In a work of research lasting over a period of years they have examined the history, the methods and the personnel of the BND; they have recorded matters never before published – conversations with senior officers and section heads of the BND, reports from agents and resident organizers, statements by both executives and victims of the secret services.

It is right that this whole complex of problems should be clarified since for a long time the BND was no normal secret service. More than any other espionage organization in the Western world it was a product of the East-West cold war, immune from any public control. Its annual budget was never discussed on the floor of the Bundestag; its position in the state was fixed by no parliamentary law. The BND's accounts are audited merely by three members of the Federal Budgetary Committee and the Chairman of the Federal Accounts Chamber; only six Bundestag deputies, the members of the Confidential Parliamentary Panel on the Secret Services, have some small insight into the organization's methods and staffing.[9]

The BND is accordingly more influential than was the military secret service in Adolf Hitler's Great German Reich. It does not in fact represent the 'monstrous underground power in Germany' which the London *Daily Express* once suspected it to be.[10] Nevertheless its informers are to be found in practically every authority, association and organization in West Germany; although the BND was intended only for intelligence-gathering in foreign countries, it followed up so many internal political trails that many a West German nonconformist felt that he was being spied on. In particular, in the Adenauer era the Social Democrats had every reason to complain of the BND's activity. Many of the BND's Old Guard, brought up in the nationalist and conservative world Greater Germany's officer corps, regarded Social Democrats as communists in disguise.

In fact the Federal Intelligence Service has never been authorized to snoop in West German internal politics. Foreign countries alone were always intended to be its field. The BND is intended to assist decision-making in Bonn; its task is to assemble information from every walk of life in a foreign country, to obtain a picture of the situation and collect intelligence, primarily on East Germany, the Soviet Union and the rest of the Eastern bloc; it is also intended to prepare analyses on countries of the Third World, to record changes in the policy of allied or neutral states, to help governments friendly to Bonn or win them over to Bonn's policy by providing secret-service assistance and to protect the interests of the Federal Republic wherever the Bonn government cannot officially appear in the open.

In other words, the BND's area of operations begins at the point where the West German government and diplomacy can no longer legitimately gather information or influence the policy of a foreign country; frequently, therefore, of necessity it works on the fringe of legality. 'We are the nation's muck-spreaders,' a West German secret-service man once said. 'If the dirt shoots up too high, the people in Bonn hold their noses. If we protect the Republic from a barrage of muck, people say: "That's what you're there for."

Lieutenant-General (retd.) Gerhard Wessel, however, President of the BND since May 1st, 1968, likes the smell of flowers. Everywhere in the two-storeyed building in Pullach near Munich which houses the BND headquarters, he surrounds himself with flowers – flowers on the

lunch-table, flowers in the garden behind the block where he has his
office, flowers on the window-sill arranged by Frau Wessel. On the wall
to the left of Wessel's desk, with its four telephones, hangs a map of the
world and in front of him, above the sofa for visitors, a 4 ft by 3 ft 6 in
photograph of the Berlin Wall at the Brandenburg Gate, the border of
the BND's No 1 area of operations – East Germany.

Wessel is a £9,000-a-year man; he has a full-time staff of 5,500 consisting of officers, civil servants and employees in equal proportions. Of
these, 3,000 work in the Pullach headquarters and a further 2,500 in
out-stations in West Germany or as resident members of German diplomatic missions abroad. Only a few hundred BND executives work in the
most secret department, the branch known as 'Agents operating in
enemy territory', which includes all agents and organizers who carry on
the genuine work of espionage worldwide. The number of voluntary
helpers, the so-called 'sources' and 'sub-sources', who also work for the
BND can only be estimated, but it is probably some 10,000, not counting casual sources used only on a single occasion.[11]

The annual budget on which Wessel's intelligence service operates is
no less secret. The official version is 'over 100 million marks'; unofficial
hints from BND officials indicate 150–180 million; Western secret-service experts estimated 450 million – probably too high. (For comparison
Washington's CIA spends $1.6 thousand million, Moscow's KGB $2
thousand million and London's SIS £7 million.)[12]

From Pullach innumerable threads run out into the country, forming
a widespread network of relationships and contacts covering the entire
Republic. There is hardly a sphere of German activity in which the
Federal Intelligence Service does not have a finger. Wessel's BND is the
parent firm for numerous business undertakings, all properly registered
with the taxation authorities and chambers of commerce; it is active in
the coffee import trade and in shipping lines; it works in the retail trade
and dispatches representatives for insurance firms and publishers.

The President of the BND is the head of the only Federal concern
selling refrigerators – and this is not all: many Germans have bought
ballpoint pens and motor-car fittings from the BND without realizing it.
Shops offering washing-machines or carpets for sale have back rooms
which are in fact reception and dispatch centres for agents, couriers and
organizers. Customer traffic in front conceals transit traffic behind. In
secret-service jargon these are known as cover firms.

In Bremen one day a man drove a tanker up to the premises of a used-
oil firm in order to dump some oil. He was not in luck; a gentleman of
the Company assured him that for the moment the firm's storage ca-

pacity was fully employed. Anyone trying to order bananas from a firm in Hamburg shown on its doorplate, in the telephone book and in the business register as fruiterers is told that the customer list is over-subscribed. Wherever the business and its salesmen apparently have no intention of doing anything, the firm with its visiting cards is no more than a façade for the maintenance of contact with agents, tipsters, investigators and recruiters. This is known in the secret service as a dummy firm.

In other places enterprises have been established such as 'Research Association Ltd', 'Society for Economic and Scientific Relationships', 'Press Cuttings Bureau' or 'Press Information Service'. In these research is in fact carried out, contacts are formed with the business and scientific worlds, newspaper articles are cut out and conversations are held with journalists. But the firms work only for intelligence purposes.

These secret undertakings deduct employment tax and social-security contributions for their employees; the dummy firms even declare value-added tax for business which has never taken place. Finally all over West Germany the BND assiduously pays rent for a number of two-room apartments. These are known as 'safe houses' and are in fact meeting points for agents and organizers.[13]

Beneath this camouflage is to be found the BND's network of Main Stations, Outstations and Substations. Frequently several subsidiaries of the BND are at work in the same place independently of each other; they exist in practically every medium-sized city and certainly in all the major cities of the Federal Republic. Overall there are one hundred outstations in West Germany, the largest being in Munich, Bonn, Köln, Frankfurt and Hamburg. The staff of the outstations varies from five in most cases to twenty in others and 50–100 in the large stations. From these – not from the Pullach headquarters – the organizers direct the agents all over the world.[14]

Dummy firms and cover firms, dummy offices and safe houses form the meshes of an intelligence network covering the entire world, its threads all running to the Federal Republic. The BND's acquisition of intelligence on foreign countries begins in West Germany.

Like a great masonic lodge, the BND maintains its friends and promoters wherever it can – in official institutions, in newspaper and radio editors' offices, in journalists' associations, in industrial undertakings and in the import-export trade. The BND requires, and is given, either officially or casually by nationals of the country concerned, identity cards and passports, contacts with foreign correspondents and the entrée into foreign businesses. Industrial and business firms, primarily those concerned in the export trade, give cover to members of the BND as their representatives and so enable them to act as observers throughout the world. They also encourage members of their firms to work for two masters – the firm concerned and the West German Intelligence Service. Members of the BND are to be found in companies with connexions in Africa, the Middle East, South America and the Far East. They canvas university professors for academic recruits.[15]

In the Federal Republic the BND's technicians listen to radio and radio-telephone traffic as far east as Siberia, using a chain of 150-ft-high radio masts along the East German border. The system of radio links is spread even wider around the Soviet bloc. Should warlike signals be received one day, a network of agents and radio operators would be activated behind the advancing Eastern bloc armies both in East Germany and the Federal Republic; between the Rhine and the Oder standby circuits have already been organized. All are provided with radio sets little bigger than a cigar box, though with very considerable range.[16]

All over the world the Pullach headquarters has recruited friends to help the BND. It maintains a direct teleprinter line to America's secret-service headquarters; it exchanges material with the secret services of all NATO countries; through its own legally resident members it observes relationships between its allies and East Germany plus the Soviet Union. For the event of war it has its emergency headquarters on the Atlantic coast of a Western country, including its own airfield and a port from which to withdraw to the USA.

The BND has been adept at helping itself. In 1958 it equipped the King of Saudi Arabia's palace guard with revolvers and walkie-talkies (for this the head of the 'Org' was rewarded with a golden sword and his interpreter with a gold watch). In 1961 it provided the opponents of Lumumba, Prime Minister of the Congo, with a printing press and courier aircraft. In 1965 it assisted Indonesia's military secret service to suppress a left-wing *Putsch* in Djakarta, delivering sub-machine-guns, radio equipment and money to the value of 300,000 marks. It awarded decorations to its foreign friends – to Hyung Wook Kim, for instance, the head of the South Korean secret service; he was later the instigator of a kidnapping affair in West Germany and was honoured with the Federal Service Cross. (In 1969 the BND were successful in persuading Kim to pardon and release the Koreans who had been sentenced in the meantime.)[17]

There is hardly a country of the non-communist world with whose secret service the BND is not in touch. It works with Israelis, Turks, Persians, Pakistanis, Swedes, Japanese, Formosan Chinese, South Americans and Afrikaners. Moreover, as its government directive requires, it maintains business relationships with countries which can hardly be said to subscribe to liberal democratic principles – Spain, Greece, South Africa and Afghanistan. In the process the BND frequently gave its friends information on West German citizens. The South African secret service, for instance, obtained from Dinser, the local BND representative, confirmation that a certain German woman journalist was politically unobjectionable before the lady was given an entry permit. The American CIA obtained the views of the BND on Germans wishing to emigrate to the United States.

This plethora of relationships, contacts and sources enables the BND to catalogue every development of importance in the world. Through its resident organizers, report centres, 'Dead letter-boxes' and courier stations, the raw material collected abroad flows into the Pullach headquarters, where it is processed. There begins what in secret-service jargon is known as 'intelligence production'.

William R. Raborn, former director of America's Central Intelligence Agency, has described this as follows: 'Intelligence, as we use the term, refers to information which has been carefully evaluated as to its accuracy and significance. The difference between "information" and "intelligence" is the important process of evaluating the accuracy and assessing the significance in terms of national security.'[18] In the BND this is the task of two divisions: Division I (Collection) and Division III (Evaluation). The intelligence-gatherers of Division I are concerned with description of source, appreciation of source and authentication; their colleagues of Division III analyse and fit the report into the overall picture.

From this process emerge the regular products of secret-service headquarters: the BND Intelligence Review and the BND Foreign Situation Report (daily), the BND Weekly Report, Situation Reports East and Situation Reports West; in addition there are monthly analyses, country studies, memoranda, forecasts and 'trend analyses'. These are then forwarded by secret channels and finally reach the 'customers', the first of which is the Federal Chancellery, then the Foreign Office, the Federal Ministry of Defence, and the Federal Internal Security Office – to cite only the most important. Items of particular sensitivity from the point of view of West German security are reported verbally by the President of the BND at the 'Chancellor's briefing conference' which takes place in the Palais Schaumburg every Tuesday morning.[19]

Such an organization disposes of secret knowledge which makes it an influential, but possibly also a dangerous, partner. During the Adenauer period, for instance, the BND became far too heavily involved in internal political intrigue and rendered far too frequent service to its many friends. One such friend was Hans Globke, State Secretary of the Federal Chancellery, Konrad Adenauer's *éminence grise*. For the information of Globke the BND, contrary to regulations, formed its own 'internal bureau', supplied with intelligence by agents from the political parties, the trades unions, refugee associations, economic concerns and official authorities. Armed with this knowledge, Adenauer could play private and party politics. Both his allies and his opponents were frequently dumbfounded and sometimes horrified at the secrets he knew: they originated from the BND.

In the mid-1950s the BND reported to the Chancellery that during an official trip to Paris Franz Blücher, the Vice-Chancellor, had visited a brothel. Adenauer's comment to Blücher was: 'Had it *got* to be a coloured girl?'

Such details, revealed in the *Spiegel* series, were inevitably alarming to Gehlen; he, after all, was responsible for the fact that the internal intelligence activities of his organization produced these and other similar spicy pieces of information. Even in retirement, however, Gehlen was still a good tactician and his come-back was to load the Social-Democrats in Bonn with responsibility for the ruination of the BND. In this he received powerful assistance in November 1971 from Gerhard Löwenthal, superintendent of Channel 2 of German television and a representative of extreme right-wing opinion in West Germany. In the periodical *Dialog* Löwenthal mounted the following attack: 'Certain statements were "purged" from BND reports on Eastern contacts of leading Social-Democrats ... which the BND's intelligence activities had uncovered. Information on BND operations with details in clear of sources used were demanded by Egon Bahr (State Secretary of the Chancellery) and were given to him; at the demand of the Chancellery a list of all cover firms and other camouflage arrangements had to be prepared. The Chancellery therefore possesses this, as it does complete details, with names in clear, of all senior personnel of the service. This is information which the particularly sensitive Pullach headquarters ought never to have released.' This was the reaction, via Löwenthal, of Gehlen's friends to the 'possible breach of secrecy by *Der Spiegel*', in other words to *Der Spiegel*'s sharp criticism of Gehlen.

The question arises how so mysterious an organization has developed and how it has contrived to maintain itself in a society striving for everything to be above-board and democratic. The answer could be supplied by a man who lives on the Starnberger See and keeps his own counsel. It is he who, more than any other individual, has built up that secret service which was once regarded as the best in Europe – Reinhard Gehlen, the founder and first President of the BND.

Anyone who wishes to learn the history and development of the BND must turn his spotlight on Gehlen, for the career of this 'Grand Old Man' of West German espionage is largely identical with the history of the BND. It is a story of professional spies and idealists, a story full of intrigue, opportunism and professional brilliance, a story unique even in the bizarre history of European espionage – a warning and a lesson for any democratic society which wishes to remain master of the faceless men.

Reinhard Gehlen had a unique opportunity to write this chapter of German history. When he was succeeded by Wessel as President of the BND in 1968, the new regime in Pullach, the coalition government in Bonn and his friends of the CIA all felt the lack of some form of war diary of the Gehlen Org and the BND – in fact a history of the West German secret service. Wessel, Carstens, the State Secretary of the Chancellery, and Helms, the Director of the CIA, asked Gehlen to write something on the lines of the Wehrmacht's war diaries; it was to be 'Top Secret' and used only for internal official purposes. Both the BND and the CIA were prepared to make the necessary material available from their archives. Gehlen, who had been promised a special retirement salary by the CIA, agreed and set to work. In doing so he was guided by the political creed to which he had always remained faithful: 'I regard communism as a mortal danger and completely reject its entire body of ideas.' (To counter this 'mortal danger' Gehlen had welcomed, on his own admission in his memoirs, such peculiar allies as Spain, Greece and Turkey, whose dictatorial systems Gehlen, the German general, whitewashes with remarks about order and decency.)

About the turn of the year 1970–71 Gehlen, then writing beside Lake Starnberg, received not only information about, but also actual copies of, the *Spiegel* series 'Pullach Intern'. Agreement had been reached between the authors of the series and Carstens, the former State Secretary, that before publication the series should be submitted to BND headquarters, not for political censorship but to check whether it revealed any official secrets. *Der Spiegel*'s authors had kept to this agreement but, contrary to an assurance given to one of the authors by Blötz, Vice-President of the BND, copies of all the *Spiegel* manuscripts had been sent to Gehlen on Lake Starnberg and he therefore had prior knowledge of the criticisms of his leadership that the series contained.

Following his own inclinations and urged on by his friends, Gehlen thereupon decided to emerge from his silence and reply to the *Spiegel* series with a book of his own. Naturally a publisher (von Hase & Koehler of Mainz) was quickly to hand and *Die Welt* bought the serial rights; the international book trade made stupendous offers. Gehlen accepted and turned his half-finished war diary, based on the BND's and CIA's archives, into a would-be bestseller for publication. Has Gehlen, therefore, made good use of his unique opportunity of stripping the secret service's faceless power of its sinister connotation, of making the secret service respectable as a legal instrument of the democratic state and so making it attractive as a profession for an intellectual elite drawn from this society?

Fortunately the authors of the present book have no need to provide their own answer to this question. Of all the critisms of the Gehlen memoirs few were so mercilessly severe as the review published in the German weekly *Die Zeit* – and it must have hit Gehlen all the harder in that the senior leader-writer of *Die Zeit* is Marion Gräfin Dönhoff, for years one of the favoured and trusted journalists whom Gehlen occasionally invited to tea and cakes.

Theo Sommer, deputy editor of *Die Zeit,* described Gehlen's attempt to 'justify' himself with the words 'A monument destroys itself' and he continued: "Gehlen whitewashes, glosses things over and angles them.' Moreover *Die Zeit* realized that Gehlen had another target besides his own self-justification – the Eastern policy of the socialist/liberal coalition in Bonn. Sommer wrote: 'His pen was apparently charged with vitriol and he was guided by an ideologically motivated distrust of the new Eastern policy.' According to Sommer, Gehlen clearly has no comprehension of the problem of integrating a secret service into the machinery of state in a democracy, particularly in post-war Germany; he says: 'Gehlen finally has the presumption to claim for the secret service a position as outrider for the diplomats, "probing and investigating without commitment" in matters of foreign policy. This idea is completely fantastic ... Such notions are only explicable in the light of a professional aberration peculiar to the secret service – the urge to progress from omniscience to omnipotence. This was the dream of Fouché, of Himmler and of Beria. It has no place in a democracy.'

Die Zeit is no less severe in its literary criticism of Gehlen's book; it is entitled *Der Dienst* [The Service], though Thomas M. Walde thinks that it should have been called 'I am the Service'. *Die Zeit* describes Gehlen personally as follows: 'So this man, long held to be the embodiment of modesty, reveals himself as the victim of an outsize ego, to whose nourishment his book is unconsciously required to contribute – "I initiated ... I gathered around me ... I continued with a clear conscience ... I as the German responsible for it all ... I proposed ... I decided ... politicians briefed personally by me ... I for my part ... my principles ... I as its Chief ... I demand ..." Gehlen presents himself as the heroic superman.' To anyone who criticizes him – the authors of the present book, for instance – Gehlen ascribes 'lack of perception and deficient capacity for judgement'.

Die Zeit certainly did not make light of Gehlen's book. It was left, however, to another Gehlen expert, W. O. von Hentig, ex-officer and diplomat, to draw the final conclusion from the Gehlen memoirs: 'Anyone looking for sensational revelations will be disappointed by the book; even more disappointed will be the historians who, contrary to earlier forecasts, will find themselves presented merely with facts and opinions widely known from the press and other books and primarily of a party political nature. Gehlen's only revelation is that the BND was a party tool of Globke's and that he (Gehlen) regarded the CIA as his model ...'[20]

The fact remains that Reinhard Gehlen, the General and founder of the BND, is a figure in contemporary history. A witness to his period he is not – that is clear to anyone reading his memoirs. Millions of readers were awaiting a 'Now I speak' book. The greatest service Gehlen could have done himself would have been to preserve his silence.

1

MAN IN THE SHADOWS

HIS enemies regarded him as the most dangerous man in Europe, his admirers as an intelligence genius. Nothing less than magical power was ascribed to this 'spy of the century';[1] he allegedly knew everything; no steel safe or secret file seemed secure when he was around. Stories were woven round him whenever he appeared, noiseless on rubber-soled shoes and invariably concealed behind dark glasses. He seldom presented himself under his true name; throughout his period in office he hardly gave a single interview; he shunned photographers.

He surrounded himself so successfully with an aura of secrecy and anonymity that superficial observers thought him capable of almost anything. A French author suspected him of being 'the real Chancellor of the Federal Republic'; an American writer saw him manipulating the levers of power of even the United States and firing tiresome espionage generals in Washington; a German émigré of the Hitler period thought that the coup of July 20th, 1944, would have succeeded had Gehlen been the conspirators' leader.[2]

The Press invented an almost inexhaustible stock of nicknames to describe his activities. In the Swiss *Weltwoche* he was 'A faceless man'; the *Westdeutsche Allgemeine* christened him the 'Man with a thousand ears'; for the *Welt am Sonntag* he was the 'Man in the Shadows'. Ex-Lieutenant-Colonel Friedrich Wilhelm Heinz, one of his rivals, characterized him as 'the product of an intellectual love-match between Mata Hari and General Ludendorff'. His indefatigable enemy, the East German writer Julius Mader, described him as the 'grey hand' whose malicious activities strangled peace and progress in Europe.[3]

This protean being is Reinhard Gehlen, Major-General (retd), until 1968 one of Bonn's most senior civil servants [Ministerialdirektor], in the Second World War head of the General Staff Section 'Foreign Armies East' (Fremde Heere Ost – FHO], subsequently founder and first President of the BND. He can be sure of his place in history. Together with Wilhelm Stieber, Walter Nicolai, Wilhelm Canaris and Reinhard Heydrich, he is among the great figures in the history of German espionage – and he did not suffer the fate of his predecessors who all lost control of the machine which they had created when at the pinnacle of their careers.

Gehlen can also lay claim to a number of other unique achievements. In the Second World War he knew more about Russian war potential than any other man outside Russia; in 1945–6 he was the only German general to take his entire organization, unpurged and without interruption, into the service of the American super-power; he constructed a West German secret service which for years was held to be the best-informed about the East in the entire Western world.

He successfully accomplished a feat unique in history in carrying the German secret services, untouched, across the gulf of May 1945. Apart from the Post Office and the railways, the BND thereby became the sole West German official institution which can trace its history back, unbroken, into the Prussian/German period. A further unique factor – Gehlen headed an organization for whose members the Second World War never, in practice, came to an end. Ever since Hitler's invasion of the Soviet Union many of Gehlen's staff had been in the front rank of the anti-Soviet crusade and they regarded the Cold War as merely the logical continuation of the war begun in 1941.

The first President of the BND and his closest associates were therefore frequently confronted with a question: what historical and political conditions had enabled ex-Wehrmacht officers, ex-members of the Abwehr [Military Intelligence] and even ex-SS officers to become the secret intelligence-gatherers of a state which had proclaimed total renunciation of the Nazi past?

For twenty-six years Gehlen, now living on his state pension, showed no inclination to enlighten the world at large on how this had come to pass. With his own special brand of myth-mongering he drew a veil over the rise, the triumph – and of course the defeats, the nepotism, the corruption and the fall in output – of the BND.

Long after Gehlen's retirement his strict instructions still held good within the BND: no outsider should gain any insight into this legendary organization. The procedures and the staffing of the BND are still largely secret; only a small circle of initiates knows its structure and internal divisions of responsibility. Not even the history of the BND's parent organization, the General Staff Section 'Foreign Armies East', disbanded in 1945, is allowed to be known. Every ex-FHO officer was instructed to keep his knowledge of the section to himself. Gehlen's reasoning was that any publicized description of 'Foreign Armies East' might enable the enemy to draw conclusions about the BND's procedures – an untenable theory since Moscow already knows all the FHO material. After 1945 the Allies microfilmed the FHO files and they are available to anyone; Soviet historians have been using them for years.[4]

Such smoke-screen tactics were typical of the artificial atmosphere of secrecy with which Gehlen surrounded himself and his organization. While he was working he would often travel under the cover-name 'Dr Schneider' and he liked to be called 'Doctor' by his staff. In his village on the Starnberger See, where he lived down a small lane at No 29, a house bought for him by the US secret service at a cost of 250,000 marks, he never visited his neighbours except at night.[5]

In 1954 Wolfgang Schraps, a reporter for an illustrated newspaper, was told that nobody named Gehlen existed. When he knocked at the door of the secret headquarters in Pullach and asked for the General, a US captain arrived hastily to say that he did not know Gehlen. Schraps replied: 'Perhaps you know a Dr Schneider?' The American said that he did not. He thought for a moment and then asked: 'What was the gentleman you were looking for called?' 'Gehlen,' Schraps answered. 'Never heard the name,' the American threw back.[6]

Gehlen even pressed his own family and his neighbours into his game of hide-and-seek. His son, Felix-Christoph, invariably introduced his father to friends as 'a salesman dealing with patents'; the villagers took a delight in protecting their James Bond from the reporters. Gehlen tells a story: 'I once received an agitated telephone call from the chemist. A suspicious car had been seen and the occupants had been asking for me. So people wanted to warn me.' Gehlen alerted the police who eventually identified the suspicious visitors as radio and television representatives of the BBC. The police and the villagers directed them to an out-of-the-way spot where they certainly found no Gehlen.[7]

This lack of information led writers and journalists to produce an increasingly outrageous series of stories about Gehlen. The list of false assumptions and nonsensical statements became endless. A London paper, for instance, described Gehlen as a member of the Prussian aristocracy, whereas his background was middle-class; Genealogical Handbook gave his birthplace as Breslau instead of Erfurt; one German newspaper maintained that only two photographs of Gehlen existed. One reporter discovered Gehlen to be a spiritual blood-brother of Stauffenberg, Hitler's would-be assassin; another journalist pictured his hero challenging Hitler to a duel – after a quarrel in the Führer's headquarters which never took place.[8]

Only those able to penetrate this safety-curtain of calculated legend and deliberate falsehood gradually came to know the man concealed behind the Gehlen mystery. Instead of a taut pugnacious James Bond they find a man of five feet seven, no longer altogether slim, almost bald and with a grey moustache; in conversation he is somewhat tongue-tied and frequently betrays the isolation in which his life has been spent as the specialist, the intelligence technician, 'the icy epitome of the military monks of the German General Staff' as the American magazine *Newsweek* once described him.[9]

In fact the story of Gehlen can only be told in terms of the military existence which has governed his life. He grew up in the Reichswehr, the 100,000-man army; he was always the pure military expert who would serve practically any regime, unaffected by almost any political or social conditions. The Reichswehr was his home; in the Reichswehr he absorbed the ideology of 'absolute realism of the Service'[10] with which its Commander-in-Chief, Hans von Seeckt, insulated from the democratic tendencies of the time a monarchist corps of officers, hidebound in feudalistic habits of thought and behaviour. The military specialist became the antithesis of the politically committed, the Reichswehr the destination of the sons of a conservative bourgeoisie resisting integration into the democratic republic.

Reinhard Gehlen felt the urge to join the Reichswehr while still at school. He was undeterred even by Germany's 1914–18 defeat with its gloomy prospects for professional soldiers, confiding to one of his schoolmates: 'The army will come back and I shall be an officer.'[11] Later he always recalled his entry into the Reichswehr with pride; never again, he told a visitor, would there be so splendidly trained and so perfectly disciplined a force as the Reichswehr.[12] Nothing seemed more natural to the young Gehlen than to seek his future in military service.

The Gehlens were Prussian traditionalists and faithful monarchists but the officer's profession had not been among their occupations. On the maternal side, however, the family tree of the Flemish aristocrats, the van Vaernewycks, did show a number of officers. For a time Walther Gehlen, the father, had dreamt of a great military career. He became a Lieutenant in 19 Thuringian Field Artillery Regiment and was in garrison at Erfurt when on April 3rd, 1902, he announced that at 5 A M that morning in his house No 63/64 Löberstrasse his wife Katharina Margarete, *née* van Vaernewyck, 'had given birth to a boy who had been given the christian name Reinhard'.

Weak health, however, forced Walther Gehlen to leave the officer's profession. One of his brothers, Dr Max Gehlen, who lived in Leipzig, was a partner in the publishing firm of Ferdinand Hirt and he paved the way for Walther to enter the book trade. Walther Gehlen took charge of the firm's Breslau branch, whither the family moved in 1908 – into the smart No 1 The Königsplatz, on the ground floor of which was 'Ferdinand Hirt's Royal University Bookshop'. The Gehlens were soon among the leaders of loyal Breslau society.

Three years later Reinhard was dispatched to the König Wilhelm High School, where he impressed his masters with his ability in mathematics and arithmetic. 'He was a cold calculator,' Herbert Urban, his school friend, recalls; 'he had a passion for figures and formulae.' He was shy and hard-working and came top of his class, but he was not exactly popular with the other boys. He gained the reputation of being a lone wolf, oddly unconcerned with the other boys' activities. Once involved in a discussion, however, he proved a wily debater.[13]

With his 'extraordinarily cool head' he soon knew where his future lay. For a short time he had debated whether to study physics but soon made up his mind to become a soldier (his father had meanwhile departed on active service as a Captain). By 1918 he was all ready to join his father's old arm, the artillery. After matriculating successfully in 1920 (he was excused the oral part of the examination because of his qualifications), he applied to become an officer and was accepted. On January 1st, 1921, Cadet Gehlen was posted to a Silesian unit, 6 Light Artillery Regiment in Schweidnitz.[14]

An uninspiring daily grind awaited him. With defeat, disarmament and inflation the Army had lost its glitter and could offer its officers little more than strenuous service, poor promotion prospects and a tightening of the belt. Nevertheless it still retained the arrogant conviction that it was the elite of what it vaguely termed the 'eternal Germany'. Thus thrown in upon itself, the Reichswehr's officer corps took refuge in the satisfaction of service, the cult of 'duty'. The term was so strictly interpreted that even brilliant soldiers like Gehlen found the climb up the narrow ladder of the military hierarchy a laborious business. Year after year passed without offering Gehlen any significant chance of promotion. He attended courses at the Infantry and Artillery Schools and received his commission as 2nd Lieutenant on December 1st, 1923. He was posted to No 2 Battery of 3 Prussian Artillery Regiment, as his old regiment was now called, and henceforth led a monotonous life of stable duties, autumn manoeuvres and mess festivities.

Relief came in 1926 when, as a dedicated horseman, he was allotted one of the coveted places in the Cavalry School, Hanover. For two years the regular lunches in the Schnurre Restaurant opposite the Cavalry School, where the cavaliers foregathered, compensated Gehlen for all the provincialism of Schweidnitz. Then, having been promoted Lieutenant in 1928, he had to return to his old Silesian garrison as Adjutant of the 1st Battalion of his regiment.[15]

But Gehlen had no intention of allowing himself to become immersed in military routine. On September 10th, 1931, he had married Herta von Seydlitz-Kurzbach, daughter of a Lieutenant-Colonel of Hussars, distantly related to Frederick the Great's famous cavalry general. Thus allied to the ancient Prussian nobility, Gehlen set his sights on another target: he wanted to escape from stable and barrack routine and enter the General Staff.

Officially there was no such thing as a General Staff. The victors of 1918 had banned it, as also any general-staff training for German officers. Unofficially, however, it continued, camouflaged as the Army's 'Troop Office' [Truppenamt]. Military Districts [Wehrkreise] had taken over the role of the disbanded Staff College, running 'Commanders Assistants Training' courses, to which only the most highly qualified officers were admitted. Gehlen sat an examination and passed through the barrier. From October 1st, 1933, he attended the 'Commanders Assistants Training' course of Wehrkreis III (Berlin). At the end of June 1935 Captain Gehlen emerged from the course having passed out second.[16]

Adolf Hitler's feverish remilitarization broke down the last barriers to Gehlen's career. Rearmament opened undreamed-of fields of activity to his energy and, like the majority of officers, he saw no reason to regret the Nazi seizure of power. In 1935 he joined the General Staff — as the 'Troop Office' was now once more allowed to call itself, and barely a year later he could at last affix the General Staff red stripes to his trousers. He plunged into the secret world of the military monks, the men who, with maps, statistics and analyses, studied the defensive battles and offensive operations of the future.

On October 6th, 1936, Gehlen attained the aim of every ambitious staff officer and was posted to the General Staff Operations Section. It remained his secret love despite the fact that, a year later, he was transferred to the Fortifications Section. Then, in November 1938, he returned to troops as regulations demanded, taking over No 8 Battery of 18 Artillery Regiment in Liegnitz. On the outbreak of the Second World War he was Senior General Staff Officer of 213 Infantry Division.[17]

This formation was a Silesian Reserve Division, formed in the Breslau Wehrkreis in the summer of 1939 and commanded by General

L'Homme de Courbière. It was to be reserve to Army Group South and advanced into Poland on the Army Group's left flank. But it was too late for the battle. When, on the tenth day of the Polish campaign, the division had an opportunity of taking part in the battle on the Bzura, Polish resistance collapsed before Gehlen could bring his formation into line. Nevertheless his superiors rewarded his efforts with his first decoration – the Iron Cross Class II.[18]

Colonel-General Franz Halder, the Chief of Staff of the Army, had taken note of Major Gehlen. Four days after the distribution of decorations Halder called him back to the General Staff, once more, as in 1937, charging him with problems of fortification. Gehlen did in fact, however, return to the Operations Section, since the fortifications section had meanwhile been disbanded and part of its responsibilities transferred to the Operations Section. As head of 'Fortifications' Gehlen soon found himself involved in the General Staff's complex concentration and war plans. For the forthcoming offensive in the West he worked out plans for possible position warfare in France; he planned a line of fortifications against the Soviets in German-occupied Poland; he designed anti-tank ditches.[19]

Gehlen now became an indispensable assistant to Halder; his name appeared with noticeably increasing frequency in the great man's war diary. Again and again Halder noted a briefing by Gehlen. On January 29th, 1940: 'Gehlen: Eastern fortifications'; on February 2nd: 'Gehlen – Jacob: Preparations for construction of defensive positions in conquered territory'; on February 13th: 'Gehlen: Details of construction of fortifications in the east. Plan for trip to the west.' Soon Halder could no longer do without Gehlen's opinion. During the French campaign he dispatched Major Gehlen as liaison officer to Sixteenth Army where no less headstrong an officer than General Model was acting as Chief of Staff; later he was sent to the Panzer Group commanded by the equally difficult General Guderian. In June 1940 Halder appointed Gehlen as his Senior Aide.[20]

In October 1940 Halder had new employment for Gehlen – he made him Head of the Eastern Group in Colonel Adolf Heusinger's Operations Section. So for the first time Gehlen came in contact with what would become his lifelong preoccupation – the Eastern Group, according to the official chart, dealt with 'Questions of overall strategy in the eastern area and the south-eastern area north of the Danube.' Russia began to exert a fascination on Gehlen.[21]

Promotion brought Gehlen into closer contact with Heusinger, the Section Head, who recognized that here was a most highly gifted staff officer. On February 19th, 1941, Heusinger wrote in Gehlen's confidential report: 'All that a staff officer should be. Far above average in personality, ability and industry. Of pronounced operational ability and capable of thinking ahead.' And a year later: 'Modest agreeable personality. Most industrious. Puts everything into his work.'[22] The friendship between Gehlen and Heusinger, later Inspector-General of the Bundeswehr [West German Armed Forces] was destined to be of historical significance: Heusinger launched Gehlen on his secret-service career; after the war Gehlen gave Heusinger a place in his intelligence organization. Each in his way was among the founding fathers of the Bundeswehr.

In Heusinger's Operations Section Gehlen became increasingly occupied with the subject 'Germany and the East'. During the planning of the fortifications in German-occupied Poland he had already seen conflict with the Soviet Union looming. Though basically anti-communist, he recoiled at the prospect of a Russo-German war. But Gehlen, the military expert, had no thought in his head other than obedience; docilely he followed his Führer's campaign of conquest into the vast expanses of the East.

He was one of the signatories of a study visualizing an offensive against the Bosphorus and Syria. He drafted an operational plan for the occupation of northern Greece. He took only a day to work out a plan of campaign against Yugoslavia. Although the background planning was done by others, he produced many ideas when Hitler's fateful decision to attack the Soviet Union had to be translated into operational plans. Gehlen played a large part in 'Operation Barbarossa'. He worked out problems of the forward movement of reserves; he drew the dividing lines between the advancing Army Groups and Armies; he solved the initial transport problems of the invasion.[23]

Halder was enthusiastic, noting, 'Very good work'. He had a special reward for such industry: On January 24th, 1941, 'on the occasion of Frederick Day', he noted in his diary: 'Presentation to each of the officers of my staff of a copy of the book *Portrait of Frederick the Great*. Present were: von Lossberg, von Mellenthin . . . Gehlen.' Three months later he pinned on Gehlen's breast the standard decoration for successful General Staff officers, the War Service Cross, Class I and II.[24]

Then the German steam-roller charged into Russia. Once more the field-grey war machine seemed to roll from victory to victory with its customary precision, smashing all resistance, checkmating every counterstroke by the defender. But Gehlen, the General Staff realist, was not deceived. By early 1942 (at the latest) he, Halder and Heusinger were forced to recognize that operations were not going well. All too patently people had underestimated the enemy; the General Staff's intelligence had failed.

From week to week Halder became more infuriated by the failures and blunders of that section of the General Staff which, under the curious title of 'Foreign Armies East', was analysing all intelligence on the Soviet war potential. 'Lapses in the intelligence service,' he wrote in December 1941 and finally on March 31st, 1942: 'Replacement of the Head of Foreign Armies East who no longer meets my requirements.'[25]

But who could satisfy the infuriated Chief of the General Staff? Halder could think of no suitable candidate. Then Heusinger proposed his favourite, Gehlen. At first Halder had doubts, since Gehlen had never been in the secret service. Heusinger, however, argued that Gehlen was an outstanding organizer – exactly what 'Foreign Armies East' required. Finally Halder was convinced – after all he himself had just written in Gehlen's report: 'Combines outstanding technical ability and unusual industry with great planning capacity and military dash. Suitable for senior General Staff appointments.'[26]

On April 1st, 1942, Lieutenant-Colonel Gehlen was posted to 'Foreign Armies East' and a month later he officially took over as head of the section.[27] The Gehlen saga had begun.

The appointment placed him in a key position in the world of secret-service activity and military intelligence. He knew little of the secret services with their spies, post-boxes and codes and he had seldom been in touch with the business of enemy intelligence.

Later he liked to say that until 1942 he had 'never had any contact whatsoever with the intelligence service'; as late as 1967 he was saying: 'I had always avoided learning modern languages since under no circumstances did I wish to go into intelligence.' This story need not be taken too seriously: as head of a group in the Operations Section he had had to work with the secret service – and collaboration had not always been harmonious; in October 1940 there had been a quarrel about spheres of responsibility with the Abwehr [Military Intelligence], ending with a sharp warning to Gehlen not to interfere in Abwehr affairs.[28]

Study of the FHO files, however, showed Gehlen how dependent the military command was on material provided by the secret service. In its kaleidoscopic history 'Foreign Armies East' reflected all the brilliance and all the shortcomings of the German secret service. It had no knowledge of the origin or the quality of the secret-service reports; it was perplexed by the manifold quarrels and intrigues of the competing secret and security services; it frequently looked down on secret-service men as mountebanks. FHO was both the beneficiary and the victim of the intelligence service.*

Gehlen knew that he could only avoid the errors of the past if he could set up his own intelligence service and improve production of intelligence, also that he must make himself independent of his secret-service competitors and their intrigues. A complete new machine was required.

* See Appendix A.

MIRACLE ON THE EASTERN FRONT

GEHLEN'S reform of his intelligence machine began with a severe setback. In April 1942 he moved into the small group of huts in the Mauerwald south-west of the East Prussian town of Angerburg where FHO was accommodated, but hardly had he done so than he added his signature to certain over-optimistic 'enemy appreciations' such as the following of April 4th: 'Russian forces at the front have suffered so severely from battle wastage and the weather that scarcely a single formation can be described as fully battle-worthy.'[1]

The fact was that he had accepted what FHO's Evaluation Group had submitted to him that day: 'The Russian reserve of manpower is now nearing exhaustion through casualties and territorial losses. The enemy cannot make good these losses. The enemy cannot again produce reserves comparable to those of the winter 1941–2 for a decisive battle.' In his 'Overall Appreciation of the enemy situation' of May 1st Gehlen's conclusion from this was: 'In view of Russian setbacks during the winter and the fact that they undoubtedly rate both our offensive and defensive capabilities very high, any counter-offensive on a broad front in the areas of Army Groups Centre and South is improbable; in addition the Russians anticipate that we shall attack in the south.'[2]

Gehlen's prognostication proved to be wrong. Soviet headquarters was not expecting any German attack in the south but rather the resumption of the offensive on Moscow. The Russians themselves struck against Army Group South.

For Gehlen this setback was an additional and conclusive indication that 'Foreign Armies East' required reorganization from top to bottom. A new system of evaluation had to be worked out; better men must take the place of the old worn-out personnel. Gehlen accepted hardly a single one of the old section heads or desk officers; one after another they were relieved.[3] Only the junior personnel or officers who had only recently joined FHO were allowed to remain. Among the latter was Captain Gerhard Wessel, the most articulate of FHO's officers and ex-Intelligence Officer of I Army Corps. He had joined the Section in

December 1941 and had already made a name for himself in intelligence work.

Wessel was born in Neumünster on December 24th, 1913, son of an evangelical pastor who had temporarily been arrested by the Gestapo for heretical statements from the pulpit. Like Gehlen he was an artilleryman and had passed through the Staff College. His fellow-officers regarded him as a reserved impenetrable personality, but Gehlen had quickly perceived that his analytical mind could be of considerable value to FHO. Gehlen had another, more personal, reason for keeping Wessel near him. Gehlen was a lonely soul, 'a very bad conversationalist, almost tongue-tied in informal discussion'. Wessel, who was a good speaker and could put a case forward convincingly, was able to help his master out of many embarrassing situations, particularly on social occasions. 'An outstandingly efficient staff officer of above-average ability,' Gehlen later wrote in Wessel's confidential report. 'Puts forward his views to his superiors with firmness and tact. Ideologically sound and physically fit . . . As a personality suitable for command positions.'⁴

Gehlen, however, thought Wessel too inexperienced for immediate appointment as his Deputy and senior General Staff officer. He needed a man who knew his Russia, and the Army Personnel Department knew where to find him; they nominated Major Heinz Danko Herre, senior General Staff officer of XLII Army Corps.

Herre presented himself to Gehlen at the end of April 1942. Gehlen told him what the problem was: Herre was to assist in creating a new intelligence service which would be able to forecast every intention on the part of the Soviet enemy. When Herre tried to say that he would prefer a post at the front, Gehlen interrupted him. 'I am sorry,' he said, 'but my staff officers must be young, have front-line experience and have knowledge of Russia. One can count on the fingers of one hand those now available who fulfil these conditions. That is why I need you. The work of the section which I have taken over has been superficial and irresponsible.'⁵

In fact Herre was exactly the type of officer Gehlen wanted on his staff. He had been born in Alsace in 1909 (his father was an Army Major) and so was comparatively young (33 in 1942). As a young officer he had served in 13 Cavalry Regiment and had acquired front-line experience in several campaigns. Moreover he knew the East; he had learnt Russian at an early age, had been friendly with Russian émigrés and had travelled in Estonia, Carelia and Bessarabia. In addition Gehlen and Herre had much in common: both were horsemen; both believed in ultimate German victory; both criticized the German master-race policy in the East – without, however, realizing that the Nazi mass crimes in Poland and Russia were a typical and entirely logical manifestation of that regime which they served so loyally.[6]

Gehlen liked Major Herre so much that he appointed him his senior staff officer. Thus had come together the most successful threesome – Gehlen, Herre, Wessel – ever known in the history of German intelligence. Henceforth their names were to be coupled with the triumphs and the defeats of that company which was then known as 'Foreign Armies East, turned into the 'Gehlen Organization' in 1945–6 and finally became the West German Intelligence Service, the BND.

In May 1942 this organizing trio began to redistribute authority and functions within FHO. Lieutenant-Colonel Gehlen was in overall command and his two assistants took over the two most important groups: Captain Wessel headed Group I, responsible for the daily situation reports on strength, locations and equipment of the Soviet forces; Major Herre led Group II which evaluated secret service reports and prepared general appreciations on the Soviet Union, other than the daily report.

The three men left the other four groups, which either were not concerned with the Russians or dealt with technical questions, undisturbed for the moment. Group III was responsible for the Balkans and Middle East; Group IV for Scandinavia; Group V included the printing and drawing offices; Group VI dealt with administrative problems.[7]

Gehlen's main problem, however, was the immediate expansion of the two groups dealing with Russia. A stream of fresh and energetic officers and experts flowed in. Tirelessly Gehlen scoured the Army's personnel agencies, always on the look-out for good staff. Wherever he could find a Soviet expert, an officer wanting a change or an Abwehr man wanting to escape from military routine, Gehlen moved in. He recruited regimental officers and eastern scholars, pastors and students, lawyers and managers – men of all sorts applied, attracted by the exacting demands Gehlen made upon his staff.

Gehlen accepted anyone who seemed suitable to him. Whether soldiers or civilians, anti-Nazi or Nazis, all were grist to Gehlen's mill, always provided that they seemed likely to raise the intellectual level of the organization. A heterogeneous company of intellectuals was soon gathered in FHO. The anti-Nazi Graf von Rittberg worked alongside the SA Obersturmführer [Lieutenant] von der Marwitz, Pastor Hoheisel with the cartoonist Hindersin; Georg von Rauch, the Russian historian, laboured on analyses and statistics with Werner von Bargen, a foreign service officer.[8]

Gehlen was adept at placing round pegs in round holes. The most promising newcomers he placed in Group I, on whose products FHO's reputation primarily depended. Their daily situation reports formed the basis for all Army General Staff planning.

Group I was organized in three 'desks' corresponding to the three Army Groups engaged on the Eastern front; each comprised a desk officer, an assistant and an aide whose duty it was to record the enemy situation on the front of their Army Group. A fourth desk dealt with partisan warfare and a fifth with questions of air reconnaissance. All desks in Group I had to produce a daily situation report on Soviet formations on their front; they had to prepare drafts of the 'Enemy Appreciation' to be given by the Head of the Section and enemy situation maps (scale 1:1,000,000) showing changes in enemy forces, results of air reconnaissance and any enemy regroupings.[9]

Group I's work centred around the 'Order of battle', the purpose of which was to provide information on enemy units. Every report of a Soviet unit was checked, incorporated into the situation report and allotted an authenticity rating. The 'Order of battle' had to show the location of a unit, its ration strength, the history of its formation, its equipment and its personnel composition. There then began a complicated process of counting, subtraction and addition, known as the 'calculation of enemy strength'. The actual fighting strength of Soviet units was calculated, their casualties subtracted and their battle-worthiness thereby estimated. The formula used was: *effectiveness* × *establishment = ration strength*.[10]

Nothing was left to chance. Changes in the strength of a Russian division or corps were recorded on an 'alterations slip'; a special note-book registered changes which had been reported but not yet confirmed; a 'movement list' showed units thought to be in process of transfer. Finally the source material for the daily situation report was passed to Group II for further evaluation.[11]

In Group II the sections responsible for the subject 'Overall Russian military situation' used an even more sophisticated evaluation procedure. One 'desk' sifted the reports in order to extract from them the operational intentions of the Soviet High Command and obtain a general picture of Russian reserves, high-level organization and defence machinery; a second desk evaluated statements from Soviet prisoners of war, reports from the German intercept service and articles in the Soviet press; a third dealt with the enemy's economic and armaments situation, a fourth prepared memoranda on the principles of Russian strategy and a fifth supervised prisoner interrogation.[12]

All these reports, memoranda and statistics were finally collated in the steel filing cabinets of a section known as 'IIc'. It maintained something which, after the end of the Thousand-Year Reich, electrified the Russians, the Americans and the British – the card-index of 'Foreign Armies East'.

The head of 'IIc' was named Ritter and he had two assistants, Lieutenant Letschert and Paymaster Wiesemann. They maintained a 'Units Card Index' and a 'Special Card Index' containing everything FHO knew about Red Army commanders, establishments, organization, training schools or field post numbers. Of particular importance were the personal files giving details of Soviet generals and all officer appointments from divisional commander upwards.[13]

Nevertheless the problem remained: where was the information to come from? What new sources could be tapped to feed the FHO analysts? From Gehlen's point of view it was here that the great weakness of the old FHO lay. One of the former section heads said: 'Most of the intelligence material we received was muck.'[14]

The trouble was that FHO had no intelligence service of its own. It merely collated and analysed enemy intelligence provided by other people. In practice this meant that FHO was dependent on a whole series of varied sources of information including Canaris' Ausland/Abwehr, the RSHA, the Foreign Office, Luftwaffe headquarters, Signals Intelligence, the Director of Artillery, Army Intelligence and OKW's Decoding Section. None of them was responsible to FHO; each was jealous of its own prerogatives within Greater-Germany's power structure.[15]

Of all these the most ready to cooperate with FHO was the Abwehr. Admiral Canaris' secret-service organization maintained on the Eastern front so-called 'Front-line reconnaissance detachments' whose task was to provide the troops with short-range information in the forward zone. These 'detachments' consisted of groups of agents who 'in the event of an enemy collapse and withdrawal' were to 'move to the rear and thence provide information by radio'; they also included intelligence officers, whose duties were thus described: 'Provision of military information and material by searching command posts, interrogating prisoners ... evaluating agents' reports, sifting and forwarding captured material.'[16]

The 'Front-line Reconnaissance Detachments' had been formed after Adolf Hitler's military steamroller had destroyed the pre-war information networks set up by the Abwehr in most of the countries of Europe. To open up new sources the headquarters on the Tirpitzufer had hit upon the idea of attaching to the advancing troops small detachments of specially qualified intelligence officers. When Hitler unleashed his war against the Soviet Union, part of Abwehr headquarters was hived off from Berlin and organized for an intelligence assault on the East.

On June 15th, 1941, sixty-seven officers, four civil servants, ten NCOs and 114 drivers, almost all from the Eastern Desk of Abwehr Division I, reported to the Intelligence Sections of the Army Groups and Armies concentrated for the invasion of Russia. According to an Abwehr order they were to 'obtain valuable material for the High Command and direct agents in enemy territory'. They were in fact only the leaders of an invisible army still awaiting their assignments in the Abwehr's agent-assembly camps. There agents originating from the east had been trained and paid 12.50 marks a day, pending call forward for employment at a further 15 marks a day by the relevant commander of a 'Front-line Reconnaissance Detachment'.[17]

As commander of this Eastern intelligence service Canaris had selected a man whom he later described as possessing 'a special gift for intelligence work'. This was Major Hermann Baun, head of the Russian desk in Abwehr I, destined to be the fourth founding father of the BND alongside Gehlen, Herre and Wessel. Baun knew Russia and the Russians as did few other German officers. He had been born in the Black Sea town of Odessa on December 17th, 1897; he could speak Russian and Ukrainian in addition to English and French and, after moving to Leipzig, had maintained his interest in Russia. He was an infantryman, promoted captain in 1937, and in September 1939 had joined Abwehr I where he was regarded as the cleverest Russian expert on Canaris' staff.[18]

On June 18th, 1941, Major Baun and his staff moved to Suleyovek near Warsaw and there set up the headquarters of 'Front-line Reconnaissance Detachment I East' with the code-name 'Walli I'. On June 19th Major Hotzel activated the detachment's radio network and the espionage war in the East had begun.[19]

On paper Walli I's force of agents was most impressive. According to Baun's orders the intelligence officer of each detachment was to use his agents to reconnoitre within a 30-mile zone ahead of the German front; any group leader, however, might use his agents 'for individual missions in greater depth (30—200 miles)'. Abwehr I's instructions laid down: 'While the group leader will remain within our own lines, his subordinates and their agents will penetrate deep into the enemy formations in accordance with their assignments. Transmission of information from and to group leaders will take place by radio.' Each group was to have two radio sets, to be dressed in Russian uniform and to be motorized. Abwehr I directed: 'Groups will be formed from members of the indigenous population (Russians, Poles, Ukrainians, Georgians, Cossacks, Finns, Estonians, etc).'[20]

This was precisely the aspect in which Baun's venture seemed likely to fail – Walli I could not recruit sufficient indigenous personnel. FHO's first request to Baun was to discover what Soviet formations were in the Baltic States. Baun had to pass the assignment on to Abwehr II which was responsible for subversion.

Abwehr II assembled 80 Estonians who had just finished their sabotage training. They were dropped behind the Soviet lines and continued to report locations, operations and movements of Soviet forces until eventually able to make themselves known to the advancing German troops. According to an Abwehr instruction their 'special recognition sign' was 'a rust-red cloth about the size of a handkerchief with a circular yellow spot in the middle'. They were gathered up for further employment as agents.[21]

'Operation Erna,' as this exploit by Estonians was known, led Baun to work out an ambitious plan: he proposed to collect long-range intelligence reaching even as far as Moscow. Abwehr II had shown him that it was possible to infiltrate agents in rear of the enemy and use them for intelligence purposes. Long before the opening of the Russian campaign Abwehr II had been in contact with opposition groups in the three Baltic States whom they had been able to use against the Soviets while keeping them in ignorance of the fact that they were working for the Abwehr.

In 'Notes for a memorandum' the Intelligence Officer of the East Prussian region had jotted down: 'Three principal liaison officers to the three countries are located on German territory; they are in fact former senior officers (Military Attachés) who receive regular instructions from Abwehr II and pass them on. The resistance groups on the other side of the frontier do not know that they are in fact under German military direction. Abwehr II's instructions are translated into the relevant language by the liaison officers and couriers who then learn them by heart. These courier agents know only the three liaison officers. Requests for information are invariably only of a general nature, so that, even if discovered, the enemy could draw no conclusions about German operational plans.'[22]

Baun now proposed to use this system in his own area. His idea was to drop agents in Russian uniform in the interior of Russia and use them to infiltrate Red Army headquarters with the objects both of confusing the enemy and giving warning of Red Army operations. Baun was not satisfied with intelligence extending over a mere 200 miles – his agents were intended to penetrate thousands of miles into enemy territory.

Baun's intelligence fantasies, however, bore no relation whatsoever to reality. His pool of agents was far too small and he was only too thankful if they were able to complete the simplest and most immediate of tasks. The 'Front-line Reconnaissance Detachments' accordingly had to confine themselves to sifting the captured files of the retreating Soviet armies and interrogating prisoners. Even these tasks they fulfilled so inexpertly on many occasions that the most fanciful speculations and conclusions reached FHO in the guise of Abwehr intelligence.[23] Baun's prestige and that of the Abwehr sank to zero; in FHO Baun's reports were frequently an object of ridicule. They gave rise to a wrangle between Baun and the FHO which, despite all subsequent collaboration, outlasted the war.

Gehlen himself was not altogether immune to this antipathy to Baun; even into the 1950s – until the final breach between the two in fact – he invariably met Baun with an attitude of suspicion. Nevertheless he was realist enough to see that Baun could offer the new FHO the intelligence service without which it was doomed to failure. Gehlen came to the conclusion that 'Walli I's' output could be improved. Baun had already succeeded in dropping his first agents behind the Soviet front and his pool of agents was being reinforced by 'converted' Russian prisoners.

Gehlen calculated that, if reorganized, this 'Front-line Reconnaissance Detachment' could provide FHO with its own intelligence service. He accordingly offered Baun closer partnership in the business. Gehlen knew that Baun felt himself constricted by the actions of Abwehr II and III which had both set up intelligence organizations for the East and had both located themselves in Suleyovek. Gehlen therefore set out to link Baun ever more closely to FHO. In the summer of 1942 Baun left his fellow-officers of the Abwehr in Suleyovek and moved Walli I to the Ukrainian town of Vinnitsa.[24]

A few months later Baun became, at least temporarily, a full-time member of FHO. FHO's personnel chart of spring 1943 for the first time shows all four founding members of the later BND on the same sheet of paper – Gehlen the head of the organization, Herre the Operations Officer, Wessel the Deputy, and Baun the Abwehr officer. Nevertheless for most of the members of FHO Baun remained a shadowy figure; none of them knew him; only Gehlen dealt with him personally.[25]

The more closely Hermann Baun became involved in the toils of the FHO, however, the more insistent did Gehlen become on improvement and expansion of Walli I's output. Baun recruited fresh agents; training of agents destined for Russia was accelerated and improved; technical equipment became more plentiful; circuits of agents were formed.

The 'Baun Agency' now began to form fair-sized groups of carefully trained ex-prisoner-of-war agents and infiltrate them through the front or drop them by parachute in the Soviet hinterland. The majority were never heard of again, but some groups did contrive to establish themselves and carry out their missions. Disguised as Soviet officers Baun's agents wormed their way into Red Army headquarters; they led a perfectly legal existence in Russian civilian life; they made their niche in factories and offices, in the administration and even in the Communist Party. They hid in forests and tried to contact anti-communist partisans.

Baun's tentacles reached even into Moscow; his secret emissaries even worked their way into Stalin's immediate entourage. One of them was Comrade Vladimir Minishsky, Secretary of the Central Committee of the Communist Party of White Russia, who had been taken prisoner in 1941 and 'converted'; he returned to Moscow as Baun's agent in the Kremlin and was prepared to work for the Germans at any time. 'Frontline Reconnaissance Detachment No 103' even had a direct line to Moscow, a radio group known as 'Flamingo' operating just outside the walls of the Kremlin. Its leader, a man named Alexander, joined a Soviet Reserve Signals Regiment as a captain, thus obtaining access to Red Army military secrets.[26]

Another line to the senior levels of the Red Army ran through the exiled Russian General Turgut. Living in Vienna and working for the Abwehr office there, he maintained radio stations in the Caucasus and Urals over which he communicated with anti-Stalinists among senior Red Army officers. The most sensational information on the Red Army, however, came from a mysterious figure in the Baun organization, a Jewish trader named Klatt, whose code-name was 'Max'. His information was so accurate that the sceptics in FHO often wondered whether Max was not a double agent feeding fake Russian material back to the Germans. No one in FHO knew the truth, which was that, via Isono Kiyosho, a journalist living in Sofia, Max had tapped the Japanese secret service, which was better informed than any other about the Soviet Union.[27]

But these star agents were not the only ones to give Baun considerable insight into Soviet secrets. The main body of minor informers also contributed. Eugeni Rohr, for instance, reported from beleaguered Leningrad on Russian rockets; Leif Mort sent in pictures and reports on Finland. There were innumerable sources, fortuitous allies and secret Hitler sympathizers working for Baun. He had good reason to be satisfied: FHO was receiving increasingly reliable information from the Soviet hinterland.[28]

But the fact that he had laid hands on Walli I was not enough for Gehlen. He required as sophisticated an information service as he could get. Accordingly he now got his hooks on a counter-espionage organization 'Front-line Reconnaissance Headquarters III East' (Walli III) which had remained in Suleyovek under Lieutenant-Colonel Heinz Schmalschläger.

From the outset Walli III had been more effective than Walli I. Schmalschläger had recruited Russian and Ukrainian anti-communists who were only too willing to be used as agents against their former Soviet masters. Their main target was the Soviet secret service and they were frequently successful in the rapid detection and destruction of its circuits of agents in the German-occupied zone. Walli III 'converted' the arrested agents and used their radio sets to mislead the enemy. Schmalschläger had over thirty captured radio sets working to Russian secret-service headquarters in Moscow and so learnt much about enemy intentions.[29]

Walli III, as a result, knew a great deal about the operations of the Soviet partisans who were conducting a threatening guerilla war against the German occupying forces. Schmalschläger's agents were so successful in infiltrating headquarters of partisan groups that, without Walli III's information, effective action against Stalin's army of the forests and the underground hardly seemed possible. This fact inevitably became an object of special attention on Gehlen's part, for in autumn 1942 the SS had annexed responsibility for anti-partisan operations and so responsibility for intelligence about the partisans became a matter of importance in the jungle warfare of the German internal struggle for power. And the main producer of that intelligence was Walli III – good enough reason for Gehlen, the strategist of the internal power-politics game, to ally himself with Schmalschläger.

Gehlen's alliance with the two Abwehr officers, Schmalschläger and Baun, guaranteed FHO a monopoly of intelligence on the East which even the SS was subsequently unable to break. Yet even the assistance afforded by the two Wallis still did not satisfy Gehlen.

One weakness, which they had never been able to master, was common to both Walli I and Walli III: they had neither the interpreters,

Soviet experts nor office staff to make a really exhaustive evaluation of captured Soviet material. Gehlen decided to set up his own organization to deal with this aspect of the Abwehr's work. The result was something which represented the real strength of the Gehlen Organization: an ingenious system of evaluation of captured material and prisoner interrogation.

The pre-Gehlen FHO had had a small section (IIz) dealing with interrogation of Soviet prisoners of war and evaluation of captured documents. Gehlen appointed Major Adolf Wicht as desk officer and he succeeded in putting order into IIz's haphazard production. Wicht, born in 1910, came from Danzig; he had taken part in the Greek, Russian and North African campaigns. He proved to possess a remarkable flair for detailed intelligence work and was later to become one of the leading figures in the BND.[30]

Wicht expanded IIz and annexed certain of the other responsibilities of Group II; eventually his desk had become so important in FHO that he was allowed to form his own Group, Group III (the rump of the old Group III moved a further number down the scale). The work of the new group centred around the interrogation of Russian prisoners, for which Desk IIIa was responsible. Subjects for interrogation were laid down by Groups I and II; prisoners were handed over by the fighting troops. Desk IIIa retained the most important and knowledgeable prisoners.

These were accommodated in a castle, known as 'Fortress Boyen Special Camp', near the East Prussian town of Lötzen, and subjected to further questioning. The camp held eighty prisoners who were under command of Major Sacharov, a Soviet officer who had gone over to the Germans. Prisoners were required to write military essays on subjects set by Wicht's staff; they were also assembled for discussions which frequently brought to light further information of value to German intelligence. Wicht laid down: 'The most intelligent and cooperative from the more important arms of the service will remain as specialists on current problems.' The camp commandant had to present an activity report monthly and Group III officers kept a continuous check on the work in Boyen.[31]

A further desk in Wicht's Group, Desk IIIb, dealt with Russian manuscript papers of a military nature. It maintained liaison officers at the Abwehr's captured material collecting centre in Warsaw and with Army Group Intelligence Sections, so as to lay hands quickly on any Red Army manuscripts. These officers perused all papers for information on the partisans and Red Army organization, equipment and training.

Captured printed material, on the other hand, was forwarded to Desk

IIIc, whence it was distributed to further desks for evaluation. IIIc itself retained any instructions or orders from the Soviet Defence Ministry; IIId dealt with newspapers, letters captured from Red Army postal service and leaflets; IIIf translated documents of special importance; IIIg collected regulations and books of Soviet origin into a library; IIIh provided additional material from its 24-hour monitoring of the Soviet radio. A final desk, IIIe, summarized the information thus gained (in so far as it was of a tactical nature) and issued it to the troops in a periodical report entitled 'Intelligence Service East – Detailed Information'. The circle was thus complete.

With the evaluation of captured equipment and a secret service, counter-espionage and enemy appreciations, prisoner interrogations and front-line reconnaissance, Gehlen at last had an organization with which he could assault his great task. 'Foreign Armies East' really began to produce intelligence.[82]

Gehlen, the perfectionist, however, gave his people no peace. He was indefatigable in his demands for improvement in the quality of his organization's work. The Chief's orders rained down relentlessly; new instructions were continually being issued, new proposals for improving the work, for more fundamental thinking and for stricter systematization. For example: 'Our communal effort must be characterized by the necessary sense of responsibility; both brains and method must be used; efforts should always be made to produce a picture of the enemy even more comprehensive than mere duty requires.' He demanded 'special care in the compilation of the card index'; he warned against reports in which 'old statements are continually repeated as new'; he urged the strictest classification of sources. On September 1st, 1943 he ordered: 'In the case of all information officers will, as a matter of principle, quote the source, if necessary giving it a rating.' He introduced five grades for sources: reliable, credible, possible, questionable, improbable. The desk officer had to attach a grading note to every report.[33]

The Chief never ceased demanding improved methods of work. In some notes for a speech Gehlen wrote: 'Enemy appreciation must in future be based increasingly on the results of air reconnaissance, Abwehr information and ground reconnaissance by the troops. Increased air reconnaisance is considered necessary.' In a memorandum of December 1943, he explained why 'efficient and systematic air reconnaissance produces valuable data for enemy appreciations ... the advantage of air reconnaissance over other sources of information (ground reconnaissance, the Abwehr, radio, prisoners' statements) is that it can quickly provide a picture of conditions deep in enemy territory.'[34]

Thus challenged and exhorted, the members of FHO achieved minor miracles of intelligence-gathering and analysis. For the first time the military leaders of Hitler's Reich were receiving soundly based information – realistic, accurate, incontrovertible. In particular, on an increasing number of occasions, forecasts of Soviet operational intentions proved correct.

FHO, for instance, gave advance warning of Soviet offensive plans in the Stalingrad area. As early as the summer of 1942, when Hitler's military leaders were still elated over the results of the second German summer offensive, Gehlen warned of a Russian counter-stroke. In mid-July he had received a report from Baun which said that, at a meeting on July 13th, the Soviet Military Council had decided to withdraw its forces to the Volga but to hold Stalingrad at all costs.

On July 15th Gehlen concluded from this: 'Developments in the enemy situation over the last few days lend credibility to this report. In the light of the situation on the fronts of Army Groups A and B Russian withdrawal is to be anticipated first to the line of the Don and, in the event of our further advance, behind the Volga while holding the north Caucasus area and the Stalingrad bridgehead.'

In October and November Gehlen gave warning of a Soviet counter-offensive at Stalingrad. On November 6th he noted that there was nothing to indicate 'that the Russians have entirely abandoned the thrust across the Don around which their plans have hitherto centred'. On November 12th he estimated that 'an early attack on Third Rumanian Army must be anticipated; its objective would be to cut the Stalingrad railway, thus endangering German forces further east and forcing the withdrawal of the German forces located at Stalingrad.'[35]

Even after the turning-point of Stalingrad, FHO was almost invariably on hand with accurate forecasts of enemy operations. In mid-July 1943 FHO announced the Soviet offensive in the Orel area a fortnight before it began; in mid-August 1943 it prophesied, ten days ahead of time, that the main weight of the anticipated Soviet offensive against the Briansk position would fall in the Sevsk area; in early March 1944, two days before the offensive opened, FHO forecast the great breakthrough operation by the First and Second Ukrainian Army Groups which destroyed the entire southern flank of the German Eastern front.[36]

FHO, in fact, now had so accurate a picture of Russian military affairs and Russian strategy that it was able to calculate beforehand what action the Red Army was likely to take. There was no Soviet formation the state of which FHO did not know; no general and no major weapon of which Gehlen's people were not aware. Every Soviet general, every Red Army commander from Brigade Commander upwards and every Chief of Staff from Corps level upwards appeared in FHO's card index.[37]

On Rodion Malinovsky, the later Defence Minister, for instance, the card index noted: 'According prisoners' statements enjoys the complete confidence of the High Command as belonging to the generation educated under the Soviets. Regarded as most competent. Author of military literature. Most demanding to his subordinates and frequently rude, unsociable, taciturn and arrogant in dealing with them.' Lieutenant-General Pliyev was noted as 'a particularly capable commander' and Colonel-General Zhdanov as 'the soul of the resistance during the siege of Leningrad'. On Marshal Kulik the entry was: 'C-in-C of North Caucasus Front at Krasnoda, probably in summer 1942 at latest; according to statements of inhabitants, aroused unfavourable comment owing to immoral conduct and was accordingly recalled and demoted.'[38]

Every piece of paper found in any Red Army office was perused in order to broaden FHO's knowledge of the enemy. It had, for instance, read the files of the case against General Chernyashovsky, who had had to appear before a Party Commission on a charge of ideological deviationism; it had examined the notes of the Secret Police detachment attached to the North Caucasian Railway Administration. Every detail was of interest to FHO.[39]

FHO frequently knew what the Soviet soldier was thinking, wanting and doing down to company level. Minutes of a meeting held on February 10th, 1944 in No 1 Company of a Guards Rifle Division were discovered, for instance; they read: 'Report by Titov, the Company Commander, on the discipline of the Company: "Communist comrades, in our Company discipline is at a very low level and for this reason the daily plans are not carried out. The soldiers do not salute their commanders. Billets are untidy and dirty. Weapons are not cleaned. Exercises are carried out listlessly." Other speakers were: Neverov – "NCOs do not look after their men and their own behaviour is intolerable. They themselves are undisciplined, as for instance Lance-Sergeant Klimov. Klimov refused to accompany his men into the sauna bath"; Meroshnichenko – "Discipline must be improved as rapidly as possible. Discipline is the guarantee of victory." Decision: The Party meeting of No 1 Company declares that the NCOs and men of the Company are undisciplined.'[40]

FHO knew the daily anxieties of the Red Army soldier and how he was punished or rewarded – in a prisoner interrogation report: 'Any

NCO from Sergeant-Major upwards can punish their immediate sub-ordinates. Officers can be punished by their immediate superiors. Strik-ing a subordinate is no longer permitted in the Red Army,' and on the scale of punishments: 'For other ranks: close or ordinary arrest (confinement in the guard room). For officers: reprimand, house arrest reduction to half-pay.'

Gehlen's office was also interested in the system of rewards. On Janu-ary 21st, 1944 the Intelligence Section of Third German Panzer Army reported: 'For destruction of a Tiger tank the tank commander receives 1,000 roubles and each crew member 500 roubles. Destruction of three Tigers is rewarded with the grant of the title "Hero of the Soviet Union".' Precise lists were kept of decorations awarded to each Soviet unit – for instance: 'Applications and grants of decorations to date in 18 Cavalry Division: "Hero of Soviet Union" – five applied for, three granted; Order of Lenin – 33 applied for, 12 granted; Order of the Red Flag – about 170 applied for, 58 granted.'[41]

Gehlen regarded it as particularly noteworthy that 'officers now re-quire authorization to marry and this is only granted if the bride can prove education up to at least tenth grade; it is further laid down that at social evenings in officers' messes officers will kiss ladies' hands and the ladies must wear long evening dresses.'

FHO kept continuous watch on the morale of the Red Army; records were maintained for every Soviet formation – on 156 Rifle Division, for instance: 'Everyone anticipates an early end to the war and the majority believe in an Allied victory. The only factor which lowers morale is the news from home about lack of food and high wartime taxation'; 215 Rifle Division: 'Morale bad owing to high casualties and bad accommo-dation. Great fear of being taken prisoner by the Germans. Political speakers not liked'; 274 Rifle Division: 'Officers regard the Soviet situ-ation as favourable. General view is that Soviet superiority is so great that the Germans cannot resist much longer'; 1324 Artillery Regiment: 'Unit fights because Germans are described as the people who wanted war and who must be driven out. Officers confident of victory and enu-merate the Soviet successes of the winter which have much impressed the majority.'[42]

FHO did not confine itself, however, to observation of the Red Army and its leaders alone. Russian industry also came under Gehlen's eagle eye, later followed by the railways, the signals service, the Party, policy and administration – in fact there was no sphere of Soviet life to which FHO did not pay attention.

For every branch of industry lists of firms were maintained showing production figures and classified in geographical areas. Records were kept of the production of tanks and assault guns; reports came in about the transfer of armaments works into the interior of the Soviet Union; one FHO memorandum dealt with 'Soviet Russian requirement for empty wagons for rail movements' and another with 'Technical terms and abbreviations of the Soviet Secret Service'.

Everything, literally everything, was gathered in – orders from the Soviet Defence Ministry (FHO possessed some 10,000 of them), every speech or pronouncement by Stalin, street maps and town plans for every locality in the Soviet Union, files of the Soviet secret service, code names of counter-espionage personnel in the Red Army. The mere titles of the book-size studies, analyses, memoranda and notes showed how widespread FHO's interests were – 'Disbandment of the Comintern', 'Ice break-up in Russia', 'Partisan handbook', Stalin's career and daily routine', 'Detailed data on firms engaged in the aircraft industry, vehicle production and rubber production'.[43]

Reinhard Gehlen, promoted Colonel in December 1942, could now be satisfied with the success of his 'Foreign Armies East'. He had achieved what no other Western secret service had succeeded in doing – communist Russia was now an open book to an enemy intelligence service. On July 13th, 1943 he announced to his staff: 'In recent days the course of the fighting on the eastern front has once more proved the accuracy in every detail of the enemy appreciations elaborated by this section. The Chief of the General Staff specifically acknowledged this a few days ago.'[44]

Henceforth Gehlen's Section was the recognized source of information for the German Eastern front. Whenever some action by the Wehrmacht was being planned, whenever either the soldiers or the propagandists wished to strike some blow against the Eastern enemy, Colonel Gehlen and his Desk IIc invariably had to be consulted.

Nevertheless Gehlen never forgot that his intelligence machine could only work efficiently if it received sound solid information from the secret-service agencies. 'Even in modern war,' Gehlen pronounced, 'espionage is of the highest importance, since front-line reconnaissance is unable to provide information on the objectives of enemy operations.'[45] FHO was increasingly dependent on an efficient secret service.

Then the SS struck a blow which placed a question-mark against the whole Gehlen edifice. In February 1944 Admiral Canaris fell and the Abwehr was disbanded. The SS death-ray was now beamed on FHO.

UNDER THE SHADOW OF THE SS

T HE blow was unexpected. Scarcely a single member of FHO really understood what the news from the Führer's headquarters implied – that Admiral Wilhelm Canaris had fallen and with him his entire organization, the OKW office 'Ausland/Abwehr' [External Military Intelligence]. A Hitler ukase dated February 12th, 1944, however, made the message of doom quite clear. Gehlen's staff read it – 'I command: 1. A unified German secret information service is to be set up. 2. I hereby charge the Reichsführer SS with command of this German information service. 3. In so far as this affects the military Intelligence and Counter-espionage service the Reichsführer-SS and the Chief of OKW will take the necessary measures by mutual agreement. Signed: Adolf Hitler.'[1]

Colonel Gehlen knew only too well what this implied: the Wehrmacht had lost control over wide areas of secret intelligence work; the SS and its secret-service expert SS-Brigadeführer [Major-General] Walter Schellenberg, had finally seized the leading position in Greater Germany's espionage system. From now on Schellenberg, with the RSHA behind him, would call the tune in German secret-service affairs.

Days passed before Gehlen knew how this change in the balance of power had come about. After the death of Heydrich, the former head of the RSHA, in May 1942, so fierce a sniping war had broken out between the Abwehr on one side and the Gestapo and SD on the other that a dramatic clash was inevitable. Basing its case on the affiliation of certain Abwehr officers to anti-Nazi opposition groups and also on the frequently defective quality of secret-service reports, the RSHA continued to press for the disbandment of the Abwehr and its incorporation into Schellenberg's SD. Step by step the RSHA witch-hunters invaded the Abwehr's preserves. In April 1943 two of the leading brains of the resistance, both of whom were Abwehr officers, Major-General Hans Oster and the lawyer Hans von Dohnanyi, were arrested on a currency charge trumped up by the Gestapo; in January 1944 further Abwehr officers came under suspicion of treason. Adolf Hitler began to suspect that the Abwehr was both a traitorous and a useless organization.[2]

Only some minor additional scandal was therefore required to arouse the dictator's wrath – and in February 1944 five of the Abwehr's staff in Istanbul defected to the Allies and exposed a considerable portion of the German espionage network in Turkey. This was enough for Himmler to lament to his Führer that 'the professional and personal failures in the Ausland/Abwehr office under Canaris' had 'risen to an intolerable level'. Hitler angrily agreed and the doom of the Abwehr was sealed.[3]

SS-Brigadeführer Schellenberg, head of the SS foreign intelligence service (Section VI of the RSHA), now saw the opportunity for which he had waited so long – that of creating a politico-military super secret service. He had a plan all ready for the distribution of the Abwehr loot among the different desks of his Section VI. Wehrmacht headquarters raised objections, however; they wished front-line intelligence and counter-espionage units, hitherto responsibilities of the Abwehr, to be allotted to the Wehrmacht. Tough bargaining ensued between Himmler and Field-Marshal Keitel, the Chief of OKW, about spheres of responsibility and the division of the booty.

Gehlen put some backbone into the supine Chief of OKW – he was afraid that the SS would lay hands on FHO's intelligence service, the 'Front-line Reconnaissance Detachments', Walli I and Walli III. Gehlen and his staff drafted a protest to Keitel for signature by the Chief of the General Staff of the Army: 'The proposed arrangement in my view implies a very far-reaching breakdown of the responsibilities of the military secret service and the transfer of many of them to the Reichsführer-SS; this causes me considerable anxiety lest the work of the military secret service suffer serious disadvantages as a result.'

The Chief of the General Staff was unwilling to protest; Keitel did, however, reject a number of important points in the RSHA plan, writing to Himmler: 'The proposed organization will lead to dispersion and therefore to a reduction of output, at least for a considerable period. This must be irresponsible at the present decisive and critical stage of the war.'[4] Schellenberg had to content himself with combining Abwehr I and Abwehr II into a 'Military Office' attached to Section VI of the RSHA; counter-espionage units and front-line intelligence in principle remained the responsibility of the Wehrmacht.[5]

This did not decide, however, under whose command Baun's and Schmalschläger's organizations should be in the future. According to a Keitel–Himmler agreement of May 14th, 1944 front-line intelligence was the responsibility of OKW but 'subject to the instructions of the

Reichsführer-SS from the technical point of view'. Gehlen was determined, in so far as he could, to stop any invasion of his intelligence service by the SD. He was suspicious of the fact that the SS had already allotted new designations to Walli I and III – they were henceforth to be called 'Main Report Centres' [Meldeleitkommandos]. Gehlen laid down the terms to be used: 'The title "Front-line Intelligence" will be employed instead of "Report Centre". The code-name "Walli" will be retained.'[6]

Gehlen succeeded in establishing even closer links with Baun and Schmalschläger. Schellenberg raised no objection to Walli I and III remaining entirely subordinate to FHO 'from the military point of view'. They retained their old titles until the very end of the war and the SS designations never became the rule. In fact the RSHA was only too happy to let Gehlen go his own way, for even the SD recognized the value of FHO's work. Colonel Gehlen became an increasingly close and indispensable partner of the RSHA.[7]

What is the explanation of this mystery? The defenders of Gehlen prefer to leave it unexplained, for close collaboration between RSHA and FHO stands in glaring contrast to the picture which his admirers like to draw of the role he played in the final phase of the Third Reich. The first President of the BND likes to present himself as a resistance fighter, or at least as opposed to the Nazi State.

'I very soon came to the conclusion,' Gehlen said after the war, 'that the cause of disaster was not the people around Hitler but Hitler himself, because he recognized no moral laws.' Being opposed to the Nazi regime, he said, he had surrounded himself with 'politically reliable' men. He went on: 'By "politically reliable" I mean people with whom I could speak frankly about the Nazi leadership and the war situation.' In this category he included his Deputy, Gerhard Wessel, and Graf von Rittberg, the head of Group I. He also maintained that he was 'a close friend of several of the victims of July 20th, 1944, for instance Roenne, Stieff, Freytag-Loringhoven, etc.'[8]

This reference to a few friendships was, in fact, about all that the story of Gehlen, the resister, amounted to. What he did not say, however, was filled in for him by his literary agents. Wolfgang Wehner, the journalist, for instance, maintained that Gehlen had forbidden his Section to use the Hitler salute and had been quite open in his opposition to Hitler's 'unbridled fanaticism'. The writer Jürgen Thorwald had 'reason to suppose' that Gehlen had been working for 'a fundamental change of German policy in the East preceded by the forcible removal of Hitler, Himmler and Rosenberg'.[9]

Thorwald had another remarkable story to tell: according to him the SS had realized that Gehlen was pursuing aims similar to those of the July 20th conspirators and there had accordingly been a bitter struggle between him and the SS – and this was a further reason why Gehlen, when head of the BND, 'rejected ex-SS men in selecting his staff'.[10]

The equanimity, however, with which Gehlen accepted many a murky figure from the ex-SS empire as a member of his post-1945 staff, hardly accords with this story. Anyone who could gather in ex-Gestapo functionaries and ex-SD men, as Gehlen did, could hardly be the uncompromising enemy of the SS which his friends would have us believe. Gehlen, in fact, sat on the fence of internal German quarrels and even to the very last hours of the Third Reich remained what he had always been – the technician, the non-political specialist. He cannot be explained merely by attaching an anti-Nazi label to him.

Ever since joining the General Staff Gehlen, the soldier, had kept himself free of any political commitment. Nevertheless, like almost all German officers, in 1933 he too had hailed the Nazi seizure of power. He had been brought up in the tradition of national conservatism with its predilection for the authoritarian state and the rule of the strong man; as a young Reichswehr officer, therefore, he inevitably welcomed a regime which presented itself as emphatically nationalistic and militarily-minded.

Gehlen did not remain long, however, under the spell of the 'national resurgence'. He was disgusted by the terror with which the regime imposed its *Gleichschaltung* and the rule of the Nazi Party closed shop. Gehlen, the monarchist, soon shed the illusion that the Third Reich was a sort of substitute for the imperial era. Proof exists that as early as 1938 he gave vent to some highly critical comments about the Nazi system.[11] For many officers the year 1938 marked the beginning of a gradual estrangement from the Nazi state – in February of that year both the armed forces as a whole and the Army in particular had lost their leaders as a result of a Gestapo intrigue (the Blomberg-Fritsch affair) and Hitler himself had assumed supreme command of the Wehrmacht.

Admittedly Gehlen regarded this affair not so much as a manoeuvre by Hitler as skulduggery on the part of the Party. In this he was not alone; many officers thought that a distinction should be drawn between Hitler and the Party. Field-Marshal von Manstein says in his memoirs that the 'widespread view' of the Army at the time was that 'Hitler did not know of the misdeeds of his followers and would certainly not approve if he learnt of them.' The immortally ironical popular expression for this wishful thinking was: 'If only the Führer knew!'[12]

Few subscribed to this point of view more assiduously than Colonel Gehlen. As late as 1942 he was still believing that Hitler could be persuaded to take a more sensible view of the situation by secret-service reports and accurate enemy appreciations. He was still so far under the spell of Hitler discipleship that professions of faith in Nazism came naturally to him. He was only too happy that the label of ideological rectitude be attached to FHO because it contained faithful Nazis such as SA-Obersturmführer Viktor von der Marwitz or the SS cavalryman Alexander von Mielecki.[13]

Again and again Gehlen warned the anti-Nazis in his Section to be extremely careful in their anti-Nazi talk. He admits that 'at least on one occasion' he 'explicitly warned' Graf von Rittberg, the head of one of his Groups; on several occasions he watered down memoranda by Major Heinz Herre, his senior officer, criticizing German occupation policy in Russia.[14]

This problem of policy in the East was the issue which ultimately forced Gehlen into opposition to his political masters. The results of the activities of the Party racial fanatics and the SS liquidation squads in German-occupied Russia became only too obvious – in their fury they were destroying the last remnants of that goodwill with which the Russians had greeted Hitler's armies as their liberators from Stalin's tyranny.

Gehlen decided that he must alert the military leaders. He had reports prepared on the attitude of the population in the occupied areas and in the Red Army; they showed clearly how catastrophic was the 'sub-humans' policy pursued by the German colonial tyrants. FHO submitted memoranda, analyses and case histories to the Chief of the General Staff and to OKW. In October 1942 Herre noted: 'We are all determined to pursue this case, to go on assembling material and somehow ensure that it reaches those in high places by the most suitable channel.'[15]

Gehlen's main supporter in his campaign was the head of his Desk IIz, Lieutenant-Colonel Alexis Freiherr von Roenne. Roenne was a convinced opponent of the regime and on close terms with prominent members of the anti-Hitler military faction. His arguments were so convincing that even the cautious and suspicious Gehlen eventually took him fully into his confidence.

Roenne was particularly knowledgeable about the mood of the population in the occupied areas of Russia. His Desk (later Group III) was in charge of the interrogation camps for Russian prisoners of war and was

T–C

daily receiving reports of the hatred for the Germans aroused by the Nazi exploitation system.

Roenne, who was a Baltic Baron, collected quite a circle of FHO officers around him, including Captain Wilfried Strik-Strikfeldt, the Section's chief interrogator; all were prepared to do battle against the Nazi exploiters wherever they could. Roenne was in close contact with Lieutenant-Colonel Graf Stauffenberg of the Organization Section of the Army General Staff; others worked with a group of Balts in the Propaganda Section of OKW. Gehlen was also in touch with the staff of Army Group Centre where the most determined opponents of Nazi methods in the East were located. FHO even discovered that some of the most eminent Nazis thought the same way; Herre noted: 'Have heard that Goebbels has sent a most sensible letter to local directors of propaganda – entirely of our way of thinking.' Opponents of the master-race programme were to be found even in Alfred Rosenberg's Ministry for the East.[16]

The fact that senior Party members were on his side made Gehlen think that Hitler could be persuaded to change course. His defender Thorwald asserts that as early as 1942 he had realized that Hitler himself was responsible for the colonial policy in the East, quoting him as referring to 'the violent methods of conquest supported by the Führer'. Historically, unfortunately, this is not accurate – entries in the diary of his confidant Herre prove the opposite.

On October 11th, 1942, for instance, Herre noted: 'The shortcomings are continually becoming more obvious, but the vital question remains: How can these shortcomings be brought to the notice of the Führer so that he himself can put an end to them?' Gehlen and Herre still thought that Rosenberg, Himmler and Koch, the Reich Commissar in the Ukraine, were primarily responsible for the state of affairs in the East. Herre was a prophet of gloom: 'No good can come of this. Much good German blood will inevitably flow in vain.' Yet he still considered that the only hope lay in Hitler, writing on November 18th: 'One wonders whether our aide-memoire [against policy in the East] has had any success. I think so. But who will submit it to the Führer and how?'[17]

Gradually, however, Gehlen and his staff began to suspect that Hitler himself might possibly be the root of all evil. Herre noted in his diary: 'I propose to put it quite plainly to the Chief that, as far as our leaders are concerned, we are now in a full-scale crisis of confidence.' Gehlen was so taken aback by this realization that he confided in his friend Lieutenant-Colonel Henning von Tresckow, Chief of Staff to Army Group Centre and one of the principal resisters. 'We agreed,' Gehlen recalls, 'that the Russian campaign could be won provided that it was soundly led both militarily and politically, but that under the prevailing circumstances it was bound to end in failure. We were quite clear that the answer to the question "What to do?" was: "It can only succeed without Number One." We were both so horrified by this admission that we broke off the conversation – we were, after all, both officers under oath.'[18]

The catastrophic development of the war situation, however, left Gehlen no choice but to urge upon Hitler a revision of his Eastern policy. The Nazi programme of conquest threatened the very existence of FHO – the day could be seen approaching when no Russian would be prepared to risk his neck for FHO's intelligence service.

On November 25th, 1942 Gehlen sent to the Führer's Headquarters a 17-page memorandum severely criticizing the failures of German occupation policy. He even equated the Nazis with the communists, saying that neither the Soviets nor the Germans had given the Russians what they longed for – 'justice, organizational ability, understanding and welfare'. The increasingly dangerous partisans, Gehlen argued, could never be suppressed without the support of the Russian population; the 'debatable notion', therefore, that the Slav was an inferior being was 'indubitably an error of the first order'. A fundamental change in occupation policy, Gehlen stipulated, was an urgent necessity. The Reich should grant the population of the East self-administration, greater cultural autonomy and the right to raise their own forces. Finally he demanded 'ruthless abolition of discriminatory practices'.[19]

All of a sudden Gehlen had appeared in the forefront of the section of Army opinion which, primarily for reasons of expediency, was opposed to Hitler's occupation policy. Without waiting for an answer from the Führer's headquarters, Gehlen pushed ahead with his own Eastern programme – and Point No 1 in it was the formation of an army of Russian anti-communists.

As early as October 1941 Strik-Strikfeldt had drawn up a remarkable plan for Gehlen's friend Tresckow: a Russian liberation army of 200,000 men was to march against the Soviets alongside the Wehrmacht and fight for a free unregimented Russia.[20]

The plan was turned down forthwith by Keitel, the Chief of OKW, but Strik-Strikfeldt and his masters were not discouraged. Everywhere on the Eastern Front German formations began to recruit Russian auxiliaries, mostly ex-prisoners of war, to arm them and use them for minor operations. Hitler repeatedly forbade the formation of further auxiliary formations, but the army invariably found some excuse for the recruitment of additional assistance. By the end of 1942 there were so many auxiliaries that Stauffenberg was able to engineer the constitution of a special headquarters known as 'General of Eastern Forces'.

In his capacity as interrogator Strik-Strikfeldt eventually unearthed a man who, he thought, had the charismatic qualities to exert enormous influence on the Russian people. This was Lieutenant-General Andrei Andreyevich Vlassov, one of Stalin's most capable Army Commanders who had been captured by the Germans in the summer of 1942. Strik-Strikfeldt saw in him the 'Russian de Gaulle', the ideal leader of the proposed liberation army.[21]

Vlassov was ready to side with the Germans and Gehlen adopted him. He allowed Vlassov to form a political organization, to recruit adherents in the prisoner-of-war camps and to make preparations for the constitution of an anti-communist army. Gehlen was careful to keep all this secret from the extreme apostles of the 'sub-humans' policy such as Himmler and Koch, also from the more moderate Nazis in Rosenberg's Ministry for the East, who were equally opposed to Vlassov. He was, after all, a Muscovite Russian who supported a centralized unified state, whereas Rosenberg's people were campaigning for the dismemberment of Russia into numerous small states and racial groups.[22] So adroit was Gehlen's diplomacy, however, that for a short time he succeeded in bringing the vacillating Rosenberg over to his side. In January 1943 the Minister for the East promised support for Vlassov's propaganda efforts provided they were confined to the Muscovite Russians.[23]

Vlassov had barely formed his political committee, however, when Himmler sounded the alarm in the Führer's headquarters. On March 4th, 1943 he wrote to the Party Chancellery that Vlassov's activities were in clear contravention of the orders of the Führer who had forbidden any truck with Russian nationalism. Before this came to Hitler's ears, however, Gehlen had taken avoiding action: he let it be known that Vlassov's recruiting campaign was necessary in the interests of enemy intelligence.[24]

Having put up this smokescreen, he gave the green light for a propaganda coup by the Vlassov movement. On April 20th, 1943 'Operation Silver Streak' began on the central sector of the Eastern Front: General Vlassov's propaganda squads inundated the Soviet positions with exhortations to desert, promising every deserter good treatment, adequate nourishment and employment in the Vlassov movement.[25]

The operation was successful. In May 1943 2,500 Red Army men deserted and a few weeks later the figure had risen to 6,500. Gehlen ordered the scale of effort to be redoubled. He appointed Strik-Strikfeldt permanent assistant to Vlassov, he made Herre available as Chief of Staff to the 'General of Eastern Forces', he propped up Rosenberg in his efforts to silence the anti-Russian fanatics in Hitler's entourage. In addition he wrote yet another memorandum, again addressed to the Führer's headquarters. On June 1st, 1943 he declared that the results of Vlassov's operations had been so encouraging that the Führer could now proceed to the next step – proclamation of an independent Russian government under the leadership of Andrei Vlassov.[26]

But the dictator would have no part of such 'extraordinary nonsense'. Hitler raged: 'I will never form a Russian army. That is fantasy of the first order.' On June 8th he decided that there was to be no Vlassov army; the Russian general might carry on propaganda at the front, but more he would not allow him. Two months later, in fact, Hitler was wanting to disband all the auxiliary formations because he had heard that some of them had gone over to the partisans. Once more Gehlen took counteraction; he persuaded the Führer's headquarters to postpone the disbandment and so at least managed to retain the majority of the 'Eastern Forces'.[27]

Gehlen was in despair. On March 16th he had written in his usual veiled terms to Roenne, who had meanwhile been appointed head of 'Foreign Armies West': 'Dear Roenne, The Company Commander [=Chief of the General Staff] has completely abandoned the struggle for these matters, at least temporarily, and the whole affair is in the doldrums. For the moment, therefore, we must tread somewhat cautiously in our propaganda on this subject, otherwise, should K [Koch] take a hand, the whole affair risks being torpedoed ... Can you not make the time to pass through here so that I can talk to someone, which one can't do over the telephone? With very best wishes, ever yours, Gehlen.'[28]

Gehlen knew that the Vlassov experiment was doomed. For the first time it had dawned on him that Germany was ruled by a maniac, open to no rational argument, a man who would obstinately pursue his own course – to the bitter end.

His involvement with Vlassov gave to Gehlen's political views on Russia a twist which remained with him even after the war. He could not forget the hundreds of thousands of anti-communist Russians who, in 1943, were prepared to make common cause with the Germans in order to break the tyranny of Stalin. His friendship with men who believed in Vlassov reinforced him in the belief that another more liberal system than that of the Soviets was possible in Russia. Only with difficulty was Gehlen later brought to realize that the Vlassov movement represented no more than a passing, highly uncertain and non-recurring opportunity to disrupt the Red regime in Russia, occasioned by the totalitarian colonialist nature of the Hitler regime. Even in the late 1940s Gehlen still thought the Soviet governmental and social system so unstable that an overthrow of the communist regime seemed to him conceivable. The example of the Vlassov movement led him, on many occasions, to misjudge the true position in the Soviet Union.

In 1943, of course, he knew that there was no possibility of a free Russia under Hitler – he was now clear that Hitler's policy was leading to disaster. Yet he hesitated to ally himself with his friends such as Stauffenberg, Roenne and Tresckow, whose purpose was to eliminate the madman in the Führer's headquarters.

Even today Gehlen still refuses to say what prevented him supporting the military resistance to Hitler. He would obviously have found it impossible to participate in preparations for a *Putsch* owing to his strict Prussian traditionalist concept of the obligations imposed on him by his oath of allegiance; in addition he may well have been horrified by the dilettante manner in which the conspirators went to work. Moreover Gehlen was so closely involved in the desperate defensive battles on the eastern front, now tottering under the blows of the Russians, that he probably feared that an abortive *coup d'état* with the civil war that would inevitably follow, would lead to the total collapse of the army in the east, followed by the Red Army flooding across Germany.

Nevertheless Gehlen allowed determined anti-Nazis to continue conspiratorial discussions inside his Section and to make use of FHO's secrets for their own purposes. He also retained Major Karl-Heinrich Graf von Rittberg who, after Roenne's departure, became the leading anti-Nazi in FHO. He was head of Group I (Daily enemy situation report) and was in the confidence of many of Stauffenberg's allies in Army Headquarters. Like Roenne, he was a devout Christian; through his cousin Helmuth James Graf von Moltke he was in touch with the resistance group known as the Kreisau Circle and he regarded the murder of Hitler as the only method of saving Germany. He was present in the 'Berchtesgadener Hof' Hotel in Berchtesgaden during the final days before July 20th when details of the attack on Hitler were discussed between Generals Wagner, Stieff and Fellgiebel. Rittberg's name had long been on the Gestapo's black list.[29]

The conspirators in FHO were in fact never certain how far Gehlen approved of what they were doing. 'The Chief' did not invite them to tell him their secrets. Gehlen puts it this way: 'I did not myself brief Graf

Rittberg about the immediate background to the preparations for July 20th. My relationship to him was such that he understood what one said to him.'[30]

Gehlen thus intends to imply that he knew about the forthcoming *Putsch* and undoubtedly he was informed in general terms about the preparations. He certainly did not, however, know dates or details. When the conspirators struck he was convalescing in Bad Elster after a bad attack of septicaemia early in July which had put him in hospital. He was probably in the same position as the head of his Group II who said: 'We were all taken completely by surprise by July 20th.'[31]

Writing his memoirs twenty-seven years later, Gehlen presents himself, if not as an actual member of the anti-Hitler conspiracy, at least as an accessory to the plans for the *Putsch*. He ascribes the Gestapo's failure to arrest him to the fact that he was in hospital in Breslau, saying: 'So I was simply "forgotten" ' – a somewhat improbable error for a machine as perfectly organized as the Gestapo, and attributed to it by a man who had intimate experience of it through his work with the SS Reich Security Department (the RSHA).

The Chief girded his loins to protect his Section from the obviously imminent retaliation by the Gestapo. His friend Roenne had already been arrested and executed, Rittberg had been carted off by the Gestapo, Captain Lindeiner and Rittberg's friend Smend had been interrogated. Gehlen managed to prise Rittberg and Lindeiner free but the bloodthirsty savagery of the Gestapo showed him that it was too risky to keep anti-Hitler putschists in FHO in future. Some of the resisters found themselves sent back to their units by Gehlen – including even Rittberg, who was shot by order of a summary court martial in 1945 for alleged subversive activities.[32]

Gehlen's reaction is reminiscent of Vlassov's attitude after the plot of July 20th. When he heard from Strik-Strikfeldt that Stauffenberg and his friends had been shot, he pretended not to know them, saying: 'One does not refer to dead men as friends. One does not know them. Never forget that, Wilfried Karlovich. I have graduated through Stalin's school. That is only the beginning.'[33]

As FHO was purged of committed anti-Nazis Gehlen's links with the SS became closer and closer, for from spring 1944 the SS was the ruling authority in secret-service matters. Gehlen had never liked the SS and had always supported the Chief of the Army General Staff in his refusal to accord it military privileges. In the year of grace 1944, however, with the Abwehr gone, anyone in Germany dealing with enemy intelligence, and therefore being a customer for secret-service reports, had to come to terms with the SS – and that meant cooperating with Schellenberg, the inscrutable and ambitious head of SD.

Gehlen had known 'Himmler's Benjamin', as Schellenberg liked to call himself, ever since the two authorities, SD and FHO, had been brought together in an operation run by the RSHA known as 'Operation Zeppelin'. This was an invention of the Eastern Group of the Ausland/SD, started in March 1942; its object was to train Soviet prisoners of war as saboteurs and use them behind the Russian lines.[34]

'Zeppelin' headquarters, headed from 1943 by SS-Sturmbannführer Dr Erich Hengelhaupt, maintained three main detachments in the East which in turn possessed advanced posts in the combat zone; the task of the latter was to carry out an immediate check of Soviet prisoners for suitability for employment in 'Operation Zeppelin'. These advanced posts, however, were entirely dependent on the goodwill of the 'Front-line Reconnaissance Detachments', whose prerogative it was to interrogate all Soviet prisoners before their onward passage to a POW camp.

If 'Zeppelin' headquarters wished to take on any particularly important prisoners, then they had to reach agreement with the 'Front-line Reconnaissance Detachments' and their controlling authority – Gehlen's Section. In practice the decision whether a prisoner should remain under army control or be released to the SD was that of FHO. Later FHO became involved in providing information for specific 'Zeppelin' operations, since in general only FHO had precise knowledge of conditions in the Soviet rear areas. The SD accordingly consulted FHO before practically every 'Zeppelin' operation.[35]

This process had begun in the summer of 1943 when Hengelhaupt was planning his first major operation. A group of 'converted' Soviet prisoners was to be dropped in Red Army uniform behind the Russian front to spread confusion and gather intelligence. Hengelhaupt had trained his agents for their secret mission over a period of months. Uniforms were ready, weapons were loaded and orders confirmed; the only thing missing was military papers to authenticate the agents as Soviet officers. The RSHA's false papers shop could not produce these unless Hengelhaupt's staff could tell it what Red Army formations were located in the agents' operational area. But no RSHA agency could answer that question; not even the SD's central card index showed where specific Red Army units were located. Hengelhaupt accordingly turned to Colonel Gehlen's FHO.

On July 7th, 1943 Hengelhaupt cabled to FHO: 'For extremely urgent operational preparations in connection with "Operation Zeppelin" the present location of Eleventh Army is requested, also if possible of its Signals Regiment, its heavy Artillery Regiment and any two infantry regiments.' Three days later Gehlen's Section replied: 'Eleventh Soviet Army is not at present in the front line. It was last identified on April 7th 1943 south-east of Staraya Russa with headquarters in Velikoye Selo. When last in line the Army included the following formations: 55 Rifle Division, 12 Guards Armoured Regiment . . . At present these formations are shown in immediate reserve or possibly further in rear, facing Army Group North.'[36]

From the end of 1943 FHO did in fact reap some benefit from the 'Zeppelin' operations in Russia. The scheme was now working so smoothly that the information produced by its groups of agents was of considerable value to FHO. The so-called 'activists' of 'Operation Zeppelin' were working at numerous points far behind the Soviet front. They included for instance: a three-man team in Moscow which infiltrated the Soviet Ministry of Transport and photographed reports on Red Army movements; a group in the Chiguli mountains which kept a watch on the rail junction of Kuibishev and was intended to recruit further groups of activists; several groups along the Moscow–Vologda–Archangel railway which, together with the indigenous population, formed resistance groups in inaccessible wooded areas.[37]

The majority of these operations were amateurish and ended in the sub-machine-gun fire of the Russian secret police. Nevertheless they produced sufficient information on conditions in Russia to make Gehlen's intelligence experts avid for more. FHO and SD moved closer together.

Coming into closer contact with Schellenberg's organization, Gehlen realized that many of the SD officers had long since lost their blind faith in Hitler's anti-Slav theories. Ever since early 1944 the cold-blooded rationalists of the SD had been advocating a policy which bore an astounding similarity to Gehlen's Vlassov programme. In the summer of 1944 they even managed to persuade their Reichsführer to execute a remarkable about-turn in Eastern policy. Himmler, who had always referred to Vlassov as a 'butcher-boy' and regarded him as a 'dangerous bolshevist' now permitted him to form two Russian divisions with resources provided by the SS.[38]

Gehlen was impressed by this unexpectedly forthcoming attitude on the part of Himmler and was only too willing to assist many an SD officer. He persuaded his friend Herre to make himself available as Chief of Staff to Vlassov even under SS jurisdiction; in January 1945 he even temporarily seconded his Deputy Wessel to act as chief of intelligence to Himmler's Army Group Vistula.[39] Moreover another SS man appeared with increasing frequency at Gehlen's side – SS-Sturmbannführer [Major] Otto Skorzeny, commander of the SS Special Service Formation [Jagdverbände].

In November 1944 Skorzeny was commissioned to set up a resistance organization in the Soviet rear areas and gain contact with anti-communist partisans. As the Operations Section of the Army General Staff noted on November 12th, these were to include: 'Resistance groups composed of Ukrainian nationalists; groups of the Polish national resistance movement which have not been altogether dispersed after being overrun by the Soviet advance; Russian anti-Soviet resistance groups to be found as deep into Russia as the Caucasus and consisting of opponents of the system, refugees etc; other anti-Soviet resistance groups composed of non-Russian elements (prisoners of war, deportees, criminals).'[40]

The link to these resistance groups, in so far as they were not already involved in 'Operation Zeppelin', was the 'Front-line Reconnaissance Detachments' and therefore FHO. Skorzeny accordingly had to consult Gehlen if he was to gain contact with the partisans. Gehlen, however, made the most of the opportunity offered by Skorzeny's Special Service Troops and Hengelhaupt's 'Zeppelin' groups to broaden the basis of his intelligence.

Gehlen worked out a plan visualizing nothing less than the concentration of the resisters and the intelligence-gatherers into a combined espionage organization behind the Soviet front. He laid down: 'If the collection of intelligence by agents under battle conditions is to be efficient, it is necessary to give it the façade of a partisan movement.' Gehlen had long since abandoned the romanticized picture of Russia painted by his German–Balt friends; he now proposed to use the Vlassov Russians merely as instruments for the collection of enemy intelligence.[41] On February 24th, 1945, Gehlen wrote to Schellenberg: 'The espionage service aimed at the Russian armed forces must be divorced from the purely Russian-national concepts of the Vlassov movement. This is necessary, in the first place to prevent the ideas of the Vlassov circle spreading too far among the agents, secondly to create an opportunity for large-scale employment of non-Russian agents.' He visualized an intelligence organization, run by FHO and the RSHA, covering the whole of Eastern Europe deep into the Soviet Union and making use of all racial groups in the East. He laid down: 'For the purpose of collecting intelligence a new non-German intelligence network will be created by formation of the necessary number of efficient groups of agents in the enemy's rear areas; it will be known as the "Secret League of Green Partisans" and will ostensibly be under Russian leadership. The principle will be: the organization to be constituted solely behind the Russian front; on this side there will be only channels of intelligence. No affiliation to Vlassov.'[42]

Without realizing it, Gehlen had thus patented the post-war organization which later bore his name. He, Skorzeny and Hengelhaupt in concert assembled all possible information about the existence of East European resistance groups. It was collated and a list of each group prepared by the 'Research Service East', an agency of the RSHA. In its 'Political Information' No 114, for instance, this agency noted: in the Mogilev area 'ex-auxiliaries and some Germans in small Vlassov groups', around Briansk 'predatory partisans and gangs of deserters' and near Orel 'medium or strong groups of Vlassov supporters numbering about 1,000 men, ex-auxiliaries with adequate armament'. Under the heading 'Activity and Political Programme' was noted: 'Sabotage of communications ... propaganda by leaflet, blowing up of bridges and railway installations, ambushes of small Red Army units ... looting, derailments.'[43]

Gehlen noted every increase in the anti-communist partisan movement – for instance: 'In the western Ukraine the nationalist partisan movement is considerably on the increase and may be considered to cause serious anxiety to the Soviet Union', or 'towards the end of the month anti-Soviet guerrillas in Hungary received considerable reinforcement as a result of innumerable atrocities committed by the Soviet occupying forces.'[44]

In addition to the 'Research Service East' Gehlen contrived to make use of other SS agencies and information centres – the 'Wannsee Institute' which had been evacuated to Plankenwarth Castle near Graz, the 'Reich Geography Foundation', the publicity agencies in Vienna, Dahlem and Frankfurt am Main, the 'Orient Research Centre', the 'East Asia Institute', the 'Havel Institute'. Information from all these was grist to the FHO mill.[45]

Cooperation between FHO and the RSHA became increasingly close and relations between Gehlen and the SD officers increasingly intimate. Consultation with FHO on their manifold subversive activities became a matter of routine to the SD. Whether they wanted information on Soviet partisans, investigations into adherents of the 'Free Germany Committee' formed by German prisoners of war in the Soviet Union, or evaluation of intelligence received by the SD from foreign intelligence services, the FHO was always on hand to enlighten its SS comrades.

FHO's information was in fact so useful that the RSHA gave almost ungrudging recognition to the work of Gehlen's Section. When he visited FHO headquarters Schellenberg flattered his host Gehlen, saying that the SD would never be able to work with the scientific precision of FHO. He asked for the secondment to the RSHA of one hundred officers, NCOs and men trained in intelligence schools; he checked with FHO his 'radio play-back' games and he ordered the SS Special Service Troops to conform to FHO directives and requirements as, for instance, the following: 'Subject: Destruction of the Vistula rail bridges. Evaluation of the most recent air reconnaissance shows several intact railway bridges over the Vistula at Cracow, Deblin, Warsaw and Torun. The main weight of supplies for the Soviet front passes over these bridges. If they could be damaged or destroyed, this would constitute a considerable relief to our own forces.'[46]

The RSHA repaid all this useful information by handing over to FHO certain highly classified Gestapo prisoners who could be used for 'radio play-back' games. In February 1945, for instance, Colonel Hoyer was placed at FHO's disposal; he was an ex-Regimental Commander who had joined the 'Free Germany' Committee while a Soviet prisoner of war, had been sent back to Germany as an agent and had fallen into the hands of the Gestapo. Gehlen noted that FHO had been given 'complete authority over Colonel Hoyer' and could 'use him as they thought fit'.[47]

Gehlen ultimately became so close an ally of the RSHA that, during the death-throes of Adolf Hitler's regime he, together with the SS officers Skorzeny and Prützmann, was charged with military direction of that macabre partisan and resistance organization known as 'Werewolf', intended to spread panic among the enemy. In an order dated November 12th, 1944, dealing with 'Battle in the rear of the enemy' the Army General Staff Operations Section laid down that 'Foreign Armies East will be responsible for cooperation with the RSHA on all matters concerning forward intelligence units.' On February 6th, 1945, the Strategic Group of the General Staff urged Army Groups to support 'Werewolf' energetically, saying: 'All units in whose vicinity "Werewolf" groups are located will take measures for the supply and welfare of the "Werewolf" groups concerned.'[48]

Anyone so determined to continue to the bitter end could be sure of the approbation of his superiors. Gehlen climbed several rungs of the ladder: he was promoted Major-General; he became Deputy Chief of the Strategic Group of the General Staff; he was even entrusted with the

General Staff's security – in the event of catastrophe he was to arrange for the Staff's immediate evacuation.[49]

Better still – Heinz Guderian, the new Army Chief of Staff, placed an almost blind faith in FHO's enemy appreciations. Guderian had been an intelligence officer under Nicolai; he therefore understood the problems of intelligence and appreciated Gehlen's achievements. He based his operational plans exclusively on Gehlen's intelligence, however discouraging it might be. This, however, aroused Hitler's wrath.

The dictator had long been irritated by FHO's realistic appreciations. Their prosaic and allegedly defeatist style infuriated Hitler – an example is the following: 'In view of the advance of strong Soviet forces against the previous front, the situation in Army Group Centre can no longer be re-established. A decision must be taken whether Army Group Centre is to relinquish its present front in order to defend the core of East Prussia or whether East Prussia must be abandoned in order to free the necessary forces. Since the Russian offensive, if successfully pursued, can have a decisive effect on the course of the war as a whole, the loss of East Prussia must carry less weight than the loss of the war.'[50]

When, in view of Soviet offensive capabilities, Guderian was trying to persuade Hitler to concentrate the German forces on the eastern front, he based his case primarily on Gehlen's appreciations such as that quoted above. Hitler, on the other hand, believed that the Russians were barely capable of a major offensive. When, on December 24th, 1944, Guderian referred to Gehlen's reports, which painted a very different picture, Hitler growled: 'This is the biggest imposture since Ghengis Khan. Who is responsible for producing all this rubbish?'[51]

Gehlen then attempted to bring his views to the notice of Hitler's immediate advisers, using secret channels to inform the OKW Operations Staff of the true situation. On January 4th, 1945, he wrote to Lieutenant-General Winter, the Deputy Chief: 'Dear General, Attached for your information I am sending you an aide-mémoire which I have submitted to the Chief of the General Staff of the Army. Since I am not authorized to pass it on, I would ask you to treat it as what it is. I would be grateful if, after you have read it, the courier could bring it back to me. With respectful good wishes, your obedient servant, Gehlen.' The courier was given a letter of authorization which ran: 'Lieutenant Athenstaedt is ordered to hand special mail to Lieutenant-General Winter, Deputy Chief of the OKW Operations Staff.' Winter promptly replied: 'Dear Gehlen, Attached I return with thanks your appreciation of the enemy situation. I have drawn the attention of the Chief of the OKW

Operations Staff to it. With greetings of comradeship and Heil Hitler. Yours: Winter.'[52]

Thus encouraged, on January 5th Gehlen reported that 'it must be anticipated that the Soviet High Command intends the forthcoming offensive to constitute a decisive step in the destruction of the German army in the East'[53] and, when Guderian went to the Führer's headquarters, Gehlen armed him with fresh statistics showing the strength of the Soviet enemy. Guderian laid this information before his Führer on January 9th. 'Completely idiotic,' Hitler shouted and demanded that the author be shut up in a lunatic asylum. Guderian lost his temper and replied: 'The man who made these is General Gehlen, one of my very best staff officers. I would not have shown them to you were I not in agreement with them. If you want General Gehlen sent to a lunatic asylum, then you had better have me certified as well.' Hitler gave way but from this moment the names Guderian and Gehlen figured on the dictator's black list.[54]

When Guderian and Hitler clashed again on March 28th, the subject was once more Gehlen's report on the enemy situation. Guderian and his 'crazy General Gehlen', the dictator raged, had misinformed him over and over again. Guderian flashed back: 'Has General Gehlen in his intelligence estimate "misinformed" about the strength of the Russians? No!' Hitler roared: 'Gehlen is a fool!' The two men were shouting so loud that Hitler sent the other officers present out of the room. Then he spoke quite quietly: 'Colonel-General Guderian, your physical health requires that you take six weeks convalescent leave immediately.'[55]

Gehlen did not survive the fall of Guderian by more than a few days. On April 9th, 1945, he too became a victim of Hitler's wrath and was dismissed as head of the Section 'Foreign Armies East'. His place was taken by Lieutenant-Colonel Wessel.[56]

4

CHANGE OF ALLEGIANCE

HITLER'S order of dismissal descended upon Major-General Gehlen when he was in the midst of secret preparations for an enterprise destined to figure as the most astonishing apostasy in the history of German espionage. He was ready to take his entire intelligence organization across into the service of the Americans even before the war had ended. It was a step he had been planning for months.

Thanks to his intimate knowledge of enemy potential Gehlen had been quick to realize that the war would end in Germany's defeat. He saw the Americans emerging as the undisputed victors. As early as 1942 he had shown interest in the military might of America; a note in Halder's diary of the spring of that year reads: 'Lieutenant-Colonel Gehlen: briefing on American armed forces.' Gehlen did not long remain in doubt as to who would be the losers of the war.[1]

He soon became fascinated by the question how an army and an administration could be preserved in a country occupied by the enemy and the fate of the Polish Secret Army provided him with his first example. In 1943 the files of the resistance headquarters, under which the Secret Army was operating, had fallen into the hands of FHO; they included plans for a rising against the German occupation forces. Thereupon, in February 1944, Gehlen prepared a memorandum revealing extensive knowledge of Polish resistance; it included this: 'The Polish underground army is under the direction of the "National Commander" (Colonel Count Komorowski, code-name "Bor"). The task of the Secret Army is to prepare for a rising and for reconstruction of the Polish armed forces.' In August 1944 Bor-Komorowski struck in Warsaw, as Gehlen had forecast, but his rising failed. Gehlen thereupon ordered an examination of the possibilities of underground existence for an illegal government and army.[2] One of the 'Front-line Reconnaissance Detachments' was ordered to analyse the history of the Warsaw rising. On Gehlen's behalf Lieutenant-Colonel Horaczek, the former head of the Abwehr office in Warsaw, was sent to interrogate Bor-Komorowski in prison. The conclusion of the inquiry was that underground resistance operations could not be effective in the long term.[3]

Based on this interest in Polish resistance, Eastern propaganda still accuses Gehlen of having initiated the formation of a German underground organization at this time. In fact he never even considered such a plan. He contemplated a very different escape route for himself and his specialists.

The idea seized upon by Gehlen originated from the bitterest opponent of Nazism in FHO, Graf von Rittberg, the head of one of his Groups. Rittberg had aired it for the first time in 1943 to his friend Major Schwerdtfeger, who says: 'In a private talk with me he raised the thought and the possibility of passing across to the Allies all the information held in FHO on the Russian army, its training, arms potential, etc, with the object of demonstrating to them the dangerous nature of their ally and so possibly assisting attempts to conclude a separate peace with the Allies.'[4]

Gehlen, the conservative anti-communist, was equally convinced that one day the West would have need of the Germans against the Soviet Union; for Gehlen and his staff, therefore, FHO's Russian intelligence would inevitably constitute a *laissez-passer* into the future. In mid-1944 Gehlen was calculating that 'the alliance between the Western Powers and the Soviet Union would fall apart as soon as their common enemy had been defeated'.

Gehlen's intention to enter the service of the Western Powers after the German defeat was finally confirmed by Winston Churchill. In his memoirs Gehlen says that 'by devious means . . . he laid hands on an appreciation of Churchill's which took far too favourable a view of our [German] situation but painted a realistic picture of Soviet potential and Soviet intentions'. Churchill's analysis, Gehlen says, described, without any trace of illusion, the future development into socialist states of Poland and the Balkan States including Hungary. Gehlen describes Churchill's appreciation as 'an explosive document' which was 'destroyed at the end of the war'.[5]

Gehlen prepared his immediate associates in FHO and Walli I for the great moment. Jaschka Jakow, a member of Göring's secret-service agency known as the 'Research Office', heard of the plan in late 1944 when he met Gehlen in a house in the Munich suburb of Pasing. Jakow recalls: 'There were three other officers in his room at the time. We were all members of the Abwehr staff and knew each other only by code-name. On this day we were given "instructions for the work of the Abwehr in the event of temporary occupation of Germany by hostile forces".'[6]

Gehlen concealed his escape plans from the suspicious men of the RSHA with considerable adroitness. SS-Brigadeführer Walter Schellenberg, who was responsible for the secret service, was given to understand that FHO must prepare itself for the eventuality of an occupation of Germany by enemy forces; in that event an intelligence service must continue to function underground. FHO began to photostat all reports and appreciations on the Soviet Union and prepared to evacuate the duplicates. As his reason Gehlen gave the necessity for FHO to continue to work even if the originals should be destroyed by bombing.[7]

Gehlen was able to make unobtrusive preparations for the actual movement since in February 1945, as Deputy Chief of the Strategic Group of the Army General Staff, he had been commissioned to plan the withdrawal by road of all General Staff Sections. Under cover of this he gave priority to the move of FHO and its card-index.

On April 4th the officer in charge of the card-index received the following 'Top Secret' instructions: 'In the event of the formation of an advance party and its movement by road ahead of the main body of the Section, it is intended that the card-index form part of this advance party. You are requested to ensure that officers, NCOs, men and secretaries are instructed that the order for movement must be carried out within two hours at the maximum and that within this period the entire card-index must be loaded. Personal baggage including blankets must be carried and may not be loaded on the trucks.'[8]

Having thus prepared for movement Gehlen drove that very day with his deputy Wessel to Bad Elster in Saxony where Lieutenant-Colonel Hermann Baun had his headquarters. With hindsight this meeting was of historic significance – one month and four days before the capitulation of Nazi Germany the blueprint for the subsequent alliance between Washington and Bonn was drawn up in Bad Elster. In the Kurhotel there the three men outlined the plan which was to guarantee them a fresh career. As the announcer's voice boomed over the radio with the news: 'The enemy continued his attack on the fortress of Breslau in strength; fighting is taking place in the streets of Rheine and Osnabrück', Adolf Hitler's three officers addressed themselves to the problem of leaving Nazism's sinking ship and seeking refuge in the democratic future.[9]

Gehlen opened the discussion with a prognostication: the war would last another four weeks at the most; it was not possible to predict whether an immediate military confrontation between East and West would follow; in any case the German army must fight on the Western side, even if only initially as an army of prisoners. Officers and men of

FHO, Gehlen continued, would receive from him an order to move from Maybach Camp near Zossen, the headquarters of the Army General Staff, into south Germany since, according to the Allied plans available to him, southern Germany was the occupation zone allotted to the Americans.

On this subject Gehlen says in his memoirs: 'I suspected that, after the end of hostilities, the Americans would be quicker than our European enemies to recapture some objectivity *vis-à-vis* the Germans.' Always anxious for some backing for his decision, Gehlen looked for 'a solid legal background for our future plans'. In the first place he sought support from General Winter, the Deputy Chief of the OKW Operations Staff, to whom he had written secret letters in the Führer's head-quarters early in 1945. After the end of the war, Gehlen also recalls, he had happened to meet Grand Admiral Karl Dönitz in Wiesbaden and had told him of his idea of providing intelligence assistance to the Western Allies; Dönitz had also agreed.

Baun stated that he too would try to move Walli I in a general south-westerly direction; he and Gehlen agreed that they would offer their services in concert to no one but the Americans. Each of them could bring with him a house-warming present – from FHO complete information on the Russian armed forces including a card-index of Red Army personalities, from Walli I a circuit of agents stretching as far as Moscow.

Baun had already prepared an operational plan for the new war against the Red Army to be conducted on German soil. After the collapse of the Wehrmacht it visualized: training and employment of saboteurs and raiding parties behind the Soviet lines; military espionage against the Red Army; preparations of arms caches for a subsequent anti-Soviet underground movement; formation of combat units of a maximum of sixty men; installation of radio reporting stations; dissemination of printed and oral anti-bolshevist propaganda.

Gehlen curbed Baun's enthusiasm, pointing out that it seemed to him more important in the first instance to set up an intelligence network, which would function on call, than to make plans for partisan operations. With this in view officers, in particular General Staff officers with intelligence training, should go to ground in mufti behind the Soviet lines and hold themselves ready to be called upon later.

Then the three prophets turned to a more immediate question: how to get in touch with the Americans. Baun offered to send some of his officers to contact American headquarters in near-by Thuringia in order, as he put it in his diary 'to get to work with the Americans'. Gehlen surmised that the US soldiers would immediately push any German officer into a prisoner-of-war camp. Nevertheless Gehlen, Wessel and Baun decided that each of them was authorized to avail himself of the first favourable opportunity to offer their services to the most senior American officer available and that each might speak in the name of the other two. The remaining members both of FHO and Walli I, on the other hand, if taken prisoner, were to give only their name and rank and were not to mention their unit or function. In any event officers, NCOs and men were only to give more detailed information on written instructions from Gehlen, Wessel or Baun.

Finally the three future allies of the Americans agreed how they would contact each other, should they become separated. They selected the letters FHO as call sign for the operation and as 'human post-box' Dr Rudolf Graber, a catholic canon, professor of ecclesiastical history and later Bishop of Regensburg. In the messages to be passed on by the Professor, Y stood for Gehlen, X for Baun and W for Wessel.[10]

On April 5th Gehlen issued his penultimate order in FHO head-quarters at Zossen. The copies of the card-index, the reports, the air photographs, the appreciations and the files were packed into fifty steel cases and Gehlen designated certain localities at Wendelstein and in the Allgäu as the hiding places for this invaluable secret-service library on the Soviet Union.

In his memoirs, *Der Dienst*, Gehlen also mentions the Hunsrück as a hiding place for the FHO material. Here his memory is at fault, for the Hunsrück was already occupied by US troops at this time. He also makes contradictory statements about the date of his meeting with Baun in Bad Elster. Whereas Gehlen refers to March 1945, Baun gives a precise date in his diary – April 4th. The entry reads: 'Y. [Gehlen] visits me in Bad Elster with W. [Wessel]. My proposal to gain contact with the Americans so that we can work with them later is approved by Y. I will make known meeting points and contacts.'[11]

Gehlen's dismissal by Hitler on April 9th caused no change in the plan. Wessel, his successor, ran the Section precisely on previous lines. Ten days later the moment came. Berlin was almost encircled by Russian forces and the Army General Staff was forced to evacuate Maybach Camp and withdraw into the still unoccupied rump of Germany. Part of it eventually reached Flensburg and the remainder moved to Bavaria, into the so-called Alpine Redoubt.

FHO also split: a small group under Lieutenant-Colonel Scheibe and Major von Kalckreuth withdrew to Flensburg; the main body under Wessel went to ground in Bavaria. Scheibe's detachment took with it one case containing photostat copies of FHO material but the bulk of the fifty steel cases moved with Wessel.[12]

A few days later Gehlen himself joined the Bavarian group and took charge of it. He travelled in one of the Wehrmacht jeeps which, in late April 1945, were dashing hither and thither in the neighbourhood of Lake Spitzing, Bavaria. The column of vehicles moved off from the lake along the 10-mile-long forest road to Valepp. There were other FHO officers in Gehlen's car.

From Valepp Gehlen, accompanied only by an aide, attempted to reach Hindelang where Lieutenant-Colonel Baun was waiting to talk to him. But he could not get through; all roads were blocked by enemy forces. On the return journey Gehlen disembarked at the house of Fritz am Sand in the Zipfelwirt region. With his rucksack on his back he climbed a spur to Elendsalm (also shown as Ödlandsalm on old maps), a state property leased to farmers by the Forestry Office of Fischbachau. 'Here,' Gehlen says, 'I found assembled the officers and staff of this group who greeted me with pleasure – six officers and three female staff assistants.'

In 1945 the tenant farmer was Ludwig Priller from Uslaw but since he was still in the Wehrmacht, his wife was running the farm. Rudi Kreidl, a mountain shepherd, was seeing to any business connected with the Elendsalm Hut for her.

The advance party had already buried FHO's cases containing the microfilms up in the mountain and laid in a store of food for several months. On the wall above his camp bed Gehlen affixed the motto: 'Laet vaeren nytt' [Never give up], that of the Flemish family of van Vaernewyck from which his mother came. A few days later Wessel arrived; he had been running the Intelligence Section in the so-called Southern Staff in Bad Reichenhall. He and three staff officers located themselves on another mountain farm some 15–20 miles from Gehlen's hide-out.[13]

As the American tanks drove through Bavaria Gehlen continued to insist that the leading troops would hardly be likely to take him to a US General but would simply put him straight into a prisoner-of-war camp. He waited for the second and third waves containing divisional and army headquarters. Every morning before sunrise Gehlen and his officers climbed up the mountain on the assumption that the Americans would not comb it further than they could drive in a jeep; every evening he returned to the hut on the assumption that the jeep patrols would only operate by day.

Gehlen's hide-out, therefore, remained undiscovered by the Americans but not by Kreidl, the mountain shepherd. Even today he still believes that SS men and a civilian with the Golden Party Badge had hidden themselves in the hut at this time. Now Kreidl had a 'deadly hatred' of the SS. He eventually descended into the valley and alerted the Americans. At the junction of the road from Lake Spitzing with that to Bayrischzell he met an American soldier. He says: 'I told him that there were SS men on the Elendsalm and that he should arrest them.'[14]

The word 'SS' was an alarm signal and so a detachment of US military police immediately moved up to the Elendsalm. They found only two wounded officers and the three girls; the others, including Gehlen, were sitting on the Auerspitze some half mile south-east of the Rotwand, waiting for the evening. The Americans issued Gehlen's people with release papers showing Elendsalm as the place of release.

The events of the next few days are part of what is called the Gehlen legend. He himself likes to propagate the story that the US detachment alerted by Kreidl climbed up to Elendsalm on May 20th, 1945, twelve days after the capitulation of the German Wehrmacht, with the specific purpose of arresting him; he displayed his pay-book and demanded to be taken to an officer of the 'Counter-Intelligence Corps' (CIC), the US Army's counter-espionage police. Twenty-six years later however, Gehlen says in his memoirs: 'We had decided not to be taken prisoner but to present ourselves to the Americans on our own initiative'; he, his officers and the three girls, so he says, accordingly went down into the valley of their own accord, 'having removed our badges of rank and red stripes [the red stripe of the General Staff on the trousers] on the previous evening'. He spent the two days of the Whitsun holiday with the parents of a friend and on the Tuesday went to the Burgomaster's office where the US Town Major was located. Gehlen records his feelings: 'In some ways I felt a grim humour in the situation that I – who after all was a Major-General in an important position during the war – should now have to hand myself over to a young American Lieutenant.' What then happened Gehlen now prefers not to admit in public.

Gehlen was taken in a jeep to Miesbach where a CIC detachment under Captain Marian E. Porter was located. The General presented himself: 'I am Head of the Section "Foreign Armies East" in German Army Headquarters.' 'You were, General,' the CIC officer replied. Gehlen continued: 'I have information to give of the highest importance to your government.' But the American was unimpressed – 'So have they all,' he replied and ordered the German off into a prisoner-of-war camp in Salzburg.

Gehlen never forgot his disillusionment over this reception. As late as 1960 the journalist Wolfgang Wehner, when writing his book *Geheim* [Secret], could quote him as saying this about the Miesbach CIC: 'The unit was a typical product of the war, formed too hurriedly and manned by the wrong people, only able to do its job by accident.'[15] Even in later days Gehlen's relationships with the CIC were never good. Those who know the General, who was not without his conceit, say: 'He expected the Americans to fall round his neck. The little man in Miesbach did not do so and Gehlen felt insulted.'

In fact, at this period, the CIC interrogators were hunting only Nazis and war criminals. The commander of the Miesbach unit was almost certainly in total ignorance of Gehlen's Section and therefore did not realize the importance of his capture. In May 1945 America's counter-espionage service had only seven Eastern experts in Germany and they were located in Heidelberg and Frankfurt.[16]

At the same period Baun and his officers were hiding from French occupation forces in Rettenberg in the Allgäu. He eventually handed himself over to US follow-up units who dispatched him too to a POW camp. It is not possible today to say with complete certainty who was ultimately the first to make contact with more influential American circles in accordance with the Bad Elster agreement. Baun's friends maintain that the credit should go to him; with American help, they say, he had already gathered his people around him in the POW camp and assured them of better living conditions – white bread and real coffee – while Gehlen was still behind the barbed wire vainly trying to attract the attention of junior CIC functionaries.

If Baun did in fact make his mark more quickly but did not avail himself of the opportunity to intercede on Gehlen's behalf, this may be a reason for the subsequent hostility between the two men. It would at least partially explain the antipathy shown by Gehlen to ex-Abwehr officers (Baun came from the Abwehr). Gehlen's supporters maintain that Baun attempted to do business with the Americans on his own account to ensure for himself the senior position in the band of German secret-service auxiliaries.

If Baun had any such plans he was working on a false assumption, for Gehlen quickly made contact with the 'right' Americans. In the next stage of his career as a prisoner of war, a camp near Augsburg, he met Strik-Strikfeldt, his former adviser, who noted that: 'Gehlen was confident and self-possessed. He had plans looking far into a new future whereas most others were merely looking back into the past.'

Matters did not go fast enough for Gehlen, however. Today he says, almost in a tone of offence: 'So far I . . . had met only American officers who regarded the situation exclusively through the official propaganda spectacles. Almost all of those I had so far spoken to thought that the Soviet Union would progress from communism towards a liberal state. Stalin was invariably referred to as "Uncle Joe". Not one I had talked to had any idea at all of the true Soviet expansionist aims. I remained some three to four weeks in the Augsberg camp until the interrogating officer came to the conclusion that I was not a valuable prisoner. He was not interested in the Russian situation.' On the contrary – one day Gehlen was pushed into a truck and taken off towards Frankfurt. Here disaster awaited him: 'When we reached Wiesbaden, despite my protests, I was committed to Wiesbaden prison on the grounds that I was a Gestapo General. Here the Americans were downright unfriendly and at times their attitude was such that I feared actual physical violence.' This mistaken view of Gehlen's role, however, did not last long.[17]

American attention was eventually drawn to Gehlen by a roundabout method. After capitulation the rump of OKW in Flensburg ('OKW North') set up a demobilization section to cooperate with the Allies in the disarmament and disbandment of the German Forces. The Germans in Flensburg, however, then became spectators of a fierce struggle between the Anglo-Saxons and the Russians for Hitler's former intelligence officers. The Western Allies set up a supervisory commission under the US General Lowell W. Rooks and the Russians a commission under Major-General Trussov to search for German secret-service material and personnel.[18] As early as May 13th Rooks was asking for production of 'a nominal roll of German intelligence officers, handbooks including office instructions, diagrams and handbooks on military intelligence channels'. The Russian request was more to the point: they wished to know the location of FHO's material and of its Chief.

At 6.15 PM on May 19th the Russian Four-Man Commission summoned Major Borchers of the Demobilization Section and subjected him to a strict interrogation. They wished to know who could give information on FHO's Red Army intelligence. Borchers replied: 'Probably only General Gehlen who is in the southern zone.' The Russian officers pricked up their ears; the name Gehlen seemed unknown to them. The next question was: 'Has General Gehlen a representative in Flensburg?' Borchers replied: 'Certain FHO officers are still here.' The Russians demanded that Borchers re-appear next day punctually at 10 AM with an FHO officer.[19]

The Americans heard of the Russian interest in FHO and reacted quickly. On May 19th they arrested Lieutenant-Colonel Scheibe,

Gehlen's representative in Flensburg; Scheibe's steel case containing the FHO photostat material had already been confiscated two days before by the US Lieutenant-Colonel Austin. For both Russians and Americans, however, the question 'Where is General Gehlen?' became increasingly urgent. American G2 (Intelligence) officers began to search for the ex-head of FHO who was said to be somewhere in the US occupation zone – this much they had learnt in Flensburg.[20]

Gehlen was eventually discovered by a G2 Colonel named William R. Philip, commandant of the Special POW Camp at Oberursel where Gehlen had been sent by the CIC six weeks after his arrest. In July 1945 the Colonel saw in a CIC memo that the much-sought-after Gehlen was in Oberursel and had repeatedly demanded to be brought before a US General Officer. Philip immediately reported the fact to his superior, Brigadier General Edwin L. Sibert, senior intelligence officer of the American occupation zone, whose headquarters were in Kronberg.[21]

So there entered Gehlen's life the man primarily responsible for furthering the post-war career of the one-time Wehrmacht general. Edwin Luther Sibert, born in 1897, was an artillery expert, an ex-Military Attaché and a Professor of Military Science. Like Gehlen he had entered the secret-service world late in life.[22] Since March 1944 Sibert had been Chief of Intelligence to 12 US Army Group which had later advanced through France, and he had studied the ideas of the German military. While fighting was still in progress in France he had been prepared to make use of Adolf Hitler's officers in the cause of American strategy. The idea had come from the German–American Gero von Gaevernitz, adviser to Allen W. Dulles, the US secret-service officer in Berne. In November 1944 Gaevernitz had suggested to Sibert that, via certain intermediaries, he should contact war-weary German commanders at the front and urge them to surrender. Sibert combed the POW camps for German officers willing to contact their fellow-officers still fighting and he had soon assembled an adequate number willing to assist the Allies to bring the war to an end.

Sibert had then radioed the War Department in Washington asking for permission to form a committee of German POWs under the Luftwaffe Major-General Gerhard Bassenge, an ex-Abwehr officer, and attach it to Allied headquarters as an advisory commission. Washington, however, turned the proposals down and forbade any fraternization with Nazi ex-officers.

Sibert came under fire from the official critics, particularly since, shortly thereafter, the surprise German offensive in the Ardennes showed how wide of the mark had been his estimate of the enemy's fighting morale. Washington initiated an inquiry against Sibert and he was regarded as the real scapegoat for the early American reverses in the Ardennes. He was in fact rehabilitated by the War Department but ever since had been wondering whether any intelligence officer could have learnt more about his enemy than he had about the Germans.[23]

He was therefore excited to see a German who arrived claiming to know everything about his Soviet enemy – and Gehlen, the prisoner, soon showed Sibert, the conqueror, how to collect intelligence about one's enemy. Sibert was astounded; he recalls: 'I had a most excellent impression of him at once.' Initially the two found it difficult to understand each other; Sibert says: 'Gehlen's English was not very good and my German was equally poor. We then got an American officer along as interpreter.'

Gehlen explained to Sibert the duties and methods of 'Foreign Armies East'; he then told him of 'the actual aims of the Soviet Union and its display of military might'. Sibert had Gehlen's exposé interpreted sentence by sentence without interrupting him once – an unparalleled occurrence. The United States, after all, were allied to the Soviet Union and US Army instructions laid down that it was the duty of every American to cut short any anti-Soviet comment from a German, even if only made verbally.

Gehlen forecast that Stalin would not allow independence to Poland, Czechoslovakia, Bulgaria or Rumania, would subject Finland to control from the Kremlin and probably wished to impose communism on the whole of Germany, including the US Zone. With her present armed forces potential, he continued, Russia could risk war with the West and the aim of such a war would be the occupation of West Germany. Sibert initially confined himself to the single comment: 'You know a lot about the Russians, General.'[24]

Gehlen then emphasized that he could prove his estimate on the basis of material available to him. Sibert says: 'Somewhere he had certain documents and evidence and he alone knew where these documents were.' The experts on these subjects, Gehlen went on, were also available; all that was necessary was to fetch the officers of 'Foreign Armies East' from the POW camps in which they were now languishing. Finally the German network of agents in the Soviet Union could be reactivated, this time for the benefit of the USA. Sibert said to Gehlen: 'I will see what I can do for you.' The two men parted with a handshake and Gehlen was taken back to Oberursel.

During the next few days Sibert broke the strict rule of the American armed forces that action should only be taken on orders. He did not inform either the Chief of Intelligence of American Forces in Europe nor General Bedell Smith, Chief of Staff to Supreme Headquarters. He says: 'Only later did I inform my superiors of Gehlen's value to us, in other words not until we were sure.'[25] US interrogators, however, soon obtained confirmation from the General Staff POWs whom Gehlen had meanwhile released from their obligation to say nothing. Gehlen fetched his fifty steel cases from their hiding places and in special camps the officers prepared their material on Russia.

Gehlen was now allowed to form the 'Gehlen staff cell', initially accommodated in the Historical Research Section and then in 7 US Army's Intelligence Centre in Wiesbaden. Gehlen and his immediate staff were treated as VIPs; even US officers were only allowed to enter the quarters of the 'cell' with Sibert's express permission. In order to brief the Americans fully Gehlen started by writing a 129-page report on himself and his work.[26]

Early in August Gehlen submitted to the Americans the first post-war product of the German General Staff – locations, strengths and composition of Soviet divisions, production figures of armaments firms in the Soviet Union, air photographs of Russian rail junctions, reports on morale of the Red Army and Russian people.

Sibert was now convinced of the value of Gehlen. He explained to Bedell Smith, the Chief of Staff, 'What we want to do with Gehlen' – the ex-Chief of FHO should create a German intelligence service, financed by the US and directed against the Soviet Union. Bedell Smith 'okayed' the project but neither he nor the head of G2 informed Eisenhower, the Supreme Commander, who had forbidden any fraternization with Germans. Moreover Bedell Smith wished to avoid compromising his Supreme Commander who had to conduct political negotiations on Washington's behalf with Marshal Zhukov, the Soviet Commander-in-Chief; he might, therefore, have been in a difficult position, had it become known that Americans and Germans were cooperating in secret-service matters.[27]

Over Eisenhower's head Bedell Smith and Sibert informed the War Department in Washington. There, meanwhile, certain circles had become suspicious of their Russian ally and US senior officers were asking themselves what the US intelligence service really knew about the Soviet Union.

The answer which came back was meagre in the extreme. America's secret services in fact knew very little about the Soviet Union. Neither the General Staff 'Joint Intelligence Committee' which coordinated the military intelligence services, nor the civilian 'Office of Strategic Services' (OSS) which dealt with espionage, sabotage, and propaganda, had access to adequate material about the Soviets. Until 1941 the US Military Attaché in Moscow had taken Soviet propaganda about the invincibility of the Red Army at its face value; his successor had swung to the opposite extreme and had not believed that the Russian army could ever recover from the blows of the German Wehrmacht.

Moreover the heads of the American intelligence services had little hope of improving their output on Russia, since they were irretrievably at loggerheads with each other. In the summer of 1945 the Americans were going through the battle which Germans and British had fought out in the 19th century – the struggle between civilians and military for control of the secret service.[28]

During World War II an all-purpose political secret service was formed, the 'Office of Strategic Services' (OSS) under Major-General William J. Donovan; it was responsible for all forms of conspiratorial activity from front-line intelligence to subversive action in the rear of the enemy. On paper it was subordinate directly to the President but soon came under the general supervision of the Joint Chiefs of Staff. The military were not in favour of OSS since they saw in it a threat to the individual intelligence services maintained by the Navy, Army and Air Force. Donovan wished to free himself once more from his military mentors and in 1944 proposed to the President that a unified secret service be created responsible to the White House alone; this, however, implied removing responsibility for secret-service matters from the Joint Chiefs of Staff.[29]

The President forwarded the Donovan plan to the Joint Chiefs and the military reaction was a violent one. They rejected any centralized system in secret-service questions and insisted that each Service retain its own intelligence organization, to be coordinated with the other two. The Pentagon even toyed with the idea of disbanding OSS altogether. This brought the State Department on the scene with a claim for control of any political secret service; if OSS was to be disbanded, it said, the section responsible for foreign policy must be transferred to the State Department.[30]

Espionage in Russia was unlikely to flourish in the midst of this sniping war. Yet the US General Staff required intelligence on Russia since the Soviet Union had meanwhile become the greatest military power in the world. Stalin's armies had quickly moved into the power vacuum left by the collapse of the German state. Step by step Russia's power had grown and her frontiers had expanded; a sinister Iron Curtain had descended over the conquered territories now in the grip of the Soviet army. In Hungary, Rumania, Poland, East Germany, Bulgaria and Czechoslovakia – everywhere in fact – the tune was being called by the Soviet military. The Russian westward march seemed irresistible; the more timorous were already calculating that, starting from her pre-war frontiers, Russia was already four-fifths on the way to Holland, Belgium and France.

America, however, the Eastern experts in the Pentagon thought, was simply the unsuspecting victim of this menace. Immediately after the end of the war the United States had demobilized their armed forces (by 1947 they had been reduced from 12 million to 1.4 million men); the Soviet Union, on the other hand, had kept theirs in being and their six million men, 50,000 tanks and 20,000 aircraft constituted a formidable threat. What had they up their sleeve? Why did they not disarm? America did not know and the American intelligence service had no spy-hole into the Eastern world.[31]

Sibert could provide an escape from this dilemma and at the same time saw an opportunity of rehabilitating himself by producing Gehlen and his organization. The War Department showed interest and in August 1945 Sibert dispatched his protégé Gehlen to Washington. Strange stories of this journey have been told – Gehlen is said to have travelled in the uniform of an American two-star general with full decorations.[32]

In fact they travelled in mufti; they had considerable difficulty in borrowing suits and even more in accommodating their belongings. They had no suitcases. Colonel Stephanus, for instance, had to use a violin case for a suitcase, making the group of German officers look like a dance band. This was of course the first time that German officers had been allowed to use a US General's official aircraft. They were flown to Washington in the plane allocated to Bedell Smith, Eisenhower's Chief of Staff. As far as Gehlen remembers, he was allowed to take with him six of his officers from FHO; they included Major Albert Schoeller, ex-deputy head of Group I (daily enemy situation report), Major Horst Hiemenz, ex-head of Group II (overall Soviet Russian situation), Colonel Heinz Herre, until 1943 senior General Staff Officer of FHO and, having been head of the training section in the 1st Division of the Vlassov Army, an outstanding expert on anti-communist trends in the Soviet Union, and a desk officer, Colonel Konrad Stephanus.[33]

The Germans arrived early in September and the first post-war German–American negotiations began. The Germans found their opposite numbers to be attentive listeners. As it happened, the American military were in a good mood, for President Truman had just decided to disband the Office of Strategic Services; from October 1st the secret foreign intelligence service of OSS was to become the 'Strategic Services Unit' under the War Department, though constituted as an almost autonomous authority. The War Department accordingly now had three secret services: the Strategic Services Unit dealing with foreign intelligence and sabotage, Military Intelligence responsible for normal enemy intelligence, and the Counter-Intelligence Corps to deal with espionage and crime within the Army. Among those facing Gehlen were Brigadier-General John R. Magruder, head of the Strategic Services Unit, and Major-General George V. Strong, head of Military Intelligence and therefore Sibert's superior. All were soon on good terms; they agreed to practically everything proposed by Gehlen.[34]

Meanwhile Gehlen had commissioned his deputy Wessel, whom he had left behind in Germany, to keep an eye out for Baun, the third partner in the Bad Elster agreement. Gehlen did not know that Baun was already in Sibert's employ; he was already experimenting with the preparation of a German intelligence organization serving the US. Sibert was playing it two ways. Wessel discovered Baun not far from Oberursel Camp, in the so-called 'Bluehouse' in the Taunus. Baun made a note of what Wessel said to him: 'I am to tell you from Gehlen that he has discussed with Dönitz [Hitler's successor] and Halder the question of continuing his work with the Americans. Both were in agreement.'

Since Gehlen in Washington could by no means be sure that the Americans would accept him, he sent word to Baun through Wessel as follows: 'If you get going, Gehlen would even be prepared to work under you.'[35] Ex-officers of FHO like to maintain that all credit for the formation of a post-war German secret service belongs to Gehlen alone, but this incident shows that to be a fairy-tale. In fact, while Gehlen was expounding the results of his labours in Washington, Baun was forming the Section I (Intelligence) and Section III (Counter-espionage) which were to form the cornerstones of a secret intelligence organization directed against the Soviet Union.

On October 10th, 1945, Baun submitted to Sibert his initial plan for an espionage and counter-espionage organization. Four days later Sibert asked for a detailed programme. Between November 10th and 28th, on Sibert's orders, Comstok, a G2 Colonel, travelled round the American zone with Baun hunting out the staff officers suggested by the latter; the majority were ex-officers of Admiral Canaris' Abwehr; they were forthwith guaranteed the protection of the American occupying power.[36]

Meanwhile, however, Washington officially held aloof. On December

10th, 1945, the War Department told Sibert in a teleprinter message that it could not give approval to the initiation of espionage activity against the Soviet Union by the Baun Group. This implied that in the European theatre of war Sibert could act on his own and do what he thought right – but on his own responsibility.

That very same day Sibert asked Baun when his organization could begin its espionage work; a month later the General wished to know when Baun could start counter-espionage, in other words penetrate the enemy's intelligence services. Under the heading 'End March 1946' the laconic entry appears in Baun's diary: 'Start of work in the intelligence and counter-espionage fields approved by General Sibert.' Here was the true beginning of the West German secret service. Baun's experts in the 'Bluehouse' were already using the first set provided by the Americans to monitor Soviet army radio traffic in Germany while Gehlen was still giving his exposés in Washington.[37]

The Gehlen legend-writers would have us believe that, immediately on his arrival in the USA, the general was faced with the question: 'What would you think of setting up for us in Europe something on the lines of your old Section, "Foreign Armies East"?' These words have clearly been put into Wehner's mouth by Gehlen himself, as also Gehlen's alleged answer: 'If I am to set up a secret service to serve the Americans, then this organization must be purely German. I must be able to choose my staff myself.' Wehner's description of the scene is: 'Gehlen's terms whiplashed down upon the table. Here was the defeated party dictating his terms, a little man with a weak voice but a man who knew what he was worth.'[38]

In 1971 Gehlen's description of his stay in the USA is considerably more modest: 'Our activity consisted of talking to War Department G-2 experts, answering oral and written questions on the Soviet Union's armed forces and drafting studies on the basis of material given to us . . . The Americans suffered from the fact that they had no sufficiently precise knowledge of the East, its mentality or its positive and negative sides.'

In fact the Americans were by no means in such a hurry to employ the ex-Chief of FHO. The mere length of his stay in America hardly tallies with 'terms whiplashing down on the table' – he was there nearly a year, until July 1st, 1946. What primarily interested the Americans was Gehlen's luggage – his studies on Russia.

The American reluctance to allow Gehlen to work for them against the Soviet Union persisted, as Gehlen himself admits, until February 1946. At that time Soviet forces occupied northern Iran and American public opinion regarded this as an act of aggression. American G-2 officers came to the conclusion that Gehlen's warnings against Russian military might were perhaps not so unfounded. The result according to Gehlen, was that 'they cooperated with us on more detailed and basic matters than hitherto'. Gehlen also noted that 'in Europe also, where Wessel had remained, there were ... certain further indications of a subsequent resumption of work'.

Baun's prospects were in fact better than Wessel's. At the end of June 1946, referring to the imminent return of the Gehlen group from the USA, he noted in his diary: 'General Sibert inquired through Colonel Dean whether I could make use of the Gehlen group which is returning from America (otherwise it would go to some camp). I replied that of course the Gehlen group should join us so that we could solve our new problem in concert.' Gehlen and his party arrived in the Taunus on July 9th; three days later Baun noted that he and Gehlen had had 'exhaustive discussions about what I had organized so far and my plans for the future'.

Baun was the expert on collection of intelligence, Gehlen on evaluation. Baun recorded that the two agreed as follows: 'The organization of intelligence must run parallel with the organization for evaluation. Each of us would run his own organization, objectives in general terms being laid down in concert. Each will handle day-to-day matters separately with the Americans. Fundamental questions will be discussed together.'[39]

Baun clearly took this agreement to mean that the German intelligence tradition was to be faithfully followed — the collection of intelligence and its evaluation should be kept strictly divorced and dealt with by two separate organizations operating independently of each other.

But for decades the efficiency of politico-military intelligence work in Germany had suffered from this division of functions and Gehlen was determined to put an end to this fundamental weakness in the German system. While still in FHO he had tried to combine the assembly and evaluation of intelligence — by close cooperation between FHO and Baun's Walli I. Baun, however, had never grasped the fact that he was not an independent operator but was really only acting as a source for Gehlen's FHO. Gehlen therefore inevitably recommended to the Americans that the collection of intelligence and its evaluation be brought under one roof.

The Americans asked Gehlen to name his price for the provision to the US government of up-to-date situation reports on the Soviet Union and the rest of the Eastern bloc. Details of the agreement, concluded in writing in May 1949 with the newly-formed 'Central Intelligence Agency' (CIA), had been discussed in Washington between Gehlen and his American opposite numbers; certain points, however, were not fixed until after Gehlen's return – in a 'Gentleman's Agreement' with General Sibert. This agreement and the subsequent contract are still secret but presumably the papers contain detailed paragraphs on cooperation between Gehlen's secret service and that of the United States.

The Federal Intelligence Service did once give some indication of the contents of the overall agreement when issuing a 'briefing aide-mémoire' on the occasion of Gehlen's retirement in 1968. According to this the agreement between Gehlen and the Americans included the following principles: 'The organization not to be an auxiliary to the American secret service but a purely German organization under Gehlen's exclusive control, contact being maintained merely through a liaison staff; the organization to be used for collection of intelligence on states of the Eastern bloc; on the establishment of a sovereign German government all previous agreements to be cancelled and the organization to be responsible solely to that government. No mission to be assigned or material to be collected contrary to German interests.'[40]

The War Department accepted Gehlen's conditions. An advisory committee was formed to settle such problems as might arise on the highest level; it included two senior officials of the War Department's secret service, the lawyer Loftus E. Becker and Professor Sherman Kent; both were later to occupy leading positions in the Central Intelligence Agency (CIA), formed in 1947 as America's central, but not centralist, super secret service. The Wall Street banker, Walter Reid Wolf, dealt with the financial aspect. The first annual budget for the Gehlen Group amounted to $3.4 million. The conclusion of the agreement between Gehlen and the War Department would probably have been a much slower process, had not Gehlen received energetic support from a Captain in the US secret service named Eric Waldmann, now a Professor of Politics and author of a book on the Federal Armed Forces. He was convinced of Gehlen's capabilities and he it was who persuaded the American military chiefs to opt for the German general. At the end of June 1946 he went to Germany and reported to his master, General Sibert, that Washington officially approved the formation of a West German secret service – but on condition that the collection and evaluation of intelligence be combined under one head and that that head be Reinhard Gehlen.[41]

Gehlen's partner Baun was not told that Gehlen was to head the organization. Baun only learnt of the decision when the two met for the second time in August to discuss staffing problems. Gehlen produced a chart showing Baun as head of the Intelligence Section and Wessel as head of the Evaluation Section. As Chief of the organization as a whole, however, Gehlen designated himself. Baun was furious, noting: 'He had not discussed this plan with me and I was presented with a *fait accompli*.' Baun did not like to raise objections in the presence of American officers; moreover he sensed that Gehlen had returned from Washington with complete freedom of authority. When he later faced Gehlen alone, however, Baun asked his fellow-conspirator from Bad Elster: 'Why have you chosen this lay-out? It completely cuts across our agreement.' Gehlen replied: 'General Sibert has appointed me to the most senior post.' Baun complained: 'Why did you not tell me of this?' In his diary he then noted: 'He had no answer to my question.'[42]

The background to his rivalry with Baun given by Gehlen in his memoirs is a simple one: There was, he says, a dispute about authority over their German auxiliaries between various US agencies; Baun's Slav temperament (he had been born in Russia) seemed sinister to the straightforward Americans. Finally Baun was unwilling to accept that a Major-General – as Gehlen was – ranked higher than a Lieutenant-Colonel – as Baun was. In fact the length of the passages on Baun in Gehlen's memoirs betrays an uneasy conscience. Ex-members of Canaris' staff still reproach Gehlen today for having treated Baun 'like dirt' and himself claimed credit for Baun's initial intelligence services to the US. Involuntarily Gehlen confirms this when he says: 'The first trial acquisition operations took place from April 1st, 1946. Reaction to the results was favourable.' At this time Baun was in charge of acquisition and Gehlen was still in the United States.

Gehlen is, of course, forced to admit that in April 1947 he relieved Baun as head of the Acquisition Section. He says: 'Herr Baun, however ... had acquired so much merit that he was entrusted with another important task by me' and that he 'retained Baun in another capacity'.

In fact Gehlen had his rival Baun on his conscience from the outset. Baun was side-tracked into another post. One day he was travelling on duty and, as was usual in the Org, was to provide certain outstations and organizers with cash – from his briefcase. Baun's driver was involved in an accident; friends of Gehlen found the briefcase with the money and spread the story that Baun was intending to embezzle it. Gehlen did nothing to stop this talk. On the contrary: Baun was called upon to leave the Gehlen Org because of this 'obscure case'. Baun, who was a sensitive man, never recovered from this stain on his honour as an officer and the damage done to his reputation. In the words of a friend he went 'morally to pieces like a whipped dog. He died an unhappy man, accused of fraud by a man whom he thought was his friend. Baun died a miserable death on December 17th, 1951.'

Gehlen rode roughshod over the lamentations of his comrade Baun. He had only one purpose in view – to build up a new espionage machine. It soon acquired a name, unofficial but revealing – the 'Gehlen Organization' or for short 'The Org'.

Gehlen started modestly. The initial staff was accommodated in two houses in the Taunus between Falkenstien and Kronberg: 'Schloss Kransberg', and a hunting-lodge requisitioned by the Americans belonging to George von Opel, owner of a wild-life park. In the near-by Blue-house the first radio sets delivered to the Org by the US Army were already humming away. Baun noted: 'Supplies from the Americans were plentiful as far as money and equipment were concerned; the petrol allowance was adequate.'[43]

Gehlen placed Baun in charge of the two sections into which he divided his organization. Baun's Section I (Acquisition) was responsible for the assembly of all intelligence material whereas Section II (Evaluation) under Wessel was responsible for analysis and collation. Overall direction of the organization Gehlen reserved to himself. He set up a small staff in a special enclosure in Oberursel Camp ('Camp King') to work out the programme of the Org's future activities.

When Gehlen issued his first orders for action the staff of the Org numbered fifty but this, of course, was not enough to implement his ambitious programme. He needed more evaluators, more couriers and more informers. In autumn 1946 he dispatched his qualified recruiting officers to gather up additional staff from the unemployed mass of ex-Abwehr and ex-FHO officers.[44]

Gehlen's emissaries had to proceed with caution, however. With Germany occupied by four different powers it was all too easy to become an object of suspicion to one of the other Allied secret services – and what could be more suspicious than the enigmatic 'Gehlen Organization', the very antithesis of all that the Allied re-educators were thinking and feeling about Germans at the time. The American counter-espionage authorities themselves were an obstacle to Gehlen's recruiting campaign. The war crimes investigators of the Counter-Intelligence Corps found it hard to stomach the fact that their rivals of the US Army's secret service should snatch many a Hitler officer from them and take him on to their pay-roll. In the POW camps the CIC and the secret service waged bitter war for every ex-Abwehr officer.

When the CIC sleuths became too openly hostile to Gehlen, he protested to his patron Sibert. Baun noted in his diary: 'The initially un-friendly attitude of the American collateral organizations and their executive agencies became somewhat less marked as a result of pressure from headquarters.'[45] The hostility of the other occupying powers, however, was an even thornier problem for Gehlen; their secret services were equally running German agents and they kept jealous watch to ensure that no one enticed them away.

At the end of the war both the British and French intelligence services had engaged Germans willing to help the West in the incipient under-ground struggle against the Russians. While on a duty visit to Hamburg, for instance, Worgitzky, who later became Gehlen's deputy, had to take refuge in the coal cellar of another Gehlen employee near the Dammtor station when it was found that the British Military Police were on his tracks. Many ex-Abwehr officers found themselves competing with former colleagues who had opted for the secret service of another of the occupying powers. Two such officers, Karl Schiffer and Gerhard Pinc-kert, discovered a particularly agreeable method of solving the prob-lem of earning their living: one day in November 1946 they both found themselves sitting on a bench facing the main gate of Eberswalde bar-racks in Brandenburg. The two did not know each other but both were in the same line of business – they were noting the registration numbers of Soviet vehicles entering or leaving the barrack gate. After a time Schiffer remarked on the aroma of his neighbour's cigarette and asked: 'Working for the Americans?' Pinckert nodded and then, smelling Schiffer's cigarette, countered with: 'And you for the French?' Schiffer confirmed that this was so. In fact their brand of cigarette gave away their employers – even in espionage circles cigarettes were an inter-nationally convertible currency in post-war Germany.

Suddenly one of the two observers had an idea: 'It would do if only one of us sat here at a time, writing in the cold. You could go and thaw out in the bar over there while I stay here on guard. I'll change places with you in an hour's time. We'll exchange notes this evening.' The other agreed and that evening each copied out the registration numbers which the other had noted. Then the two gentlemen took leave of each other politely, went to Eberswalde station and took a train for Berlin – Schiffer into the French sector and Pinckert into the American.[46]

The incident shows that the intelligence services of the Western Powers were finding an adequate supply of German underlings ready to work against the Russians. Gehlen realized only too clearly that he must press on with his recruiting campaign if he was not to be left at the post by rivals in the race for former espionage experts.

About this time the British were toying with the idea of setting up a service of their own formed from ex-members of Gehlen's staff. Early in 1946 the British authorities assembled in Ostend fifty German ex-staff officers who had been primarily employed on the Eastern front. They were interviewed by interrogators of '9 Research and Intelligence Section' of the British Army; the head of this unit, Major Netler, was looking primarily for officers who had previously served in FHO and at the end of the war formed part of the group which had withdrawn to Flensburg under Majors Scheibe and Jürg von Kalckreuth. One of the British interrogators, Captain Pistorius, eventually discovered Lieutenant-Colonel Adolf Wicht, whom he looked upon as a sort of substitute Gehlen. In 1943–4 Wicht had been in charge of Group III of FHO responsible for the evaluation of captured material and the interrogation of prisoners of war; he was regarded as one of the most talented members of Gehlen's staff.

Pistorius put a proposition to Wicht: 'Would you not place at our disposal your knowledge of the Red Army? Thereby you would be helping the West if it came to a fight with Russia.' Wicht was not willing. As relations between the Soviet Union and the Western Allies deteriorated, however, Pistorius and his master Netler put increasing pressure on him. On January 7th, 1947, when Wicht heard that his release was imminent, he made some concession to the British: he was not willing to enter their service but would, as he put it, 'write down what he knew about the peculiar features of Soviet strategy'; his subject was to be 'Soviet ideas and principles in winter warfare'.

Nevertheless the British left no stone unturned to persuade this particular Soviet expert to join them. On April 9th, 1947, Captain Merdes, another member of Netler's staff, drove him in a military vehicle from Munsterlager to Schöppenstedt in Brunswick where Wicht had hidden certain of his wartime documents. Merdes even entertained his guest in a British officers' mess. The British were repeatedly making attractive offers. Merdes, for instance, said: 'We would like to send you to Berlin. You have no need to worry about accommodation or salary. Since you speak Russian we would even give you a language allowance.' But Adolf Wicht refused. He left the British and later joined Gehlen.[47]

Despite the frequently superior material attractions offered by their rivals, Gehlen's recruiters were more successful, for they knew how to appeal to the nationalist and conservative sentiments and *esprit de corps* of ex-officers. Even more important, they knew how to appeal to the ineradicable anti-communism of the ex-serviceman, that emotional complex in which the totalitarian anti-bolshevism of the past Nazi era was inextricably linked with their humiliating experiences of Russian military victories and the atrocities committed by the Soviet soldiery. As time went on many of the FHO officers had developed a curious love–hate attitude to all things Russian, making them ready to do almost anything against the Soviet Union. None of them anticipated anything but the worst from the Russians – they had not even been prepared to trust their own Russian minions, the supporters of the anti-bolshevist General Vlassov.

The attitude of mind of the men in FHO is illustrated by a small note in a file, dating from the final phase of the war and carrying Gehlen's signature— 'As was only to be expected, in the areas of Germany occupied by the Red Army treatment of the civil population is horrible. Bestial murder, rape of women and girls and the most senseless destruction are the order of the day and are apparently approved as retribution for atrocities allegedly committed by Germans.'[48]

The key phrase is 'as was only to be expected'. What they saw and heard after 1945 accorded precisely with their anti-bolshevist concepts – the policy of violence pursued by the Soviets and their German minions in Central Germany, the destruction of non-communist systems of government in Eastern Europe, the voracious expansion of Soviet power behind the Iron Curtain. Without giving adequate thought to the motives and reasons behind Soviet behaviour, they saw themselves justified – this, exactly this, was what they had always thought the bolshevist enemy would be like. As a result, when Gehlen's recruiters canvassed for 'The Org' in POW and refugee camps, in bars and private houses, their arguments struck a chord.

Wehr, an ex-officer recruit, describes the arguments used by Gehlen's people thus: 'One must do something against the threat of bolshevism; one must reconstruct the old organization for the sake of German security and this can only be done with the help of the Americans.' Friedrich Hecker, an ex-Abwehr Captain, says: 'I myself belonged to the Gehlen organization for a time. The presence of old friends and the common front against the communist East attracted me to it.'[49]

When they approached a candidate, Gehlen's recruiters first demanded from him his 'word of honour as an officer' and a pledge of absolute secrecy. Then they told him that Gehlen was working under American sponsorship but that his organization was 'a purely German undertaking, under no circumstances to be directed against the interests of our country'. One must visualize war between East and West, they continued, and obviously German officers must side with the West.

Major-General Gehlen, the argument ran, personally guaranteed that the duties required were decent and above-board. 'Dirty tricks,' such as sabotage and subversion, would be dismissed as methods unworthy of an officer. The General had set the tone with his directive: 'We shall often be compelled to do dirty business. For this we require gentlemen with clean hands.'

Many were won over by the prospects of a gentleman's career. Others, whose only experience was that of the soldier or staff officer and who were wondering how to adapt themselves to civilian life in de-militarized post-war Germany, were only too glad to work at their old trade once more. Gehlen's recruiters could offer many material attractions – accommodation, 'Care' parcels and Chesterfields. Many officers hitched themselves to Gehlen's star. Two ex-FHO officers, Fritz Scheibe and Horst Hiemenz, had already opted for the Org. They were joined by Captain Gerhard Boldt and Lieutenant Blossfeldt, both ex-FHO, General Horst von Mellenthin, Kleikamp, ex-head of unit counter-espionage, Lieutenant-Colonel Reile, ex-Abwehr, and Kretschmer, a former Wehrmacht Attaché – to name only a few.[50]

So once more the predominant influence in the organization and development of a German secret service was that of the military. For the third time in the history of German espionage secret-service work was conducted according to military rules – no civilian had the entrée to the Org, no political authority, whether German or American, had the right to participate or even supervise. The Org had been constructed by military men and to them military intelligence was the primary aim and purpose of a secret service. Methods of work in the Org bore the stamp of the military hierarchical and patriarchal cast of mind.

Moreover, as an ex-General Staff officer, Gehlen regarded his organization as something more than a normal secret service. For him it was a reservoir for officers who had lost their vocation but to whom, thanks to his connections with Washington, he could one day offer the opportunity of rebuilding an army and a General Staff.

Accordingly Gehlen offered Adolf Heusinger, his former master, a place in the Org. Heusinger recalls: 'Herr Gehlen thought that it would certainly be wise for me to keep myself up to date on the development of the military situation in the East.' The ex-Lieutenant-General accepted with pleasure. Heusinger's experience was that of other ex-officers; they were initiated and then employed by Gehlen. Gehlen's confidant Heinz Herre says: 'It was important at the time to get as many officers as possible off the streets.' One after another they joined Gehlen – Ernst Ferber and Josef Moll, both ex-General Staff officers, and

Lieutenant-Colonel Heinz Günter Guderian, son of Gehlen's old patron, the Chief of the General Staff.[51]

In later years, of course, when they had become Inspectors or senior officers of the West German armed forces, none of these people had any wish to recall their service in the Gehlen Organization. Heusinger, who was only too well aware of the traditional German prejudice against secret intelligence organizations, played it down, saying: 'My activity had nothing to do with agents'; after becoming Inspector-General of the Bundeswehr he maintained that he had worked as a 'freelance writer'. Moll, the Inspector of the Army, said that he had run 'an independent business' in Stuttgart; Guderian, the Armoured Corps Inspector, had laboured in a 'scientific research institute'.[52] In fact for all these people service in the Org was a direct continuation of their military career. Nothing seemed to them more natural than to join their friend Gehlen's ex-field-grey column; in his organization he seemed to be perpetuating the military service which 1945 had interrupted.

In the tough conditions of the post-war period, moreover, it was hardly likely that Gehlen's organization would be used for civilian-type assignments. In the furore of the Cold War people were tempted to think only in military terms. The Red Army was threatening Europe and only strength potential, numbers of divisions and armaments statistics seemed to count. Such considerations overshadowed any more sophisticated political thinking. Moreover the object of the Org was to present a picture of an enemy who evoked violent emotions, emotions stemming from the unexorcized past of the Germans and the bourgeois hatred of communism.

Nevertheless Gehlen recognized that the new secret service could not be a purely military organization. The staff of the Org came from too varied a background to be forced into the straitjacket of military discipline and a military hierarchy. Members of the headquarters should, Gehlen decided, as far as possible be equal in status. Military ranks were seldom used and each member of the staff was given a cover-name, by which he was to be addressed even by those who knew his real name. Gehlen himself became 'Dr Schneider' or 'Doctor' for short.[53] The substitute for military discipline was the ritual of an oath-bound brotherhood of secrecy.

Every new member of staff was greeted by the Chief in his headquarters with a handshake. He was then presented with a 'Solemn Declaration' which he had to sign before being admitted to the organization – 'In the knowledge that the Org can only fulfil its duties satisfactorily if maintenance of the strictest secrecy is guaranteed, I undertake on my honour that, unless otherwise required for a specific reason, I will only communicate, whether orally or in writing, matters concerning the business and personnel of the Org to superior or subordinate members of the staff or agents, if and in so far as this is necessary in the interests of duty. I accordingly acknowledge that I shall be contravening this solemn declaration if, without special permission, I disclose, whether orally or in writing, facts, events or details of personnel to persons outside the organization or to members of the staff and agents who are neither my superiors nor subordinates. If discussing matters which need be only partially disclosed in the interests of duty, I will not disclose more than is necessary to superior or subordinate members of the staff or agents. If disclosure is not necessary at all in the interests of duty, I will not do so either to superior or subordinate members of the staff or agents.' Should he leave the organization any new member of staff had to guarantee maintenance of complete secrecy. Paragraph Two of the declaration stipulated: 'I recognize that, should I contravene the obligation to preserve secrecy, I can be punished.'[54]

Anyone signing this declaration was pledging himself to a conspiratorial existence. Initially he was not allowed to tell even his closest relatives who his employer was or why he was away from home so frequently. If he was wise he concealed his employment, not only from the British and French but even from the Americans as well. Overnight he had become a member of a secret society with its own rites and code of honour, insulated from the outside world. A short training course, later increased in length and intensity, grounded the newcomer in the ways of the Org and turned him into a fully regimented and effective member of the brotherhood. Such schooling was essential because the recruits who flowed into the Org were heterogeneous in the extreme. Few of them had experience of secret-service work; many had spent their war service in front-line units and knew nothing of intelligence. For the newcomers to the trade Gehlen had a training programme all ready and prepared.[55]

A so-called 'educational' directive from the Chief initiated the newcomer into the rudiments of espionage. It laid down that: 'When a new member of staff has been recruited and screened, his training will follow a definite plan geared to his future employment. On conclusion of training a report, showing results achieved, will be submitted to the head of the Group.'

Strict instructions hammered into the newcomer the fact that almost everything in Reinhard Gehlen's Org was secret. The whole instructional period was designed to show that all members of the espionage machine, great or small – the heads of groups, the organizers, informers, agents and the army of volunteer helpers from the 'tipster' to the 'investigator' – were no more than threads in a great network which must remain invisible. An organizer, Gehlen's instructions laid down, must 'know all about his informers; informers, on the other hand, should know nothing of their organizer, not even his real name. It must be explained to the informer that collection of intelligence is a highly secret matter and must never be discussed with anyone at any time.'

It was impressed on all members of the Org that they must show the utmost vigilance *vis-à-vis* their agents – 'The agent is a trader in intelligence; his organizer should establish a correct business relationship with him but beyond that have no personal contact. Meetings should take place only in restaurants or other public places, never in a house since it might have built-in microphones. The agent should not know more than is absolutely necessary. On leaving him, ensure that he is not following you.'

According to the training instruction, however, the organizer should possess some 'human ties' with an informer. The greatest caution was recommended in recruitment and selection of informers – 'An informer will be found by the tipster; his personality and circumstances will then be established by the investigator; during this process neither tipster nor investigator must appear in person. The informer will only be approached personally, and then engaged, by the recruiting officer.' Once in the service of the Org, the informer 'should not change his mode of life, do nothing to draw attention to himself, not embark on major expenditure, always be aware of the danger of discovery'. The rule for organizers was that 'when in the company of an informer he should be kept continually aware of the dangers of his surroundings (his friends, etc)'.

Organizers were ordered to exercise special caution when an informer returned from an assignment. The rules laid down: 'All may be in order; alternatively he may have been "converted" or he may have a "tail" (a follower) to find out whom he is working for. The following security precautions should therefore be observed: at the first meeting do not speak to him, simply arrange a second meeting-place, then call him and arrange a third meeting. Meanwhile it will be possible to find out if he is being shadowed.' Gehlen's pupils were also given similar instructions concerning a specially important figure in the espionage organization, the courier; they said: 'In this case particular attention should be paid to capabilities and state of health which are essential for anyone taking up the work of courier. The candidate must display caution, circumspection, presence of mind and punctiliousness. Physically he must be strong, agile and athletic. His is the most dangerous of all employments since he is the most frequent user of the railway with material on him.'[56]

Having thus passed through their training, Gehlen's new staff officers were in a position to occupy posts in the headquarters or out-stations of the Org. The Chief could now really begin to satisfy his American masters' requirements for information. By January 1947 he was ready.

Gehlen had presented himself in Washington as the man who knew a great deal about the Soviet Union and could unravel almost any Soviet secret. The Americans now demanded more, and yet more, information about their Russian opponents. But how was the Org to obtain it? Baun proposed that contact be re-established with the circuits of Russian agents and radio operators previously run by his Walli I; they were still there, he said, and ready to work for Gehlen. Gehlen encouraged Baun to go to work, although later he liked to say that he never shared his chief intelligence officer's optimism. In fact Baun was merely pursuing the plan which Gehlen himself had worked out a few weeks before the German capitulation. At that time he had visualized combining the German intelligence service's remaining circuits of agents in Russia and Poland with the anti-communist guerrillas in those countries and thus tapping a further source of agents. Until the very end of the war Walli I and its subordinate agencies had actually been in contact with groups of agents working in Russian headquarters; Otto Skorzeny's SS Special Service Troops had also infiltrated parties of Russian agents behind the Soviet front. FHO had been working on the formation of an agent/guerrilla army even into May 1945. Then communications had been severed.

Baun nevertheless believed that he could re-establish his contacts. He ordered his radio operators to call up the old informers[57] and then – too late – was forced to admit that it was 'an attempt made with inadequate resources'. He could register no success, for the agents in Russia had 'cut themselves out' – secret-service jargon for severance of contact with an agent. They neither heard the call-signs from the Taunus nor were they in a position to answer them. As the German forces and their intelligence officers became increasingly distant, their Russian henchmen had sunk their radio sets in lakes or buried them in woods; the majority of the informers had reported to Soviet counter-espionage agencies. They had no intention of risking their necks for the defeated Germans.

Gehlen used this, the Org's first set-back, as a pretext for an intrigue against his rival Baun, in which the old antipathy between the General Staff officers of FHO and the men of the Abwehr showed its face once more. He held Baun personally responsible for the absence of radio communications with the East and disparaged him to the Americans. Moreover Baun was still trying to emancipate himself from Gehlen's authority as laid down by the US General Sibert. Colonel Dean, the US liaison officer to the Org, accordingly ordered that Baun be put in cold storage. Baun was forced to accept ex-Colonel Dinser, a friend of Gehlen's, as Chief of Staff in his section. Baun lamented: 'Gehlen was even prepared to issue orders that Dinser and I must live together and that he should work in my room.'[58]

The Americans were now pressing Gehlen to expand his organization and at last to provide up-to-date information from the East. Colonel Dean laid down the target date as July 1st, 1947 — by that time a network of agents was to be set up in what Baun called 'the enemy zone', in other words the Soviet Zone of Germany, Poland and the Soviet Union. The US liaison staff were in a hurry, for after the failure of the Foreign Ministers' Conference in Moscow in the spring of 1947 and the Red Army's hold-up of Western military trains to Berlin, the possibility of war with Russia could no longer be excluded. But what the potential enemy in Moscow was actually planning, whether the Soviet Union was really girding its loins for a showdown — that Washington did not know.

To be sure of Stalin's plans one of the Western secret services would have had to have an agent or an informer (a 'source') sitting in the middle of the Kremlin. But no such source appeared and no informer was sending radio messages from Moscow. Any statement to the contrary is either pure invention or a product of the Gehlen legend. The truth is by no means so breathtaking. Gehlen had no super-spies and no star agents in the Soviet think-tanks. He did, however, know how to make use, at the right time, of an incomparable source of information but for its exploitation General Staff precision work was required — his sources were the German prisoners of war in the Soviet Union.

In fact in the German prisoners of war the Soviet Union, mistrustful and xenophobic as ever, was harbouring in its own country an army of 3.1 million spies. From the simple soldier to the general each was an expert in some field — the soldier, sailor or airman knew about weapons, aircraft or ships, the farmer about agriculture and the craftsman about industrial products.

Huddled in cattle trucks, millions of Germans travelled through the vast expanses of Russia, from Finland to the Black Sea, from the Volga to Siberia. They carried out their set tasks in industry, in the kolkhozes, in the forests and in the mines. In their hutted camps were to be found engineers, geologists, miners, telecommunications specialists, chemists and railway workers. They built roads, they tunnelled mine-shafts, they lifted railway tracks, they were even employed as craftsmen in armaments works. Many of them learnt Russian and so could understand things not intended for their ears. They noted bottlenecks in the supply of raw materials, stoppages of production, rises in output figures and percentages of delivery quotas; they learnt of harvest failures and they knew the mood of the population.

Initially employed only as manual labour, the 'Plennys' (as the German prisoners were known) gradually came to occupy more important posts and their knowledge widened. As soon as they had gained intimate knowledge of some works, then, in accordance with Moscow's POW policy, they were immediately transferred to some other camp and therefore to some other concern. But this meant that the cattle trucks once more rolled through the country, past airfields and industrial areas, meeting troop trains, crossing bridges and passing through railway stations. The 'Plennys' gazed through the slits in the trucks and passed the time in counting runways, coke ovens, trucks, river crossings and railway tracks.

As head of FHO Gehlen had based his appreciations primarily on statements from prisoners of war and deserters. From the outset, therefore, the Germans in Russia represented a potential source of information. So in the summer of 1947 he started where he had left off in the spring of 1945 – with a system of detailed interrogation. It was more productive than any intelligence-gathering by individual agents in the Soviet Union could ever have been. Moreover it was the most humane espionage undertaking in post-war history, for it did not claim a single victim. Its code-name was 'Operation Hermes'.[59]

Members of the Gehlen Organization were permanently located in the West German reception camps for returning prisoners of war. When the arrival of a fresh convoy from Russia was announced, they were ready with their pencils and their questionnaires. Almost everyone who returned, whether soldier or civilian internee, passed through the office of the Gehlen representative, who asked him in what camps he had been and in what industry he had worked. Gehlen's men also noted names of stool-pigeons and of instructors on the 'anti-fascist courses' in the Soviet camps. Anyone who, as a result, was thought to be under communist influence was not questioned by the Org but was registered in a special card-index as a potential enemy.

To the returning POWs this process was presented merely as the official registration of personal details, but it was in fact the first step in the assembly of intelligence data. Completed questionnaires were forwarded to the Org's headquarters in the Taunus and there the headquarters officers checked the information from camps and places of work against the archives of FHO.

A few weeks later a man would knock on the door of the returned prisoner's home and introduce himself, saying that he came from a German organization which was admittedly working for the Americans but was acting exclusively in the interests of Germany; he wished to put one or two questions. To the more cautious he would display a blue pass from the 'Historical Research Institute' in Wiesbaden; the really suspicious he invited to visit the nearest CIC agency which would vouch for his visitor and his quest for information. 'After initial hesitation,' one of Gehlen's staff says, 'almost all these home-comers began to talk. They had been through the hell of imprisonment; they had suffered in Russia and they knew the country as no one from the West had known it before. Hardly any of them hated the country or its inhabitants. Each of them remembered some touching incident when some Russian had passed a morsel of food to the starving prisoners. But they knew about Soviet communism and had seen through it.'[60]

Like pieces of a mosaic, every detail produced by these returning POWs was fitted together by Gehlen's interrogators. The Org soon knew about grain production in the Ukraine and oil deliveries from Baku; but it also knew more than any other Western intelligence service about advanced submarine production and the manufacture of motor vehicles. Sometimes dozens of reports would come in from some out-of-the-way camp about a single arms factory. Taking each statement individually it was all small beer – typical of secret-service work. Each 'Plenny' could only tell what he himself had seen, experienced or heard. Nevertheless, from the multiplicity of reports a reasonably accurate picture could be constructed.

A good illustration was the information received from the Black Sea port of Balaclava near Sebastopol where there was a submarine refit yard. Prisoners from camps 7299/6 and 7299/16 worked in the port as bricklayers and mechanics. When they returned to Germany they were among Gehlen's most important 'sources'. One of them, for instance, reported that in the spring of 1947 Colonel Tutuso, head of the Secret Police in the Crimea, had been relieved of his post. For any Western secret service it was, of course, of interest to know whether Tutuso had fallen into disfavour and might therefore be a candidate for 'conversion' and used for counter-espionage purposes. For weeks Gehlen's investigators searched for prisoners returning from Balaclava and eventually they found them. One of the 'Plennys' said the Colonel Tutuso was an Old Guard revolutionary and a friend of Stalin; his transfer to Tiflis was in fact a promotion. Asked how he knew this, the ex-prisoner replied that he had been a Secret Police driver; having learnt Russian he could overhear conversations between the NKVD men. Moreover he had moved Tutuso's furniture and in the process had seen a personally inscribed photograph of Stalin; he had also heard that Tutuso was being moved to Tiflis. He knew too about Tutuso's successor in the Crimea: he was called Major-General Kalinin and was a relative of the former Soviet President of the same name, whom he resembled, particularly about the chin and nose. 'The NKVD people talked about him,' this particular informant recalled, 'saying that Kalinin was very strict but gave an impression of distinction and education.'

Gehlen's interrogators were always looking for cross-checks. One source 'with relatively good knowledge' of the port of Balaclava, for instance, reported the delivery of coal from the Donetz and cement from Kerch by freighter and lighters. Since he had not been on the ships himself, the interrogator asked him how he knew the cargoes and ports of origin. 'From fellow-prisoners who had to unload the stuff,' he replied. To check whether the source's other information was accurate, Gehlen's agents questioned prisoners who had unloaded coal and iron ore in Balaclava and only when confirmed by information from other ex-prisoners were the source's other statements recorded. These included the fact that, in addition to two auxiliary cruisers, there were a number of small submarines in the port moored together in sixes. 'Total numbers varied considerably,' the source said; 'frequently, but at irregular intervals, quite a number of submarines would leave and return a day later.' In the record of interrogation it was noted: 'Source reckons the maximum number of submarines at 36.'[61]

In the Crimean town of Simferopol prisoners were employed as sweepers in a veterinary hospital. Behind a range of hills one of them was continuously hearing the sound of engines. He reported: 'I crept up the hill and, although I did not get a complete view of the countryside, I could make out some twenty tanks of various types including the T24, the German 'Panther' and the German Mark IV with a long gun of about 7.5 cm calibre. I also saw an engine being lifted from a tank with a small crane.' One prisoner had witnessed the 1947 May Day parade in Simferopol. The Org's interrogator noted what he had seen — 'after the motor-cyclists came five guns of about 15 cm calibre drawn by small tracked vehicles which must use very little fuel. The guns had dust-covers on the muzzles; there was no sign of a muzzle brake.'

Frequently the interrogators returned discouraged from their question-and-answer sessions; obviously they knew only of the results which they themselves had achieved and these often seemed to them highly unilluminating. One of Gehlen's people complained to headquarters: 'A normal week consists of two good reports, one moderate report and six fruitless visits entailing a maximum waste of time and energy. Moreover one should not forget the psychological effect on the agent – he travels through the city by tram two days running; he walks considerable distances in the heat; he talks to the source for hours on end and when he closes his notebook, he has frequently achieved nothing.'[62]

There were, of course, ex-prisoners who refused to cooperate with the Org. One such was a Lieutenant from a Mountain Infantry unit, whose cover-name was 'Kurt Rosen'; he had been captured near Lvov on August 4th, 1941, had spent eight years wandering through Russia, both European and Asiatic, and eventually, after several attempts had succeeded in escaping. In the late 1950s, writing under the name of 'Clemens Forell', he published an account of his adventures in the expanses of Russia which became a best-selling novel. Millions both in Germany and abroad were fascinated by the book *So weit die Füsse tragen* [So much foot-slogging] and by the similarly entitled television film. Kurt Rosen was not prepared to provide the Org with information. The agent who interrogated him noted morosely in his report: 'The last conversation, with which this report deals, took place on March 6th, 1950, and a further meeting was arranged for March 10th. R did not come, however, but sent the attached letter. The following reasons for his refusal to give further information may be conjectured: either he is really afraid of reprisals from the Russians, should they occupy West Germany, or he has let his imagination run riot and is afraid that precise questioning will expose him as a fraud. There is, however, a third possibility: that as a result of his experiences in the Soviet Union he has suffered mentally as well as physically.'[63]

Rosen, however, was an exception. As a rule the returning prisoners answered the Org's questions with the greatest alacrity. Then another agency of Gehlen's organization had to work out how valuable these statements were; this was the Evaluation Group in Oberursel, of which ex-Colonel Herre had meanwhile assumed control. Each evening and each night Gehlen's interrogators wrote down what they had elucidated during the day. Since there were no secret channels of communication between agents and headquarters, the interrogator simply put his report in an envelope and dispatched it by post to a cover-address in Frankfurt am Main. There the mail was collected by couriers and taken to Gehlen's camp in the Taunus, which was sealed off by the US Army.

In Oberursel Herre and his staff compared the ex-prisoners' information with other statements and then registered it – together with FHO's old intelligence. As an instance – suppose the ex-prisoners all agreed that four dry-docks were under construction in Balaclava, then, with the help of his FHO records, Herre could calculate the capacity of the submarine refit yards on the Black Sea.[64] If there were specific questions outstanding, headquarters would send some expert to carry out a further interrogation, probably an ex-naval officer who knew Balaclava from his time in the Navy and who was able to elicit more precise information with the help of maps, aerial photographs and sketches.

During one such visit one of the ex-prisoners remembered that he had in his luggage a small piece of red stone. It came from a chemical works in Djerzhinsk, from a restricted area which Germans working in the concern were not allowed to enter. One of them, however, was allowed in – as driver of a dust-cart. His job was to collect waste products and cart them to a special rubbish dump inside the restricted area. On one of his journeys it occurred to the Germans that these little red stones might be used to make a spark. He pocketed a stone and rigged himself up a lighter which he successfully slipped through all the searches made by the camp guards.

No spy, however highly trained, could have smuggled specimens of material out of these works since they were closely guarded. The ex-corporal, now ex-dust-cart driver, however, brought his lighter with him to West Germany. Gehlen's interrogator exchanged it for a packet of Camels and sent it to headquarters. Since the Org did not yet possess its own laboratory, the flint was simply placed in an envelope with a note as to its origin and, via the US liaison staff, dispatched to Washington by courier aircraft. A few days later Washington sent a congratulatory telegram which, however, contained the urgent warning to send such finds in metal containers in future. The US secret-service scientists had analysed the flint as radio-active material.[65]

The reports produced by this mine of information constituted by the ex-prisoners were not, however, forwarded direct to the Americans. The Org's Evaluation Section used them to construct personal card-indexes, an order of battle of major Soviet formations and lists of Russian military establishments, arms firms and kolkhozes. They formed the basis of the Org's analyses and appreciations on every aspect of the Soviet Union – industry, armaments, communications, armed forces and morale of the population. These analyses were frequently of book size. They were drafted in German and passed to the US Liaison Staff which then forwarded them to the War Department in Washington.[66]

The effect of Gehlen's reports on the US military and secret service in the autumn of 1947 was that of an alarm signal. The USA had already mothballed most of her warships; the bomber fleet of the Second World War had largely been scrapped and the fighting troops had returned home. The Soviet Union, on the other hand, was raising her production of both tanks and aircraft. Washington found the Org's information all the more interesting in that Gehlen was now in a position to produce intelligence on Soviet forces in East Germany. In late 1947 the Org started 'short-range intelligence' (as opposed to 'long-range intelligence' from Russia itself) – the assembly of information on the Soviet-occupied zone of Germany.

Although Gehlen had certain individual agents operating in the zone, in this case too he received most of his information from so-called non-secret sources – the refugees. Here he was admittedly in competition with the Western intelligence services. The American CIC, the British SIS and the French Deuxième Bureau all maintained interrogators in the refugee camps in their zones to register and question Germans escaping from the Soviet Zone.

But Gehlen outwitted his fellow-conspirators. In practice it worked like this: in the refugee camp at Kornwestheim in Württemberg was a group of interrogators from the American CIC. The new arrivals from the Soviet zone, however, remained remarkably tongue-tied in front of the US inquisitors; they would give their personal details, but when asked about dismantling of factories, communist party functionaries or the presence of Soviet troops in their home town, they became evasive. They had in fact been advised not to enlighten the Americans by a man named Schmidt, the schoolmaster in the camp school. He would say: 'You don't know that the Americans won't pass on your statements to the Russians.' Schmidt, on the other hand, the new arrivals trusted; they told him where they came from, where they had worked and what they had seen.

Schmidt was continually on the look-out for what he called the 'good German' and would talk to them in his hut in the evenings. He would generally end by saying: 'You really should not keep your knowledge to yourself. After all the Russian is our enemy and what you have told me about the local dignitaries of the Socialist Unity Party is of real interest. I know a gentleman who would be very interested in you, not an American but a German who is working for our common cause.' In fact

Schmidt, the schoolmaster, was acting as the Org's 'tipster' in the camp. In view of his opportunities for making contacts an old friend already working for Gehlen had recruited him — with coffee and cigarettes. Schmidt told his Gehlen friend about knowledgeable newcomers from the Soviet zone and arranged for them to meet.[67]

In talking to the refugees Gehlen's investigators were primarily interested in 'possible connections in East Berlin and the Soviet zone of occupation', as their cautious phraseology put it. In other words they were collecting 'clues to people', information about Soviet officers and German employees in Russian agencies who might be subjects for an 'agent approach'. They were also interested in letter-headings and stamps of Soviet agencies — for copying.

As in the interrogation of returning POWs, a high percentage of the information produced by the refugee was of no importance. The fact that the Soviet Lieutenant Sokolov, living in the Parkstrasse in Zwickau was intelligent, twenty-seven years of age, married, brutal and obstinate was of no consequence; equally uninteresting was the information that the German licensing agency was under the supervision of a Russian Captain named Olech who lived at No 42 Frankestrasse, Berlin-Karlshorst (home telephone: 050023; office: 55 16 44), always wore mufti and was regarded as well-read and a fanatical communist. Such reports came back to the interrogator from the organizer with the comment: 'Useless. Not worth sending on to headquarters since it contains nothing of interest.' The same source, however, might produce the following lead-in: 'All written applications for inter-zone trade must pass through a German–Russian translation bureau in the Friedrichstrasse, Berlin. V., an employee of this bureau, is pro-West and is very susceptible to money; he is the old-style bon viveur, likes his food and smokes American cigarettes when he can get them.' The organizer's comment on this was: 'Tip could be good if following questions could be answered: How, when, how often and how intimately was source in contact with this man? Number of house in Friedrichstrasse.'[68]

Thousands of these personal reports streamed into the Org's headquarters in the Taunus. Countless scraps of information about conditions in the Soviet zone were registered by Gehlen's sections. As time went on the Org blossomed into a great official institution. The accommodation available in the Taunus, which was temporary anyway, soon became too small. Gehlen had already pleaded for something more spacious so that the families of his staff could be accommodated. As soldiers they had been separated from their wives and children for years and, in addition, they were forbidden to have contact with the outside world. Finally there was always the danger that some member of one of the staff's families might be kidnapped.

In the autumn of 1947 Herre and Colonel Leabert, the US Liaison Officer who had succeeded Colonel Dean, went on a voyage of exploration through the US Zone. Both had a fairly clear idea of what the secret-service headquarters should be: it should have enough space to accommodate all the sections in adjacent buildings; it should not be actually in a town but not too far away from one. The German and the American inspected every barracks occupied by US troops, 'but,' Herre recalls, 'we found nothing suitable'.

The two were about to return from Stuttgart to Frankfurt when Herre remembered a complex of buildings where he had once been on temporary duty during the war; it was the 'Rudolf Hess Settlement' in Pullach, a small place about six miles south of Munich on the banks of the Isar near the 'Grosshesseloher Suicide Bridge'. What Leabert and Herre discovered in Pullach was precisely what they wanted: a compound containing some twenty single- and two-storied houses, huts and bunkers, all surrounded by a wall a mile long. It had been constructed in 1936 to house the staff of the Führer's Deputy Rudolf Hess and had also temporarily been the residence of Martin Bormann; in April 1945 Field Marshal Kesselring had had his headquarters there. Since 1945 it had been occupied by the Postal Censorship authorities of the US Army. After inspecting the area Leabert decided: 'This is where we must go.'[69]

The American censors were forced to evacuate and on December 6th, 1947, Gehlen and his staff moved in. The date gave the area its new name – 'Camp Nicholas' (the German equivalent for Santa Claus). The staff brought their families with them. Gehlen, with his wife Herta, his daughters Katharina, Herta and Grete and his son Felix-Christoph, was allotted Bormann's two-storied house, the 'White House' in the centre of the estate. It was in typical Nazi style: over the front door was the German eagle in stone, but holding nothing in its claws since the US censors had chipped away the swastika; on the main wall of the great ground-floor dining-room ladies with ample bosoms were weaving ears of corn into yellow necklaces; in the garden slender young men stood on pedestals in gymnastic postures; a fountain played.

In next to no time the camp in Pullach had become the headquarters of a German secret service – despite the facts that the Stars and Stripes flew above the entrance gate, passes were checked by American soldiers and missions assigned by American officers. By early 1948 Gehlen had transferred 200 of his staff to Pullach and shortly thereafter he informed the married members that wives and children could now be accommodated. The Org became a great secret-service family.

The admission of families had two objects – to make the ex-soldiers feel at home and also to provide the Org with office staff, for the majority of the wives took jobs as secretaries. Children went to a kindergarten inside the camp or to a school run by wives whose husbands were also members of the Org. Many of the boys and girls in that school have followed the family tradition and are still working today as secretaries or desk officers in the West German Intelligence Service. Many ties were formed between the members of this secret society. Gehlen, who was a great family man, found a place for many of his relatives in the Pullach machine. He also liked playing the role of match-maker and was instrumental in arranging the marriage of his secretary to a secret-service general.[70]

All Gehlen's arrangements were designed to make his staff independent of the outside world. A hospital was set up to ensure that they were cared for medically; a mess, provided with American rations, offered the staff and their families a menu such as no other German could enjoy in 1948. The Chief contrived to instil the solidarity of a military headquarters; the atmosphere was welcoming. And the policy paid – more and more men were ready to follow the general's star. More important still, the ex-soldiers of the staff were ready to take any risks to ensure that 'the firm', as the Org was referred to internally, produced results.

This was all the more necessary in that in 1949 Gehlen and his Org changed masters. Until that time the Org had been under G-2 (Intelligence) of the US Army and, this being so, strict limits were set on the objects of Gehlen's activity. The Org's primary object was to provide the US military with military information from the East. The US officers of the Liaison Staff asked a few political questions, although as early as 1946 Gehlen had begun to pry into the political secrets of the Eastern bloc.

In the spring of 1948 Gehlen was involved in a serious disagreement with Colonel Leabert, the head of the US Liaison Staff, over the question whether the Org should deal solely in military espionage. Leabert issued Gehlen with a categoric order to confine himself to military intelligence in the Eastern bloc. Gehlen refused. Leabert thereupon threatened that the Org would lose its independence and be subordinated to US Headquarters in Germany. Gehlen would then have no prerogatives of any sort.

Leabert did in fact withdraw his order but Gehlen, who was most touchy and very conscious of his position, refused to cooperate further with Leabert and in August engineered his replacement. In doing so Gehlen was logically pursuing his basic idea. He wished to free himself from the tutelage of G-2 and ally himself with the CIA, which had been formed in 1947. He seized the opportunity of a directive from the US military urging greater economy, to hand in his resignation, proposing, as he says in his memoirs, 'to disband the Organization in view of the disparity between resources available and tasks allotted'.

Long before this, however, Gehlen had initiated negotiations with the CIA which ultimately produced an English-language contract signed in June 1949 and a German-language equivalent signed on June 23rd. In alliance with the CIA Gehlen's initially military Org turned increasingly towards political, economic and technical espionage against the Eastern bloc.

The name 'Pullach' became synonymous with secret service efficiency.

AGENTS, AGENTS, AGENTS

MONTH by month Gehlen's organization grew; more and more ex-soldiers joined the ex-General. They worked all the harder for him when he indicated to them that their purpose was one which Adolf Hitler's warriors understood only too well. Their object was to commit the US occupier on the German side and exploit the differences between Washington and Moscow in order to save the Germans from the worst consequences of the war begun and lost by the Hitler regime.

As early as the beginning of 1947 Gehlen had confided to one of his staff that he was reckoning on the possibility of war between Russia and America; even should there be no armed conflict, he said, Europe faced a decade of growing tension. Meanwhile he was toying with a fantastic notion – that the Russians and Americans would tear each other to pieces and so give a rearmed Germany the opportunity to create a new order in Europe. Pending this, the Americans must be anchored to Germany and brought into the game on the German side.

By a series of accidents Gehlen was now in a position to exert decisive influence on American policy towards Germany and Europe. Ever since the War Department in Washington had commissioned him to continue his intelligence work in the East, his voice had contributed to the US picture of Russian influence expanding irresistibly across Europe. Like most of his Western contemporaries Gehlen supported the view that the Russian steam-roller would continue to grind its way forward. He could see no reason for the Soviet Union suddenly to halt its westward march begun during the war – particularly when faced by a Western Europe threatening to sink in a welter of regimes lacking credibility, economic disorder and communist bids for power.

Today we know that this picture was a false one. Russia's westward advance came to a halt where the war had left it – on a line from Lübeck to upper Adria. Louis J. Halle, the American historian, says: 'We could not know, at the time, that an expansion which had already covered so much of the distance to the Atlantic seaboard and the western Mediterranean would stop before reaching them.'[1] Nevertheless the Soviet Union remained a source of continuous political unrest throughout the world; in view of the unhappy state of Western Europe Stalin was inevitably tempted to expand Moscow's influence in non-communist Europe by an obstreperous policy of blackmail. Western Germany above all, in disarray and ruled by war-weary occupying powers, seemed to him an easy prey.

Stalin's decision proved to be a bad miscalculation, for it led Washington to commit itself to the support of free, but sick, post-war Europe. From this time on America's leading military men saw the Soviet Union no longer as an ally but as their potential enemy of the next war. And it was Gehlen who kept the US strategists in a state of alert; seventy per cent of all the US government's information on Soviet forces and armaments came from the Gehlen Organization.

Their commission from Washington enabled Gehlen's staff officers to continue to do what they had learnt and what they had always done. They probed into troop strengths and military movements, they calculated strength potential and production figures, they listed military personalities and postings of senior officers in the East. They had little sense of the political niceties or of ideological motives; their concept of the mentality of the super-power in the East was frequently distorted by their picture of an enemy of almost diabolical cunning. In the essentials of military intelligence, however, their efficiency was unrivalled.

In a very short time these capabilities ensured for the Org a monopoly in secret-service matters such as no other Western espionage organization could boast. The Org was able to put its Western rivals in the shade because it was operating in its own back garden – the Soviet-occupied zone of Germany. Nowhere else could it have recruited so many assistants or aroused such passions; nowhere else were Germans of almost all ideologies and parties more determined to expunge the results of the Second World War.

In the Eastern Zone a small group of communist activists under the protection of the occupying power had set up a regime which was a challenge to everything held dear by democrats and patriots. Under it power was wielded by hard-core communists; marxists of all shades of opinion had been forced to combine in the 'Socialist Unity Party' (the SED) which had then been transformed into an all-embracing centralist party on the Soviet model; land and industry in private ownership had been expropriated, the bourgeois parties emasculated and the citizenry deprived of their liberty.

Nothing could reconcile the Germans to a system imposed by force and the occupying power. 'Changes in the machinery of state had not been brought about by changes in the basic order of society; on the contrary, with the aid of an official and administrative machine which had been developed into a central engine of power, changes in the structure of society were imposed'[2] – not even socialists could stomach that. The State of Walter Ulbricht and Wilhelm Pieck could hardly count on loyalty from anyone – from workers to bourgeoisie.

This State, which no German wanted, was now the target for Gehlen's informers and he could be sure that everywhere he could find willing hands to help him. The Org's first great successes were scored in the Eastern Zone. It was a triumph of military intelligence – how could it be otherwise? One of those primarily responsible was ex-Captain Dieter Keuner (not his real name); from his house in Berlin-Wilmersdorf he had organized a circuit of agents in the Eastern Zone.

Keuner had served on the Eastern front during the war and joined the Gehlen Organization in 1947. Initially he had merely been one of the Org's agents but had rapidly risen to be head of an out-station in West Berlin. His staff consisted of twenty organizers, each of whom ran ten agents; their informers were residents of the Eastern Zone who were required to report every detail of military interest.[3]

Among the organizers the most important was ex-Colonel Kurt Tölle (not his real name), Keuner's former regimental commander. Keuner had recruited him shortly after becoming head of his out-station. Even Tölle, however, had to climb the regulation promotion ladder of the secret service. First he journeyed through the zone, recruiting staff among his former fellow-officers; with them as 'sources' he became an agent, until finally headquarters in Pullach appointed him an organizer. Tölle had a fixed monthly salary of 700 marks, 200 marks less than Keuner. Nevertheless to Keuner, the head of the station, his subordinate Tölle was always 'the Colonel' – the proprieties had to be observed. This, however, did not prevent the ex-Colonel from standing strictly to attention before the ex-Captain.

As organizer Tölle mobilized a group of five agents to obtain information from the Eastern Zone. One of them was Walter Zentner (not his real name) who had known Tölle for years; they had served together in the Wehrmacht. Tölle had knocked on the door of Zentner's house in 1947 and recruited him for the Gehlen Organization. During his first months as an agent Zentner himself went into the Eastern Zone, visited former comrades and asked them to note down for him the registration numbers of Soviet military vehicles, to make sketches of airfields, watch Red Army exercises and to report on the morale of the population in the zone.[4]

Zentner's currency was cigarettes, coffee, tinned milk and chocolate. Once a month he travelled through the Russian Zone exchanging these desirable goods for information. It was a profitable business for all concerned until, one day, Zentner heard that one of his informers had been arrested by the People's Police. Thereafter he kept out of the zone and made his informers come to West Berlin. They came quite unsuspectingly, for among the friends and fellow-officers from whom the first circuits were formed, strict precautions seemed unnecessary. In any case the informers reacted unfavourably to any sign of lack of confidence and would then frequently peddle their wares to some other Western secret service. Anyone who could offer news or secrets from the Russian Zone had no need to worry about takers. Berlin was the great exchange mart for intelligence. Americans, British and French were all prepared to buy whatever was on offer.

Zentner was able to recruit a hard core of good informers. He soon had ten available who reported to him whatever they heard, read or saw in the Russian Zone. None of them knew any of the others. Zentner met them one at a time, always at a different meeting place and invariably on a Saturday or Sunday. There was the baker's assistant from Döberitz, for instance, who reported how many loaves his bakery delivered daily to the Russian barracks; a washerwoman in Eberswalde counted Russian soldiers' shirts; in Potsdam a former regimental friend of Zentner's observed the number of barrack windows lighted in the evenings and the number in darkness compared to the previous week; an informer in Schönwalde rummaged in a rubbish dump for letters and scraps of paper bearing cyrillic characters and took them to Zentner in West Berlin each weekend. Zentner paid his agents a fee in Western currency for every piece of information – 20 or 30 marks, sometimes even 50 marks. As reward for the scraps of paper from the rubbish dump he would push a packet of cigarettes across the table. Travelling expenses he refunded in Eastern currency.

In August 1947 Zentner also recruited a nineteen-year-old building worker, Klaus Imhoff (not his real name). He came from Niesky in Oberlausitz and had merely come to spend a weekend in West Berlin. After visiting a cinema he went to a restaurant near to Zoo Station for a bowl of soup. There he came across Zentner, who happened to sit at his table and talked to him. Zentner soon knew Klaus Imhoff's life history: his father had been killed in Russia and his mother was bringing up three children, working in a factory. Klaus, the eldest son, had had to become a builder's labourer but wanted to be an architect.

The two agreed that life was impossible under the Russians and the

SED functionaries; the only question was how to get rid of them. Zentner said that the first thing to do was to tell the West everything that happened in the zone. He knew an ex-Wehrmacht officer who collected such information and passed it on to an agency which in turn informed the American authorities.

Then came the vital question from Zentner: as a building worker had Imhoff access to Soviet barracks, for instance? Imhoff said that he had no means of entering a barracks but he had often observed troop trains in Niesky bringing Soviet soldiers and tanks from Poland. Zentner said that it was important to know how often such trains arrived, how many tanks they carried and what their destination was; Imhoff should keep his eyes open and pass on what he had seen next time he visited West Berlin. Imhoff promised to appear again.[5]

With this promise Klaus Imhoff had become a member of the Gehlen Organization. 'What mattered to me,' he said later, 'was to give the Ivans and the SED a smack in the eye. I felt that morally it was both my right and duty to fight the communist enemy in our country. I did not think of myself as a spy but as a resister against the occupying power and their quislings in Pankow.' On the street, in the tram or among his friends Imhoff made a note of anything which seemed to him of interest. Every Saturday he took the train to East Berlin and in the afternoon the metro to the Western sectors. In some bar he would find Zentner sitting with a *Tagesspiegel* spread out in front of him.

Early in September 1948 Imhoff happened to meet his schoolfriend Hubert Maus (not his real name) near the Soviet war memorial in Niesky. Maus had joined the People's Police and from him Imhoff learnt that the police were receiving military training and were being equipped with heavy weapons. Inexperienced though he was, Imhoff realized the implications: the Soviet Zone was secretly arming. Imhoff went to West Berlin at once and hurried to Steglitz. He left the metro at the Schlossstrasse, turned into a side-street and entered a Schultheiss bar. He went straight to the table where Zentner was waiting with his *Tagesspiegel*.

Imhoff reported what he thought was sensational news. Zentner too was impressed. His report, written shortly afterwards, was as follows: '9718. [Zentner's code-number] Source Klauss Imhoff from Niesky, who was in school there until 1947 with Hubert Maus and passed his finals at the same time as Maus, has reported to No 9718 that, a few days ago he met his friend Maus near the Soviet war memorial in Niesky. Maus is now serving in the People's Police. Maus told source K.I. in strict secrecy that he was now a soldier. His police unit was training near Weimar on machine-guns and mortars. Maus thought it likely that the police would later be equipped with artillery and tanks (T34s). When source K.I. asked whether the police were being trained on these weapons by Russians, Maus replied that the Russians supervised but the training was done by officers of the former German Wehrmacht. Evaluation of source K.I.: Have known source for one year and his information has invariably proved accurate. 9718.'[6]

On the following Monday Zentner took the report and submitted it to his organizer Tölle, who initially wished to write it off as a figment of the imagination. He thought it inconceivable that the Russians would allow Germans to handle heavy weapons. 'I then talked to him like a Dutch uncle,' Zentner recalls. 'I was convinced that there was something in this report. I told him: "That fellow Imhoff is not fabricating." ' Tölle countered: 'But what about Imhoff's informant, the policeman?' Zentner pleaded: 'But at least pass the information on. Perhaps the Americans already know more.' Tölle allowed himself to be argued round and drove to the house of Keuner, the head of the out-station, where the organizers always delivered the products of their informers in the zone.

When Keuner read Zentner's report, he said solemnly: 'Colonel, what you've got here is a winner.' Twenty-two years later Keuner said: 'At the time we were getting a lot of reports which led me to say, as I read them: "Well now, there's someone who has thought up a splendid story to extract one or two little rewards from our briefcase." In sifting the material one had to have a good nose to smell out fact and fiction. In this case, however, I felt instinctively that there might be something in it.' When Tölle had gone Keuner wrote a report for the Pullach headquarters. Then he dialled a telephone number and said: 'We must see each other tomorrow; it's urgent.' The answer came back: 'Nine at four.' Nine was the time of day and four the code number of the meeting place – the monkey-house in the Berlin zoo.

Next morning Keuner engaged a visitor to the zoo in conversation in front of the monkey-house; he took a *Telegraf* from his pocket and showed the gentleman an article in the newspaper. The man asked Keuner if he would lend him the paper and Keuner said that he would. Then the two parted. Keuner had been relieved of his *Telegraf* and of an envelope which he had pasted inside it – containing the report from Niesky. The report was now in the Org's internal postal system. That evening the courier entered the offices of the US military airfield at Tempelhof. A few minutes later an American conducted him to a twin-engined courier aircraft, a Dakota. Some American officers and also some civilians were already on board, the latter all members of Gehlen's organization.

On landing in Frankfurt the courier looked for a car with German markings among the US vehicles parked at the airport. He quoted a four-figure number to the driver, who checked it against a row of figures on a notepad. In front of one of the hotels in the middle of Frankfurt the courier got out, leaving his briefcase on the passenger's seat of the car. The driver took it on to a semi-detached house in Bad Nauheim where there lived certain officers of the Org who acted as liaison between headquarters in Pullach and its outposts in Berlin. Zentner's report was sent on its way to Munich by another courier travelling from Frankfurt main station on the south-bound US military train.

Finally the report arrived at a villa near the Nymphenburger Schloss in Munich; violin-playing could be heard through the windows and a doorplate announced that the owner was a music teacher. The fact that he possessed a code name and a number, however, showed that the alleged musician was responsible for another of Gehlen's agencies. His house was in fact the centre of communications from the Org's out-stations such as Bad Nauheim, Stuttgart and Bremen. This was the last relay post for mail between headquarters in Pullach Camp and its agents in the Russian Zone.

An hour later the report from West Berlin was on the desk of Colonel (retd) Dinser of the Acquisition Group. One of the staff recalls that its effect was that 'of a steam-hammer'. For the first time the West learnt that the decision had been taken to remilitarize the Soviet Zone. The 'Barrack Alarm Squads' [Kasernieste Bereitschaften], later renamed the 'People's Barrack Police' [Kasernieste Volkspolizei], heralded the formation of an army in the other half of Germany – long before West German politicians had thought of any such thing.[7]

A lively debate took place in the higher ranks of the Org over the credence to be placed in the report from Niesky. It is no longer possible to discover how the various men around Gehlen voted but several of those involved remember Gehlen's own view quite clearly: 'The Doctor' declared at once that he thought it possible that the Soviet government was preparing to re-arm the Eastern Zone. A process was beginning which Gehlen had always visualized – the revival of the German Army.

Gehlen ordered a special staff to be set up in Pullach to study the transformation of the People's Police into a military force. All heads of out-stations and organizers were ordered to divert their agents and sources on to Project 'People's Police', as Keuner himself had already done. Gehlen sent word to Keuner that the source Imhoff should be given a special reward – a 'Care' package. In the Eastern Zone ex-Wehrmacht officers found themselves once more being visited by old friends. The visitors were particularly interested to know whether they or any wartime mutual friends were being employed by the People's Police. Young policemen suddenly found themselves being invited to drink a glass of beer. Military manoeuvre areas were surrounded by people picking mushrooms.

In the headquarters of the Soviet forces in Zossen and that of the People's Police in Berlin the plans for arming the police were still held under the highest security grading, but by using all possible channels, the Org soon knew the organization, strength and equipment of these embryo East German forces. The special 'People's Police' staff in Pullach worked as if it were a twin to the Russo-German Police Headquarters forming the East German forces, first on paper and then in cadre.

By spring 1949 the Org was able to calculate and inform the Americans what planning goals had been set for the 'Barrack Police' for the end of that year – twenty-four regiments of infantry, seven artillery regiments, three tank regiments, two engineer regiments and three signals regiments. The strength of each unit was to be 1,250 men and the total strength of the 'Barrack Police' 48,750. It was an extrapolation exercise in the best traditions of the German General Staff. In the autumn of 1949 a senior People's Police officer defected and handed over to the Org the secret plans for the formation of the first 'Barrack Police' units, by then already complete. They checked precisely with the forecasts made by Gehlen's experts in the spring.[8]

The discovery of the 'Barrack Police' showed for the first time how effectively Gehlen's organization was watching military developments in the Soviet Zone. The time was now past when the Org had to content itself with interrogating refugees from the East and acquiring its military knowledge that way. It now had its own spies between the Elbe and the Oder and their numbers, though small, were growing month by month. The Org's next success was not long in coming and it was a copybook example of successful espionage – Gehlen's investigators uncovered one of the East's greatest military secrets.

In the spring of 1949 Pullach began to receive agents' reports referring to curious flying objects to be seen in the Soviet Zone. One report, for instance, said: 'This flying object looks like a rocket; at first sight it appears to be a new type of aircraft without wings or propeller.' Officers and technicians of the Western air forces asked themselves whether the observers were the victims of some optical illusion or whether they had really seen some novelty produced by the Russian aircraft designers. Gehlen's air-force experts came to the conclusion that it must be some new Russian aircraft. They were supported by a further report which said that this sinister flying machine developed an enormous speed; it also made a whine, unlike the noise of the conventional engine.[9]

One of those racking his brains over this whining sound was a German ex-fighter pilot living in Spandau and working for the Org as an agent under the code-name 'Horst'. Horst was not affiliated to one of the Berlin out-stations but worked for an ex-General Staff Colonel (code number 8035) in the Gehlen agency in Bad Nauheim. Horst informed 8035 that he could hear the whining noise coming from Schönwalde airfield north of Berlin, where Soviet air force units were stationed. He would like to pursue the matter; could the organizer please send him a camera.

The organizer in Bad Nauheim was hesitant – if Russian soldiers or German police caught a man with a camera, particularly near the airfield, that would be the end of his agent. 8035 was all the more unwilling to accept this risk since Gehlen was always admonishing his staff to put 'security before output', in other words it was preferable to forgo information rather than risk one's own people. Horst was insistent, however, and finally won his point after headquarters had instructed all commanding officers to inquire from their agents in the Russian Zone about the wingless and propeller-less flying object.

One Saturday Horst went out to Schönwalde, dived into the birch woods round the airfield and began to look for mushrooms, a favourite pretext used by everyone's agents wishing to approach a barracks or an airfield. The whine he had heard in Spandau suddenly rose to a scream and one aircraft after another flew low over him. Horst photographed the machines with his Leica. When the aircraft had vanished, he heard Russian voices and saw a flat roof carrying a thin aerial rising from a tall thicket about twenty yards away.

Horst photographed the roof and antenna, crept back and returned to West Berlin. Over the telephone he then informed Gehlen's officer in Bad Nauheim of the results of his excursion to Schönwalde. Late that evening 8035 left for Berlin to meet his agent in a Wilmersdorf restaurant; he took the camera and film, leaving Horst a packet of Camels. On Sunday the organizer was back in Bad Nauheim and shortly thereafter a courier left for Munich with the film.

In Munich officers and engineers of the former German Luftwaffe sat down with US Air Force officers and began to analyse the pictures. As soon as the Germans saw the aircraft with their red stars, they were reminded of their own 'Wundervögel' [Miracle birds], the jet-propelled Me262 and He172. The Soviet fighters were of exactly the same type, Gehlen's people thought. An explanation was now also found for the earlier report that the aircraft had no wings: when previously observed the aircraft had clearly been banking at 90 degrees preparatory to landing and this had resulted in an optical illusion. The remaining information was quickly extracted from the photographs. The roof obviously belonged to a ground station and the aerial was identified by the experts as part of a beam transmitter.

The Pentagon reacted somewhat anxiously to the photographs and information from Pullach. The only possible conclusion from Gehlen's material was that the Soviets now possessed a weapon comparable to the first US jet fighter, the F86 Sabre. The Org accordingly received a further assignment: if possible find out constructional details of the Soviet aircraft and the fuel used.

Gehlen first set to work a section of his staff which secret services often underestimate but which frequently provides the decisive clue in conventional espionage affairs – that of the archivists. All the home addresses of prisoners returning from Russia, together with their statements, were registered in the Org's archives. Gehlen ordered a search for men with knowledge of the Soviet aircraft industry. One of the archivists found a report on the aircraft works in Tiflis and the name of an ex-prisoner who had stated in the Friedland reception camp that he had worked a metal press in Tiflis.

Gehlen dispatched a specialist interrogator to the ex-prisoner, who proved to be a peasant in Upper Bavaria. Twenty years later the officer can still remember the interview: 'We sat in the kitchen. I asked the man whether he had worked on metals for aircraft while in Tiflis. He said – I could hardly understand him, he was so broad – that he had worked a light metal press. I asked him: "Did the upper surface of a plate shine or was it dull? Were the edges porous, granulated or smooth and sharp? Did a whitish coating form on the metal if left in the rain?" "Well now," the peasant replied, "I pressed the metal but I didn't take much notice of it. But wait there a minute." He rummaged in a chest and placed a roughly-shaped pot on the table, saying: "There's your metal." While in Russia he had secretly constructed this pot out of the metal concerned, because he did not want to go on spooning his cabbage soup out of an old jam tin; on the lid was engraved a horseshoe surrounded by gentians.' Gehlen's officer bought the pot for 50 marks; Gehlen later had the lid sent back to the ex-prisoner as a souvenir of his time as an aircraft worker in Tiflis. With this pot, however, the metallurgists in

Pullach and their American colleagues could now determine the composition of the metal.[10]

It remained to find out what fuel the Soviet jet fighter used. The Org's experts set about their task with General Staff thoroughness. Some of their agents blocked a stretch of railway line near Chemnitz and held up an approaching train of tank wagons carrying fuel for the Red Army. When the train halted, the Russian escort in the guard's truck clearly thought that this was only a temporary stoppage and neglected to put out sentries. Thereupon a man climbed on to one of the tank wagons, opened the circular cover and lowered an empty beer bottle into the tank. He waited for a second or two, pulled up the bottle, closed the lid, climbed off the wagon and disappeared into the night. A few minutes later the train moved off again. The signalman and engine-driver each received 20 West marks from the Gehlen organization and the agent with his beer bottle 30 marks – all three were working for the Org. The tank wagon did in fact contain what the Pullach chemists wanted – fuel for jet aircraft.

When the US F86s first met the MiG-15s (the aircraft which the Org had investigated) in Korea, it was clear that the Russian electronic equipment was considerably superior. Pullach received a further request: the Americans wished to know what the electronic equipment of the MiG-15 was. Once more Gehlen's people set to work but this time the Org could not help. Electronics remained a mystery to Gehlen's machine.

Against Gehlen's advice the US Secret Service then began to search on its own account for an East German informer who could procure for them the electronic gear of the MiG-15. A promising candidate seemed to the Americans to be a certain Captain Lange-Werner belonging to a Barrack Police unit stationed near Kamenz airbase in Saxony; he undertook to do some spying. The US Secret Service was impatient and charged on regardless.

One day in 1953 a car with US markings appeared before the police barracks near Kamenz and a US secret-service organizer asked at the guard room if Captain Lange-Werner could come to the gate. He arrived. What his comment to his organizer was about this as a form of secret meeting, we do not know. Three months later he was arrested, brought before an East German court, condemned to death for espionage on September 8th, 1953, and later executed.[11] It was left to the Formosan secret service to persuade Kum Sok No, a North Korean air-force pilot, to fly to South Korea with a MiG-15 and land there. On September 21st, 1953, Kum Sok No handed the Soviet jet fighter over to the Americans and received a reward of $100,000.[12]

Gehlen's successes and the Lange-Werner fiasco, however, persuaded the US secret services to leave the Org in sole charge of espionage in the Soviet Zone. Gehlen could now work undisturbed. Beyond the Elbe stood a growing force of military spies, ready, indeed determined, to give the General in Pullach all the information he wanted. Heinz Herre, head of the Evaluation Group, says: 'At that time they would come and ask what we required. We would tell them what we wanted; they would vanish and reappear again a few days later with the goods.'[18] From suitcases and rucksacks the informers fished out Russian service revolvers and military identity cards; they counted the number of stars and bars on the shoulder-boards of senior Russian officers; they produced reels of photographs of airfields and ammunition dumps; they stole pay-books, medals, rubber stamps and official instructions.

One day a Russian general in Jena sounded the alarm: a secret, 'officers only' training film on tank tactics had disappeared from his safe. East German and Russian military police cordoned off Jena railway station and searched pockets, suitcases and parcels of the passengers and passers-by. Two workmen carrying a sack of coal were allowed through the barrier and the guard permitted them to stow their sack in a goods wagon destined for Berlin. At Berlin-Friedrichstrasse Station the two men transferred their sack to the metro and departed in the direction of the Zoo station. At the bottom of the bag was the film – a present for the Gehlen Organization.

One day an old rickety delivery van with a tarpaulin cover skirted the Potsdamer Platz and stopped in West Berlin in front of the first tobacco shop. The driver asked to be allowed to telephone. He dialled a number and said: 'I come from Günter in Oranienburg; I am bringing you an interesting load.' Shortly thereafter one of Gehlen's Berlin agents appeared and took over the 'load' – a Red Army soldier whom 'Günter' had filled up with vodka and then smuggled into West Berlin in his friend's van.

In some cases agents simply sent their hot potatoes through the post, giving a fictitious sender's name and address and consigning them to Schöneberg parcels office. An ex-member of the Org says: 'We did not actually get a rocket that way but sometimes it was as good as a film – a sub-machine-gun arrived in a violin case; a *Täglicher Rundschau* wrapper contained a piece of paper giving names, ranks, equipment and duties in a complete Russian regiment; in a box labelled "Glass – With Care" we received some specimen rocks from the uranium mines in Aue.'

In Berlin intelligence could almost be picked up on the street. On May

28th, 1949, Agent 9415 reported that he had 'once more met a certain E.S. who comes from my home town Riga and is bilingual in Russian. Since about mid-1946 he has been used as interpreter by certain Eastern Zone firms when doing business with the Soviet Military Administration.' E.S. was 'still in contact with certain officers of the Soviet Administration who sometimes asked him to do them a personal favour such as obtaining a light meter, photographic equipment, radio valves, etc, in other words things not easily obtainable in the Eastern Zone . . . Asked what he could do, S vouchsafed that he was also in personal contact with certain German typists who might be prepared to give him carbon copies of their work. S also thinks that he might be able to persuade certain officers to defect to the Western Zone, bringing important information with them.'[14]

In Falkensee Agent 8219 discovered a lady who could speak Russian and was consequently acting as housekeeper to a Russian Major. The agent reported to Pullach: 'I proposed the following plan to her: While she was with the Major (I assume that she is on intimate terms with him) she should try to lay hands as unobtrusively as possible on secret papers, orders, instructions, etc.' The lady had apparently declared 'that she would in fact be in a position to obtain some of the above'.

An army of Gehlen agents watched every military movement – the sentries on the barrack gate in Bad Langensalza, the coloured signs on Red Army vehicles in Gotha, radar installations at the Schottheim air base, the addition of concrete tracks to the Jena–Gotha autobahn. Hundreds of observers noted the registration numbers of Soviet military vehicles, recorded the time and place of their appearance, listed aircraft numerals and jotted down details of uniforms.[15]

The information which daily came flooding into the Org's report centres in West Berlin was mostly small beer. Soon, however, it became so unmanageable in quantity that the Org began to streamline and compartmentalize its Eastern-Zone work. A report centre under ex-General Kleikamp, former Chief of Intelligence to Army Group South, collected all intelligence material and forwarded it to Pullach; the Org's agencies in West Berlin, however, divided the work between themselves. Centre 120a, for instance, dealt with military espionage in Thuringia, an agency known as 'Waldkapelle' [Forest Orchestra] under Moritz, an ex-Criminal Police officer, specialized in the interrogation of refugees, Centre V/2663 carried on counter-espionage, and so forth.[16]

At the same time the Org set up a courier system in the Eastern Zone to relieve agents of the necessity of bringing their material in person to the West Berlin report centres. The whole zone was covered by a network of 'dead-letter boxes', regularly cleared by couriers. Subsequently the Org added a series of radio operators and radio stations in central Germany. One of the first operators in the zone was Karl-Heinz Schmidt, a former submarine coxswain now working as a glazier in Luckenwalde. In mid-1952 he and his wife were trained by Gehlen's radio specialists, were allotted two special radio sets and formed the first radio station known as 'Siren'.

Schmidt was followed by other radio operators, all equipped with the American '12 WG' set which enabled them to listen to the Org's broadcasting service. The majority of the operators admittedly belonged to the reserve network, only to be activated in emergency. The Org did not, however, think that it could afford to allow its reserve operators to remain entirely idle and they were employed as couriers, sometimes even as agents. An example was Franz Pankraz, an ex-naval radio operator, now working as a mechanic in the transmitter-assembly section of the nationalized works in Berlin-Köpenick. The Org had designated him as a reserve operator for emergency but at regular three-weekly intervals he received radio messages from West Berlin ordering him to clear certain 'dead-letter boxes' and deliver their contents through courier channels.[17]

For Gehlen, of course, any restriction of the Org's activity to purely military intelligence was unsatisfactory; it was not enough merely to spy on troops, barracks and airfields. In the event of war, for instance, it would be important to know how quickly the enemy could concentrate and so communications in the Soviet Zone also came into the Org's purview. Most important of these was the traditional means of military movement, the railways.

As early as 1948 a West Berlin organizer, whose code-name was 'Schröder', had discovered an old wartime friend occupying a senior position in the State Railways of the Soviet Zone and apparently at the start of a brilliant career. He was called Herbert Richter, an ex-officer who was at that time in charge of the Railways Directorate in Güstrow, Mecklenburg. Richter was prepared to provide information about the running of the railways and Red Army rail movements in the north of the zone. Every six weeks Schröder went to Richter's office and collected his material. As a result the Org was familiar with the contents of many of the railway administration's files, for Richter rose higher and higher in the railway hierarchy; he became head of the Construction Group in the railways office in Wittenberge and finally Chief of Construction and Production in the main railway depot, Berlin. Schröder, the organizer, followed him like a shadow as Richter rose.[18]

Another Gehlen agent in the East Berlin railway headquarters was waiting to smuggle his material to the West. This was Ewald Misera, manager of the Traffic and Service Department in the General Office. He reported regularly on Soviet movements of troops and equipment, on the demands made on the railways by their Soviet masters and on loading and discharge of goods. He photographed the general activity reports of all the railway regions, railway time-tables and personal notes on the ten senior members of railway headquarters. Anything he did not know the Org obtained from other railway employees such as Walter Flentge, Inspector of Railways in Magdeburg, or Gustav Miecklev, an assembly-line inspector in Rostock.

Observation of the railways led on to that of road traffic and shipping and here too the Org found helpers in influential positions. Karli Bandelow, a construction engineer and senior desk officer in the State Secretariat for Motor Traffic and Roads, provided information on bridges in the Eastern Zone, his office's telephone directory, politico-economic plans and minutes of internal conferences; Käthe Dorn, personal secretary to the managing director of the Motor Traffic and Roads department's planning section, handed over construction plans for bridges and roads; Rolf Östereich, a dispatcher in the maritime electrical department of a nationalized firm, gave the Org a picture of maritime equipment in the Eastern Zone; Gramsch, a section head in the General Directorate of Shipping, reported on military transports, loading schedules and bottlenecks in production.

Gehlen's organization expanded at an increasing rate; one activity after another in the Soviet Zone came under its microscope. Walter Schneider, a desk officer in the Ministry for Reconstruction, gave Gehlen 'a complete picture of the Ministry . . . and of the construction combines in the Republic'; Christoph Kommerek, business manager of the inland water transport office in Altenburg, infiltrated people into Poland; Vitalis Dalchau, dealer and interpreter for the J. V. Stalin electrical works in Berlin-Treptow, provided information on automated cement works, export deliveries and design engineers.[19]

Gehlen's requests for information became more comprehensive as the months went by. A stream of instructions told organizers and agents what to look for. A 'General Assignment for all concerned' was issued, urging every member of the Org to 'establish what war economy measures are being taken in the East German Republic irrespective of whether they come from the occupying power or the East German government, to record distribution of manpower between the various branches of the economy and to report any measures of a police, internal or external political nature, whether taken by the East German government or the occupying power, together with their effects, practical and psychological, upon the population.'[20]

Subsequently orders became more detailed. Organizer 9980 received the following: 'On the occasion of your meeting today with Informer 99801 you are requested to instruct him as follows: An expert assessment is required of the electronic products exhibited at the Leipzig Fair by the Soviet Union and its satellites. Interest is primarily concentrated on long-wave technique. New prospectuses and catalogues on the subject are desired.' The Org's West Berlin branch X/9592 was given 'Intelligence Assignment No 5 Transport' which ran: 'Until 1950 one to two trains per month carrying uranium ore ran from Czechoslovakia via Bad Schandau and Frankfurt am Oder to Brest-Litovsk. In the last three years no reports on these have come to hand. You are requested to inquire of sources in Bad Schandau and Frankfurt am Oder whether anything is known of an alteration to the routing of these trains or whether any other information on the subject can be given.'[21]

Gehlen was continually pushing his outposts further into the innermost circles of the East German regime and eventually he had placed agents in the very centre of enemy power. He wished to know the thinking in that small circle of the initiated who were even then preparing to proclaim the Russian Zone as the 'German Democratic Republic'. They were the men who enjoyed the confidence of Ulbricht, the Secretary of the Socialist Unity Party – German old-guard communists, the Soviet advisers and their German henchmen from the ranks of the bourgeoisie.

One of the regime's influential apparatchiks opened the door for the Org into the secret world of the East German governmental machine. This was Walter Gramsch, formerly a senior employee of the State Railways and a Captain in the reserve, born in 1897. Having played some part in the resistance movement of July 20th, 1944 (he had been considered for the post of transport expert in a Goerdeler government), he had been arrested by the Gestapo; after the war he had become a senior civil servant [Ministerialdirektor] in the *Land* government of Saxony-Anhalt. Gramsch, who was a Social-Democrat, was furious with his communist masters when the Socialist and communist parties were forcibly amalgamated in April 1946. When proceedings of inquiry were opened against him by the communists for alleged membership of a Nazi organization, the breach between him and the Socialist Unity Party became complete.[22]

Nevertheless Gramsch succeeded in clearing himself of all suspicion and even in regaining the goodwill of the Party bosses who admitted him into the Party. By August 1947 he had already become head of the Transport Section in the 'German Administration for Trade and Supply' – it was the start of an astounding career. At the same time, however, one of Gehlen's investigators heard that Gramsch was opposed to the regime and recruited him into the Org. He was even permitted to choose his code-name himself.

'Brutus', as Gramsch became, was the Org's first really influential agent in the future 'Democratic Republic'. He rose higher and higher in the transport bureaucracy of the Soviet Zone. Between 1949 and 1953 he served in turn as head of the Planning Section in the Administration for Trade and Supply, Section Head in the German Shipping and Entrepot Trade Agency, Head of the Chartering Section in the Directorate-General of Shipping and finally Head of the section entitled 'Use of Shipping and Ports' in the East German government's State Secretariat for Shipping.[23] The Org had thus placed an agent in the immediate entourage of Gehlen's most dangerous opponent. This was Ernst Wollweber, the State Secretary, an old secret-service hand and German communism's top sabotage specialist.

Wollweber was the son of a mine-worker and had been both a docker and a deck-hand; he was a communist of long standing and had been trained in the Military Espionage School in Moscow; before 1933 the Party had looked upon him as 'the best saboteur in the world'. When the Nazis seized power he set up an organization in Copenhagen working for the Soviet secret service, the Subversion or Z [Zersetzungs] Apparat. It consisted of 20–25 men, primarily Danish, Norwegian, Swedish and German communists. Its task was to sabotage shipping belonging to the potential enemies of the Soviet Union – Hitler's Germany, Italy and Japan.[24]

Any ship flying the flag of these countries was a target. Wollweber invariably used the same method to put them out of action – his agents placed a dynamite charge in the ship's bilge between the outside of the hull and the hold. The detonating mechanism was set so that the charge would explode when the ship was on the high seas. One ship after another blew up – in 1934 the Italian *Felce* in the Gulf of Taranto, in 1935 the Japanese freighter *Tajima Maru* after sailing from Rotterdam, later the Dutch *Westplein*, the Japanese freighter *Kazi Maru*, the German *Claus Böge*, the Rumanian freighter *Bessarabia* and the Polish steamer *Batory*.

Wollweber's sabotage exploits, however, came to an end before they could bring the Soviet Union any significant advantage. In 1940, when the Germans occupied Denmark, his organization had to move to neutral Sweden. There an attack on the Finnish ship *Figge* miscarried; Wollweber and some of his agents were arrested by the Swedes and sentenced to three years' imprisonment a few months before Hitler's invasion of the Soviet Union.[25]

After the war Wollweber asked the Soviet secret service for an assignment in the Western Zones; he had no wish to do 'office work' in East Berlin. The Russians, however, refused, fearing that Wollweber would quickly be detected in the West and put out of business. Their fears were not unfounded, for as early as 1946 Gehlen's Org had had its eye on Wollweber as a sabotage specialist. He was no stranger to Gehlen – the Org's archives contained the complete record of the proceedings of the 1940 Stockholm court against the shipping saboteur Wollweber, alias Fritz Köller. In the Second World War the area for which Gehlen's 'Foreign Armies East' was responsible included Sweden and he had many informers in the Swedish officer corps.

In 1946 Wollweber took over an innocent-sounding post in East Berlin. He became Deputy Head of the Directorate-General of Shipping. To Gehlen, however, this was a red light. He could not believe that the communist expert on ship sabotage was now going to build them instead of sinking them.[26]

In Gramsch, the head of one of Wollweber's sections, therefore, a man had appeared at just the right moment, who was able to keep his master under observation. As a socialist and former anti-Nazi resister 'Brutus' was soon able to establish himself in Wollweber's good books and his reports confirmed what Gehlen suspected: Wollweber remained faithful to his trade – sabotage. In the maritime school at Wustrow on the Baltic Wollweber had at any one time two hundred men under training as captains, ship's engineers and radio operators; twenty of those completing each course were given some special form of training.

They learnt how to handle explosives; they were told how to form cells for subversive warfare and how to transmit secret information. There followed fundamental political indoctrination at the Karl-Marx College at Klein-Machnow near Berlin. Finally they went to the technical school maintained by the Ministry of Transport (Shipping Division) in the former university area of Ladebow near Greifswald. Here all Wollweber's old procedures were taught – how to 'salt' bunker coal with explosive, how to set a time fuse, etc. Brutus provided full details of Wollweber's curriculum. Students were urged, he said, to mix sand with the lubricating oil for steam or diesel engines, to put compasses and sextants out of action, to set off bunker fires by spraying the coal with paraffin, to saw through rudder chains when at sea and soak cargoes with water.[27]

'The "Wollweber Organization",' Gramsch reported to Pullach, 'is roughly divided into four operational groups – "seaports", "inland ports", "railways and other transport" and "Allied supply lines". Assignments are divided between these various groups which are responsible for preparing acts of sabotage. Issue of the executive order for sabotage is the prerogative of the Soviet Army High Command or the senior luminaries of the Soviet Communist Party.' A headquarters note on Gramsch's information read as follows: 'The "Wollweber Organization" is fully integrated into the Eastern Bloc secret services which are working against the West. Owing to the inevitable overlaps it is often difficult to tell whether one is dealing with an operational group, a base or an agent of the "Wollweber Organization".'[28]

A series of further shipping mishaps soon betrayed the hand of Wollweber. On January 25th, 1953, the liner *Empress of Canada* caught fire in the port of Liverpool; on January 29th flames swept through the world's largest liner, the *Queen Elizabeth,* and on January 30th there was a fire on her sister-ship, the *Queen Mary.* The main cable to the engine-room of the British aircraft-carrier *Warrior* was cut with an axe and a similar case of sabotage occurred on the aircraft-carrier *Triumph.* An explosion tore the hull of the aircraft-carrier *Indomitable.* Acts of sabotage were also reported from the destroyer *Duchess,* the aircraft-carrier *Centaur,* submarines, cruisers, transports and supply ships.[29]

Gehlen's staff were naturally not prepared to say whether Brutus had been able in every case to expose his master Wollweber as the instigator of these acts of sabotage. Nevertheless there were many indications that Brutus' information was setting the Org on the track of Wollweber's agents in North German ports. As early as 1952 Gehlen agents had infiltrated the dockers' organizations in Hamburg and Bremen. They wormed their way into dockyards and fitting-out berths, into pay offices and issue depots. And their target was not solely dynamite; they were also checking ships' cargoes.

For Brutus had alerted Gehlen to the existence of a further organization bearing the mark of Wollweber, the object of which was to circumvent the Western embargo on goods for the Eastern Zone. Wollweber attempted to bribe West German customs officials and frontier police to allow goods into East Germany. He forged export licence documents and diverted via Scandinavia machinery consigned to central Germany.

In the trans-shipment ports of Hamburg, Bremen and Lübeck,

Gehlen's agents investigated all cargoes which seemed to be destined for Wollweber and on many occasions Brutus' information enabled them to sabotage his smuggling trade. Gehlen's people still chuckle over one trick which they managed to play on the East Berlin importers. Wollweber had apparently bought a complete factory plant from some Western country and this became known to the Org in time for action to be taken. Gehlen thereupon decided that half the machinery should be allowed into the Eastern Zone but that the second consignment should be stopped, so that Wollweber was landed with only a portion of the machinery and plant, having paid for all of it.[30]

Wollweber could barely move without being observed by Gramsch. All his habits and goings-on were reported to Pullach. His note in the Org's central card-index read: 'W has few friends; he likes to keep in the background. He trusts very few people and, as a precaution, even has his "friends" watched. His rooms are invariably locked. He regards women merely as temporary distractions. W is often to be seen amusing himself with ladies of easy virtue in the Johanneshof Hotel in the Johannes-strasse; he has frequently been seen dancing.' 'Gustav', his bodyguard, however, was invariably present. Gramsch reported: ' "Gustav" is fifty years of age, of medium height, slim and has a thin angular face and bushy greying hair.'

Gramsch also took note of the women in Wollweber's life. They included the head of the female staff, Maria Weiss, 'deputy Director-General of Shipyards and Shipbuilding in the Soviet Zone, a malicious denouncer and the terror of everybody', a secretary named Klara Vater, née Creutzburg – 'has long been thought to be Wollweber's mistress' – and his private secretary Fräulein Müller – 'often Wollweber's "travelling companion" and as such on terms of intimacy with him'.

Even more important, however, were Gramsch's reports on Wollweber's political views – he was, after all, later to become Minister of State Security and a member of the Politburo. The Pullach archives recorded that Wollweber was 'not entirely uncritical of conditions in the Eastern Zone' – 'during a fact-finding tour in Chemnitz in November 1952 Wollweber said to a restricted company in the Chemnitzer Hof Hotel: "Why do we always abuse the capitalism of the West? Freedom to acquire capital, after all, is the only method of stimulating competition and so raising both the quantity and quality of production." On several occasions, also in a restricted company, W has emphasized that there was "nothing wrong in combining the doctrines of Lenin and Stalin with the empirical values of the West". He has frequently said: "We have much to learn from the West." '[31]

The Org could hardly have had more precise information about one of the most important men in the East German regime. Yet the work of Brutus/Gramsch was only the beginning of a process of infiltration into the very seats of power of the Peoples' Democratic Republic. The Gehlen Organization worked its way deeper and deeper into the inmost political circles of the other half of Germany. It penetrated even into the office of East Germany's first Minister-President, Otto Grotewohl. Once more it was an opponent of the Socialist Unity Party regime who became a source of intelligence for Gehlen. He was Karl Laurenz, a lawyer aged forty-eight.

Laurenz was a Social-Democrat who had been accepted into the Socialist Unity Party on the amalgamation of the Socialist and Communist parties in 1946. He was a staunch anti-communist, however, and three years later was expelled from the Party and placed temporarily under arrest – as an enemy of the People's Republic. In his own way, however, he retained his connexion with the regime – his fiancée, forty-two-year-old Elli Barczatis, worked for the most exalted governmental functionary of the Socialist Unity Party. She was, in fact, senior secretary to Grotewohl, the Minister-President. In 1953 one of Gehlen's Berlin organizers met Laurenz who told him that, as a former Social-Democrat, he regarded Grotewohl, his fiancée's employer, as a traitor to the Socialist Party. Gehlen's man pricked up his ears. He persuaded Laurenz to recruit Elli Barczatis to work for the Org and Laurenz was successful.

Across the secretary's table came government decrees and minutes from ministries; she read letters from the Soviet High Commission and directives from the East German politburo; she wrote letters and speeches for Grotewohl; she arranged agendas for ministerial meetings and typed government decisions; she recorded Grotewohl's conversations with Soviet functionaries and East German ministers.

In the evenings, however, Elli Barczatis returned to her flat in Köpenick, where she met Laurenz who had been working during the day as an interpreter for the East German authorities. She told him what she had taken down in shorthand, recorded, typed or reproduced during the hours she had spent in the office of the head of government. Every other day Laurenz crossed into West Berlin and there met Gehlen's organizer. He handed over copies of Grotewohl's secret papers; what he could not bring in writing he reported verbally. 'The Barczatis,' an old Gehlen hand said, 'were a tender plant which came into full bloom for us in Grotewohl's office.' In fact, 'The Daisies' (the Barczatis' code-name) were among what the Org called the 'highest-quality sources' ever tapped by Gehlen in East Germany.[32]

For intelligence value Walter Gramsch and Elli Barczatis could hardly have been bettered. They were actually in the offices of the men who took the decisions and exercised the power. But Gehlen had even greater ambitions. He wanted to lure the actual wielders of power themselves into his net and in the case of Kastner, the corpulent jovial Vice-President of the Peoples' Republic, he succeeded.

Hermann Moritz Wilhelm Kastner, born in 1886, had been a land-owner in Saxony and professor of constitutional and administrative law; he had acted as defence counsel to anti-Nazis under the Third Reich and had himself been arrested by the Gestapo. After the war he had been one of the founders of the Liberal-Democrat Party and then its Chair-man. He had entered the orbit of the Western secret services in 1948. Kastner had just moved from the office of Minister of Justice in Saxony to a post in the German Economics Commission of the Eastern Zone when he received an appeal from an old friend, Bishop Wiencken of Meissen. The Bishop had formerly provided refuge for those persecuted by the Nazi regime and he was now enraged by the political blackmail exercised by the Socialist Unity Party. He urged Kastner 'not to close his eyes to the fresh injustices here in the East'. He went on: 'Under Hitler you helped many people; now you must do something once more. Above all the West must know what is going on in the Eastern Zone.'

The Bishop also knew how to inform the West. He had met a certain Dr Carol Tarnay working for the American secret service and in the Franciscan hospital on the Burggrafenstrasse, West Berlin, the Bishop introduced his friend Kastner to this agent. Kastner promised Tarnay to tell him everything 'that the American government ought to know'.[33]

Kastner kept his promise. He reported on all the conclaves in which, as time went on, he acquired a seat and a voice – the Central Committee of the Liberal-Democrat Party, the so-called Economic Commission, the Presidency of the People's Congress, the National Council of the National Front, and finally the Cabinet of the East German Republic. He described his conversations with Soviet politicians, diplomats and gen-erals and passed on their views. The US secret service, for instance, knew that, after two bottles of vodka, Max Fechner, the Minister of Justice, had stripped off all his clothes and rolled himself up in a carpet and that each time she pronounced a death sentence Hilde Benjamin, the Vice-President of the Supreme Court, lit her candles, read the Talmud and listened to the music of Bach. Kastner knew all about Ul-bricht's position, also that at home Grotewohl was henpecked by his wife Johanna.[34]

With the utmost calm Kastner passed on all he knew about the luminaries of the German Democratic Republic. He listened politely when Luitpold Steidle, a committee member of the East German Christian-Democrats, an ex-Colonel of Adolf Hitler's Wehrmacht and now Minister of Health, expatiated at a cabinet meeting in the summer of 1950 on the sinister role which could be played by espionage. He had vivid memories, Steidle said, of the German Abwehr's preparations in the summer of 1939 for the invasion of Poland. He himself had seen how, years before, German agents had taken measurements of every bridge, every road and every railway line in Poland. When war broke out, even the most junior NCO could find his way by means of maps accurate to within inches.

Ulbricht leant forward and interrupted the Minister: 'You see,' he said, 'that is the way the imperialists prepare for war – against us too, against us too. We must be very much on our guard against spies.' The Ministers nodded and agreed with the First Secretary. Kastner, the Deputy Prime Minister, waxed indignant over the machinations of Western spies. 'They are terrible, these prying eyes,' he said, looking angrily round the room.[35]

After such meetings 'Helwig' (Kastner's code-name) would generally send a report to West Berlin. His home was his channel of communication to the West; he dictated his reports to Gertrude, his second wife; she then typed them and hid them between the books in his library. Each Thursday evening Kastner would bring back the minutes of the cabinet meeting which had taken place that day. Each Friday Frau Kastner would conceal the reports in her suspender-belt and brassière, climb into her husband's official car and tell the driver to go to West Berlin. The Peoples' Police on the sector boundary would salute when Frau Kastner showed her special pass authorizing her to visit West Berlin. In the nunnery of the Franciscan Hospital, however, Tarnay, the agent, was already waiting and to him she handed the papers.

One day in the early 1950s, however, Tarnay told her that he had found an organization which would be even more grateful for Kastner's information than the US secret service – the Gehlen Organization. After discussion with the Americans, Tarnay had changed his allegiance.

Having thus gained touch with a senior East German politician, Gehlen was tempted to play high politics with Kastner. He was a believer in the theory that there existed in the Kremlin a group whose liaison officer in East Berlin was the leading Soviet diplomat Vladimir Semyonov and which wished to install Kastner as head of the East German government. Such a possibility obviously had to be exploited in the hope of liberalizing East Germany and then freeing it completely from the clutches of the Eastern Bloc; this might be done with the assistance of his informant Kastner. In fact Kastner did enjoy the confidence of the Russians; Semyonov, the Political Adviser to the Soviet Military Administration, regarded him as a friend and Army General Chuikov, the Russian C-in-C in Germany, frequently asked his advice. The Russians looked upon Kastner as a possible partner in the event of a German settlement, in other words should Moscow be prepared to forgo integration of East Germany into the Eastern Bloc and permit the formation of a re-united, non-communist but neutralized Germany.[36]

In the Kremlin, however, there were divided views on policy towards Germany; on one side were the supporters of sovietization, on the other the protagonists of the neutralization plan. The latter were prepared to accept German–Soviet collaboration on traditional lines and a re-united bourgeois Germany provided it was divorced from the West. Kastner's view was that 'attempts to bolshevize Germany would fail; communism was not suitable as an article of export from Russia to Germany'. This he said in 1950 in an interview with the Swedish newspaper *Aftonbladet*; he also said it to the Russians, frequently and emphatically. Knowing that he had Russian support, Kastner campaigned more and more recklessly against Ulbricht and the Socialist Unity Party. He became highly unpopular with his colleagues for his tiresome speeches. Finally he lost his seat in the cabinet; he had already been expelled from the Liberal-Democrat party for hindering cooperation with the Socialist Unity Party.

Kastner was not to be intimidated, however; he made public gibes about the 'Socialist Unity Party revolutionaries who were in fact nothing but simpletons'. Kastner felt sure of himself since his Soviet friends did not desert him. A political discussion between Kastner and Semyonov frequently began with the Russian and the German quoting passages from Goethe's *Faust* at each other. The two enjoyed joking about Ulbricht's spurious culture or the domestic habits of Wilhelm Pieck, the East German President. Semyonov had a story according to which Pieck would return in the evenings from his official residence in the Schloss Niederschönhausen to a lodging in the servants' quarters near the Schloss; there he would put on carpet slippers and a workman's apron and take his evening meal at the kitchen table. Kastner chuckled: 'And all off the same plate with a spoon,' to which Semyonov added 'The pudding all mixed up with red cabbage and noodle soup — horrible!'[37]

The Russians continued to support Kastner. Under Soviet pressure the Liberal-Democrat party was forced to readmit him and the government to appoint him head of the 'Committee for Promotion of the Interests of the Intelligentsia' in the East German Republic. Then, with the death of Stalin, came Kastner's unique opportunity. This was the moment for which Gehlen had waited so long – Kastner's Russian friends wished to give the ex-Chairman of the Liberal-Democrats (and Gehlen's agent) a high political post.

This was on June 13th, 1953. From all over East Germany reports came in that the population was becoming increasingly vocal in its antipathy to the government's regulations laying down new working norms. The same day Semyonov, who had meanwhile been promoted High Commissioner, alerted his government in Moscow, reporting that public opinion was turning increasingly against the government led by Grotewohl, the Minister-President, and Ulbricht, Secretary of the Socialist Unity Party. Semyonov recommended that the Socialist Unity Party's monopoly be temporarily abolished and a new government with bourgeois leanings installed.

Gehelen's organization learnt of Semyonov's secret report from one of its own sources – an interpreter in the Soviet High Commission was working for Pullach. Even more important to Gehlen was the news that, on this same June 13th, Semyonov had invited Kastner to head the government. For three hours Semyonov tried to persuade his German friend to accept the offer, but Kastner hesitated and before he had made up his mind, events overtook him. The rising of June 17th, 1953 wrecked Semyonov's plan; it forced Moscow first to protect and then to support the Ulbricht regime. The chance of a bourgeois middle-of-the-road solution in East Berlin never returned.[38]

All this did not prevent Kastner and his wife from continuing to work for Gehlen, however. As one of Gehlen's staff put it, Helwig and his wife 'bred like rabbits'. For years Gehlen and his Russian experts were kept informed by Kastner about the main lines of Soviet policy towards Germany. Nobody in Pullach doubted the authenticity of Kastner's information; as time went on, however, Gehlen's experts began to wonder whether, in the conclusions Kastner drew, he was not dancing to someone else's tune. To the more sceptical of Gehlen's staff senior Soviet officers seemed to be showing over-conspicuous goodwill towards Kastner after he had been outlawed by the East Berlin leaders. Some of those in Pullach thought they knew why – that the Kremlin knew perfectly well that Kastner was a channel of information to the West and that the Soviet diplomats were merely using him to pass across doctored information on Moscow's policy towards Germany.[39]

Whatever reservations the Pullach headquarters may have had, however, Hermann Kastner continued to provide the Org with information. As a friend of Semyonov Kastner may have been in a different category from Gehlen's other agents in East Germany, but in one respect they were all alike – Kastner, Gramsch and Elli Barczatis did not regard themselves as agents; they considered themselves as patriots keeping the West informed about conditions in the East. They were not, therefore, spying; they were giving information. Moreover the Gehlen Organization did not present itself as a secret service; it appeared instead as a West German agency occupied in unmasking before world public opinion the machinations of the illegal East German state and in protecting the West against bolshevism.

If money was paid or accepted, this was done as reimbursement of expenses. Gehlen sent his star agents Christmas parcels containing caviar, champagne and salmon, though admittedly one of the recipients lamented: 'We would have preferred butter; caviar we can get from the Russians.' On the lower levels, however, among the secret-service foot-soldiery, neither caviar nor champagne were to be seen. There payment was made in much smaller coinage. As with all secret services, bribery and blackmail were often the order of the day in the Org.

Distressingly, use of these methods became more frequent as recruitment of agents became more difficult. The post-June 17th terror, the counter-strokes of the communist security services and above all the increasing lassitude of the people in East Germany complicated the work of the Org – and the greater the requirement for agents beyond the Elbe, the more questionable did the Org's recruitment methods become. A beer in a West Berlin bar or a visit to a Western cinema were often enough to lead some innocent into the jungle of the Org and its secret web. Gehlen's recruiting officers pursued East German visitors to West Berlin as ferociously as head-hunters.

Werner Moch, for instance, born in 1934, merely wanted a glass of beer; the fact that he got a great deal more than that was due to a stranger who accosted him. Moch tells the story: 'He was called Erwin Martin. After one or two glasses he asked me: "Would you be willing to take letters across to the East?" I replied: "Yes." Then Erwin took me to the Cafe Rieger in the Naunynstrasse; there we met Herbert Steinborn and Hans Schröter. I realized that Erwin had the job of finding people who could be recruited into Steinborn's business ... Steinborn said to me that I would get ten marks each time I took letters across to the East. As the business was very brisk, Steinborn gave me a telephone number through which I could reach him. He asked me to collect information about Soviet troops in Germany, for instance by looking for pieces of paper with Russian writing in waste-paper baskets, noting vehicle numbers and photographing jet aircraft. I was also to recruit people.'[40]

Anyone unwilling to sign up with the Org at once, however, found that recruiting methods could be somewhat crude. Gehlen's agents, for instance, used blackmail to compel one East German citizen, 'E.H.', born in 1925 and headmaster of a school, to do some spying. In the mid-1950s 'E.H.' told his story: 'Four years ago one of my colleagues told me that he was going over to the West. Before leaving he said that he would like to introduce me to two of his friends. We drove into West Berlin for this meeting, to a café known as the Zigeunerkeller. At this first meeting my colleague's friends were very genial. No one talked politics . . . They paid the bill but asked me to sign it. When I showed surprise, they said that they would draw the money from an agency concerned with military fugitives from the German Democratic Republic; it was a welfare centre for visitors from the Eastern Zone. I accordingly signed.'

A few weeks later the headmaster's colleague left East Germany. The story continues: 'When he departed, he had had to leave behind certain valuables and papers to which he was very attached. He wrote to me and asked me to bring them to him in West Berlin. I drove over there and met the two men once more. This time they laid their cards on the table and demanded that I join a secret service of which – as I then learnt – my colleague was already a member. I asked for time to think it over. I returned to East Germany and, when I did not reply, received two postcards and one letter containing veiled threats. I decided to meet them once more. On this occasion they said to me: "Either you accept or you will be denounced to the people in the East." I accepted.'[41]

Ex-Captain Kurt Heinz Wallesch, who lived in Leipzig, had a similar experience. During the war he had commanded a battery of 84 Artillery Regiment. When he refused to work for the Org, the agent concerned threatened to tell certain East German agencies that Wallesch had been concerned in mass shootings in the Leningrad area.

At first the Org had little difficulty in recruiting East Germans in West Berlin. Immediately on the sector boundary so-called 'boundary cinemas' showed Western films for East Berliners at reduced prices. There is no proof of the statement that film theatres such as 'Fox' and 'W.B.T.' were semi-financed by the Org. The fact remains, however, that they were useful for contacting agents. Werner Moch describes the procedure: 'I spoke to visitors to these cinemas and asked them whether they would like to earn some money on the side. If they agreed, I took them to Steinborn, usually in the Cafe Rieger in Berlin Kreutzberg. I recruited over thirty-five people in this way. For this I received initially 5 to 10 marks and later 50 marks per week.'[42]

After the popular rising of June 17th, 1953 'Care' parcels were distributed in West Berlin to anyone from East Germany – an ideal opportunity for Gehlen's recruiters to accost potential agents. They were also active among refugees from the Soviet Zone who registered in the West Berlin or West German camps.

In the camp at Berlin-Marienfelde the following happened to Werner Hunter (not his real name): 'A man spoke to me in the camp canteen, offered me a glass of beer and invited me to go on a pub-crawl in West Berlin. We met three evenings running. He always paid since I had no Western money. One evening he said to me: "I know how you could come by some money." Then he explained his plan: "There is an agency in West Germany which is very interested in the East German Barrack Police. You are a mechanic. Look now, go back to the zone and volunteer for the Barrack Police and in particular for a tank unit. When you're there, report to me everything you see and hear. Do that for two years and then we'll get you out and pay you 20,000 Westmarks. We'll also ensure that you get a good job in the West." I did not want to; I had come across because the people over there had been pressurizing me to join the Barrack Police. Then my new friend said: "One day there'll be a Wehrmacht over here again and then you must join it. It's all the same whether you do your rifle drill over there or here. But if you do it over there, you'll get paid by us".' 'Hunter' agreed to join the Gehlen Organization. For two years he spied on the Barrack Police. Then once more he fled to West Berlin – but he never got his promised 20,000 marks.[43]

Whether as volunteers or conscripts, one man after another joined the West German army of agents. Gehlen's web spread itself ever more closely over the East German Republic. On December 23rd, 1953 *Neues Deutschland*, the Socialist Unity Party's official newspaper, lamented: 'The Gehlen Organization has hitherto scored certain successes in the recruitment of agents in the German Democratic Republic.' It was a crass understatement. Almost every sphere of life in East Germany was an open book to the Org.[44]

6

THE ORG: ITS MEN, ORGANIZATION
AND METHODS

THE Org's agents were watching and listening; Gehlen's web spanning the East became closer and closer knit. As his spies probed wider and deeper into East Germany, however, both the Pullach headquarters and its espionage army underwent a change. The leaders of Gehlen's Org began to inject system into the espionage business, hitherto carried on partly as an adventure. Until the early 1950s the Org had largely existed on improvisation; now bureaucratic methodology was the order of the day.

With the appearance of the West German 'economic miracle' the Org's management was inspired to reconstruct their machine on the lines of that force which had long since displaced the military in the front rank of society – industry. The Org took on the form of a large-scale business enterprise. Economic considerations competed with the military standards which had previously been the sole yardstick for Gehlen's organization. Nicolai, the head of the imperial secret service, had once said that 'the secret service is a gentleman's trade'; the saying now became: 'The secret service is good business.'[1]

Gehlen turned the Pullach headquarters into a 'Directorate-General' [Generaldirektion] and he himself assumed the title of 'Director-General' [Generaldirektor.] The main outside offices and representatives were constituted like those of a major business undertaking. There were 'General Agencies' [Generalvertretungen], 'District Agencies' (Bezirksvertretungen], 'Sub-Agencies' [Untervertretungen] and 'Local Branches' [Filialen]. Within this organization, however, the administrative picture was still that of a military secret service.

Gehlen divided his headquarters into a large number of Departments [Hauptabteilungen], Sections [Abteilungen], Groups [Gruppen] and Desks [Referate] which were continually being changed and reorganized. Certain of the departments and sections did, in fact, remain constant. Among them was the Administrative Section which dealt with questions of personnel and finance and was responsible for: the central card-index, the central registry, training, technology, logistics and eco-omics. Department I dealt with the collection and evaluation of foreign intelligence, Department II with precautionary measures in the field of psychological warfare and Department III with the 'assembly and evaluation of intelligence at home and defence against secret-service assaults on West Germany'. Department I was subdivided into sections for army, air force, navy, economic intelligence and political intelli-gence, all further sub-divided into country Groups.[2]

At the head of the Departments and more important Sections Gehlen placed only his closest associates, mostly ex-General Staff officers and experienced Abwehr men. Colonel (retd) Dinser, a war-disabled officer and Gehlen's cousin, was responsible for evaluation; ex-Lieutenant-Colonel Horst Wendland, formerly head of the Army General Staff Or-ganization Section, continued as the Org's Chief of Organization; Lieutenant-Colonel Oscar Reile, formerly in charge of counter-espionage in the Abwehr Office in France, headed Department III. Finally Gehlen's old assistants from the FHO days, Lieutenant-Colonels Wessel and Herre, took turns in running the intelligence-gathering machine.[3]

Separate lines of communication ran from the headquarters Depart-ments to the next most senior organizations, the General Agencies [Generalvertretungen – GV]. 'Line 1', for instance, connected Depart-ment I in Pullach with the General Agencies responsible for foreign intelligence – Munich for Austria and Czechoslovakia, Darmstadt for Poland and the USSR, Bremen for East Germany. 'Line 2' connected Department III with the General Agencies in Karlsruhe (for counter-espionage in the East) and Stocking.[4]

The General Agencies were the operational headquarters for espion-age in the East. They were therefore largely independent; for instance they had their own budget, though they were dependent on the main headquarters for personnel. It was the duty of General Agencies to open up new channels of information, to direct and control the subordinate agencies, to sift information coming from the Local Branches [Filialen] and forward it to the relevant sections in Pullach. They had full-time staffs, divided into specialist desks for military, economic, political and technical matters. The General Agency in Karlsruhe, for example, had a staff of sixteen distributed among three Sections – Personnel and Train-ing, Economic, Espionage and Counter-espionage. Many successful Pul-lach careers started in the General Agencies – for example Reile, Felfe the double agent, and the present head of the BND Private Office were all originally in Karlsruhe.

At the head of the General Agencies Gehlen placed his most experienced men. His friend Alfred Benzinger, an ex-Sergeant-Major of the Field Security Police, headed the General Agency in Karlsruhe; General Kretschmer, ex-Military Attaché in Tokyo, ran that in Darmstadt; in Munich Colonel Joachim Rohleder, the Abwehr's counter-espionage expert, was in charge and in Bremen Lieutenant-Colonel Hermann Giskes, the Wehrmacht's Radio Security expert. The latter was succeeded by ex-Colonel Hans-Heinrich Worgitzky, formerly Chief of Intelligence to Army Group Centre and subsequently Vice-President of the BND.[5]

Next below the General Agencies came District Agencies [Bezirksvertretungen – BV], to be found in almost all major cities in Germany, often more than one in the same place. The BV were responsible for giving general assistance to the GV; their staffs were small. They trained newly-recruited agents, gave them their orders and controlled them. The BV acted as a screen between the GV and subordinate offices and were responsible for correspondence with the out-stations. Operationally they checked potential agents for reliability and supervised recruitment of new staff by the lower level, the Sub-Agencies [Untervertretungen – UV].

The UV were the true front-line headquarters of active espionage. They were located in medium-sized towns and were responsible for recruitment, training and direction of agents and informers. They collected the resulting reports and forwarded them to the BV. The BV and UV were the preserve of the ex-Colonels and Lieutenant-Colonels. Head of the BV in Frankfurt, for instance, was ex-Colonel Cox (not his real name), late of the Abwehr, who had good contacts in Spain; Lieutenant-Colonel Westphal, late of the Luftwaffe, ran Sub-Agency X in West Berlin. The ex-soldiers, however, sometimes had to share these posts with ex-SS officers; UV 1600, for instance, was under ex-Hauptsturmführer [SS Captain] Caspar and BV North under ex-Obersturmführer [SS Lieutenant] Hans Sommer.[6]

The lowest rungs of the ladder were the Local Branches [Filialen] or out-stations, set up along the zone boundary and in West Berlin. They were the advanced report centres for agents and informers. From them the organizers directed their men in East Germany, usually three to five per organizer. Gehlen left the running of the Local Branches to ex-officers who had learnt the espionage trade only while in the Org. They were mostly Majors; Werner Haase, for instance, an ex-regimental commander, was in charge of Local Branch 120a and Gärtner, late of the Luftwaffe, of Local Branch X/8970.[7]

All the Org's agencies masqueraded as business firms. The Munich GV, for instance, concealed itself behind the title 'South German Industrial Sales Ltd' with an office at No 50 Emil-Geis-Strasse. 'Industrial Sales Ltd' in fact did no business at all. GV North was lodged in a Bremen villa under the title 'Used Oil Sales Ltd'. UV 17 at Nos 1–2 Am Langenzug, Hamburg, called itself 'Agro', a trading firm. GV 'L' at 36 Gerwingstrasse, Karlsruhe, presented itself as 'Zimmerle', manufacturing venetian blinds. In some cases friends and acquaintances from the business world allowed the secret service to use their names and firms as cover. The UV at No 33 Robert-Blum-Strasse, Mannheim, for instance, appeared as agent for a champagne firm. The only one of all these whose title came near the truth was the 'Swabian Industrial Agency' located at 68 Werastrasse, Stuttgart. Here Gehlen's 'Technical Service' designed and manufactured all that varied equipment without which the Org could not operate – radio sets, invisible inks, special paper, containers for films and reports. The establishment manufactured flat-irons in which films could be carried, electric light plugs with built-in microphones, cigarettes which could contain rolled-up-reports and thermos flasks with built-in cameras.

The Local Branches were mostly camouflaged as insurance agencies, tax advisory firms, translation bureaux or literary agents. An employment agency was another favourite form of cover; General Kleikamp, the Pullach headquarters' personal representative in West Berlin, had his office in the 'Berlin Employment Agency' in the Buggestrasse, Dahlem. Many of these concerns did in fact arrange insurances, advise taxpayers and sell books. Meanwhile, however, the intelligence business flourished in a back room.[8]

West Germany and West Berlin were soon covered by a network of Gehlen agencies. The whole lay-out was so complicated that no outsider could form a picture of all the Org's ramifications. Gehlen was continually emphasizing that the secret service must screen itself from the main body of its own staff and that members of the Org should only know as much as was necessary and as little as possible.

The only contact between the inner circle and agents or informers was through the 'safe houses', one- or two-room apartments in which the organizers met their men. There new recruits were trained in the rudiments of espionage; there the organizer would receive their reports or give them their assignments – if he did not do so in some bar or on a park bench. The organizer in his turn knew only his Local Branch and his Senior Organizer and the latter only the UV above him. Only the head of the UV knew where the BV was located and only the head of the

BV knew the way to the GV. Only heads of GVs were allowed into the Pullach headquarters – and that only if they enjoyed Gehlen's personal confidence or had been ordered to report. Entry into Pullach was forbidden to all other members of the Org, whatever their rank.

Gehlen made no attempt to specialize his subordinate agencies by subject or area of the territory which was his target, East Germany. All the main lines of clandestine communication ran to West Berlin and so, independently of each other, all the General Agencies and most of the District Agencies set up Sub-Agencies or Local Branches there. Their staff members were kept in ignorance of the fact that other branches of the Org were working in the city in parallel with them. As far as the agents in the Zone were concerned, only a few desk officers in headquarters knew where all their lines of communication led. Two or more agents could therefore be spying in some nationalized concern without knowing each other; one of them was probably reporting to a Local Branch in West Berlin and the other to one in Wolfenbütel. The Local Branches too avoided any specialization in their work since that would have made them easily detectable to the enemy. One Local Branch, for instance, had informers in heavy industry in Saxony, an agent in Thuringia, a West German businessman who brought back economic and military information from his trips to East Germany, the head of a section in the East Berlin Foreign Ministry and a mining engineer who reported figures of steel production.[9]

The Org's security precautions were continued right down the line. Agents had to use 'dead-letter boxes' to ensure that they (or the enemy counter-espionage agents) never came face to face with their organizer or their immediate superior. The spy would place a container with his information in the 'dead-letter box', which would then be cleared by a courier – also unknown to the agent – and the material taken across the frontier. The courier would leave in the 'dead-letter box' a fee plus further instructions. Other East German informers were told to travel to West Berlin and there post their material to a cover address either in one of the Western sectors or in West Germany. The main principle was that the agent should never know the man giving him his instructions.

Such a regular system of precautions, however, was not enough for the super-cautious Gehlen; to mislead the inquisitive, he kept part of his organization continuously on the move. He would open Sub-Agencies, leave them in operation for a month, then close them again and post their staff to other out-stations. Over the heads of his General Agencies he would open Local Branches whose existence or purpose were known to Gehlen alone.

Gehlen himself was always on the road, inspecting and supervising his shadowy army. Agents who seemed to him particularly smart would suddenly receive an order to travel from East Germany to Frankfurt am Main and present themselves at some definite time at a certain table in the café Kranzler. Thence a man would take them to an apartment where they were awaited by a gentleman whose most striking characteristic was the size of his ears. The man seemed extremely well informed and would keep his visitor talking for hours. Seldom did the visitor realize that he had been talking to Gehlen. Another example: a certain cover firm dealt in radios in its salesroom and in intelligence in its back rooms; one day a customer wearing dark glasses tied the salesmen in knots with detailed questions about the construction of radio valves – it was Gehlen, the amateur technician.

In an engine factory in Chemnitz two of Gehlen's agents who did not know each other took copies of the design plans of a piston and dispatched them, each to his own Local Branch. Headquarters in Munich, however, received a third copy. Via another of the Org's agencies Gehlen had placed a third informer in the factory; he sent his material to a Munich cover address which Gehlen had arranged without the knowledge of anyone else in the Org.[10]

Such interference by Gehlen often infuriated the heads of the General Agencies. Jealous of their independence, they behaved as if they were barons in their own right and only unwillingly acknowledged the authority of their emperor. Visitors from Pullach were often kept waiting in some anteroom for hours before the head of an out-station was ready to receive the gentleman from headquarters. The head of a General Agency frequently regarded himself like an Army Commander at the front and looked upon the men of Pullach as chairborne warriors, like the officers of the wartime OKW, who had seldom ventured out of their headquarters to visit the front.

The moguls of the General Agencies were blood brothers with the American Military Police. In particular they were dependent on the goodwill of the MPs if they spent all the money allotted them for operations by Pullach. In this event, in order to pay their own staff, they would convert whole lorry-loads of American cigarettes, delivered by the US Army as rewards for intelligence services, into dollars on the black market. As soon as the transaction with the black marketeers was complete and the Germans had disappeared with their dollars, the US Military Police would appear, confiscate the cigarettes and return them to Gehlen's people, who would then repeat the process – after again regularizing the matter with the police.

These aspirations to independence on the part of their subordinates caused the Pullach headquarters to assert their position of authority in the intelligence battle. A stream of directives was issued on cover, controls and counter-controls. An instruction of June 27th, 1953 laid down that the agents and informers were the 'pillars of intelligence' but that these foot-soldiers were by no means all on the same level. 'The agent is a dealer in intelligence, with whom the organizer should have a correct business relationship but no personal ties. The agent should always be encountered with suspicion.'[11]

The informer, on the other hand, deserved to be treated with confidence: 'The informer is a man of confidence with whom the organizer has personal contact outside his official duties.' There was a whole series of differing categories of informer or 'source'. They included: 'infiltration' sources – informers who had worked their way into important posts in the civil service, industry, the Party or the sciences in order to spy on the enemy's administrative machinery; 'verification' sources – informers located near important targets and able to report continuously on what they saw there; 'travelling' sources – informers who had occasion to collect information while on official journeys; 'transit' sources – informers who kept watch on regularly used stretches of railway line or autobahn and noted troop movements, repairs or the construction of new lines or bridges; 'counter-espionage' sources – informers working inside the enemy's espionage organization, who could report the enemy's intentions, the extent of his knowledge of the Org and could mislead him by feeding him false information ('play-back' material); 'casual' sources – for instance informers in Western anticommunist organizations who reported to the Org such information as came to them from East Germany and statements by refugees; and finally 'high-level' sources – informers in very senior positions who were able to produce documentary material from the safes of closely-guarded headquarters.[12]

As time went on the Org became more cautious in its choice of informers. In the early years personal acquaintanceship had been thought sufficient to guarantee that a man was trustworthy; later, however, a systematic screening process was applied to every potential recruit. The first indication of a possible informer who might be suitable to work for the Org usually came from a man already working for Gehlen – the 'tipster'. He had to set out in detail how he had made the candidate's acquaintance, whether he was related to him and, most important, whether the candidate had previously worked for another secret service.[13]

An example of such a report: 'Ref: G. Vladimir. Source: Leo. Aged about 43. Is a Russian, born in Estonia. During the war served as an NCO in a German unit fighting the bolsheviks and was wounded in the eye ... G. is very avaricious for money and therefore not very discriminating in his choice of occupation.' And another: 'Being employed as a commercial traveller, Sch. could be used both in Vienna and East Germany as investigator and contacter; this depends on his potentialities which must first be discovered.' Yet another 'tip'; 'After discussion with P.L., referred to above, he stated that he was in a position to maintain communications with the localities listed below, alternatively, through couriers to be designated by us, to contact informers already located there. Following localities might be considered: 1. Rostock: Source: ex-Sergeant-Major of the German Wehrmacht, aged 40, average education, working in a shipyard. 2. Görlitz-Frankfurt am Oder: Merchant, formerly of German, now of Polish, nationality; travelling representative; free to visit localities mentioned above; had already been recruited for work by L.'[14]

Any 'tip' had to be forwarded to headquarters in Pullach. They alone decided whether the clue should be followed up. If they decided in favour, one of the General Agencies was commissioned to assign an 'investigator' to the case. The investigator inquired into the man's personality, way of life, environment, knowledge and characteristics. He had to proceed in accordance with directives issued by headquarters. They stipulated: 'The investigator must endeavour to judge the candidate as far as possible in the light of the following points: in judging character any negative qualities which may be apparent should by no means be forgotten. If a candidate does not show a sense of realism, he is in no way qualified for secret-service work. The informer must be able to give a faithful photographic description of what he has seen in enemy territory. A conspiratorial turn of mind is essential for secret-service work; if this is not present, secret-service employment is unthinkable.'[15]

The investigator had to set out his findings on the candidate in writing and forward them to headquarters. On July 27th, 1954, for instance, an investigator reported: 'The above-mentioned M. was born in Aussig on May 12th, 1913; he was a regular officer in the German Wehrmacht. Until December 31st, 1953 he was in Soviet captivity at Stalingrad, Voroshilovgrad, Kharkov and Dniepropetrovsk. He is a qualified economist by profession. In addition to German, which is his mother tongue, he allegedly speaks good Russian and English. Would like to do secret-service work.' Another report read: 'Sch. is an Austrian but an ardent German nationalist. He left the church and married but has lived apart from his wife since 1939 and was officially divorced in 1952. Has good commercial training. Possesses a typewriter.' One investigator waxed enthusiastic: 'Personally I regard Dr P. as a completely impeccable and excellent character suitable for secret-service work. Should he be approached, reference may be made to me.'[16]

Once the reports had reached Pullach, neither the 'tipster' nor the investigator were told whether their labours had brought a new spy into the Org. Once again the decision was solely that of headquarters; if they took a favourable view of the candidate, some out-station was ordered to engage the man.

For this purpose the out-station employed yet another class of person – the 'convenor' or 'contacter'. For candidates living in East Germany, the contacter had to find some pretext which would bring them to West Berlin. When a candidate arrived the 'recruiter' went into action and it was on his empathy and eloquence that the success of the recruitment largely depended. Inevitably the moment arrived when the recruiter had to put the question whether the candidate was prepared to do intelligence work; the answer showed whether the investigator had done his work well. If the meeting was taking place in East Germany rather than in West Berlin the candidate's reaction might literally be a matter of life and death for the recruiter. An unwilling candidate might always betray the recruiter to the police. Certain of Gehlen's agencies found this too risky and arranged for the 'approach' to be made in bed. They engaged East German girls who would 'contact' important candidates.

West German candidates were approached in a similar fashion. One report says: 'As ordered, contact with L. was pursued. At the first meeting on October 15th, 1953 in Vienna it emerged that his speciality is Rumania.' The establishment of contact was often difficult – 'Since Herr A.A. is an extremely cautious person, we agreed to make the approach as follows: The gentleman in question brought him greetings from "Gustav" and handed him half a playing card. If this fitted the other half of the card already in his possession, there was no obstacle to frank discussion.'[17]

In many cases there were unfortunate scenes if the person approached did not react as the Org's men wished. One recruiter became indignant: 'The way in which a female applicant is checked and passed on from one person to another is not right. It gives rise to the suspicion that we are trafficking in girls – as happened in this case.' One informer who had already been recruited complained: 'In accordance with my verbal agreement with the gentlemen in Munich I was to ... undertake investigation work entirely independently and on my own. Please do not therefore worry me with stupid trial assignments. The fact that I have been in practice for sixteen years should vouch for me.'[18]

Recruits resident in the East were naturally of particular importance to the Org. Once they had agreed to go into the intelligence business, they and their recruiter agreed on some innocent remark which, when written on a postcard, would summon them to West Berlin to receive their first assignments.

The recruiter had to send a report to the Pullach headquarters detailing his conversation with the candidate. A Gehlen directive of October 10th, 1952 stipulated that it must provide answers to the following questions: 'Where, when and under what circumstances did I make the acquaintance of the person with operational potentialities? What concrete possibilities of acquiring intelligence does the person possess, alternatively what possibilities might he or she open up? (Precise details are to be given here of place, target, activity, place of work, position, number of people, name of superior, where keys are kept, etc.) A character sketch of the person should be given to show suitability for intelligence work. Are there prospects of opening a report channel? What demands does the person concerned make?'

The new recruit would eventually receive a postcard telling him that all was well with his relatives in West Germany or that his sister Friedel was about to have a baby or that the family would like at last to have a reunion celebration. The key was the closing words which might be: 'Heartiest greetings, Yours, Fritz.' This was the agreed signal for a meeting with the man who would in future, direct and care for the new recruit – his organizer.[19]

Though in Gehlen's scheme of things the informer and the agent were the real operators in an intelligence service, the organizer was in fact the heart and soul of operational intelligence. Whether a spy, left to himself in enemy territory, produced good or bad intelligence depended primarily on the way in which his organizer handled him. Gehlen's organizers frequently showed a solicitude for their informers rare in international concerns.

Organizers would frequently disregard unwise orders from headquarters or one of the agencies in order not to jeopardize their men. In cases when agreed warning signals were no longer getting through to a man, the organizer, on his own initiative, would often warn him of the threat of arrest – against the strict headquarters order forbidding travel into East Germany. In 1953, for instance, a West Berlin organizer heard that his informer in an arms factory at Suhl, Thuringia, had been blown and was threatened with arrest. The organizer obtained the uniform of an officer of the East German police who had recently defected, packed it in a suitcase and travelled to Suhl. He changed into police uniform in the lavatory of Suhl station, went to the porter at the factory and ordered his man to be sent to the gate. When the man appeared, the bogus police officer declared him under arrest and took him away – to West Berlin.[20]

At his first meeting with a new informer the organizer placed him under contract; he swore him to the 'strictest maintenance of secrecy' and gave him the code number under which he was to be known in the Org. The informer himself was usually allowed to choose his code name. In one of the Org's 'safe houses' the organizer then gave his informer his first lessons in espionage. The informer was told how to prepare a report – 'a report should be submitted on every target'. The informer's code number appeared at the head of each report together with a serial number.

To enable the agency or headquarters to establish the time taken by a report in transmission, the informer had to record two times: the 'tactical time', in other words the day and time at which the observation was made, and the 'recording time', in other words the day and time when the report was written. The organizer then had to note a 'time of receipt'. If the informer was using a so-called 'sub-source', he had to proceed as follows: 'When the sub-source is used for the first time, give the following: age, profession, position, whether an ex-soldier, where and for how long, rank, married or unmarried, residence; what is relationship of our informer to him and what is the quality of that relationship – distant, close or a relative? Give short character sketch (garrulous, drunkard, some political motive).'

Every report had to explain 'method of acquisition' – 'How did source obtain the material?' Then followed the text of the message. In the event of 'visual acquisition' the informer, sub-source or agent had to ask himself four questions: 'When did I see it? Where did I see it? What did I see? What did it look like?' The instruction stated that the report 'must be precise, clear, short but comprehensive'. Gehlen's training programme specified: 'The informer should be as fully trained as possible in observation and description; he should first look at an object, then describe it and finally sketch it. This must be practised frequently so that the eye becomes used to taking in as much as possible, indeed everything.'

The organizer also had to teach his informers the following: 'Should an informer obtain original material, he must first report the fact since it carries with it the risk of discovery; he may only produce the material on receipt of the necessary authorization.' Instructions for writing reports in invisible ink were: 'Write the secret text between the lines of the cover-text, using a thin paint-brush or splinter of wood wrapped in cotton-wool; use block capitals and do not press hard. The ink lasts three to four weeks.'[21]

An informer approaching a 'dead-letter box' in order to leave in it a report to be forwarded to his organizer was not to carry the report in an envelope in his briefcase but place it in an outside pocket of his jacket or overcoat so that, in the event of danger, he could tear it up and throw it away. Only after checking that all was in order at the 'dead-letter box' was the informer to place his message in an envelope and then in a container. Once he had left the 'post-box', a further figure in the intelligence world soon appeared – the courier.

Gehlen ordered that: 'Before he actually operates, the courier must get to know the journey in question. He should travel the route several times "unloaded" and observe: When, where and at what intervals are passes and luggage checked? What is the form of check – full or spot check? Does it include a body-search and is this done arbitrarily or only when there are grounds for suspicion?'

When travelling through East Germany the courier always had to have a 'cover-story' ready for the East German police, in other words he must be able to produce a convincing, though fictitious, reason for his journey. To avoid exposing couriers to unnecessary risk, the Org employed several of them for any one message; they worked on an east-west relay system. The first courier, for example, would place a message from Leipzig in a 'dead-letter box' at Magdeburg, a second would then take it to another 'dead-letter box' near the zone boundary, a third would take it to some woods on the frontier and hide it in a thicket on the Western side. There a fourth courier would collect it and deliver it to the nearest Gehlen agency.[22]

Sometimes a message would take two or three weeks to reach the organizer. At this time the Org had no radio links to its agents. The most original courier channel was thought up by some of Gehlen's people in West Berlin. In 1953 they trained a swan on Glienick Lake to carry espionage material in small plastic bags under its wings from Potsdam to the west bank and return to the east bank with instructions – passing a bridge guarded by Russian sentries who threw chunks of bread to Gehlen's courier as she paddled by.

If a report arrived from an informer in code or written in invisible ink the organizer had to decipher it or render it visible by heating or wetting it, depending on the type of ink. He then sent to Pullach through the official channel not only the text in clear but also the informer's original production. Even the envelope and, in the case of packages or parcels, the paper and string had to be forwarded to headquarters, since these things had a value of their own – orders and money could be sent back to agents and informers using normal East German materials which would consequently excite no comment.

The organizer had to be continuously on the watch to ensure that his communications to his informer were not cut. The informer was under obligation to give some sign of life every seven days. From time to time an organizer and his agent would agree on a meeting in West Berlin. Many informers regularly met their organizer to report. Regulations laid down that an organizer should only deal with one informer to avoid several agents being compromised, should the organizer fall into enemy hands. Owing to lack of suitable organizers, however, they frequently ran three or four informers in East Germany. Pullach's order that an organizer should never allow his informer to know his real name also remained largely a paper exercise. Many organizers in fact even put their informers up for the night. Since most of these secret-service front-line soldiers were addicted to alcohol when off duty, many friendships were struck up between the spies and their 'bell-wethers'.[23]

In written correspondence with headquarters, however, the organizer had to follow instructions slavishly – in his own interests, since form and content of a report frequently decided an organizer's career. He would get a black mark if he had not extracted the last detail out of his informer. In this event there would follow a stream of 'supplementary questions' as in this note on 'a report by informer S.': 'Why was no attempt made to establish the location of 117 Pioneer Brigade? Why is there no report on the port of Rostock? Why does source report nothing of what he saw during his journey from Rostock to Leningrad and return? Did he see ships; if so, when, where and which? Does he know anything about minefields? Where was a pilot taken on board and why? Nothing is said about the port of Danzig. Why does source give us nothing? This is devastating!'

On a 'report by informer E.' one of the Org's agencies fulminated: 'Even worse than the previous report! Observations are inadequate. There are no precise dates or details. Obviously source has been badly taught about what he has to do and to report – or alternatively is not interested.' The agency then wished to know: 'What gives anyone to suppose that a division is located in Prenzlau? The figure given of about 4,000 men does not constitute a division. Who assumes this and why? Where are the headquarters? How are they indicated (signs, etc)?'[24]

In the face of so censorious an attitude on the part of headquarters most organizers preferred to follow the rule that a report should be 'short, factual, exhaustive and credible'. They noted every detail but were careful to abide by the instruction: 'Do not put leading questions. Never force the pace; let the informer tell his own story. He should himself make any sketches as best he can; they are not to be embellished by the organizer.'[25]

A completed report by an organizer looked like this (the subject was the observation of a Soviet barracks): '*TZ* [Tactical time] 14/12/1952, 4.55–12.48. *FZ* [Report written] 14/12/52. *EZ* [Date of receipt] 14/12/52. *Source:* XXXX. *Description of source:* already known. *Estimate of source:* completely calm and sensible before departure. Determined to carry out his mission satisfactorily. *Method of acquisition:* visual acquisition on journey to ZZ and during period spent there. *Cover story:* Father Tony R., mother Miezl R., son Johann . . . looking for a former workmate named Joseph Wagner in ZZ with object possibly of obtaining employment for him here. *Alternative story:* looking for his sister in the vicinity. Source answered questions put to him without hesitation; his account and his answers seem fully convincing.'[26]

When questioning an informer the organizer had to note down everything: when the informer got up, when he started work, how long he worked and what he did in his spare time. Most important of all, the informer had to describe in the utmost detail how he had reconnoitred his target, how he had obtained possession of the key to the safe, for instance, and whom he had contacted. Then the organizer had to report whether the informer had been nervous, depressed or in specially good humour. At the conclusion of the report the organizer had to state whether his informer's statements seemed credible and if so, why.

Organizers soon realized, however, that they might well do themselves harm by giving too accurate a description of the attitude of their informer. If a spy was reported as temporarily depressed, Gehlen's security representative would frequently decide that he must be put out of circulation at once as a 'security risk'. Organizers were naturally unwilling to lose a good informer because of some temporary loss of equanimity. They therefore generally described their sources as extraordinarily calm, balanced and thoughtful.

An optimistically phrased report was also to be recommended because headquarters paid for every scrap of information. A source was rewarded according to the value and frequency of the intelligence he produced; a single report might earn him 20–100 Westmarks. (On his own admission Gehlen himself was drawing a monthly salary of 1200 marks tax free in 1952.) The organizer and his informer therefore had to draft their report in such a way that 'supplementary questions' were unnecessary and the informer was certain of the maximum reward. Headquarters did not, however, distribute their largesse without having first consulted the informer's personal file which was held in Pullach. This file included the 'Personal Questionnaire' (completed by the investigator), the *curriculum vitae* (drawn up by the informer), the 'worksheet' and 'training report', both written by the organizer.

For the personal questionnaire the investigator had had to find out whether the spy had a means of livelihood but 'was not averse to earnings on the side'. In his *curriculum vitae* (part II) the informer had had to list his dependants and describe any 'friendly relationships' with other people. In the 'worksheet' the organizer had answered questions about 'presence of mind, circumspection, knowledge of human nature and manners'. From the 'training report' headquarters knew 'how the trainee behaved on an operational mission' and whether he had completed 'training in invisible inks' and 'training on keys'. All this formed the basis for the classification allotted by headquarters to any report from the informer transmitted by his organizer.

Headquarters classification also decided what measures the Org would take to bring a threatened informer to safety. The more important the source, the more strenuous the efforts made by the Org to screen and protect him from the enemy. Gehlen's basic instruction on agents said: 'If an agent or informer perceives that he is being shadowed by the enemy, he must report the fact at once; depending on the degree of danger and the practical possibilities, he will be placed in cold storage, transferred, removed, dropped or brought to safety.'

At the outset of their association organizer and informer agreed on a 'warning notice' for use should the informer be in danger. It consisted of a postcard carrying an agreed text to be sent as soon as the informer became apprehensive of discovery or arrest. Headquarters had laid down the form and the wording even of these postcards – 'For the various degrees of danger it is recommended that the following messages be passed: if thought to be under surveillance: "Dear Maria, heartiest greetings on my return, Your . . ."; after a house search: "Dear Friend, we were recently visited by a nice aunt. Best wishes and greetings, Your . . ."; if questioned and released: "Your friend sends you heartiest greetings . . ." In all three cases this message means: cease work.'

Organizer and informer also agreed on some innocent-sounding code-word, known as the 'pressure signal', to be used should the informer be pressurized and 'converted' by the enemy counter-espionage service. Receipt of this code-word meant to the organizer that henceforth only 'play-back' material was to be expected from his informer. The warning signals could, of course, also be used in reverse direction. From its counter-espionage sources the Org would often learn that one of its informers had been blown. Then it was the organizer who had to send a post-card with a concealed warning. For high-level sources escape lines were prepared beforehand; they were given timely information of 'safe houses' where they could go to ground in East Germany and of the 'guides' who would send them on their way westwards. In the event of any difficulties with German or Allied authorities at the frontier the fugitive was ordered to contact an officer of the American CIC forthwith; he was then to give this officer his 'emergency number', a combination of figures which identified him as a member of the Gehlen Organization.[27]

Headquarters requests for information, however, were not confined to the work and security of their informers in enemy territory; they were equally interested in the work of their organizers and local branches. All organizers had to produce a detailed activity report every month. Brevity and accuracy were required in everything, as the papers of one of the Org's out-stations show.

June 1950: 'Activity report for period 16/5/1950 to 15/6/1950. Activity centred on attempts to obtain Polish identity papers. In all, five reports and four personal questionnaires were submitted. Of the reports two concerned intelligence operations already initiated and the remaining three were of a counter-espionage nature.' Two months later: 'Activity report for period 16/7/1950 to 15/8/1950. During this period activity centred on the recruitment of suitable Poles and the acquisition of Polish identity papers. The search was also continued for a Polish-speaking interrogator, also for a frontier guide and frontier crossing into Czechoslovakia.' A month later: 'Activity report for the period 16/8/1950 to 15/9/1950. During this period a total of eleven reports were submitted, of which two were of counter-espionage nature, three concerned recruitment of an interrogator, three recruitment of an informer for the Polish area and one with the acquisition of Polish identity papers; two special reports concerned SBONR [a Russian émigré organization] and Caucasians (15 pages). In addition one list of Polish refugees was submitted.'[28]

Only by obtaining an overall view of the work of all its out-stations could headquarters evaluate the intelligence material received and fit it into the general picture of the situation prepared and continuously improved by the analysts of the Evaluation Section under Colonel Dinser. The reports and indications from the out-stations formed the raw material; in Pullach this had to be worked up into what Colonel Leabert and his US Liaison Staff of fifty called 'intelligence' – situation reports compiled from secret and non-secret sources, checked and compared over and over again. In these all the various reports were allotted their due place and weight.

The Americans were continually urging haste upon their German minions in Pullach; the Berlin blockade and the Korean war had long been casting their shadows over the world political scene. The US experts kept reminding Gehlen's people that espionage reports must be dealt with quickly since they rapidly became obsolete; reports on enemy troops, they calculated, lost ten per cent of their value per day, in other words in a week they had lost two-thirds of their significance. Gehlen agreed to improve his methods of evaluation. A new assessment scale was introduced; more rapid evaluation was the aim.[29]

Soon the Americans were able, on occasions, to get answers to their intelligence questions after the lapse of a mere few days. The US Liaison Staff passed the Org's situation reports to Washington by radio or courier aircraft; the usual addressees were the Org's partners in intelligence – initially the War Department's 'Strategic Services Unit' under Major-General Magruder, then Rear-Admiral Sidney Souers' 'Central Intelligence Group', the forerunner of the Central Intelligence Agency (CIA). On the formation of the CIA, America's central secret service, it increasingly became the main customer for the Org's material; this was dealt with by the staff of Loftus E. Becker, Deputy Director of the CIA, and relevant parts of it were forwarded to the office of the Head of Army Intelligence, Major-General Alexander Bolling. Almost all Gehlen's American allies of the early days had meanwhile been appointed to senior CIA posts – Becker, Sherman Kent, Edwin Sibert. They all helped to cement the alliance between the CIA and Gehlen's Org.

The Washington generals, however, were still not satisfied with Pullach's intelligence. Russia and the states of the Eastern bloc still largely showed as blanks on the maps of the US General Staff. Gehlen turned further east.

ADVANCE TO MOSCOW

THE first orders for the great operation issued from General (retd)
Alfred Kretschmer, head of General Agency 'H' in Darmstadt.
Service instructions appearing on January 25th, February 26th and 28th,
1953 told the staff of the Gehlen Org that the great man in Pullach had
laid down fresh objectives. In addition to short-range intelligence, in
other words espionage against the German People's Republic, the Org
was now to proceed to long-range intelligence-gathering in the other
states of the Eastern bloc and finally to distant intelligence in the interior of the Soviet Union itself.

Gehlen's first object was to move his spies further eastward, into
Poland, Czechoslovakia and Hungary. Within the Acquisition Department in Pullach he set up a special section, designated by the number 50
in internal correspondence, to plan operations in the more distant East;
'50–R' was in charge of intelligence of Russia and '50–S' of that in
Eastern bloc states other than East Germany and the Soviet Union.

General Agency 'H' under Kretschmer was in operational command.
In his instruction of February 28th addressed to Sub-Agency 'K' in Augsburg Kretschmer said: 'The first necessity is to inform leaders in the
field of this mission and of the methods leading to its fulfilment. A
situation must be reached in which, throughout the area for which the
sub-agency is responsible, watch is kept for leads into Poland, Czechoslovakia, and the USSR from the Soviet-occupied zone and from the
Federal Republic: such leads must be investigated as to suitability for
our purpose and then be developed into channels of communication.
The procedure to be initiated may be graphically described as follows:
throughout the area of the sub-agency a searchlight should be directed
on to Poland, Czechoslovakia and the USSR; such lines or connecting
links as appear in the searchlight should be "spotlighted" with the
object of providing detailed answers to these two questions: "What is
it?" and "What might be developed therefrom?" '[1]

Poland headed the list. That country formed a strategically important
pivot between the Soviet Union and East Germany; it was allotted

Priority 1. Gehlen decreed: 'Any information from the area beyond the Oder-Neisse line is of interest.' But Poland was difficult to penetrate. As early as June 1950 an organizer had reported to Pullach: 'Recruitment of agents for Poland is proving somewhat difficult at present because all intelligence agencies outside the Eastern Zone are concentrating their attention on Poland. It would be helpful if visits could be made to camps in which Poles are accommodated as, for intance, those at Ingolstadt, Würzburg and Neu-Ulm. It is difficult, however, for anyone with an identity card showing German nationality to enter these camps.'

In fact the Org's only possibility of penetrating Poland lay in the recruitment of Polish refugees and Soviet deserters. The Org maintained informers in the Bavarian refugee camps whose duty, in the words of an organizer, was to 'discover suitable persons or those otherwise of interest, to inform me and then place me in personal touch with these people'. Russian émigrés working for the Org were also despatched on a search for people with Polish connections.[2]

The Org's investigators swept up almost every Pole who left his country for political reasons. Gehlen's men appeared in all Polish camps and organizations, pretending that they were collecting information for some American agency, since Poles were unlikely to be prepared to help a German secret service. Initially Gehlen's investigators were interested primarily in military questions, listed in a working paper supplied to them from headquarters. They asked where in Poland Russian troops were stationed, how fully accommodation was occupied, where the Russians had supply installations and where their manoeuvre areas were.

Almost more important to the Org, however, than these military details was the refugees' knowledge of living conditions in their home country. Every refugee could tell Gehlen something he needed in order to develop an intelligence network in the East. If the Org was to infiltrate its own agents into Poland it had to know what routes to use to cross the frontier ('Get the refugee to make a sketch, specify method of transport'), where, when and by whom checks were made in the frontier zone, and what identity papers were demanded, recognized or refused. The Org's main interest, however, lay in the answer to the question: 'What possibilities are there of evading these controls?' Each Polish refugee was asked to state: 'When and where did he succeed in crossing the frontier (description of the country, precise indication on a map of the route followed).'[3] Armed with this information Gehlen's planners began to prepare to infiltrate agents into enemy territory. Here again the Polish refugees could help. The interrogators tried to discover persons whom a spy might contact, whether some relative, friend or acquaintance of the refugee might be willing to cooperate. Gehlen's men were continuously on the road recruiting agents for the Polish operation and collecting genuine identity papers. A Pole working in the 'Control Centre' of the International Refugee Organization (IRO) in the Warner barracks, Munich, produced a nominal roll of Polish refugees. Another Pole gave names of twenty-two of his fellow-country-men who had fled from Poland to West Germany in 1950 and was rewarded with 100 marks for his pains. An interpreter in the IRO camp at Fürstenfeldbruck undertook to keep a look-out for possible agents and to collect Polish identity papers.[4]

In the summer of 1950 an informer reported that he had 'arranged various meetings' with a Pole, S.M., living in Munich – 'it was agreed that he would place at our disposal Polish refugees who seemed suitable'. A certain I.K., also from Munich, was reported to 'travel on duty to the Displaced Persons camp outside the city. At a meeting he declared himself ready to give names of Poles lodged in this camp.' Another Pole, W.B., was prepared 'to go to Poland as an informer and there set up a safe house which could be used by designated agents'. Yet another Pole, G., signed on as a radio operator but the recruiting officer reported that 'he insisted on a minimum subsistence allowance to be precisely specified beforehand and also on adequate preparation, for instance assembling and testing his set'. A German ex-Captain, W.B., produced a good tip; he had been taken prisoner by the Poles in 1945 and in his POW camp had become friendly with a Polish officer 'who was particularly conspicuous for his violent opposition to everything Soviet or Russian'. W.B. suggested that he might 'give some courier going to Poland a short note for the Polish officer in order to establish contact with him'.[5]

Germans who had any contact with Poles were harnessed into the operation. A certain Karli Bandelow, employed in the East German State Secretariat for Motor Vehicles and Road Transport but working for the Org, took photostat copies of minutes of meetings with Polish engineers and noted any who seemed approachable. Another, Christoph Kommerek, in the nationalized Inland Water Transport Office in Altenburg, set up an infiltration channel into Poland via shipping lines on the Oder. The Org also recruited East German railway guards and merchant seamen for espionage work in Poland.

A note on an East German seaman by one of Gehlen's recruiters read as follows: 'He said that he and two others from his ship had been sent to the Danzig Quay in Stettin for cleaning and repair work. I thereupon gave him precise instructions on matters of interest to us; I went into the greatest detail about ports, the country, installations, ships, military establishments, naval units, coastal defences, flying-boat stations, etc. I also raised the question of the recruitment of other informers from his ship and in other ports.'[6]

Even Russian officer defectors were prepared to place their Polish contacts at Gehlen's disposal — against adequate remuneration. A former Red Army captain, for instance, who had previously been working for the US secret service through ex-Colonel Rolin, one of their organizers, made a present to Pullach of two tiny circuits. The record reads: 'Circuit 1 consists of: 1. Koller jnr living north-west of Breslau. 2. Liaison — Koller snr living in the US sector of Berlin–Friedenau. 3. Courier — Mayer. Circuit 2 consists of: 1. Kuberski, a construction engineer at Lodz. 2. Liaison — Schwartz, an aircraft construction engineer. 3. Courier — Mayer.'

Thus Gehlen's agents worked their way into Poland. An informer named Alfred Pietruszka arranged courier lines and post-boxes; an agent named Adolf Machura collected economic information; another informer, Wilhelm Alrichs, kept watch on barracks and troop movements in Danzig; yet another, Henryk Skowronek, reported from Gogolin anything which seemed to him noteworthy.[7]

New men were continually presenting themselves to serve in Gehlen's Polish espionage machine. Agent ODT 738–18, whose real name was Conrad Wruck, brought his entire family into the Org. He later told a Polish military court: 'My sister, Stefania Wazna, living on the Baltic in what used to be called Zoppot, was instructed in the use of invisible inks. I also made use of my father, Albert Wruck. My brother Stefan, who was doing his military service at the time, gave me information about barracks in Grudziadz (formerly Graudenz) and Bydgoszcz (formerly Bromberg). My uncle, Marian Niemczyck, who worked in a state saw-mill, gave me details of production and personalities in the timber industry and obtained for me a plan of his works.'

ODT 738–18's methods were a good illustration of the way in which a Gehlen agent built up his circuit in enemy territory. He continued: 'I also recruited other people outside my circle of relatives. My friend Gelhar, who had remained in the West, asked me to look up his wife Jadwiga. She advised me to visit her uncle, Wiktor Krogul, who lived at Olsztyn, in the south near Czestochowa. I went there. Krogul was working in a hospital and doing duty for the senior administrator who was away. He was living with a certain Leocadia Berend, an officer's widow. She encouraged him to work with me and he helped me – he gave me two identity cards forgotten by patients in the hospital.'[8]

So Gehlen had his foot in the Polish door and he could now further expand his East European network. His informers advanced into another of the neighbouring People's Democracies – Czechoslovakia.

German foresters in the Bayerischer Wald conducted Gehlen's agents to unguarded frontier crossings. The Czechoslovak authorities, however, were alive to the Org's movements. As early as October 25th, 1950 an informer had reported: 'Stricter frontier control has been initiated since October 1st. Continuous patrols are maintained day and night; they consist of small groups of four or five young men aged between 20 and 25 and have been observed actually on the frontier. They are no different from the other Czech frontier guards but have been given special training by instructors from the MVD frontier service.' Nevertheless the Pullach headquarters was soon satisfactorily informed about military affairs in Czechoslovakia; the Org's agents, however, were primarily interested in the Soviet forces in the country.[9]

An informer in Prague reported that the Red Army had recently been issued with a shell which 'could be used both from a mortar and as a bomb'. It included 'an ingeniously simple but safe detonator; if the missile is used as a bomb, the detonator, without further setting, enables it to explode either at some precisely pre-calculated height, giving a shrapnel effect, or on impact'. This shell, the informer reported, had been invented by technicians in a lathe and machine-tool factory at Kharkov. The design had been further developed by a Czech engineer conscripted by the Russians. Manufacture of the shell had been in progress since spring 1949 in a munitions factory at Kurgan in the Soviet Union.

Gehlen passed this report on the bomb or shell to the US Liaison Staff in Pullach. This produced a request from the Americans for a specimen of the detonator itself. A fortnight later Gehlen handed the Americans a parcel containing, not only the detonator, but specimens of the metal and explosive used together with complete technical and ballistic data. Gehlen was also able to present them with something even better – the Czech engineer. The Org's couriers had smuggled him and his entire family across the frontier.

By this time Gehlen also had spies in the Skoda arms works; a shorthand typist in the Ministry of Commerce in Prague kept him informed on trade between Czechoslovakia and East Germany; a technical draughtsman handed over the plans of the 'magnetic/metal/ceramic triode LS 500 (cathode-ray tube)', an important component of the guidance mechanism in weapons and missiles.[10]

Another country of the Eastern bloc had long been on the Org's list for investigation – Hungary, and it was discovered that a Hungarian Lieutenant-Colonel in Budapest had started to form an anti-Russian resistance organization. On April 4th, 1948 Gehlen dispatched a liaison officer to advise this officer against undertaking any form of resistance 'since, in view of Soviet counter-espionage methods, any opposition groups would be quickly broken up' – in the words of a written directive from the Org's local branch in Vienna. The emissary proposed instead that any anti-Soviet faction in the Hungarian army should 'collect information of a military, political and economic nature about the country and the Russians'. The Lieutenant-Colonel was in agreement and the first information from Hungary began to flow into the Pullach headquarters.[11]

Simultaneously Gehlen set up an out-station in Bad Reichenhall; it was manned solely by Hungarian émigrés and a Honved [National Guard] Lieutenant-Colonel named Kollenyi was in charge of it. In Salzburg Kollenyi maintained a group of interrogators who contacted Hungarian refugees and trained them for employment as agents in Hungary.[12]

As Hungary became increasingly important in Gehlen's scheme of things the sections of the Org dealing with that country began to transfer their activities more and more to Austria. Although Austria was still subject to Four-Power occupation, it offered an ideal base for Gehlen's espionage work in the East. From Austria it was easier to infiltrate agents unobtrusively into Czechoslovakia or Hungary and in addition it was easier to contact soldiers and agencies of the Red Army.

As early as 1948 one of Gehlen's reconnaissance parties had visualized Vienna as a future operational base. The party reported to Pullach: 'The casual visitor by no means gets the impression that he is in a city occupied by various victorious powers. All sectors are equally accessible to him and basically there are no controls; he can therefore move about with complete freedom provided he possesses valid identity papers.' On the other hand Vienna was equally a target for the enemy intelligence services and in addition the communists had a foothold in the Austrian police. In an 'Instruction' to its staff in Vienna the Org accordingly warned: 'You are threatened with danger, not only from the Russians but also from the Austrian gendarmerie. Here too, therefore, you must be cautious.'

The Org's agencies in Austria, therefore, primarily those in Vienna, were constantly being urged to check the security of their people. The watchword was 'Danger of abduction'. One organizer reported: 'On checking the accommodation of informers to see whether an abduction could be easily engineered, we came to the conclusion that, in his present lodging, XXXX is the most exposed. The street is little used ... the house is situated only some 200 yards from No 10 Soviet District. Please, therefore, ensure that, in order to regularize the position, XXXX receives as soon as possible the Czech identity papers already requested.'[13]

The views of Gehlen's advance party on 'Security measures by the Soviet occupation authorities' were as follows: 'In bars or restaurants of the Soviet sector frequented by Soviet citizens one or two civilians are invariably to be seen who, by their appearance, are unmistakably Russian. They sit for hours over a glass of beer or wine, talk to each other practically not at all and are primarily employed in watching any Russians in uniform. If any of the latter are approached by a civilian and a conversation begins, one of the spies gets up and passes close by the soldier in order to overhear what is being said.' Even in the Prater Gehlen's scouts spotted 'Soviet spies both uniformed and in mufti'. After 10 PM, however, surveillance ceased 'since at this time the junior ranks must be in their billets'. Thereafter only 'officers of the rank of Lieutenant upwards are to be seen; they go about nonchalantly with Austrian girls and are also addicted to alcohol'.

The Org's first problem was the recruitment of Austrians in a position to contact Soviet soldiers. In a secret memorandum headed 'The Austrian as informer' the Pullach headquarters urged psychological sensitivity upon the German recruiters whom it despatched to Vienna: 'For our purposes the Austrian, particularly the Viennese, is a problematical assistant. Any Viennese in responsible positions desire, not unjustifiably, to avoid all difficulties with the Soviet occupation authorities. In general, therefore, collaborators will only be found among the "dispossessed", the unemployed or the down-and-outs. The main sources of informers will therefore be the refugees from German minorities and ex-members of the Nazi organization.'[14]

Headquarters also reminded its Viennese recruiters of the historical factors to be considered: 'In most cases the Viennese feel themselves to be German-Austrians. It must be remembered, however, that the parents or grandparents of the people in question were probably Czechs, Poles or Hungarians, etc. The organizer must therefore be tactful in his approach to avoid exacerbating inferiority complexes.'[15]

In fact it emerged that the Org's informers were to be found primarily among the 'dispossessed', those who had been sentenced and had their property expropriated after the war for holding office or being otherwise active in the Nazi Party. Close relations between them and the

Org's representatives developed with special rapidity if Gehlen's man could present himself as an ex-comrade from the Waffen-SS. One informer reported as follows on a meeting with a candidate named Joseph Schürmer: 'When I divulged to him that I was an ex-member of the Waffen-SS, he opened up completely and offered to assist here in Vienna both in word and deed.' Schürmer became an agent of the Gehlen Organization.[16]

Many of those offering their services to the Org were dubious characters. One organizer recommended as an informer a certain 'Hermine': 'A Sudeten German woman who has suffered severely from the Reds. She wants no more in life than to drive the bolshevists out of Europe.'

Another of the Org's informers was faced with criminal proceedings before a court in Salzburg and headquarters made efforts to have the case quashed. The correspondence on the subject had its comic side: 'Ref: V-86567. You are hereby informed that 86567 has completely changed his appearance; he now has a moustache and side-whiskers and has changed his hair-style so that, compared with a photograph of June 1953, he is entirely unrecognizable. You are nevertheless requested to pursue the quashing of the case in Salzburg and, if successful, to report the fact.' A counter-question from headquarters elicited this somewhat acid reply: 'Ref: Change in appearance of V-86567. The fact that 86567 had a moustache and side-whiskers was not the subject of some rumour but was reported in this office's message of October 24th, 1953. Since the change of appearance, however, made him more conspicuous than ever, the moustache and side-whiskers disappeared ten days ago and, except for his new hair-style, he now looks as he always did. What progress is there at present in the quashing of the Salzburg case? 86567 will in any case wish to go home for Christmas. Please do all you can to enable him to do this.'[17]

In Vienna were also to be found women who would work for the Org as 'convenors' or 'contacters'. The Org placed special emphasis on women, for an internal instruction headed 'Defection Work in Vienna' included this: 'An additional method is the recruitment of ladies of easy virtue to visit localities frequented by Soviet citizens.' These girls attempted to contact Soviet officers and soldiers, took them back to their flats and there introduced them to the Org's recruiters. One of the most active of these sirens was 'Anni', whose personal card showed that she was born in 1928, was 5 ft 7 in tall, had an oval face with brown eyes and blonde hair and as 'distinguishing mark' a 'scar under the chin'.

She had been discovered by one of the Org's informers who, in his Report No 60, said: 'In March/April this year Anni made the acquaintance of a Soviet Air Force Lieutenant-Colonel in the Dobner Bar. She came to realize that the Russians are not all barbarians but that some are men like us, as she put it. Subsequently there was established between the two a relationship which still exists today. She cannot pronounce his name because of the sibilants which she cannot manage. The christian name is Peter.' Gehlen's man, however, was even more interested in the following: 'Peter likes his drink but has a weak head, particularly for wine; he has to keep a very tight hold of himself to avoid making gaffes in the presence of other Russians. He has already told Anni several times that he has no wish to go back to the Soviet Union.'

Anni declared herself ready to arrange a meeting between Peter and the Org's informer in one of the Western districts of Vienna; a condition was attached: 'If information is likely to be required frequently, it would be wise to help her re-establish herself either as a hostess or barmaid in some bar. It would be enough to provide her with two reasonable evening dresses and she could then arrange her employment herself.' At a subsequent meeting Anni said that she could obtain a position in the Moulin Rouge, a haunt of Russian civilians. She would require, however, not only an evening dress but a pair of shoes.

The informer at once made a 'proposal' to the Org's out-station in Salzburg: 'For the purchase of the above-mentioned articles a sum of 700 Austrian schilling will be required. It would further seem wise to disburse to her, as her first month's wages, a sum of 1,000 Australian schilling, to ensure that she remains keen to feed to us not only Peter but also other members of the Russian occupation forces.' The calculation paid off. Anni arranged contact with the Russian Lieutenant-Colonel who proved willing to cooperate; she also introduced other Russian officers to the Org's informers.

A report dated December 2nd, 1953 shows how industrious Anni was: 'Most recent meeting with Anni took place on November 28th at 10 PM in a dance hall in District IV. Anni was sitting alone; at an adjacent table sat a Major and a Lieutenant (artillery or tanks – no badges – bright red piping and button-holes); both were drunk and were asking Anni to drink with them, interspersing their invitations with vulgar Russian swear-words. They asked the waiter for vodka but he had only slivovitz; accordingly they soon departed, inviting Anni to go with them but she refused owing to their crude behaviour. Next meeting in a café on November 30th, 1953.'[18]

Anni was soon faced with competition in her new profession. 'Tamara' lured air-force officers and Russian Navy sailors into her flat by promising to sell them wrist-watches. 'Helene' ensnared a sergeant named Ivan in Traiskirchen. 'Tosca' and 'Alfa' brought over two officers named Sergei and Michail. 'Anita' traded wrist-watches with an artillery lieutenant named Alex. 'Maria' inveigled Russians into a bar. 'Rosemary' became friendly with a Russian officer's family who wished to learn German (the Org provided the tutor). 'Margot' struck up a liaison with two engineers named Viktor and Alexander.[19]

Once these female assistants had piloted their tame Russians home, the visitor was given too much to drink. Later the black-market dealer in watches arrived – in fact one of Gehlen's informers. It was his duty to find out whether the Russian concerned was ready either to desert to the West or enter the service of the Org.

At this point the art of the 'approach' came into its own once more, exercised in this case in accordance with the provisions of a 'Defection Aide-Mémoire No 1' issued to all heads of local branches: 'Guiding principle: No approach without a personal check. Second principle: take your time, be workmanlike, be on your guard against provocation. Danger No 1: Enemy provocation. Danger No 2: An unwise remark – this can irretrievably wreck the best-laid plans. Therefore: careful personal check and discovery of all forbidden subjects which might cause your man to break contact.' Only after all this should the approach be made. The aide-mémoire continued: 'What is approachability? It is the sum total of all the components of a Russian's character, of his living conditions both at home and abroad and of his general disposition which might lead to a readiness to collaborate.'

If the Russian was ready to be talked to, the informer must present himself 'as an individual, as a friend or business partner, never as representing any group of people of any sort'. The reason: 'The Soviet citizen, in particular the Russian, will open up – if he does so at all – only to someone in whom he has confidence, to a friend whose intentions towards him are good.' The Org accordingly used primarily Russian émigrés; they knew how to offer good bait to Soviet nationals.[20]

Gehlen's recruiters sent full-scale shopping lists to their headquarters 'to assist in contacting Soviet elements'. On October 20th, 1953, for instance a Ukrainian informer asked for 'two Swiss wrist-watches (Doxas), two less expensive wrist-watches, three pairs of nylon stockings (dark, size 9–10), specimens of women's materials in silk or light wool (provided later orders can be met) and a consignment of fountain pens, Biros and ball-points.'[21]

Numerous Soviet officers fell for the Org's offers and began to produce material of interest to Gehlen – reports on the morale of the troops, information on weapons and equipment, secrets of the Soviet occupation administration. As time went on Soviet officers developed an aptitude for dealings on the Vienna intelligence stock exchange. One of Gehlen's Ukrainian informers made contact with a Russian administrative officer who travelled from Budapest to Vienna every fortnight. The Ukrainian asked the Russian to get him a Zorkiy camera, whereupon the Russian replied: 'Surely you would be more interested in a gas mask or a steel helmet.' The Russian was able to bring with him, however, official regulations, service manuals, identity papers, official correspondence and Russian provincial newspapers. The Ukrainian reported: 'He is most anxious to earn money and likes good living; he is determined to sell the material he brings at a good price.' The Org bought it for 6,000 schilling.

Pullach's agencies, however, were also collecting intelligence on their own account. Their agents combed rubbish dumps near Soviet troop locations for official regulations, private mail and telephone directories. An instruction from Local Branch 'Erich' read: 'Try to discover fresh dumps and extend your area of activity. For every article specify where and when found.' Chamber-maids, hired by informers for a few schilling, searched rooms occupied by Russians in the Imperial Hotel, the Grand Hotel and the Esplanade for shreds of letters or notes. Agents stationed outside Red Army barracks noted the registration numbers of Soviet vehicles – a sure clue to any Soviet troop movements.[22]

A 'Report on St Poelten barracks' read: 'In the grounds in front of the house, on the road leading to the main barrack entrance, was a patrol of four infantrymen (strawberry-red shoulder-boards) armed with sub-machine guns; they demanded the identity papers of every soldier who passed. In the opinion of source this is the building of the DKA (Dom Krasnoi Armii) – Red Army House or the barrack dining-hall.' In another report an informer recorded: 'Ref: Soviet vehicle numbers. In period 1/7/53 to 15/7/53 following vehicles with Soviet registration numbers were observed: 2/7/53 – District I – Opernring, 1430 hrs, green jeep C-2-58-46; 11/7/53 – District I – Burgring, 1730 hrs, green truck C-2-54-46; 11/7/53 – District V – Reinprechtsdorferstrasse, 1630 hrs, light-green truck E-7-48-97.'[23]

Simultaneously a flourishing underground courier service operated from Austrian airfields; it provided rapid transport for mail or small parcels to anywhere in the world, without inspection by customs or censorship authorities. Many pilots were only too ready to carry some 'Press Service mail' for a fixed fee.[24]

The ring of eyes and ears around the Soviet Union became denser. The Gehlen Org had its agents and informers almost everywhere. So Gehlen set in motion the great underground offensive into the real centre of power – the Soviet Union itself. There a vast war machine was forming which held the West spellbound. Gehlen's American masters were demanding more and more up-to-date information from the Soviet Union.[25]

Gehlen's planners thought up ways of infiltrating Russia. The main action was known as 'Operation Pfiffikus'; it involved informers in East Germany contacting any German who had reason to travel to the USSR – students, professors, engineers, scientists. One Gehlen agent tried to foist a camera on an East German actor who was going to Leningrad with his company – 'to take a few pictures during a trip round the port'. Anyone who could hand a Soviet soldier over to the Org was promised according to a Gehlen directive, 'a graduated fee depending on the importance of the source discovered'.[26]

What Gehlen really required, however, for his intelligence operation into the Soviet Union were the espionage professionals – agents, radio operators, couriers. These could only be men – or women – who had been born and brought up in the Soviet Union, who knew the manners and customs of the country, were filled with hatred for the Soviet regime, were both courageous and determined to fulfil their secret-service missions. Such people seemed to be available – fugitives from Russia, the Ukraine, Georgia, Armenia and the Baltic States had been knocking on Gehlen's door ever since Munich had become the main centre of the Russian émigré movement.

There were the 'old' (post-World War I) émigrés including the ageing White Army officers. Then there were the 'new' émigrés – German collaborators, people deported by the Nazis and the survivors of Vlassov's army; they were hiding from the Russian repatriation officers. Finally there was the 'third wave' – soldiers and officials who had deserted since the end of the war. All these were living in the IRO camps and they had organized themselves into associations, societies and small groups – forty-four of them in all. Each in his own way dreamt of a return to Russia – a Russia liberated from the Bolsheviks.[27] This Russian colony offered the various secret services operating in West Germany a literally inexhaustible source of information. However impenetrable the Iron Curtain might seem, into the houses, the camps and the association offices of these émigrés ran the secret channels of communication; Red Army deserters found refuge with friends; Russians received letters from relatives in the Soviet Union; exiled politicians were in radio communication with partisans in the Ukraine. Gehlen's intelligence sleuths were clearly unlikely to neglect such a reservoir of information.

Admittedly some of the exiled Russians made a good thing out of the curiosity of the secret services. One of the Org's informers spent hours writing down what a deserter named 'Anatol' said he had seen in the Caucasus eight weeks previously – the formation of a Soviet tank division; he described with equal precision the armament of the tanks and the character of their officers. When one of the members of the Evaluation Section read the report, however, he recognized 'Anatol' as an old friend who had told the same story to FHO back in 1942. A sailor named 'Vladimir' who had ostensibly deserted from the Russian Navy in 1949, offered the Org the 'Soviet Union Air Defence Mobilization Plan, to be completed by 1951'. He was asking $1,000 for it. When the informer concerned balked at the price Vladimir lowered his sights: 'I paid 300 marks for it myself; if you want the plan, I will let you have it cheaper. I am in urgent need of money.' Pullach wrote off the plan as a forgery and 'Vladimir' as a prisoner of war captured in 1943.[28]

In many cases such forgeries were the work of the Soviet secret service, which had been quick to realize how to make use of the market in intelligence. It issued a stream of false reports to mislead the Org. As early as 1949 an informer in one of the émigré organizations had warned Gehlen: 'The Russians are spreading false information of a military nature on a vast scale. They expect your agents to demand payment for these false reports from their masters. Source K. considers that ninety per cent of all intelligence reaching the Americans is fake.'

The Org's investigators soon discovered that a group of former Russian officers was passing false information through an ex-SS-Obersturmführer, whom they had introduced into the Org.

Gehlen's strategists soon discovered that the émigré organizations in West Germany were by no means necessarily under the leadership of orthodox anti-bolshevists. In many of them Soviet secret-service stoolpigeons were to be found attempting to penetrate the Gehlen Organization and reporting its Russian informers to Soviet headquarters in Berlin-Karlshorst.

One of Pullach's investigators came to the conclusion that in a certain émigré organization known as 'NTS, people working directly for the Soviet Union are recklessly given cover and support'. In another émigré society, the 'League of the Andreas Flag', an informer detected an ex-Lieutenant-Colonel Solomin of the Soviet Secret Police who, 'when in his cups, would tell stories of his prowess in shooting Russian colonels and generals for attempted desertion to the Germans'. Vigilant though they were, Gehlen's men could never be sure whether they were dealing with figments of the imagination of some harum-scarum intelligence-peddler, or with doctored material fed to them by the Russians.[29]

There was only one way out of this dilemma. The Org had to find agents whom it could send into Russia on its own account – and Gehlen's attention was drawn to a group of émigrés prepared to do exactly this. They were the 11,000 Letts, 4,000 Estonians and 5,000 Lithuanians who had settled in West Germany after the annexation of their countries by Stalin. More than all the other émigrés they were hoping that one day their countries would be liberated and that they could return. The Western powers encouraged them in this day-dreaming, for Washington, London and Paris refused international legal recognition to the Soviet annexation of the Baltic States. Gehlen dispatched his recruiters to the camps occupied by these people. He used primarily German Balts from Riga who presented themselves as spokesmen for the American secret service and spread the story that America would liberate the Baltic States. This crusade, they said, must be planned ahead of time and the USA had formed an organization to prepare for this battle of liberation – by collecting enemy intelligence. For this purpose, the recruiters' argument continued, scouts were required and they must necessarily be Letts, Estonians and Lithuanians with local knowledge. They were to collect military intelligence on the Soviet Baltic coast and join forces with groups of anti-Soviet partisans.

Such an appeal to patriotism was not without its effect, and numerous volunteers presented themselves for this dangerous mission. They were initially taken in charge by officers of the US secret service. These Letts, Estonians and Lithuanians were given an employment contract guaranteeing them $100 per day for every day spent in Soviet territory. On conclusion of their mission they were to receive a special bonus payment of $1,000. The Americans also undertook to care for any who became casualties while on duty; for an agent wounded or incapacitated on duty the contract provided 'after free medical treatment' for a 'payment up to $5,000 depending on capacity for work. Should the agent lose his life $5,000 will be paid to his dependants.'[30]

Agents, who had to speak perfect Russian, were submitted to a test in an American camp in Bavaria; while there they were entitled to weekly pay of 100 marks, free board and lodging and American cigarettes. The programme of the acceptance test provided for: 'Investigation of a colliery by day and night including preparation of a sketch and the avoidance of security guards – all under control of an officer. Later the examinee will be captured by a patrol; he must have a completely watertight story and answers ready. Any sketches or other incriminating articles must be so concealed that they are not detected by the patrol.'

If he passed the test the candidate was flown to Fort Bragg in North Carolina where he was given basic training. Dressed in a frogman's suit he learnt how to swim across a lake at night; he was taught how to enter an airfield undetected in full daylight and how to survive for three days in the woods without food. Pupils then had to march for five days through a wooded area towards a defined objective, spend five days reconnoitring a target and return to base within a further five days. No lifts were allowed.

Training in America for these Baltic spies lasted three months during which time they were paid $125 per week. Finally they were trained for the normal form of secret-service transport – parachuting. The majority of the volunteers were young and at the Fort Bragg airfield their training included somersaulting both forwards and backwards, jumping from a 60-ft tower and finally three jumps from an aircraft at 2,000 ft. They were taught to bury their parachutes on landing and remove all traces of their arrival. Finally these Letts, Estonians and Lithuanians were handed over to the Gehlen Organization in Germany which now became responsible for preparing them for their mission on Soviet territory. This was done in a castle in Bavaria where the Org's Russian experts gave the agents individual instruction on their objectives. One agent, for instance, was told to work his way into a Leningrad shipyard as a mechanic; while still in Bavaria he was given the name of the foreman who would offer him the job; he studied a plan of the yard and soon knew all about its production and capacity. Another agent was directed to a factory near Riga manufacturing aircraft parts. A third was to make his way to Königsberg and report on the extent of the coastal fortifications. A fourth was taught about the organization and leading personalities of the partisan groups operating against the Soviets in the Lithuanian forests.[31]

Meanwhile the Org took its precautions to ensure that the agents could sink unobtrusively into the enemy countryside and operate with some prospect of success. They were fitted with Russian clothing; their 'cover story' was substantiated by Soviet identity papers, work permits, trade-union documents and ration coupons. The Org tailors sewed into each quilted jacket thirty Swiss watches – for bribes or rewards. Considerable sums in roubles were also hidden in the clothing. (A Western secret service helped in their procurement. Since Russians are suspicious of high-denomination notes, agents were only given five- or ten-rouble notes.

Now came the question how the agents were to reach their operational area. There was one way – the sea. The Org had already discovered that it was possible to land men by boat on the Baltic coast but this method was only practicable with the assistance of the British secret service. In 1949 the British Admiralty had instituted a protection service for West German fishing trawlers in the Baltic. For this purpose some of the former German Navy's E-boats had been reactivated; they carried no weapons, had German crews but flew the British flag.

These boats were under command of a man who has become one of the great bogies of East German propaganda – Rear-Admiral Hans-Helmut Klose, born in Rostock in 1916. At the end of the war he had been commanding No 2 Fast Patrol Boat Training Flotilla and had experience of operations against the Russian Navy. Legend credited him with the capacity of knowing where his E-boat was at night merely by sticking his thumb into the 'flooded field' (naval slang for the Baltic). When Gehlen's staff were cudgelling their brains over the question how the Letts, Estonians and Lithuanians whom they had trained for the Russian operation, were to reach their operational areas, their minds turned to the then Lieutenant-Commander Klose and his E-boats. Klose could put the agents ashore and pick them off again when they had completed their mission.[32]

American secret-service officers contacted their British colleagues of the Naval Intelligence Service. The British agreed, on condition that the German boats would occasionally deposit British agents also on the Baltic coast. The E-boats were refitted for their secret mission in Portsmouth and Vegesack – they were equipped with additional tanks, radar and direction-finding gear. Meanwhile Klose journeyed through West Germany hunting out old comrades who had turned into landlubbers. After long talks with their old commanding officer some of them gave up their jobs and packed their bags.

In the dusk two or three men would then board one of the three E-boats. They were Gehlen agents on their way to spy in the Soviet Union. They immediately disappeared below deck. Immediately thereafter the three boats left their moorings and each steered a different course into the open sea. By dawn they were in the Bornholm area and threaded their way individually through the swarm of West German fishing boats heading for the Baltic salmon-fishing grounds. Radio communication from the E-boats was restricted to two-letter signals according to a special code. These were broadcast blind to several monitoring stations without call-sign, answer or acknowledgement.

On reaching the most easterly of the German fishing boats two of the E-boats would stop and the third, carrying the agents, would continue alone towards the Baltic coast, After dark that evening it would be standing off a landing area previously located by special electronic equipment and chosen for its security from the enemy counter-espionage services. There a reception committee would be waiting on shore to assist the agents to disembark safely. The E-boat would creep within about three miles of the shore with muffled engines and then put off a rubber dinghy equipped with an outboard motor and direction-finding gear. Agreed direction-finding signals came from the coast to assist the landing operation. The agents coasted in to land and handed over their dinghy to others waiting to return to Germany.[33]

The method proved successful. One after another groups of agents invaded the Russian Baltic area. On September 30th, 1951 Boleslav Antonovich Petansk (who later defected to the Russians) landed in the area of Uzava with a group of agents, two radio sets, weapons and 80,000 roubles. On October 20th, 1952 Sigurd Kumich, similarly equipped with radio sets and heading another group of agents, made contact with a partisan organization in western Courland; he was to make his way to Riga and there set up an out-station for the Org. Cooperation between Gehlen's agents and anti-communist partisans proved so fruitful that Soviet Latvia's State Security Service reacted nervously.

One of the reasons for this nervousness was the fact that, try as they might, the Russians could not catch Klose's boats. The boat which had carried out the landing in the Uzava area in September had been spotted by observers of the Latvian Soviet Republic's counter-espionage service under Colonel Albert Janovich Balodis. The Russian Navy had immediately been alerted and two destroyers, six frigates and eight patrol boats had set out to chase the mysterious E-boat. It was sighted by the pursuers on the high seas between the Latvian coast and the island of Gotland. The Russians manned their weapons; the boat was clearly visible.[34]

But they could not catch it. The distance between the fugitive and its pursuers continued to increase and shortly thereafter the little ship had disappeared – thanks to its superior speed. A few days later at a reception in Moscow a Russian diplomat complained to the British Naval Attaché that it was not very friendly for unknown E-boats to operate inside Soviet territorial waters; the Soviet Union would no longer tolerate this. The Attaché replied that it was equally unusual for Soviet ships to carry out firing exercises against certain patrol boats; the British Admiralty would no longer tolerate that.

For a long time the Russian Navy puzzled over its failure to catch this boat. Only later did it learn the reason; the E-boat was unarmed; its automatic guns and torpedo tubes had been dismantled. Laden with torpedoes, guns and ammunition the Russian boats could not keep up with it. At first the Russians thought that it was always the same E-boat which they chased. They soon realized, however, that there were three of these swift boats operating in the Baltic.

Since the E-boats could not be caught, the Latvian counter-espionage service turned its attention to Gehlen's groups of agents. Colonel Balodis of the Latvian State Security Service adopted a wartime strata-gem. He commissioned Budris, a secret police officer, to form a group of ostensibly anti-communist partisans to try and establish contact with the genuine partisans. In the woods of Courland a deadly cat-and-mouse game began between the agents and their pursuers.[35]

The Org, however, continued to infiltrate its agents into the Baltic States. The E-boats moved their landing areas southwards where they were secure from the Budris group and fresh agents set to work in southern Courland and in Poland. Information from the Baltic came in so well that Gehlen was inspired to open a second clandestine sea line. In 1953 the Org reached agreement with the Americans for the landing of agents in the Crimea.

Two American patrol boats were shipped from West Germany to the Turkish Black Sea coast, where their German crews were accommo-dated in a sealed-off area. Once more patrol boats set off carrying agents and once more Gehlen's informers were making their way into Soviet territory. The Black Sea operation had been in progress for over three months when suddenly the trap snapped shut on Gehlen's agents in the Baltic. One of the E-boats had landed agents on the coast of Poland but the Polish counter-espionage service had captured them all. Presumably there was treachery afoot.

Meanwhile Budris had succeeded in penetrating the Latvian partisan groups and part of the resistance organization was already at the beck and call of the Russian secret service. In 1954 Budris even attempted to establish radio contact with the agents' headquarters and so, in 1955, the Org called the operation off. Hans-Helmut Klose left his secret-service trade and returned whence he had come – to the Navy; he is today Rear-Admiral Commanding German Naval Forces in the North Sea. Reinhard Gehlen, however, had to look for new infiltration routes for his intelligence-gathering operation in the Soviet Union.[36]

*   *   *

Initially he had no alternative but to try the old methods once more. He therefore turned to the more reliable among the anti-communist émigrés in the hope that they might assist him to penetrate the Soviet Union. He first formed a circuit of agents along the Danube extending into Rumania; from there he hoped to find some entry into Russia. An organizer, reporting on a new and important informer, said this: 'He is personally well acquainted with one of the protagonists of the Rumanian National Committee (the government-in-exile) who has agents among the Danube merchant seamen; he is accordingly in a position to provide intelligence on the Danube basin, the course of the Danube to its mouth and Reni, perhaps also on Transylvania.'

Gehlen exploited every opportunity offered him by the Russian émigrés. He even contacted émigré leaders living in other countries, provided they were considered to carry enough weight. Even the briefest of 'tips' was enough – the following for example: 'Ref: Istomin, Konstantin Evseyevich – ex-Colonel, 11bis. Av. Colonel Bonnet, Paris 16, Tel: AUT 4478. Has quite remarkable contacts with highly-placed French and British personalities; is also in touch with their intelligence services to whom he passes information on Russian émigrés resident in France. Very anti-communist in his views.'[37]

Many of the Russian émigré organizations were prepared to undertake missions into the Soviet Union for the Gehlen Organization. In particular, with Gehlen's help, the nationalist 'NTS' dispatched parachutists who were to make their way as far as Moscow; most of them, however, were discovered and arrested by the Soviet counter-espionage authorities. 'ZOPE' [Zentralvereinigung politischer Emigranten aus der UdSSR – Central Association of Political Emigrés from the USSR] located in Munich thought up another method of extracting intelligence from Russia. One of the Org's agencies reported: 'Ref: Activities of ZOPE – Munich. Source: Tamara. Above-mentioned source (known to me for years as confirmed anti-communist) appeared on August 1st of this year and asked for my assistance in the following matter: ZOPE proposed to give certain German students with a smattering of Russian the opportunity of visiting the Soviet Union (Moscow and possibly other university cities). Travelling expenses, accommodation and pocket money would be paid. The purpose would be to interest the students in problems and questions concerning the youth, student society, the churches and the literary elite in the Soviet Union. Ten or more persons might apply for this trip and so there would be a possibility of selecting particularly suitable students. The students in question would be expected to make friends with suitable persons in the Soviet Union who might become permanent pen-friends. Naturally neither the German students nor the Soviet citizens concerned would know that ZOPE was behind this project; a "Press Information Service" would be given as cover.'

Gehlen's people, of course, would have nothing to do with such hare-brained schemes, particularly since the Org considered that ZOPE was showing 'signs of degeneration'.

IN PURSUIT OF 'ENEMIES OF THE STATE'

Lieutenant-Colonel Hermann Baun, the first head of the Gehlen Organization's Acquisition Service, was in revolt against his Chief. As an honest intelligence officer the Org's next task, outlined to him by Gehlen, shocked him. He had never imagined that the new German secret service would be called upon for work of this sort. In his distress he confided to a friend: 'Gehlen is becoming megalomaniac. He actually wants to play Gestapo for the Americans. We won't go along with that.'

Gehlen had told Baun that the Org now had to set up a State Protection organization to track down communist infiltrators and break up the circuits of red agents. It was not enough, Gehlen had argued, merely to observe the enemy in his own country; he must be prevented from gaining a foothold in West Germany. Gehlen, the dogmatic anti-bolshevist, was convinced that the aim of the Soviet Union was to bolshevize Central and Western Europe, either by attack from without or by seizure of power from within using *Putsch* methods.

To his critics, moreover, Gehlen could reply that his American masters wanted him to undertake such counter-espionage work. The initiative for the formation of the counter-espionage group had in fact come from Washington. At the height of the Greek civil war in the summer of 1947 Gehlen's US liaison officers had urged the Org to search for communist agents in the American occupation zone and to keep under observation people suspected of communist leanings. Gehlen's closest associates, however, had warned their Chief against trespassing into the internal political field.[1]

Baun was the spokesman for those who did not like the idea of the Org sleuthing for the Americans. He told Gehlen flatly that it could not be the task of a German intelligence service to hand German nationals over to the American authorities.

In a last-minute effort to dissuade Gehlen from his plan Baun proposed that, instead of setting up a politically questionable state-security service, the existing organization, a section of the Org known as IIIf, be expanded; the enemy in West Germany, he said, could equally well be dealt with by the traditional counter-espionage method, infiltration of agents into the enemy intelligence service. If they or 'converted' enemy agents pointed out who the Eastern spies operating in West Germany were, then these people could be reported to the US counter-espionage authorities; the Americans themselves could then arrest the spies. Baun concluded: 'In secret intelligence work only counter-intelligence is productive of success.'[2] A few weeks later Baun was able to demonstrate how effective IIIf could be in paralysing the enemy's espionage.

On March 5th, 1948, a nineteen-year-old Czech girl named Bozena Hajek, a student of philosophy, registered in the refugee camp at Regensburg. She said that she had fled from Prague and wished to emigrate to America. She had to complete a questionnaire (No 3488) including a list of all her relatives. As with all completed questionnaires from refugees, Bozena Hajek's personal details were forwarded to Gehlen's Org. As a matter of routine the documentation section checked whether any of the relatives named appeared in the Org's card-index. Bozena had recorded that her brother-in-law was named Vojtech Jerabek and on his card Gehlen's archivists found the following: 'Jerabek, Vojtech: Captain on the staff of the Czechoslovak Army. Together with Captain Ottokar Fejfar has been running the Czech military secret service in Karlsbad since June 1st, 1947. Informers report that the operations of Czech agents in West Germany are directed from this office. J. is married to Slavka, née Hajek.' The Org at first suspected that Captain Jerabek was trying to send his sister-in-law Bozena to work as a Czech agent in the USA. Inquiries of informers in Prague, however, showed that she had in fact left Czechoslovakia for political reasons. The Org's Section IIIf was tempted by this news to try, via Bozena Hajek, to establish contact with her brother-in-law in the Czech secret service and recruit him for their own counter-espionage work.[3]

The Operations Desk of the Acquisition Department made available to IIIf a man who was ideally suited to make a confidential approach to Bozena Hajek – a good-looking Czech with charm. His code-name was 'Ondrej'. In the Regensburg camp Ondrej quickly gained the confidence and affection of the girl and he soon found out that, when visiting his relatives in Prague, Jerabek had frequently complained about the communist regime. Ondrej was thereupon ordered to go to Prague with messages to her parents from Bozena; then he was to establish contact with Jerabek, being vouched for by the latter's relatives in Prague. On

August 4th the head of IIIf dictated a 'Submission to the Chief': 'Ondrej departed 1700 hrs. Mission: to recruit Captain Vojtech Jerabek for the Org.' At the head of the report Gehlen wrote the operation's code-name: 'Operation Bohemia'.

Two-and-a-half months later, on October 22nd at 9.32 PM, Ondrej went up to a black Tatra car in front of Karlsbad Station. 'Do you want to go into town?' the driver asked. Ondrej replied: 'No, towards Joachimsthal.' The driver then said: 'Get in the back.' After this regulation exchange of passwords, which had been relayed to Ondrej in a letter from Bozena Hajek's parents, the two left Karlsbad – on the back seat Ondrej of the Gehlen Org, at the wheel Captain Jerabek of the Czech military secret service.

Jerabek stopped on a wooded track near Karlsbad. 'My father-in-law has confidence in you,' he told his passenger. 'It is dangerous to have confidence these days. What do you want from me and what have you to offer?' Ondrej replied: 'We want information from you about the organization and activities of the Czechoslovak intelligence service, in particular about the activities of agents in West Germany.' 'And what reward would you propose for that?' Jerabek asked. 'We would pay you well and in dollars,' Ondrej replied. 'And what would I do with dollars in Czechoslovakia?' Jerabek asked. Ondrej replied: 'The money would be a great help to you in Germany.' 'But I first have to get there,' Jerabek said. 'That too can be arranged,' was Ondrej's reply.[4]

After this exchange Jerabek took Ondrej back to Karlsbad Station telling him to wait in Prague for an answer. The next day Gehlen's informer, using invisible ink, wrote his report for IIIf in Pullach. He recorded his conversation with Jerabek word for word; he even reported the number of cigarettes Jerabek had smoked. Ondrej hid his letter in a 'post-box' under a bench; some unknown courier took it on its way to Munich.

At the same time another of the Org's informers in Prague reported that the communist regime was preparing a purge of the officer corps. It was not possible to say, however, whether this implied danger for Jerabek. Nevertheless IIIf alerted Ondrej; he was to tell Jerabek that he was on the Reds' shooting list.

This warning decided Jerabek. During the night November 8th/9th, 1948 Ondrej conducted him across the frontier into Bavaria. Jerabek did not come alone; he brought with him Captain Fejfar, who worked with him, and Major Tyr of the Prague Defence Ministry.

In Bavaria officers of the American CIC took over the fugitives and brought them to their local office in Nuremberg. There Fejfar and Tyr handed over to the Americans their secret-service offerings – lists of Czechoslovak agents in West Germany and the key to the code used by the Prague secret service for its radio traffic. A few days later the CIC arrested eighteen agents of the Czechoslovak intelligence service and a further twenty-eight persons with whom they had been in contact were placed under surveillance. Jaromir Koska, the star Czech agent, was sentenced to twenty years' hard labour by an American military court.[5]

For the Gehlen Org 'Operation Bohemia' was its first great counter-espionage success. Prague's military intelligence service took two years to recover from this blow. The Czechs were still trying to replace their arrested agents when the Org uncovered another network – a spy-ring run by the Yugoslav secret service.

This time the clue was provided by the French. On August 27th, 1949, an informer reported to Pullach: 'In April 1949 a Yugoslav espionage circuit was discovered by the French Sûreté in Friedrichshafen. Among others arrested (on April 9th) was a Yugoslav named Levec who had been acting as an agent of the Yugoslav intelligence service in the French occupation zone of Germany since 1947. On the subject of the US Zone Levec stated the following: "Head of the Yugoslav intelligence service in Germany is a certain Topic, alias Mimara, a museum custodian by profession. He is a member of the Yugoslav Restitution and Reparations Commission in the US Zone. In 1947 T. was expelled from Säckingen by the French for currency offences; he went first to Berlin and thence to Frankfurt am Main; he is now in Munich." '

The informer also had the names of further agents and organizers of Belgrade's secret service – for instance, Lieutenant Doran, a member of the Yugoslav Mission in Frankfurt, Blagojevic, an agent living in Stuttgart ('carries out assignments for the Yugoslav Mission in Baden-Baden'), Lieutenant-Colonel Podkonjak of the Berlin office of the Yugoslav intelligence service, Major Franjo Ozbolt, secret-service representative in the Yugoslav Liaison Mission in Baden-Baden and Captain Dusan Padjan, Ozbolt's aide. The Yugoslav secret service's German agents also came into the Org's ken, for instance General K. (ex-Luftwaffe) on whom an informer reported: 'In January 1949 K. was using the cover-name "Miller" and was with the Yugoslav Liaison Mission (Major Ozbolt) in Baden-Baden; he dictated to S.H., a short-hand-typist, a report on the formation of a modern air force.'

For six months Gehlen's agents kept the Yugoslavs under observation; everyone they contacted was shadowed. Then the Org handed to their US liaison officers in Pullach the results of their investigations.

The Americans expelled the Yugoslavs. The Belgrade secret service had to organize a new circuit of agents.[6]

Over and over again Baun referred to such counter-espionage successes as these when emphasizing to Gehlen his worries about the formation of an internal German counter-espionage organization. But his master did not listen to Baun. On the contrary – the successes of his own counter-espionage led Gehlen to claim that his was the only agency which could guarantee the internal security of West Germany. In his eyes the East's spies constituted a major threat to the existence of a German democracy. But he also maintained that the East's political sympathizers, who were ready listeners when communist agents and agitators attacked the Western way of life, were equally menacing.

In numerous talks with his staff Gehlen would conjure up the vision of the 'Bolshevik Trojan horses undermining West Germany in preparation for an assault by the Russians or a communist seizure of power by subversive means'. Gehlen felt himself called upon to protect the rump left to his country between the Elbe and the Rhine from subversion and upheaval. The result was a widespread system of spying in which many of the Org's staff became prominent as anti-communist witch-hunters. The West German secret service turned into an internal German fighting force in the cold war.

Gehlen was well aware that after its experiences with the Gestapo and in the East with the SSD, German public opinion was extremely sensitive to any snooping or spying. In his memoirs, therefore, he denies that the West German secret service ever engaged in internal intelligence activities while under his leadership, at least not until the formation of the BfV (Internal Security Office) in 1950. He says: 'I am convinced that, while I was in office, not one single message giving the results of internal political intelligence operations was ever sent to Bonn' and later: 'Equally we never kept any German politician under surveillance.' The facts tell a different story.

Once more a German secret service became entangled in the minefield of internal policy and propaganda. Nicolai, with his internal intelligence service, had initially merely been collecting intelligence about external enemies on German soil but he had turned into the persecutor of the internal opponent; so now, although initially it had had no other purpose than to guard against agents of the communist powers, Gehlen's internal intelligence system degenerated into one for political snooping.

The first targets for the internal intelligence system were the numerous Soviet agents who had infiltrated the West German refugee camps after the end of the war in order to persuade Russian émigrés to return to the USSR and hamper recruitment by Western secret services of agents with local knowledge for their operations in Russia. A swarm of Org informers went out to put these red emissaries out of business. Detailed observation of the refugee camps and émigré circles soon enabled Gehlen's men to recognize their enemy.

One informer reported, for example: 'In my view K. is a member of the circuit of Soviet agents here; his job is to canvass people for a return to the Soviet Union; his area of activity is the main railway station.' And another – 'K. has been active as a Soviet agent in Munich since 1948; previously he was in Lübeck, Hamburg and Schleissheim Camp (near Munich). K. has two identity cards in the name of Kolin – stateless. In Munich his contact in the Soviet Military Mission was a certain Wernik, who in turn was subordinate to Ssonin (Colonel) in Frankfurt.' And a third: 'Gudrun S. has long been suspected of acting for Soviet intelligence. At one time, allegedly on behalf of the Soviets, she had a liaison with Georg H., the musician. Source is firmly convinced that she has returned to West Germany on some mission for the Russians.'[7]

The Org's investigators followed up every trail which seemed likely to lead them to Soviet agents. A certain Irene Hellwig in Fellbach near Stuttgart, for instance, was suspected of being the sister of the Russian Marshal Sokolovsky; a certain Nina Kikodze was 'notorious for sowing dissension and hatred among Georgian émigrés'. Any suspicious person was registered in the Org's card-index.[8]

Later the Org's counter-espionage work was extended to include German communists. In April 1950 one of the CIC's lists of informers disappeared and was discovered in the headquarters of the Bavarian Communist Party. The Americans alerted the Org which soon found out how the list had got into the hands of the communists. From then on the German Communist Party and its alleged underground organizations were kept under sharper surveillance.[9]

Soon Gehlen was no longer satisfied merely to shadow Soviet agents and West German communists. The field of action for the Org's agents became wider and wider; to communists were added left-wing pacifists, national-conservative visionaries, neutralists and Russo-romanticists. All these were equally suspect to the Org since they weakened what was known in Pullach (and not only in Pullach) as the anti-bolshevist defensive front. As the circle of those to be kept under observation expanded, however, Gehlen became increasingly determined to take into his service the ex-functionaries of the Nazi police machine. Many of the ex-Gestapo and SD surveillance experts seemed to the non-political

Gehlen to have the experience required to assist his hunt for enemies of the state.

Later, through his official biographer, Jürgen Thorwald, Gehlen spread the story that 'on principle' he had 'rejected' any SS man; in fact, however, from the summer of 1950 he accepted numerous recruits from the ruins of the old SS empire.[10] Within the Org he justified his acceptance of these ex-SS men by arguing that he had had to prevent them from resuming their activity on behalf of the Eastern Secret services; they were also particularly suitable, he said, to undermine the East German State Security Service, which was largely manned by ex-SS men.

Initially Gehlen did actually believe that he could dispense with the assistance of ex-members of the RSHA. Although he had worked with the SD on many occasions during the war, he had always kept his distance from it. As head of FHO he had been quite prepared to make use of the RSHA but he would allow it no influence in his secret-service army. After 1945 Gehlen avoided almost all contact with Himmler's infamous disciples. Five years later, however, when he was once more occupied with Russian intelligence, applications came in from ex-RSHA experts. Their *curricula vitae*, which reached Gehlen among their recruiting papers, read like recommendations from some competitor in the secret-service trade.

Desk C2 in Section VI of the RSHA had been responsible for 'Operation Zeppelin' (see pp. 38–9 above); this had dispatched members of all Soviet nationalities behind the Russian lines to blow up bridges, distribute subversive propaganda and collect intelligence. They had gone off the air as the Soviet forces advanced deeper into Germany and by the end of the war there was complete wireless silence in Operation Zeppelin. Here they were, however, suddenly coming to life again – on the employment application forms reaching Gehlen. There was, for instance, a group named 'Wilhelm' in the forests of Vologda, Jaroslav and Tybinsk; there was 'Operation Theodor' in the Tambov-Voronezh area, 'Operation Josef' in Moscow and in Georgia 'Operation Mainz' with groups in Tiflis, Telavi, Batum and Kutais.[11]

What the Knights of the Death's Head could offer to Gehlen all sounded most promising. One memorandum read: 'Despite all their shortcomings a considerable number of Zeppelin groups were functioning up to the last and there is every reason to think that they are still active today in many places, particularly in the Baltic States, the Caucasus and the forests of Vologda.' One of Operation Zeppelin's operations officers even reported an intelligence circuit still completely intact: 'A few years ago an ex-instructor of Georgian activists under Operation Zeppelin, a man whom I know well personally, received news from his informer in Istanbul that contact with Dr X. can be re-established via Turkey, also with Group Y. which has settled in the north-western part of Georgia. He is in possession of the passwords agreed with Dr X and Group Y.'

These groups in far-off Russia, the SS men implied, were only awaiting a signal from Germany in order to resume their activity. One ex-SS-Sturmbannführer reported that the final radio instructions sent to them had been: 'War against the Soviets will be continued in the foreseeable future. Groups will be called up at the right moment. Until then intelligence activity should cease but contact between groups should be maintained as far as possible.' For the ex-SS men 'war against the Soviets' was a foregone conclusion and so in their memoranda they submitted to Gehlen that: 'In the event of future hostilities timely preparation of an operation on the lines of Operation Zeppelin could render decisive assistance to military operations.' Clearly the implication was that only ex-members of the RSHA could initiate these preparations in time.[12]

Gehlen did not reject these offers. They were all the more attractive in that the applicants could promise him some comprehensive archives on Russia – the personnel card-index, library and maps of the SS 'Wannsee Institute' in Berlin where Russian experts had analysed every book, newspaper and periodical from the Soviet Union. The ex-SS men ordered up picks, spades and shovels. They then dug in the gardens of Nos 56–58 Grosse Wannsee, where the RSHA research institute had once been located. But they were out of luck; they could only produce one or two empty and decaying boxes. The Russian secret service had discovered the documents in 1945, some in the garden of the Wannsee Institute but most of them in the Austrian castle of Plankenwarth, where the material had been evacuated towards the end of the war.[13]

These fruitless earth-moving operations in Wannsee only reinforced Gehlen in his determination to employ ex-members of the RSHA. The Russians could only have learnt that the boxes were buried in the garden from SS functionaries who knew what they were talking about. Gehlen's conclusion was that he must bring as many as possible of these knowledgeable SS secrecy experts under his own control.

The fact that another of the SS prognostications proved untrue did not alter this decision: 'Wilhelm', 'Theodor', 'Josef' and 'Mainz' did not respond. All the Operation Zeppelin groups which the RSHA strategists had reported to Gehlen as ready for action, proved to be corpses; not a

single radio call-sign received an answer. The men of the RSHA, therefore, were of no use for Russian intelligence but for the hurried expansion of an internal German counter-espionage service they seemed to
Gehlen highly suitable. He needed the pen-pushers of the Gestapo and
SD for a task for which they were only too well equipped – the pursuit
of 'enemies of the State'. The decision on who was to be regarded as a
foe of Western democracy was all too frequently taken by survivors of
Hitler Germany's police machine.

Gehlen threw the Org's doors wide open to ex-Gestapo and SD men
and many an illustrious figure from Nazism's engine of domination came
through them. They included SS-Oberführer [Colonel] Willi Krichbaum, a friend of Reinhard Heydrich, the Gestapo's 'Frontier Inspector
South-east' and one of the most savage opponents of the anti-Hitler
military resistance when head of the Secret Field Police; others were
SS-Sturmbannführer [Major] Fritz Schmidt, formerly head of the Gestapo office in Kiel, and SS-Sturmbannführer Dr Emil Augsburg of the
Wannsee Institute, one of the SD's most influential Eastern ideol-
ogists.[14]

Gehlen had some use for all of them. The former SS-Hauptsturmführer [Captain] Caspar took Sub-Agency 1600; the former
Gestapo Inspector Max Staudinger joined the Pullach headquarters; ex-
SS-Hauptsturmführer Franz Göring headed an Org agency known as
'Ton'; the Org's agencies in Austria were headed by ex-SS-Sturmbannführer Josef Adolf Urban, formerly head of the SD office in Budapest, and Dr Bruno Kauschen of Desk C2 in Section VI of the RSHA. A
place was even found for the egregious SS-Obersturmführer [Lieuten-
ant] Hans Sommer; in the autumn of 1941 he had planned – behind the
Wehrmacht's back – to blow up the Paris synagogues in order to incite
the French to anti-Jewish measures, but his manoeuvres had been so
maladroit that the Wehrmacht had expelled him from France. Sommer
became head of District Agency North.[15]

In 1963, as a result of the treason trial of the ex-SS man Heinz Felfe,
Gehlen's BND was labelled as being far too ready to employ ex-
members of the 'Order of the Death's Head'. State Secretary Globke
played the matter down, saying that SS men accounted for less than
one per cent of BND personnel. Conservative members of the BND,
however, spoke of five per cent; other observers estimate the figure of
voluntary and full-time ex-members of the RSHA, the Gestapo and the
SS 'Front-line Reconnaissance Detachments' who at some time worked
in the Org and in the BND even higher. Gehlen himself says: 'Their
numbers were small.' The fact remains, however, that after the Felfe

trial a Munich lawyer was fully employed dealing with nothing but claims for compensation against Pullach by ex-SS men who had been prematurely retired. For Gehlen such statements originate from the 'fairy-tale empire'.

The ex-disciples of the Order of the Death's Head brought into the Org a crusading mentality which turned it into the spearhead of an anti-communist witch-hunt. They had had instilled into them the anti-Slav 'sub-human' theories of the SS and so these former SD men were obsessed with an undiscriminating anti-communism compounded by rancour over their defeat in 1945 together with a residue of the crazy racial notions of the SS. These ex-SD and ex-Gestapo members of the Org frequently gave way to that hatred of all things Russian which had been instrumental in bringing the Third Reich to its downfall.

Criticism of Hitler's exploitation policy in occupied Russia was much frowned upon in these circles. The author of an internal memorandum entitled 'The Russian Emigrés' said complacently: 'Irrespective of whether Germany will be a good or bad ally in a fight for the liberation of Russia, from the purely military point of view every enemy of the Soviet Union will be in the same situation, should it come to conflict.' For these members of the Org anyone who had once worked with them in some SS agency was considered reliable. A report on the ex-SD intelligence officer Alarich Bross stated that he was 'absolutely reliable from the political point of view' and another ex-SD man, Hans Brachmüller, was stated to be 'politically completely impeccable'.[16]

Rigid anti-communism and a reluctance to rethink the old-established dogmas were in fact regarded with indulgence by many of the original members of the Org, whose thinking differed little from that of the ex-SS functionaries. The Org, after all, had chosen as its Head of Personnel Hans Schröder, a graduate of the Nazi Leadership School in Bernau, head of the Nazi Party organization in a foreign country, and then a Section Head under Ribbentrop; it had deliberately refused (in Walde's words) 'to allow a machine which had been salvaged from the general bankruptcy adequate time to reflect on this bankruptcy'. The Org could therefore hardly object if the ex-SS men continued in their old ways. Some of the books written by Lieutenant-Colonel (retd) Reile, one of Pullach's authorities on counter-espionage, give the impression that the Org had become a nest of anti-democratic reactionaries. He regarded the sentiments currently expressed about Nazism merely as a 'flood of lying propaganda in which we are being submerged'.[17]

In this atmosphere, it was only too easy for the view to gain ground

Reinhard Gehlen: front cover of *Der Spiegel* in September 1954

Left: Lieutenant-Colonel Walter Nicolai, Head of IIIb, the military secret service in World War I. *Right:* Admiral Wilhelm Canaris, Head of the military secret service in World War II

Reinhard Gehlen as Head of FHO in Army Headquarters, Mayerbach Camp near Zossen, early 1945

Left: SS-Brigadeführer Walter Schellenberg and SS-Obersturmbannführer Otto Skorzeny, Commander of the SS Special Service Troops. *Right:* General Andrei Vlassov, captured by the Germans in 1942 and Gehlen's ally in the fight against the Soviets

Gehlen at a 'social evening' in the FHO mess

Left: Major-General Lowell W. Rooks, Head of the Anglo-American Control Commission in Flensburg. *Right:* Lieutenant-Colonel Scheibe of Gehlen's staff who handed the first FHO files to the US Army in May 1945

Left: Lieutenant-Colonel Hermann Baun who ran Gehlen's intelligence service during the war. *Right:* Lieutenant-Colonel Heinz Herre who, together with Gehlen, negotiated the agreement between the German intelligence experts and the War Department

The 'Elendsalm' hut near Lake Spitzing in Upper Bavaria where Gehlen hid in 1945

German soldiers returning from captivity in Russia in the spring of 1949

The American special camp at Oberusel near Frankfurt, the first headquarters of the Gehlen Organisation

Kransberg Castle in the Taunus, one of the first out-stations of the Gehlen Organisation

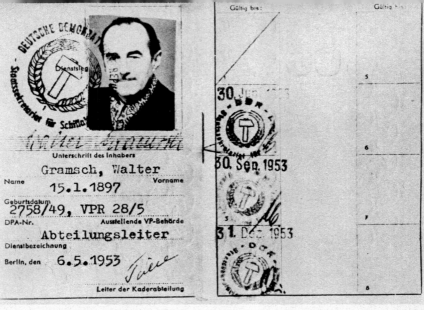

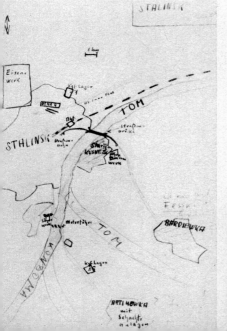

Identity card of Walter Gramsch, head of the 'Shipping and Ports' section in the East German Ministry of Shipping

Left: Sketch of the Soviet town of Stalinsk drawn for the Gehlen Organisation by a released prisoner-of-war. *Right:* East German Lieutenant-Colonel Siegfried Dombrowski, one of Gehlen's star agents from 1956 to 1958

Hermann Kastner, Deputy Prime Minister of East Germany and Chairman of the Liberal-Democratic Party

One of the rare post-war photographs of Gehlen – taken in Hannover in 1958

The Soviet-American zonal boundary in Austria, one of Gehlen's most important areas of operations until 1955

East German Ministry of State Security in Berlin-Lichtenberg

Russian torpedo-boats used against the West German spy boats in the Baltic in 1950–55

The *Empress of Canada* sabotaged in 1953 by Wollweber

Leaders of the Nazi Police and Secret Service Organisation: Reinhard Heydrich *(third from right)*, Head of the RSHA; Heinrich Müller *(fourth from left)* Head of the Gestapo; Walter Schellenberg *(second from left)* Head of the SD

A German ex-E boat used to land Gehlen's agents on the Baltic coast

Gehlen's secret-service
rivals in West Germany:
(above) Graf von Schwerin
(Security);
(right) Otto John
(Internal Security)

Left: Konrad Adenauer, the Federal Chancellor, with State Secretary Hans Globke, Gehlen's superior. *Right:* Hans Joachim Geyer, a Gehlen agent 'converted' by the East German security services, at a press conference in East Berlin in 1953

Gehlen's East German opponents: Wilhelm Zaisser, Minister of State Security *(second from left)* and his deputy, Erich Mielke *(centre)*; Otto Grotewohl, Minister-President *(left)*; Wilhelm Pieck *(right)*, President, handing Zaisser his letter of appointment in February 1950

Left: Wolfgang Lotz, the Israeli agent trained by the BND, who operated in Cairo from 1961 to 1965. *Right:* Brigadier-General Hans Heinrich Worgitzky, Vice-President of the BND from 1957 to 1967

Left: Gerhard Bauch, the BND's Cairo representative, 'blown' by the Lotz affair in 1965. *Right:* Heinz Felfe, the Russian spy, in SS uniform in 1940

Left: Gerhard Wessel, as Brigadier-General in autumn 1963, Gehlen's successor as President of the BND from May 1968. *Right:* Gehlen sailing with his daughter

Left: Horst Ehmke, Minister in the Federal Chancellery and responsible for the BND since 1969. *Right:* Dieter Blötz, Vice-President of the BND since May 1970

The offices of the President and Vice-President of the BND

Inside Pullach Camp

that the Org had an historic mission – to protect West Germany from communists and left-wing extremists. Anyone suspected of opposition to the State or to society soon found the Org's men on his heels. Investigators had no compunction in reporting a man to Pullach on the slightest suspicion. Even a visit to relatives in East Germany was enough to attach a taint of espionage to a West German in Gehlen's eyes.

A source named 'Short', for instance, suspected an ex-Lieutenant who had been a prisoner of war in Russia of being an agent because he occasionally travelled to East Germany. The man had been born in Dresden in 1918. Short reported to Pullach: 'During his convalescence in T. he travelled to Dresden on several occasions to see his parents; on return he always had large sums of money, although in the hospital he was only paid pocket money. He has a fiancée, daughter of a large hotel-owner in S. He is reputed to be suspected as an agent.' The report led to detailed investigations, carried out by ex-SS members of the Org. Not only the ex-Lieutenant but also his fiancée and her father were kept under surveillance for weeks. Spies of the Org infested the hotel in order to detect any possible meetings of agents.

The results of all this observation did not justify the effort involved. There were no meetings of Eastern agents in the hotel nor were the main suspects working for a communist secret service. The 'sums of money' which had made the investigator suspicious were the rewards, not of conspiratorial, but of business activity. The ex-Lieutenant was in West Berlin selling china and silver from his parents' house. Even with this explanation, however, the 'case' was not closed. It is still on record today – in the card-index of a secret-service headquarters in Pullach, for anyone who has ever been registered by the Org remains on the list – and this still applies to the BND, the Org's successor.

The ease with which an ordinary citizen could find himself registered on the secret service's card-index is illustrated by the case of 'E.S.' and his wife. On December 4th, 1962, one of Gehlen's men reported on the couple: 'Ref: E.S., Munich 13. The above-named S. (according to the telephone directory) carries on a wholesale cosmetics business in his flat; he is listed in the business register. According to the concierge he is married to a Czech; there are no children but a student is said to live in the flat. All are most peculiar people; they speak to none of the other inmates but keep themselves completely to themselves. S. has very many visitors but it does not seem that business visits are involved since no parcels are taken into or out of the flat. The concierge suspects that some underhand business is going on in the flat.' The gossip of a concierge, passed on by an informer, was enough to cause Pullach to investigate more closely. A female agent, pretending to be a 'dealer in cosmetics', accordingly visited the firm of S. and 'was received by Frau S.'. The report on their conversation reads as follows: 'The woman said that she had come from the Sudetenland to Germany before the war to live with her aunt. To my question whether she was a Sudeten German she replied: "I suppose so." The woman is about forty-eight years of age, blowsy and speaks with a Slav accent. Frau S. gave the impression of being very nervous; her flow of speech was almost continuous, perhaps to conceal her nervousness.' E.S. and his wife were accordingly registered in Pullach's card-index of suspects.[18]

Gehlen's investigators left no stone unturned to uncover the 'Trojan horses of bolshevism' in West Germany. Denunciation and speculation were the order of the day. Any contact with relatives in East Germany immediately aroused the suspicion of the sleuths and set them moving. An informer's report on a woman, 'M.I.', living in Munich read as follows: 'Frau M.I. has private means; her son H. is attending the Technical High School here and is said (despite his age!) to have a very good high-level post in a business here. About two months ago the family visited the other brother, who lives in the Eastern Zone; they stayed there about a fortnight. The other son is allegedly a factory owner (!?) and very well-to-do. On their return to the Federal Republic the family bought themselves a new Ford Taunus 17M. The family lives an extremely secluded life, associates with no one and avoids talking to other inmates of the block. The son who lives here, however, did once say to one of the younger inmates that he would like to study but unfortunately had not matriculated. The mother, on the other hand, told one of her neighbours (the only one to whom she speaks) that her son was studying at the Technical High School and at the same time had a leading position in a business here.'[19]

A single sentence from one of the Org's spies was often enough to label someone as a communist. On February 12th, 1960, an informer reported from the Interpreter Institute in Heidelberg: 'To judge from her behaviour and talk the Secretary of this school (Adenauer's interpreter in Moscow) is one-hundred-per-cent communist.'[20]

Quite unabashed, one informer reported to headquarters that his 'Source P.' had been opening the letters of a Russian émigré in Munich: 'When asked by source why she received so much mail, she replied that these letters were in answer to her advertisement about a room. Exercising the necessary caution, source opened one of these numerous letters (none were registered); it gave no indication of sender but he found inside 200 marks in twenty-mark notes and a completely meaningless letter, something like "Struggle on and don't give up." Source then resealed the letter and handed it to the addressee. He asks, however, to be told of a method of opening letters unobtrusively since in this case he considers further observation to be most necessary.' The Org's headquarters directed that the woman should be kept under observation. The directing officer also instructed his informer that letters should be steamed and then opened by running a pencil under the strip of adhesive. It is difficult to see what reason the Org had for thinking that this Russian woman was involved in secret-service activities since Source P. had described her as follows: 'She is paralysed in both legs, uses crutches or an invalid carriage when on the street.'[21]

A Russian woman receiving money in envelopes, a family visiting their son in East Germany, an interpreter's behaviour and talk – such reports from the internal German counter-espionage service show that the Gehlen Org's potential anti-communist complex was fast turning into a well-nigh ludicrous 'enemy of the state' psychosis. If the professional purveyors of suspicion thought anyone to be questionable, they were entered in their card-index. It soon included not only persons suspected of espionage, but a variegated collection of communists, neutralists and East-West 'bridge-builders'.

Gehlen's attention was drawn to this latter group of people during the summer of the Korean war, when the East-West cold war threatened to develop into a hot war. At this time Gehlen conjectured that Stalin would take advantage of the US commitment in Asia in order to strike in Europe. He accordingly gave orders for 'unreliable elements' in West Germany to be discovered and listed so that the police might take them into preventive custody in the event of emergency.

In Hamburg, for instance, Gehlen's investigators searched for communists among the dockyard labourers. The gentlemen concerned knew the Elbe waterfront well, for they had all spied in Hamburg before 1945 when they had been members of the SD office there. In one yard the storekeeper noted each evening the names of workers who seemed to him suspicious, and what they had said to each other. The reports and the lists went to one of the Org's out-stations manned exclusively by ex-Gestapo and ex-SD men. In Hannover the sleuths placed on their black lists, among other people, the journalists of *Der Spiegel*. The editor, Rudolf Augstein, was labelled as a 'dangerous element' (he was known in the Org as 'red Rudi').[22]

The Org's informers could count upon large-scale assistance from officialdom, as the following report shows: 'Together with a Criminal Police official, whom I know well, we today searched through the card-index of the Residents Registration Office, looking for K., but . . . unhappily without result. We found only a "G.K." who had moved to Swabia some time ago. The name was equally nowhere to be found in the card-index of the Aliens Office which I also searched with an official whom I know personally. I will continue the search in the Labour Exchange and the Health Insurance Office but results are unlikely since K. is probably living here, or has registered with the police, under another name.'[23]

All members of the German Communist Party were subject to automatic registration. Even leading Social-Democrats, however, also appeared on the Org's lists; they included Erich Ollenhauer, the Party Chairman, and Herbert Wehner, whom Hans-Heinrich Worgitzky, head of one of the General Agencies, described as 'a most dangerous enemy of the State'. Gustav Heinemann was also listed by informers as a dangerous 'element' after he had broken with Adenauer and been instrumental in forming the All-German People's Party [Gesamtdeutsche Volkspartei].[24]

Even relatives of 'suspect' politicians were kept under surveillance. Ollenhauer's nephew, for instance, was suspected of being a communist. Informer 2679 reported: 'In amplification of the report by 2707 already forwarded, you are informed that the Hermann Ollenhauer mentioned therein is a nephew of Erich Ollenhauer, Deputy Chairman of the Social-Democrat Party. The nephew was temporarily with his uncle in Bonn and moved to Wilhelmshaven in October 1950.'[25]

Supporters of Gehlen would have us believe that the Org's 'internal security precautions' were discontinued in the mid-1950s. This is contradicted, however, by the fact that informers' reports dated 1963 exist – and they reveal the methods employed by Gehlen's spies.

A report forwarded to Pullach on January 7th, 1963, for instance, recording a meeting between his 'Source II' and a certain 'Doctor of Philosophy F.K.', reads like a denunciation from the days of the Third Reich: 'Dr K. stated that he had always been in favour of co-existence with the Soviet Union and in this connexion he referred to Bismarck's Russian policy. When source objected that there was a great difference between the Russian Empire and the present-day Soviet Union, Dr K. took no notice and changed the subject.' Conclusion: 'Source is not sure whether Dr K. is merely a so-called "re-insurer" or whether he has genuine communist leanings. In any case the greatest caution must be exercised in further investigation of this case, since source considers him a very sly fox.'[26]

In 1963 one of Gehlen's informers even infiltrated a female spy into the office of the President of one of the Provincial Parliaments [*Landtage*]. The lady, who had already been working for the informer concerned in one of the Ministries of this *Land*, was recommended by his 'Source R.R.'. On June 20th, 1963, he reported as follows to his Local Branch which passed the report on to Pullach with its approval: 'Frau N.M. acts as secretary to the . . . parliamentary party. Source describes her as very good and most efficient. For some time she has been working as secretary to the President of the Provincial Parliament and naturally knows much that goes on in parliament and its parties. As source reports, she would be willing, on the side, to pass her knowledge and observations to the relevant German agency.'[27]

Gehlen made use of anyone, from a secretary to a cleaner, who could help to spy on suspects. An entry of May 1958 in the Pullach card-index reads: 'Steinmann, Käthe; Hamburg. Earmarked for dispatch as a "daily" to the house of some suspect. St. is reliable and quick-witted, has common sense and is a loyal German. Husband was a Lieutenant decorated with the Knights Cross for valour. Tip from V 16 601, in whose house St. previously lived.'[28]

The Org did not confine itself to observation and registration of individuals; it also concerned itself with organizations, firms, parties and societies as such. On June 13th, 1958, for instance, the Org's Agency 'Ton' (run by ex-SS-Hauptsturmführer Göring) received the following 'Verification Mission': 'Verification is requested of the "Study Group for Economic Advancement" Ltd, Hamburg, Tel: 36 59 51. The study group is allegedly planning a German exhibition in Moscow and a Soviet exhibition in the Federal Republic. You are requested to establish: (*a*) Who are the main leading personalities? (*b*) Purpose and aim of the study group's activity. (*c*) With which business circles does it work? (*d*) What is the standing of the study group?'

Individuals and agencies who (in the words of a directive from one of the Org's agencies) 'cooperated in West Germany with "Peace Committees" in the Soviet Zone', were also shadowed. On occasions Pullach had to issue warnings to prevent overlaps in the approaches made to various organizations. An organizer in Local Branch X/9592 was told: 'You are requested to make no attempt to approach the headquarters of the East Prussian Nationals Society in Hamburg since an agent of another out-station is already active therein.'[29]

The Org's investigators were so assiduous in their hunt for unseen enemies of the State that many of the staff became uncomfortable and several resigned from the Org. One was an ex-SS man employed on the compilation of lists of suspects in Hamburg. He recalls: 'I was surprised to be told that these lists were drawn up in agreement with senior government agencies in Bonn; even the Chancellor (Konrad Adenauer at that time) was said to have expressed a personal wish for them. The whole affair seemed to me unlike a military intelligence organization, in which I would gladly have worked once more. It looked to me more like dirty spy work.'[30]

The SS man's suspicions were correct. The rigid anti-communism of Gehlen's internal sleuths proved attractive to those political forces which were even then preparing to decide which way the new German State should go. The men around Adenauer inevitably saw an ally in the Gehlen Organization and the first contacts between Gehlen and Adenauer were quickly arranged. Backstage in Bonn and Pullach there was formed an unholy alliance between the secret service and a political party.

CAPTURE OF THE CHANCELLERY

G EHLEN was now within sight of the ultimate goal which he had set himself at the end of the war. He was determined to use his contact to Konrad Adenauer to achieve the last point in his ambitious programme – acceptance of his secret-service organization into the official German State machine. Para III of the agreement concluded with the US War Department in 1946 had laid down: 'When a sovereign German government is constituted ... the organization to be responsible solely to that government.'[1]

Nevertheless, five years after the formation of the Federal Republic the Gehlen Org was still only a private German-American agency. Powerful interests had combined to prevent Gehlen's organization from entering the service of the West German State. In the Federal Internal Security Office [Bundesamt für Verfassungsschutz], in the Blank Office (the future Federal Ministry of Defence), in the staffs of the Allied High Commissioners and among the senior ranks of the US Army – everywhere was to be heard the phrase coined by Sefton Delmer, the senior *Daily Express* correspondent: 'Gehlen and his Nazis are coming.'[2]

Gehlen saw in this all the more reason to put his money on Adenauer. As early as 1948 he had ordered his staff to prepare a detailed biography and character study of Adenauer. Twenty-two years later a member of the Org's central staff recalled: 'Gehlen sensed at a very early stage that Adenauer was the man who would form the first government of the Federal Republic. Gehlen knew the attraction exerted on West Germans by the bourgeois parties.' Whether this is mere *post hoc* self-glorification or whether Gehlen did in fact make an astute judgement of personalities, the fact remains that he was anxious to get in touch with the man who could assist him to liberate the Org from its American obligations.

Through intermediaries Gehlen let it be known that he would like an interview with Adenauer in order to discuss with him 'questions of West German security'. The BND's tame historians put the first meeting at 1950 but the memory of the older members of the Org is more accurate.

On September 14th, 1948, a Soviet military court in East Berlin condemned five Berliners to twenty-five years' forced labour for resistance to the occupying power and the next day the Parliamentary Commission in Bonn, the forerunner of the Bundestag, gathered in protest against the Russian sentence.[3]

That evening, with various of his party friends, Adenauer was ruminating about their lack of knowledge of the Soviet Zone. One of the Christian Democrats remarked that Gehlen and his organization knew a great deal about it. Adenauer said: 'Who is Herr Gehlen?' When told, he expressed a wish to see the man and a few days later Gehlen was standing in front of him. What the two discussed on this occasion we do not know, but they must quickly have realized that each needed the other: with his manifold opportunities of acquiring secret information Gehlen could give Adenauer a decisive advantage over his rivals in the forthcoming struggle for the Chancellorship; Adenauer, on the other hand, could guarantee to the Head of the Org pride of place in any West German secret-service system.

One of Adenauer's former political aides explained: 'Gehlen seemed to Adenauer to be of interest from two points of view. In the first place he could keep Adenauer up to date on developments in the Eastern Zone and this was of particular importance since his (Adenauer's) two most dangerous political opponents, Jakob Kaiser in the Christian-Democrat Party and Kurt Schumacher of the Social-Democrat Party, were very well informed on the Soviet Zone. Secondly Adenauer realized at once that, with his knowledge, Gehlen could exert influence on the people to whom he purveyed this knowledge – the Americans.' Moreover Adenauer and Gehlen were in agreement in their estimate of the political situation: both reckoned with the possibility of war between East and West and both saw West Germany threatened by a communist fifth column. Adenauer was primarily afraid of communist agitation in the Ruhr – Gehlen set up out-stations in Bochum and Essen. Adenauer also thought that the Hamburg dockers would be susceptible to communist blandishments – Gehlen reinforced his Hamburg out-station.[4]

Gehlen could offer more, however, than intelligence on the East and security for West Germany. To Adenauer the links which Gehlen had long since formed to other Western countries, must have seemed equally valuable. These were not confined to the fifty US liaison officers who appeared every morning in Pullach Camp and read the messages which came in to the Org's sections and desks. The Americans had soon ceased to act as occupiers. Under the influence of the daily situation reports on the East which painted Moscow's policy of pressure in the blackest of colours, the US secret-service officers inevitably came to accept the political views of their German partners. Senior US secret-service officers were soon pleading for an end to the occupation regime on this side of the Elbe and the incorporation of West Germany into the political, military and economic alliance of the West. The Americans were urging Gehlen to join a united Western secret-service front against communism.

The first actual invitation came from Switzerland, from an old friend of the German soldiers, the Swiss Colonel Max Waibel. He had been an exchange officer in the Infantry School at Döberitz, had run the Swiss Army's Intelligence Service during the war and had then been Military and Air Attaché at the Swiss Legation in Washington. Early in 1948 he had been instrumental in arranging contact between the Gehlen Org and the Swiss counter-espionage authorities. Waibel visualized that, by co-operating with the Org, he would achieve, not only better information on the Soviet Union, but also a coordinated defence against communist subversion. Here, as it happened, the Pullach headquarters could help, for chance had placed it on the trail of communist agents working into Switzerland.[5]

One of Gehlen's informers was given a tip to keep his eye on the Hotel Terminus in Baden-Baden. This hotel, Gehlen's investigators discovered, served as a meeting point for members of the Polish and Czech Military Missions in Baden-Baden, all of whom were working for the Eastern secret services. As manager the Poles had installed one of their own countrymen named Rassek, who worked for all three intelligence services at the same time – Russian, Polish and Czech. Rassek ran the courier network; it went to agents of the East in West Germany, but also to spies in France and Switzerland. For this purpose Rassek employed girls who appeared in his bar as hostesses and were 'frequently ordered by Rassek to accompany gentlemen in whom he was interested up to the rooms of the hotel', as one of Gehlen's investigators reported to Pullach.[6]

Gehlen's agents were soon in a position to prove that the Russian, Polish and Czech secret services were sending agents into Switzerland from bases in the French Zone. The Swiss counter-espionage authorities thereupon offered to arrange a contact between Gehlen and the French intelligence service in order that all three might keep a combined watch on the espionage lines running between Switzerland and the French Zone. Gehlen was hesitant, however, since the French secret service, the 'Service de Documentation Extérieure et de Contre-Espionage' (SDECE) was still suffering from its penetration by communists during the resistance period. In addition the French were regarded as amateurs in the trade; in Berlin, for instance, they made use of a host of intelligence-peddlers who either invented information from the Soviet Zone or passed on reports doctored by the Russians.

The Swiss counter-espionage authorities, however, assured Gehlen that the key positions in SDECE were increasingly being occupied by officers who had worked in General de Gaulle's counter-espionage organization during the war; within the SDECE, they said, the Gaullists were waging savage warfare against the ex-members of the communist resistance and the Gaullist secret-service men merited Gehlen's support. The Americans also urged Gehlen to do business with the French. The US secret service had barely any contact with SDECE but was most anxious to gain some insight into the policies of Paris.

Gehlen agreed to the establishment of contact with the French and the partnership between the Org and SDECE later developed into an alliance no less friendly than that with the American CIA. Members of the Org who had fought in Italy during the war then established contact with the Italian intelligence service and officers who had worked for Canaris in Madrid, did likewise with the Spaniards. Carstens, the State Secretary in the Chancellery, later said: 'There was thus established in the early days a partnership with the Western secret services which was not without influence upon the subsequent political and military cooperation between the Federal Republic of Germany and its allies.'

For Adenauer the head of an organization with such manifold connexions was an indispensable member of his immediate entourage. The two were already working smoothly together when the Federal Republic was formed. After holding his first cabinet meeting on September 20th, 1949, Adenauer went straight back to receive Gehlen for a formal discussion and Point 1 on their agenda was the future of the Gehlen Organization. Washington showed no hesitation in releasing the Org to the Federal government forthwith. Adenauer, however, feared that the British and French might make difficulties since they regarded the American-run Org with some suspicion.

Gehlen was vitally interested in a solution to this problem, since once the Federal Republic had been proclaimed, the fact that the Org cooperated with a foreign power might label it as an agency working against German interests. Gehlen found a loophole: if the Chancellor and the leader of the Social-Democrat opposition, he suggested, formally declared that a German American secret-service alliance was essential to the security of the Federal Republic, then the Org could be at the disposal of the Bonn government as well. The deal was clinched. As Carstens later reported, Adenauer gave 'agreement to continuation of the work under American trusteeship' and Dr Schumacher, then leader of the opposition, also agreed. Henceforth important reports from the Org were addressed to the Chancellery. Gehlen had his foot in the door of the West German decision-making machine.[7]

The Allied High Commissioners supported Gehlen's position. The Bundestag had just promulgated a law altering the criminal code to provide for a sentence of hard labour for espionage or disclosure of State secrets. On August 30th, 1951, the Allied High Commission issued a law restricting the application of this change in the criminal code in favour of Allied secret services and thereby indirectly in favour of the Org. Paragraph 92 of the Federal law stated: 'Anyone who, on behalf of an agency situated outside the area to which this law applies, deliberately collects intelligence on administration, agencies, concerns, installations, associations or individuals situated within the area to which this law applies, who sets up an intelligence service for this purpose, canvasses for such activity or supports it, will be punished with imprisonment.'

In their Law No 62, however, the Allied High Commission amended this: 'Neither the German criminal code nor any other criminal regulations issued by the Federal or *Land* governments are applicable to: information of any sort given or intended to be given to the governments of the United States, the French Republic or the United Kingdom, their occupation authorities or their occupation forces; the establishment or maintenance of relationships with the governments of the United States, the French Republic or the United Kingdom and their occupation forces.'[8]

This Allied High Commission law gave the men of Pullach a unique and exceptional legal position. Armed with full authority to collect information for the US occupation authorities, the Org could now legally pursue its surveillance, within the Federal Republic, of actual or supposed enemies of the state.

Gehlen's informers listened in West German universities, they kept watch in industrial concerns, they spied in official agencies. They ferreted in the card-indexes of Residents Registration Offices, Health Insurance counters and labour exchanges; they carried out personal checks on applicants for the new Federal civil service, on journalists, trade unionists, politicians, clerics, professors and industrialists. In amassing this internal German dossier Gehlen was from the outset pursuing his personal aim, to consolidate his position in the place where he had long considered that his true master was to be found – the Federal Chancellery in Bonn.

In the Palais Schaumburg on the Koblenzer Strasse Gehlen had soon won the respect of a man who knew how to exploit the Org's secret information for the benefit of the ruling Christian-Democrat party. This was Dr Hans Globke, under the Third Reich a desk officer in charge of nationality questions in the Reich Ministry of the Interior and interpreter of the Nazi anti-Jewish legislation; in the Chancellor's office he was the 'Vice-President', the most senior civil servant and head of personnel; he ran the administrative machine with such ability that even two decades later Ehmke, the Minister in the same office, described him as 'an ace'.[9]

Even before being officially appointed State Secretary in October 1953 Globke was functioning as the real head of administration in the Palais Schaumburg. From the outset Gehlen put his money on Globke. On his side Globke at once recognized the opportunity offered him by Gehlen — the acquisition of secret information for the exercise of personal power. Globke was never in doubt: one day the Org — all of it — must become the Foreign Intelligence Organization of the Federal Republic. He was equally in no doubt as to who should then exercise supervision over it — not some Federal Minister, but the Chancellery, in other words Hans Globke.

With Adenauer's approval Globke set up a special Chancellery fund from which he financed his specific missions for the Org and with this money Gehlen began to step up his internal intelligence service. The formation of the new Federal Ministries and agencies offered him good opportunities for the recruitment of fresh staff, sources and agents. One of the members of the National Assistance Department, formed in 1949 under Dr Hans Lukaschek, described how Gehlen's canvassers worked: 'About this time I was visited in Bad Homburg by a man whom I seemed to have met before. He had been a Colonel on the General Staff of the Army. He would not give me his name but was clearly in the service of the Gehlen Organization. He asked me to give him the names of persons suitable for employment as agents both among my acquaintances and among the numerous applicants for employment in the Department of National Assistance.' The ex-Colonel's visit was productive, for the statement continues: 'I gave this gentleman a number of names. Lukaschek had also received him and had also given him some names.'[10]

Staff members of official agencies who thus became agents of Gehlen produced names of relatives or acquaintances in East Germany but they could also purvey office secrets which included much tittle-tattle. The Pullach headquarters, however, did not just throw this stuff into the waste paper basket; in many cases they made use of it for purposes of political denunciation.

The truth was that many of the reports and analyses produced by Gehlen's counter-espionage service followed a perfectly straightforward rule of thumb: the Adenauer government was ranged in a common front with the USA against the bolshevik world enemy; therefore – anyone in the Federal Republic who was politically or personally opposed to Adenauer was at the very least suspect; if he were not already a communist, he was anyway a neutralist and therefore fair game for the doctrines of communism. This uncomplicated standpoint explains why Gehlen and the senior members of his staff regarded any Christian-Democrat government as synonymous with the state, although for tactical reasons they still valued their contacts with the Social-Democrat Party leaders. Nevertheless in their eyes the Social-Democrats were always suspect; Adenauer and his Christian-Democrats were the only people who counted.

Close though his relations with the Chancellery were, however, Gehlen found that he had some genuine competitors. His secret-service monopoly was disputed by a group of German intelligence experts who had nothing to do with Pullach and whose bond was their resistance to the Hitler dictatorship.

This opposition originated in attempts to give the Federal Republic a political police designed to keep the opponents of democracy under observation and track down foreign spies. After the collapse of 1945 the Germans had had no police authority; a Control Council law forbade surveillance of political activities by any German police agency. Only the Allied secret services and their German minions were permitted to carry out political-police duties. As the occupation regime began to fade away, however, the West German politicians demanded the return of their authority over the police. They had in mind something on the lines of the Weimar system – special authorities incorporated into the normal police organization but with executive powers.[11]

West Germany's Allied masters, however, were not prepared to grant their protégé a political police – memories of the Gestapo were too vivid. In a 'Police Letter' of April 14th, 1949, the Allied Military Governors did nevertheless authorize formation of an agency, directly subordinate to the Federal Chancellor, for the collection and distribution of information relevant to the security of the State. A name, which appeared for the first time in the Basic Law, was found to designate both the agency and its sphere of operations – 'Verfassungsschutz' [Protection of the Constitution]. It was to be kept strictly divorced from the police and to have no executive powers; the general sense of the 'Police Letter' was openly stated — 'to prevent the resurrection of a political police in Germany'.[12]

The agency was eventually named the 'Federal Internal Security Office' [Bundesamt für Verfassungsschutz – BfV]. Before it could be constituted, however, the Ministries of the Interior in Lower Saxony and North Rhine–Westphalia had set up Internal Security Sections and were taking active internal security measures. Not until the spring of 1950 was the Federal Government able to submit a law for the constitution of the BfV and it immediately aroused violent debate because — as the Allies desired – the agency was to be subordinate to the Federal Chancellor's Office. The Social-Democrat opposition objected to such a reinforcement of the personal power of the Chancellor. The Bundestag accordingly allocated authority over the BfV to the Federal Minister of the Interior and in a law of September 27th, 1950, it defined the duty of the BfV as: 'Acquisition and evaluation of information and intelligence ... concerning tendencies aiming at suspension, alteration or disturbance of the constitutional order in the Federal Republic or in a *Land*.' The BfV was instructed to concentrate initially upon keeping under observation communist or right-wing extremist intrigues.[13]

In a 'Federal Government Instruction on the Formation of a Federal Internal Security Office' dated November 7th, 1950, Adenauer attempted to safeguard his influence over the BfV: the Chancellor's agreement, the instruction stated, was required for the nomination of a President for the Office. Globke proposed as the first President one of Adenauer's personal aides – Ernst Wirmer, brother of one of the resisters executed after July 20th, 1944. Once more, however, the Social-Democrats objected and Adenauer had to bow to their veto. He left the choice of a head for the political secret service to the responsible Minister, Dr Robert Lehr, Minister of the Interior.[14]

So eventually there arrived to head the Internal Security Office a man whom Adenauer did not particularly like and whose effect on Gehlen was that of a challenge. This was the liberal-conservative lawyer, Dr Otto John. From 1937 to 1944 he had been legal consultant to Lufthansa; he was a friend of the existing head of the House of Hohenzollern, Prince Louis Ferdinand, had worked with Major-General Hans Oster, the anti-Nazi Chief of Staff of the Abwehr, and was one of the few survivors of the anti-Hitler resistance.

Four days after the abortive *Putsch* of July 20th, 1944, John had escaped imminent arrest in Berlin by taking an aeroplane to Madrid; from there he had been taken to England. He had initially worked in

England as adviser to the 'black' propaganda station 'Soldatensender Calais' [Forces Network Calais]. John had been recommended by his old resistance friend, Jakob Kaiser; he had the support of President Heuss and so had good prospects of acceptance as President of the Internal Security Office. Gehlen, however, attempted to prevent his nomination. When the US Security Director in the Allied High Commission asked the CIA for a personal check on John, the CIA informed Gehlen and Gehlen sounded the alarm.[15]

Gehlen, the ex-General, was incensed that John, the émigré, should have had the audacity to address German POW Generals with inadequate respect. Worse still – John had assisted the prosecution at the trial of Gehlen's idol, Field Marshal Erich von Manstein, and Gehlen therefore regarded him as a contributory to the sentence imposed by a British Military Court. After the war John had carried out the political screening of German POWs on behalf of the British 'Control Office for Germany and Austria'; anti-Nazis were placed in Category A, the politically indifferent in Category B and Nazis in Category C – and they included Field-Marshals, Generals and Admirals. On John's classification depended their prospects of a return home, for those in Group C were initially retained in internment.[16]

The Manstein trial in 1948 also raised the question of the view to be taken of the behaviour of a German officer under the Hitler regime. The British members of the Court Martial on Manstein basically regarded him merely as a first-class soldier, particularly when he swore that he had only heard of the murders of Jews after the end of the war. Elwyn Jones, the prosecutor, thereupon called John into court. John was not, as is often maintained today, acting as assistant to the prosecution; rather he was the legal trustee for the Nuremberg Military Tribunal of the files and documents of Eleventh Army, which Manstein had commanded in Russia. Among these documents was Eleventh Army War Diary, by which the prosecution set great store. A certain passage in the War Diary was pasted over. John says: 'Elwyn Jones asked me to hold the page up to the light and challenged Manstein to read the words which had been pasted over. They were: "The new Commander-in-Chief does not wish officers to be present at shootings of Jews. This is unworthy of a German officer." '

Manstein was unable to explain why this sentence had been pasted over; he had to admit, however, that he had signed the War Diary regularly. The court's views on the Field Marshal underwent an abrupt change. They no longer regarded as a gentleman an Army Commander who tried to use lies to exonerate himself from knowledge of genocide.

The verdict was eighteen years' imprisonment for Manstein.[17]

For Gehlen, the Manstein-worshipper, it was self-evident that John ought never to be head of any official agency. He took up the cudgels against John on two fronts; his CIA friends were given to understand that a list existed on which John figured as a sympathizer of the pro-Russian espionage and resistance group 'Red Orchestra'; in the Chancellery Gehlen pointed out that, with John heading an internal security agency, the young republic would never gain the confidence of the millions of ex-soldiers. When the US Director of Security, however, put forward Gehlen's arguments, he received no support from his colleagues in the Allied High Commission. The British replied that John, the anti-Nazi, would be a counterweight to Gehlen, the ex-General. The French supported the British.

In the Federal Cabinet Lehr, the Minister of the Interior, put his finger on the real point of the objections to John: they were all, he stated officially, an act of revenge on the part of the generals' clique. Adenauer reluctantly gave his agreement. On December 5th, 1950, John took over as head of the Cologne office, but only in an acting capacity.[18]

Gehlen left no stone unturned to prevent ratification of John's appointment. Ultimately the argument was even to be heard that John was in the pay of the British – consequently an object of suspicion to Adenauer, whose policy was based on alliance with the American superpower and reconciliation with his neighbour, France. The real reasons for the opposition to John meanwhile became crystal-clear when General Busse, Manstein's former Chief of Staff, handed to Lehr a 'protest by the Generals' against John's appointment as President of the BfV on the grounds that he had interrogated German officers under degrading circumstances.

Such spite was too much for Lehr and he pressed Adenauer hard to confirm John's appointment. The Chancellor gave way and in December 1951 John was officially appointed President of the BfV. He lost no time in pointing out to Gehlen's representatives that counter-espionage was one of the most important tasks of his office. To Gehlen's personal aversion to John, therefore, was now added an actual rivalry between the Org and the BfV. Gehlen now had to watch lest the BfV squeeze him out of counter-espionage and internal intelligence altogether.[19]

In effect the BfV did begin to expand and invade the Org's preserves. It was primarily the head of the BfV's Acquisition Section, ex-Abwehr Captain Richard Gerken, who was planning to expand his office. He set up 'Federal Intelligence Offices' in Lübeck, Hannover, Kassel, Munich and West Berlin and 'Coastal Intelligence Offices' in Hamburg and Kiel, all responsible to the BfV. Simultaneously out-stations appeared in the *Länder* which Gerken partially manned with ex-RSHA men – he had himself belonged to the RSHA after the fall of the Abwehr.

Although the *Land* authorities resisted the expansionist efforts of the BfV in Cologne, they themselves set up further intelligence agencies – the *Land* Internal Security Offices. These in their turn organized out-stations whose very title, 'Intelligence Posts', was enough to remind Gehlen that his monopoly in the secret-service field was threatened. Moreover the formation of the *Land* Internal Security Offices led to the creation of even more organizations – the Internal Security Sections in *Land* Police headquarters, which soon extended their tentacles into local police inspectorates, commissariats and districts.

A matter of special vexation to Gehlen was inevitably the fact that the BfV annexed primary responsibility for counter-espionage which had previously been the prerogative of the Org alone. Moreover no law existed authorizing the BfV to do this; it had simply quietly annexed this responsibility – and no political authority had seriously tried to prevent it. The Ministers of the Interior of the *Länder* did not give their approval to this semi-legal activity on the part of the BfV until October 1954.[20]

The BfV was already too strong merely to be circumvented by the Org. So, since he could not eliminate John, Gehlen tried to conclude a truce with him. He visited John in his Cologne office and John went to Pullach for a return visit. At dinner Gehlen raised his glass in a toast to his rival, saying: 'We wish to forget the past. To good cooperation.' John remained discreet, merely replying 'Prosit.' Nevertheless John too had his reasons for cooperating with Gehlen. He was well aware that the Head of the Org was a perpetual visitor to the Chancellery and there poisoned the atmosphere against him. The Chancellor did not like John anyway; he had seen him once – and that was apparently enough. Adenauer had said: 'I don't like him.' He had even incited the Org to snoop into Dr Otto John's private life.[21]

Early in 1952 Adenauer asked Gehlen to investigate whether it was true that the President of the BfV maintained contacts in the Soviet Zone, worked with East German business concerns and had a fat bank account in Switzerland. Today Gehlen is disinclined to remember this request, but old Gehlen experts can recall that the Org was able to pin nothing on John. John probably knew nothing of this snooping; the little he did hear, however, about the meetings between Adenauer and Gehlen he found sufficiently shocking. Hitherto John had always regarded Adenauer, the Catholic Rhinelander, as a violent anti-militarist, whose *bête noire* was any General, particularly of the Prussian variety.[22]

Chancellor Adenauer, however, seemed to have accepted ex-General Gehlen without reservation. His new adviser from Pullach could put forward his views with such precision and was so attentive to the interests of the Chancellor and the Christian-Democrat Union that, in his little closed circle, Adenauer would frequently address Gehlen as 'My dear General'. He placed visibly increasing reliance on the Org's reports and appreciations and on occasions even sent the BfV's monthly reports to Pullach for checking. When, at the end of 1953 the BfV was unable to produce a list of communist agents in West Germany which Adenauer wanted, the Org was asked to furnish it. A few days later the Org's list was on the Chancellor's desk.[23]

Gehlen's position in the Chancellery was so unassailable that John thought it wise to sing his praises in public. Gehlen found this all the more acceptable since he had need of John as an ally. Other anti-Nazis were threatening Gehlen's vital interests – and this time in a field which he had always considered his special preserve.

For some time the Western Allies had been pressing Adenauer to come to their assistance with a German defence contribution. The High Commissioners expressed the wish that the Bonn government set up a military liaison office with which the Allies could discuss detailed plans for the remilitarization of West Germany. The Americans thought they knew who could undertake this task – the officers of the Gehlen Org, who had been dealing with basic military questions for years. As Head of the German/Allied Liaison Office, therefore, the US representatives proposed their favourite, General Gehlen.[24]

The British and French, however, would not accept the US protégé – he was altogether too inscrutable for them. Sir Brian Robertson, the British High Commissioner, proposed another candidate to Adenauer, the ex-Tank General Gerhard Graf von Schwerin. Adenauer agreed. So, with a small staff, Schwerin moved into a couple of rooms in the Palais Schaumburg as 'Adviser to the Federal Chancellor on Security Questions'; he himself was on the ground floor but in the attics, later taken over by the BND, his staff opened an 'Internal Services Centre', the cover-name for Schwerin's office, demilitarization still being officially in vogue.

Schwerin was responsible to the 'Agency for External Affairs', the embryo Foreign Office; this too was accommodated in the Chancellery but was not under Globke, the Head of the Chancellery Office. Initially, therefore, Gehlen and his friends did not realize that Herbert Blank-

enhorn, a senior civil servant [Ministerialdirektor] in charge of the
Agency for External Affairs, had given Graf von Schwerin the task of
building up a military secret service. The idea originated from Adenauer; he wished to be informed on the military situation in East
Germany before taking the decision on West German remilitarization –
and by an intelligence service not (like the Org) dependent on the Americans.

Schwerin had to admit to Blankenhorn that he had little experience in
secret-service matters. Blankenhorn thereupon advised him to entrust
the task to ex-Major Joachim Oster, who had joined Schwerin's office in
May 1950. Oster was no more experienced in secret-service affairs but
he knew what to do. His father, Major-General Hans Oster, had been
Head of the Central Section in the Ausland/Abwehr, one of the closest
associates of Admiral Canaris, the real organizer of the military resistance to Hitler, and had been executed in April 1945. From the old
Abwehr Joachim Oster collected Lieutenant-Colonel Friedrich Wilhelm
Heinz and with his aid began to build up a military secret service.

Oster undertook to organize the headquarters while Heinz ran the
external services. Since, however, Adenauer wished to avoid the appearance of creating yet another secret-service machine, the two had to
evacuate the Chancellery. They moved initially to Bad Godesberg, later
to Frankfurt and finally to Wiesbaden; camouflaged as an 'Institute for
Contemporary Research' (later rechristened 'Archives for Contemporary History') they carried on military espionage in East Germany. Working from West Berlin, Heinz directed a number of informers
in the East.[25]

Adenauer soon issued his first requirement; the miniature secret service was to enlighten the Chancellery on the concentration of Soviet
forces opposite the Federal Republic. A fortnight later Heinz submitted
a detailed report on the dispositions of Soviet forces in East Germany; it
showed clearly their concentration areas and possible lines of advance.
Adenauer showed the report to his cabinet and the Ministers were impressed. Globke passed the report to the American secret service and
they confirmed its accuracy.

Gehlen, however, was taken aback; here was dangerous competition
in his own original field. He saw his position seriously threatened. He
already felt that he was being harried by the legatees of Oster, the
resistance martyr, who were accusing him of employing far too many
ex-Nazis in his organization. Every one of his rivals seemed to have
belonged to the Oster circle: Joachim, Oster's son, had helped his
father, John had acted as contact man for the group and Heinz had been

a member of a strong-arm squad formed by Oster in September 1938 to arrest Hitler.

Gehlen made no bones about the fact that he did not like the way things were going. This was borne in on Oster when he tried to contact Gehlen and discuss collaboration with him. Only after prolonged efforts would Gehlen agree to talk at all – and then not in Pullach but in a Munich 'safe house'. Graf Schwerin reports: 'Gehlen's attitude at this meeting was icy; he was impervious to any proposal for collaboration.' It was an experience which Joachim Oster was not likely to forget.[26]

Gehlen was determined to drive a wedge through his opponents before they could squeeze him out of his secret-service domain; he took as his target the weakest member, Lieutenant-Colonel Heinz, since he was regarded in the trade as something of a mountebank. Heinz had been a Free Corps officer, a desk officer in Canaris' office and then a regimental commander in the Abwehr's 'Brandenburg' Division; he had been arrested by the Gestapo after July 20th, 1944. After the war he had set up a private intelligence agency in the Baseler Strasse, Berlin-Lichterfeld and was soon specializing in the sale of information on locations and strength of Soviet forces in the Eastern Zone. His customers were initially the American and later the Dutch and French secret services. Many reports he sold simultaneously to all his customers.

Both to his agents and his customers Heinz made use of a highly marketable trade-mark – the name of Canaris. He did not, of course, tell them that his master had not always taken him seriously. The French, however, were more impressed by the reports of their informant Heinz (code-name 'Tulip'). Heinz was linked to the French intelligence office in Koblenz run by Captain Elsaneaux; his contact in Berlin was 'Courby'. Whenever 'Tulip' summoned 'Courby' to the Baseler Strasse, the French secret service was sure to receive some sensational report from the Russian Zone.

'Fabulous intelligence successes; brilliant, highly interesting and important reports,' a French secret-service man noted on Heinz. Gradually Heinz became so valuable to the French that they allowed him to move from Berlin to Neuwied in the French Zone and run his network of agents in the Russian Zone from there. 'Tulip' continued to produce.[27]

This mass-production of intelligence, however, soon aroused the suspicion of Gehlen. He had meanwhile heard a rumour that in 1946 Heinz had betrayed one of the Org's informers to the Russians. At that time Gerhard Pinckert, who had set up a network of agents in Saxony and Thuringia, had been sentenced to a long term of imprisonment by a

Soviet military court. Pinckert and Heinz had known each other in Canaris' office and in the Brandenburg Division. The old hands of the Org still maintained today that Pinckert warned Gehlen against Heinz thinking him altogether too dubious a character.

The fact remains that Gehlen ordered his staff to avoid all contact with Heinz. Whether he also warned the French secret service, we do not know. It seems likely, however, since one day the Koblenz office cut 'Tulip' out and commissioned 'Courby' to take charge of Heinz' network in Berlin and the Russian Zone.

The new man, however, discovered that in fact Heinz had no network of his own at all. All the agents whose names Heinz had given him said that they were working for the US secret service; they had left Heinz because he never paid them for their information. 'Courby' was able to produce receipts signed by Heinz. The only conclusions to be drawn from all this were as follows: either Heinz had been passing doctored material from Russian sources and had been a Russian agent seeking to mislead the French secret service, or he had simply invented his information in order to make a profit. Heinz' friends put forward an even more innocent tale: that Heinz had always been prone to let his imagination run riot and that he had simply 'spiced up' press reports from the zone and made capital out of those – a profitable business at the time, particularly in Berlin.[28]

The fact that Bonn had commissioned so controversial a figure to construct a military intelligence organization made Gehlen's battle against the Oster group all the easier. He could not himself, however, conduct the campaign against this secret-service black marketeer. He was already suspected of an obsessive thirst for power and so he had to set someone else on to Heinz. The 'someone else' was Otto John – though John did not realize it.

Through intermediaries Gehlen passed word to John that Heinz had intrigued against him in the hope of becoming head of the BfV himself. A hint that Heinz was working for the Russians also seems to have made some impression on John. The Head of the BfV opened a file on Heinz and this was soon embroidered by all sorts of insinuations from Jan Eland, a Dutch secret-service man who had previously worked with Heinz in Berlin. In September 1953 John, the head of political intelligence, set out to overthrow Heinz, the head of military intelligence. He submitted his dossier to Ritter von Lex, his immediate superior in the Ministry of the Interior, and to Globke, the head of the Chancellery Office. Theodor Blank, Heinz' master and the successor to Graf von Schwerin (who had resigned), was told nothing.

Globke was able to add a little spice to the Heinz file for the benefit of Adenauer. Heinz had published a book entitled *Sprengstoff* (Explosive) and in this Globke found a sentence on the Rhineland separatist period which was clearly aimed at Adenauer: 'Burgomasters of cathedral towns, obsessed with pan-European ideas, supported them [the separatists] by silence and inactivity.' Adenauer ordered the hesitant Blank to dismiss Heinz and on September 29th, 1953, 'by mutual agreement' Heinz asked for his release; Oster also resigned. Gehlen had eliminated his competitors in the military-intelligence field. In vain had Heinz warned his enemy John: 'Gehlen and his people are set on seizing control of all German secret services. You are standing in his way just as I did. He will get you too.'[29]

Gehlen's next stroke of good fortune was the entry into the 'Blank Office' of certain of his closest associates, his former deputy Gerhard Wessel, for instance, and his former master Adolf Heusinger. They quickly took measures to ensure that their friends in Pullach were solely responsible for enemy intelligence and they supported Gehlen's claim for acceptance into the Federal Service. They worked out an organizational plan for the proposed Federal Ministry of Defence involving the creation of yet a third focus of secret-service activity – the Military Security Service [Militärischer Abschirmdienst] or MAD for short.

The authors of this plan, with Gehlen behind them, took care that the MAD could constitute no threat to the Pullach machine. The MAD was to be responsible only for counter-espionage within the armed forces and was not to have an independent intelligence-gathering organization of its own. In the summer of 1955 Gehlen submitted this plan to Adenauer and he gave his agreement. The co-authors of the plan then occupied key positions: Colonel Josef Selmayr, the Org's expert on South-east Europe, became head of the Security Office, to which all MAD Groups were subordinate; Colonel Wessel took charge of the section in the Defence Ministry responsible for military intelligence; Colonel Ernst Ferber, a member of the Org, became Head of Personnel in the Defence Ministry.[30]

The cornerstone of Gehlen's edifice of power, however, was still lacking – acceptance of the Org into the Federal service. Gehlen and his partners were unable to agree upon this for years. The British and French continued to insist that, until the Federal Republic had attained complete sovereignty, it might not possess a secret service in its own right. In addition the British and French politicians, military and secret-service officers feared that via the US-controlled Gehlen Organization

American influence over Federal policy would increase – and in this they were not far wrong.

There were other obstacles: the German politicians feared the access of power inherent in the Org's official recognition; Gerhard Schröder, the Federal Minister of the Interior, was opposed to the Foreign Intelligence Service being subordinate to the Chancellery Office; Blank, who was in charge of defence, thought that there were 'too many ex-SD people' in the Org; Schumacher and Erler, the Social-Democrat leaders, demanded strict parliamentary control over the secret service. Gehlen himself doubted how long his support from Washington would last – and one incident confirmed his doubts.[31]

When Adenauer visited America in the spring of 1954, among those invited to a dinner in the German Mission in Washington was Major-General Arthur Trudeau, Head of US Army Intelligence. Trudeau confided to the Chancellor his worry that the CIA should be supporting a West German espionage organization. He was doubtful of Gehlen's reliability; he was also unable to see what political advantages accrued from supporting a shadowy organization run by an 'ex-Nazi officer'. Trudeau's warning seems to have had its effect on Adenauer, for the General was invited to a further prolonged interview in the Mission. Trudeau repeated his criticism of Gehlen.

Gehlen, of course, learnt of this conversation. He immediately protested in writing to Allen Dulles, the Director of the CIA, who at once made representations to Eisenhower, saying that General Trudeau had damaged vital US interests by his intervention. Eisenhower summoned Trudeau and dressed him down. The Joint Chiefs of Staff and Secretary of Defence supported Trudeau, but the CIA proved stronger. Trudeau was relieved and dispatched to a US Far Eastern command.[32]

The danger to Gehlen's espionage empire became ever clearer. With the return of sovereignty to West Germany and the basically anti-communist mood of the time, the moment was propitious for an inflationary growth of secret organizations and clandestine intelligence services. Hans-Joachim von Merkatz, a Bundestag deputy, thundered: 'It is an intolerable situation that a nation should be the target for seventeen or eighteen intelligence services.' In addition to the Org, the BfV and the MAD there was an 'Industrial Warning Service against Activities Damaging to the Economy', the 'Eastern Bureaux' of the political parties and the trades unions, cold-war organizations financed by the Western secret services, post-war organizations such as the 'Anti-inhumanity Combat Group' and the 'Investigating Commission of Free Lawyers', an 'Information Bureau West' and all sorts of obscure investigation centres,

East European Institutes, refugee associations and so forth.[33]

Gehlen knew that he must soon extract a decision from Bonn if he was not to be the spectator of the gradual disappearance of his secret-service authority and its erosion by his competitors. He was almost at the point of resignation when the fall of his rival John gave him a new lease of life.

Early on July 21st, 1954, all the Western secret services were alerted: John, the head of the BfV, had not returned to the Hotel Gehrhus in West Berlin, where he was staying for the tenth anniversary cele-brations of the anti-Hitler *Putsch*. At this moment the West German security expert was lying in a house belonging to the Soviet secret ser-vice in Berlin-Karlshorst – 'heavily drugged', as John told the Federal Supreme Court in Karlsruhe in December 1956, or 'dead drunk' as Gehlen's friends still maintain today. Probably the crossing of the fron-tier into East Berlin by the head of Bonn's counter-espionage service during the night July 20th/21st, 1954, will never be explained; either he was unconscious, having been drugged by Wolfgang Wohlgemuth, a doctor working for the Russians, or he was half-seas-over because, em-bittered by the restorationist upsurge in the Federal Republic, he had drunk too much whisky and had allowed himself to be persuaded by Wohlgemuth to go to the East and there raise the red flag against the alleged revival of Nazism.

Long before the mystery had been clarified, however, one man – Gehlen – was quite clear about John's crossing of the frontier. When asked in the Ministry of the Interior what explanation he could give for John's departure, Gehlen merely replied: 'Once a traitor, always a traitor.'[34]

Gehlen now felt strong enough to raise the ante for his entry into Federal service. The John affair, he explained in Pullach, showed who were the only people capable of protecting the State – German officers. If the Federal government now approached him for his services, he would dictate his terms. To Erich Mende, later Chairman of the Free Democrat Party, he said: 'Now, after what has happened with John, they must first come to me here and ask me to do something for them. No harm if I am now somewhat unforthcoming; that will merely in-crease their readiness to meet my demands.'[35]

In fact Konrad Adenauer was ready in July to push a plan through his cabinet to take the Org into Federal service with an initial annual budget of twenty-six million marks. According to a proposal by Gehlen administrative responsibility was to lie with State Secretary Globke and political supervision to be exercised by a Bundestag panel. Two Ministers, however, Blank and Schröder, raised objections. Schröder in particular, who had been John's master, had disliked Gehlen's continuous intrigues against the Head of the BfV. Decision on the problem was once more shelved.[36]

Gehlen now turned for support to the party upon the good conduct of whose functionaries he had always kept a sharp eye – the Social-Democrats. He found a willing ear in Fritz Erler, a Social-Democrat Bundestag deputy anxious to counter the accusation that his Party was interested in neither the external nor the internal security of the Federal Republic. By feeding him political reports from East Germany, primarily from the higher levels of the Socialist Unity Party, Gehlen contrived to interest him in secret-service matters. In any case the Social-Democrat leaders had their own security problem – they were afraid of communist infiltration. Gehlen promised to keep his eye on members of the Social-Democrat party who attended courses, meetings or demonstrations in East Germany.

Nevertheless Gehlen had little time left. Even America's CIA was losing interest in its German auxiliaries in Pullach. The Org had suffered heavy losses in East Germany; agents of Gehlen had been sentenced by East German courts; the Org was becoming an international by-word. Moreover the Americans were becoming irritated that Gehlen was operating primarily on behalf of Bonn while Washington was footing the bill. At the end of June 1955 it was rumoured that the US government had cancelled payments to the Gehlen Organization. The knowledgeable consider this rumour a subterfuge by Gehlen to force through acceptance of the Org into the Federal Service.[37] Be that as it may, on July 11th, 1955, the cabinet decided to accept the Org into Federal service as 'an agency affiliated to the Office of the Federal Chancellor'. So after ten years of battles, triumphs and intrigues Reinhard Gehlen had reached his goal and the Org had found its final form. A new designation appeared to impress the public: Federal Intelligence Service – *Bundesnachrichtendienst* (BND).

The cabinet's commission to the BND consisted of a single sentence: it was to collect information abroad which might be of importance to the Federal Government and assist it in taking decisions.[38] The cabinet had no wish to say more and a curtain of silence descended over the BND. In vain the Social-Democrats and Federal Party pressed in the Bundestag for some law to fix the BND's position. Adenauer refused, thereby contravening Article 87 of the Basic Law which prescribed that any senior Federal agency must have some basis in law. Owing to this congenital defect the BND never entirely succeeded in ridding itself of the stigma of illegality or in gaining the position in the public esteem which was its due. This state of affairs was in no way altered by Adenauer's agreement to the formation of an all-party Confidential Panel of Bundestag deputies to exercise some form of parliamentary control over the BND. For years the parliamentarians had dust thrown in their eyes by briefings in Pullach; where a measure of supervision and caution was required, these secret-service tyros were satisfied with the great Gehlens' word that all was in order.[39]

Those who know Gehlen have been amused to read in his memoirs the emphasis which he places upon his insistence on objectivity, also the fact that he kept the Social-Democrat leaders informed on secret-service matters. Such briefings of leading Social-Democrats were always discussed with Globke beforehand and Gehlen would frequently meet Globke in the evening to talk over them afterwards. The two would congratulate themselves that they had once more succeeded in giving the Social-Democrats, and later their Party Chairman Erich Ollenhauer in particular, the picture of the situation desired by Adenauer – an obvious abuse of the BND's monopoly of foreign intelligence under Gehlen.

Under cover of the elastic word 'security' Gehlen was able to prevent any check of his personnel before their acceptance into the civil service or other government employ. Once more he showed lively solicitude for his staff. When the reorganization of the Gehlen machine began in August 1955, he combined numerous medium-sized outstations and small local branches into major agencies and so assured himself of sufficient posts in the higher civil-service grades. He himself became a senior civil servant [Ministerialdirektor] with the title of President of the Federal Intelligence Service. Gehlen now ruled over a total of 540 civil servants, 641 office staff and 64 employees.[40]

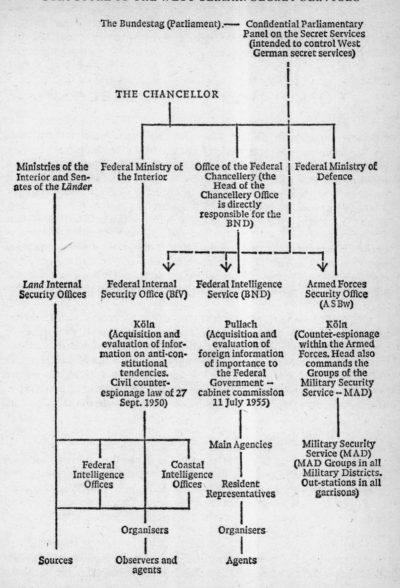

STRUCTURE OF THE WEST GERMAN SECRET SERVICES

The Bundestag (Parliament).—— Confidential Parliamentary Panel on the Secret Services (intended to control West German secret services)

THE CHANCELLOR

Ministries of the Interior and Senates of the *Länder*	Federal Ministry of the Interior	Office of the Federal Chancellery (the Head of the Chancellery Office is directly responsible for the BND)	Federal Ministry of Defence
Land Internal Security Offices	Federal Internal Security Office (BfV)	Federal Intelligence Service (BND)	Armed Forces Security Office (ASBw)
	Köln (Acquisition and evaluation of information on anti-constitutional tendencies. Civil counter-espionage law of 27 Sept. 1950)	Pullach (Acquisition and evaluation of foreign information of importance to the Federal Government — cabinet commission 11 July 1955)	Köln (Counter-espionage within the Armed Forces. Head also commands the Groups of the Military Security Service — MAD)

Federal Intelligence Offices — Coastal Intelligence Offices

Main Agencies

Resident Representatives

Military Security Service (MAD) (MAD Groups in all Military Districts. Out-stations in all garrisons)

Organisers — Organisers

Sources — Observers and agents — Agents

COMMUNIST COUNTERBLAST

T HE rejoicing in Pullach over the Org's new official status was short-lived. Messages flowed in to the BND Headquarters showing clearly that there was a serious threat to the very existence of Gehlen's intelligence network in the East. The BND was faced with an opponent of its own calibre – the East German Ministry of State Security [Ministerium für Staatssicherheit], MfS for short.

As the months passed the silent war between the two German secret services increased in intensity; as with all internecine struggles it became visibly more bitter and pitiless. Moreover the contestants were not equally matched: whereas one followed the traditional rules of gentlemanly espionage, the other preferred the methods of the political all-in wrestler – particularly since he knew that he had the edge over his opponent.

The truth was that, in contrast to the West German secret service, the MfS and its executive organ, the State Security Service or SSD [Staatssicherheitsdienst], was able to arrest any opponent and read the letters of any citizen. It could engineer fake trials and manipulate indictments. It knew that it had the backing of an authoritarian State and Party machine and was immune to any public criticism. From telephone tapping to kidnapping the Mfs and SSD could make use of the whole range of police practices, always with one end in view, expressed thus by the Minister of State Security: 'We are a sharp sword with which our Party will inexorably strike down its enemy.'[1]

The authority and functions of the SSD showed that in the MfS the conspiratorial traditions of German communism, the spy system of the Soviet Secret Police and the police-state doctrine of the Gestapo had all combined to form a highly dangerous mixture. The midwives of the MfS had been communist conspirators, Soviet secret-service men and Gestapo commissars.

Its history can be traced back into the 1920s, to the so-called 'Apparat' (machine), the name invented by German communists for the illegal revolutionary organization which every communist party had to create following a decision of the Comintern in the summer of 1920. This secret party-within-a-party included only the most furtive and activist comrades. When, early in 1923 Comintern headquarters in Moscow thought it saw a possibility of a 'German October', it ordered the German Communist Party to set up three 'apparats' – a military (or M) apparat for the training of assault squads, an intelligence (N – Nachrichten) apparat for secret investigations and a terror (or T) apparat for the organization of political assassinations.

The German Reich was divided into six regions, each headed by a politico-military director who was to run the revolt by his 'apparatchiks' in his region.[2] Among the most intelligent of these directors was a schoolteacher and ex-Lieutenant named Wilhelm Zaisser, born in 1893, son of a janitor at Essen-Rüttenscheid High School; in 1918 he had been an officer in the occupation forces in the Ukraine, where he had become a communist. He seemed to his Russian colleagues (directors were closely supervised by Soviet Generals) to be so bright a star in the intelligence world that, when the German October Revolution failed in 1923, they took him along to Moscow.

Zaisser went to the 'M School', an espionage academy run by the Red Army; he undertook henceforth to work for the Russian military secret service. At the M School Zaisser met another German espionage graduate, the ex-merchant seaman Ernst Wollweber. He was the son of a miner in Münden, Hannover, and was earmarked by the Soviets to form a sabotage organization in Western Europe.[3]

In 1925 Zaisser's and Wollweber's paths diverged; Wollweber returned to Germany while Zaisser went to China, Manchuria and finally into the battles of the Spanish Civil War. There he met yet a third old member of the German Communist Party and a comrade from the apparat – Erich Mielke, born in 1905, who had been a *Red Flag* reporter and had escaped from Germany in 1931 after the murder of two police officers in Berlin.[4] So the three future Ministers of State Security in East Germany knew each other well.

The three next met in Moscow after the outbreak of the Russo–German war and, according to their lights, Zaisser, Wollweber and Mielke all busied themselves with working out a police and intelligence system for post-war Germany. Zaisser was the leading spirit. He had meanwhile entered the service of the Soviet Secret Police, whose chief, Lavrenti Beria, had snatched him from the NKVD prison in which he had been languishing since the time of the Stalinist purges. Since then Zaisser had been his liberator's adviser on German questions – Beria had had a finger in the formulation of Russian policy towards

Germany since the early days. When Beria fell in 1953, he carried Zaisser (who was by then Minister in East Germany) down with him.

It was no doubt due to the influence of Beria that in 1942 Zaisser took charge of the 'Anti-fascist School' in Krasnogorsk, through which passed all German prisoners of war earmarked by the Russians for important posts in the post-war German administration.[5]

In Krasnogorsk Zaisser lit upon a group of ex-Abwehr officers and ex-Gestapo and SD functionaries who could provide him with what he lacked: experience in the systematic surveillance of the German people. These ex-officers and ex-officials of Adolf Hitler had it all at their finger-tips – counter-espionage, counter-intelligence, a sophisticated police system of thought-control, detection of 'anti-State elements' before they had even thought of perpetrating an act of resistance. Among their spokesmen was Lieutenant-General Bamler, a former Section Head in the Abwehr, a friend of Canaris and on good terms with Heydrich, the late lord and master of the Gestapo. Bamler had been taken prisoner by the Russians in 1944 and had been used by the Soviet Secret Police to spy on refractory prisoners.[6] He was only too ready to help Zaisser set up a new German police and intelligence system.

Zaisser visualized a central Ministry of State Security, organized on the pattern of the Soviet State Police, using methods in the field reminiscent of the Gestapo and SD and simultaneously employing the infiltration technique of the old communist 'apparat'. The main lines of the plan had already been drawn up when the Red Army entered Berlin. Zaisser and his immediate associates followed close behind; Bamler together with Zaisser's other new recruits remained behind in the prisoner-of-war camps.

The first essential was to man the more important police headquarters in the Russian occupation zone with reliable German Communist Party veterans. Zaisser took charge of the Police Presidency in Leipzig; Mielke, in the Saxony Ministry of the Interior, organized the political police and Joseph Gutsche, an ex-director of a communist region, became head of the Criminal Police in Saxony. Saxony had clearly been selected as a testing ground for the secret police in the Soviet Zone. Zaisser was in fact planning to create his State Security Service, working from Leipzig. Initially, however, his Russian comrades showed little desire to approve the formation of a German political police.[7]

The end of the war had given the Soviet secret services unlimited power in central Germany and they had no intention of sharing it with the German communists. Two mighty organizations of the Stalinist state watched over the Germans in the Soviet Zone – the Ministry of State Security or MGB and the 'Central Administration for Intelligence' or GRU; the former had its headquarters in St Antonius Hospital in Karlshorst and a staff of 800 distributed in the cities and regions of the zone; the GRU had a 250-strong headquarters in Wünsdorf and branch offices in Erfurt, Leipzig, Magdeburg and Schwerin.[8]

The MGB and GRU, however, had too much on hand to be able to dispense with German assistance. They had to guard the Soviet occupation forces against spies, penetrate West Germany, keep an eye on parties and organizations in the Soviet Zone and hunt Nazi criminals. The Russians accordingly had to recruit German auxiliaries. Late in 1945 special sections entitled 'Kommissariat 5' (K5) appeared in the provincial and district offices of the Peoples' Police. They were to assist the Soviet security authorities to discover and arrest political criminals (or those considered to be so under Allied Control Council Law No 10).

The Russians were careful to allow only limited powers to the K5 desks. They were only permitted to concern themselves with political offences in which the Soviet occupation authorities were not interested; the relevant Soviet officer had to give agreement in each case. Moreover the Russians forbade any central directing authority for the K5 Kommissariats. They did not relax their control until the end of 1946; at that time an agency was formed in the East Berlin Administration for the Interior authorized to issue instructions to K5 desks and commissariats in the Criminal Police offices of the *Länder* and of districts.

Zaisser and his friends gradually ensured that the K5 organization acquired secret-police powers. It was given executive authority, it became increasingly divorced from the normal police administration and its duties were extended. It was not now designed to deal primarily with Nazi criminals; its new brief read: 'Surveillance and suppression of enemies of democratic reconstruction.'[9]

From August 1947, K5 took over duties hitherto reserved to its Russian masters and it was accorded legal powers. It could now order arrests and confiscate the property of prisoners. It could demand the dismissal of citizens of the Soviet Zone from public office and place them on probation.

A year later the Russians authorized creation of a second secret-police force to track down enemies of the regime in all spheres of the economy. This was the 'Commission for protection of the people's property' headed by Erich Mielke; it sent secret emissaries into all industrial concerns in the zone and spied out saboteurs and anti-communists in managements.

However, the increasing popular resistance to the sovietization of the zone, and the successful work of Western secret services eventually forced the Russians to suppress their last doubts about creation of a German State Security Service. Only one agency remained suspicious – the Advisory Section in MGB headquarters whose duty it was to supervise the SSD experiment. But it was unable to curb the enthusiasm of Zaisser who, in mid-summer 1949, on the eve of the proclamation of the German People's Republic, had been commissioned to form a State Protection Corps. At last he was able to create what he had always wanted – a State Security Service.[10]

With an initial allocation of five million East marks Zaisser proceeded to construct a state within the state of workers and peasants. He combined the K5 organization with Mielke's guardians of the people's economy and moved the whole concern into No 22 Normannenstrasse, Berlin-Lichtenberg, until then the offices of a financial agency. On February 8th, 1950, Zaisser's headquarters was given its name – Ministry of State Security. The Minister's deputy was State Secretary Mielke.[11]

The new authority was organized into a number of divisions [Hauptabteilungen] and groups. Its primary tasks were threefold: defence against Western espionage, detection of the last opponents of the regime and enemy intelligence in the West. These tasks were accordingly divided among the main divisions: Division I was to protect the East German armed forces against Western influences, Division II to infiltrate Western secret services (counter-espionage), Division III protected the economy, Division IV countered Western espionage, Division V detected underground organizations and kept its eye on parties and the churches, Division VI protected heavy industry and the arms industry against spies.

These MfS divisions soon covered East Germany with a fine-spun web of SSD agencies, listening posts and informers. The Ministry's tentacles penetrated down to the local level. There were sixteen security districts with divisions corresponding to those of the Ministry; these in turn ran local agencies in all main cities and areas; these were the true front-line headquarters of secret-police activity.[12]

Zaisser set great store by the formation of the local agencies, for theirs was the task of recruiting the army of agents and informers who were to keep watch in businesses, factories and authorities for enemies or critics of the Socialist Unity Party regime. These local agencies usually had a full-time staff of about forty, consisting primarily of 'operatives', as the SSD termed its organizers. The most conspicuous 'operatives' were the so-called 'commissioners', maintained quite openly by every local agency in all major industrial or agricultural concerns. They engaged informers, of whom there were two categories: 'secret informers' who worked in an honorary capacity, were only given minor tasks and filed reports on their own initiative, and 'senior secret informers', who received a small monthly salary, directed and controlled a number of informers and were entitled to arrange meetings on their own. There was also a third group of informers affiliated to no local agency and known as the 'secret staff'. They were directed from a District Office or from the Ministry itself; they were, and still are, regarded as the key figures in underground SSD work; they were infiltrated into known anti-regime circles or enemy espionage groups.[13]

In addition to all these there existed an 'Agency 12'; this had members in every main East German post office to check letters, parcels and packages; 'Division O' monitored telephone traffic in East Germany. More important still – the SSD set up two central detention prisons and sixteen further detention establishments in which it could arbitrarily isolate detainees from the outside world. The SSD alone decided on initiation, prosecution and conclusion of legal investigations; the SSD's final report influenced the measures taken by Public Prosecutors; the SSD decided on sentences to be pronounced by the courts.[14]

So the mighty MfS machine was now in operation; new men moved into the positions prepared by Zaisser. This was the moment Bamler and the converted prisoners of war had been waiting for in the Soviet Union; Zaisser summoned them to serve in the SSD. He had quickly realized that he could never build up an effective state security system with the old-guard communists alone. He needed the old surveillance experts who had been given a new ideological twist in Krasnogorsk; he also needed the growing East German generation of academics, trained in the 'Free German Youth' movement and the Socialist Unity Party.

Zaisser had studied the history of the Russian State Police long enough to know that even communists can visualize more desirable professions than service in the secret police. The SSD therefore had to be made attractive, to be presented as the state's *corps d'élite*, the Order of the omniscient, keeping watch over the well-being of the new socialist society. Such glorification of the SSD was not without its dangers since it inevitably aroused the suspicion of the Party bureaucrats who thought of themselves as the élite. The comrades of Division S (Security) of the Central Committee of the Socialist Unity Party

anyway thought that Minister Zaisser was giving himself far too independent air *vis-à-vis* the Party.

The anti-fascist purists of the Party, moreover, raised their eyebrows
over many of the men chosen by Zaisser. They were prepared to accept
General Bamler, formerly of Canaris' staff, as adviser to the MfS, but it
was altogether too much for them when they came across ex-Gestapo
functionaries as members of the SSD. SS-Hauptsturmführer Louis
Hagemeister, for instance, who had been a desk officer in the counter-
espionage section of the RSHA, appeared as head of the Interrogation
Section in the SSD District Agency in Schwerin; SS-Untersturmführer
Johann Sanitzer, who had been in charge of Desk IV A 2 in the Gestapo
office in Vienna, appeared as a Major in the SSD District Office in
Erfurt; SS-Scharführer Reinhold Tappert, who had been a specialist
in Security Police headquarters, reappeared in the SSD agency in
Berlin.[15]

The Party establishment, however, was equally unenthusiastic about
the younger members whom Zaisser gradually recruited into his organization. They came from academies and high schools; they had been
brought up as cold rationalists and had learnt to judge the communist
state by technocratic rather than ideological criteria. Many of them
were not even members of the Socialist Unity Party; Zaisser had relaxed
the rule that an SSD man must be a Party member.

Here was proof of the fact that the SSD was no exception to the
historic rule that a dictatorship's secret policemen are often more
astute than the regime they are supposed to protect. In their peculiar
way the SSD investigators were in closer touch with daily life in East
Germany than any other authority; they knew the real situation in the
country and in addition their Chief favoured some liberalization of Ulbricht's tyranny. The men around Walter Ulbricht were well aware of
this but they remained silent so long as Zaisser continued to deliver the
goods. And Wilhelm Zaisser's SSD *did* deliver: his listening posts
covered every section of the Republic and he was able to detect and
liquidate many opposition groups.

Anti-communist visionaries in West Berlin had involuntarily presented the SSD with its first major success. They were to be found in
Berlin's impenetrable jungle of East-West cross-currents, in which
democrats genuinely indignant over the injustices of Ulbricht's regime
mingled with fanciful busy-bodies and secret-service agents avid for
information. From this undergrowth arose an extremist association entitled the 'Anti-Inhumanity Combat Group' [Kampfgruppe gegen Un-
menschlichkeit – KgU].

The KgU had been founded by Rainer Hildebrandt, a confirmed anti-Hitlerite; his purpose had been to form a political association to mobilize Western public opinion against the concentration-camp system in the Soviet Zone and to hunt for missing persons in the zone. With this in view he allied himself with Dr Heinrich von zur Mühlen, an ex-Abwehr man who ran an intelligence organization in the zone known as the 'Hoffmann Bureau'. But the KgU under Hildebrandt and Mühlen was rapidly swept up by the American secret service, whose attention was drawn to it by the increasing number of East Germans whom Hildebrandt succeeded in recruiting into his tracking service. The US Colonel Wallach, head of the CIC's Berlin office, was particularly attracted by the KgU's manifold possibilities of obtaining information. Wallach became the organization's real master and financier.[16]

In 1950, however, the place of the CIC was increasingly being taken by the CIA and the head of the CIA's Berlin office held the view that the only method of damaging the communist regime was by sabotage. His watchword was: 'That zone has to go bang, bang!' The two KgU leaders, however, were unwilling to adopt this course – and so the CIA squeezed them out of their own association. To replace them the Americans found a willing helper in Ernst Tillich, a Social-Democrat and a theologian, the typical anti-communist crusader. He filled all important posts in the KgU with a squad of ex-Criminal Police officials and issued orders to prepare for acts of sabotage.[17] Things began to 'go bang' in the zone. Socialist Unity Party propaganda photographs were set alight with phosphorus; the Finow canal bridge at the Zerpen lock was damaged; railway lines were blown up. Wolf and Starke, two of the KgU's new officials, proposed that East Germany's electricity supply be paralysed by the demolition of high-tension pylons; in a secret depot in the Clausewitzstrasse, Berlin-Charlottenburg, KgU men issued explosives and raiding parties armed themselves to carry out Wolf's and Starke's instructions.[18]

The saboteurs went about their business in so dilettante a fashion, however, that Gehlen began to fear that the KgU might jeopardize the Org's work in the Russian Zone – members of the KgU and the Org's agents worked together on occasions. Through Hans-Georg Scharlau, one of his agents who had been a KgU driver, Gehlen learnt of harebrained plans being cooked up in the chemical laboratory of KgU headquarters in Nikolassee. Gehlen warned Colonel Wallach against giving further support to these saboteurs, the Org had always refused to participate in sabotage. Gehlen severed all connexion with the KgU but Wallach was still unwilling to drop it.[19]

When he eventually made up his mind to do so, it was too late. Zaisser struck; in March 1951 the SSD arrested the KgU leader in Brandenburg and shortly thereafter an entire group was blown. During the night September 8th/9th, the KgU network in Saxony was swept up. Shortly thereafter Roland, the KgU's headquarters night-watchman, disappeared with an armful of documents – he had been an SSD agent.[20]

Zaisser's haul of documents soon led to another blow, this time against the 'Investigating Commission of Free Lawyers in the Soviet Zone', a sort of sister organization to the KgU. This too was working with the US secret service and it too fell victim to infiltration – the SSD had fed in an agent as secretary in the Commission's headquarters.

By the spring of 1952 all the more important members of the 'Investigating Commission' had vanished into the cells of the SSD, which enabled the Russians to track down many of the Commission's informers – a timekeeper in the German Internal and External Trade Association, the head of a division in the Stralsund Construction Company, a civil engineer in the Machine Tools Ministry, the manager of an incandescent lamp factory in East Berlin.[21]

All these documents and prisoners' statements uncovered so many trails into the Western secret-service undergrowth that the SSD could now turn on its greatest opponent – the Gehlen Organization.

Zaisser collected together everything the SSD knew about the West German secret service. Every press report on the Org was analysed, every statement by an arrested Western spy was evaluated. Bamler too could make a contribution here – he had served in the same artillery regiment with Gehlen and had also been in the 'Foreign Armies' section of the General Staff. The MfS also turned to the Russians for assistance. Sixty MGB officers combed the camps for German POWs who knew Gehlen; they interrogated seventy witnesses, including ex-Colonel Karl Schildknecht, who had headed a group in FHO, and ex-Lieutenant-General Hans Piekenbrock, a former section head of the Abwehr.[22]

In cases where sources of information evaded the SSD's clutches, they arranged to capture them by force. On February 13th, 1953, an SSD squad kidnapped Major (retd) Wolfgang Höher, one of Gehlen's organizers in West Berlin; SSD agents had first slipped a drug into his glass of wine in a bar on the Wittenbergplatz. While under arrest Höher gave much information about the Org, later published in a brochure entitled 'Agent 2996 speaks'. Armed with this information, the SSD opened a silent offensive against the Org. Once again Zaisser used the well-known infiltration technique and alleged anti-communists were to be found trying to gain contact with the Org in West Berlin.[23]

Before the SSD could achieve a breakthrough into the Org, however, Zaisser's position collapsed. After the death of Stalin he had been tempted by superficial signs of dissolution in the Ulbricht regime to take a hand in the Politburo's party struggles and work for the fall of Ulbricht. The popular rising of June 17th, 1953, however, put an end to his plotting and he was forced to leave both the MfS and the Party. Ulbricht celebrated his victory over the remnants of the Zaisser machine; he demoted the Ministry to a State Secretariat, subjected it to strict Party control and placed at its head Ernst Wollweber, the sabotage apparatchik. In a secret oration Ulbricht thundered: 'The Politburo has established that the leaders of the Ministry of State Security have failed. The Ministry ... has promoted tendencies of arrogance *vis-à-vis* the Party and has tolerated formalistic and bureaucratic methods of work. Party work was hampered by the senior functionaries of the Ministry.'[24]

As a result of this self-immolation of the SSD, however, and of the continuing popular unrest, Gehlen's agencies both in West Berlin and in East Germany became over-bold. In the rush of events after June 17th an increasing number of East German citizens were prepared to work for Gehlen. The Org's local branches were unable to cope with the flood of work. Unchecked material began to flow through the Org's channels; agents were engaged without sufficiently careful screening. Everyone wished to exploit this unexpected situation and cast caution to the winds. The security experts did not perceive that numerous SSD spies were infiltrating Gehlen's agencies.

One of these was a writer named Hans Joachim Geyer; his assignment was to infiltrate Gehlen's local branch X/9592 in West Berlin. Under the pseudonym Henry Troll he had written the John Kling series and other detective novels and he had always dreamed of playing a John Kling role himself. The first opening was offered him by the Gehlen Org in 1952, first as investigator in East Germany and then as a desk officer in the local branch X/9592. Then, however, Geyer fell into the hands of the Eastern counter-espionage service and was 'converted' by them. Since then he had spied for the East Germans – at night, when the local branch offices were untenanted.

From autumn 1953, therefore, 'Grell' (Geyer's code-name) was in a position to photograph every document which had been placed in the branch's safe during the day – personal details, informers' reports, accounts, cipher keys. Among the papers which he photographed with his Minox camera was the list of all sixty informers maintained in East

Germany by X/9592. Every morning a courier smuggled Geyer's material across into East Berlin.[25]

As a double agent Geyer's position was absolutely ideal. He was a friend of the head of the branch; during the day he read the informers' and agents' reports; he was in charge of the security of the files; he had access to the branch's strong-room at all times; he had a duplicate key to the steel cupboard. Then he committed a stupid error and in one fell swoop destroyed everything that he had taken months to build up.

Early in October 1953 the head of the branch thought that the office needed an additional secretary and commissioned Geyer to engage a girl. Geyer placed an advertisement and a number of applicants appeared. During the interviews, however, he assumed his John Kling role and gave himself such an air of mystery that one of the applicants became suspicious. She found it peculiar that Geyer, who presented himself as an industrial representative, would only meet her in seedy cafés, wished to know all about her relatives and was interested in her men friends. She suspected that he was in the white-slave trade and alerted the police.

About 10 AM on October 29th two criminal-police officials rang the doorbell of Geyer's rented apartment and asked for the alleged industrial representative. Geyer was not there. When he returned an hour later and heard of this visitation, he lost his nerve and thought that he had been discovered. He collected some documents and files, locked his apartment on the inside and jumped through the window into the garden. By midday he had gone to ground in East Berlin.[26]

His flight was the signal for a manhunt after the Org's informers. All over East Germany SSD flying squads, which had been ready for weeks, took action and arrested numerous Gehlen agents; they included members of the Ministry for Reconstruction, police officers, an editor of the *Berliner Zeitung* and leading functionaries of the East German bourgeois parties.

A radio message from East Germany addressed to Gehlen's local branch X/9592 read: 'We have been blown. Arrests are raining down.' Disillusionment and bitterness spread among the Org's informers. All realized that it had never suffered so severe a blow. The Geyer case had shown how slackly the security regulations had been applied: Geyer ought never to have been employed in the branch since his family lived in East Germany and were consequently subject to any form of pressure by the SSD. Organizers had been instructed not to run more than five informers in East Germany – and X/9592 was running sixty.[27]

The Org's agents became so vocal in their discontent over the Geyer set-back that Gehlen thought it necessary to comfort those who had not yet been blown. The Pullach headquarters issued Directive No 852 sv 'Ref: Security of our methods'; it read: 'The large-scale publicity in the Eastern press about the Geyer incident will naturally cause anxiety to all informers and lead them to wonder whether a similar incident could not take place within their own ranks. This subject must be dealt with at forthcoming meetings with Eastern Zone informers. The confidence of our workers in the Eastern Zone must remain unassailable and they must continue to feel that they are in good hands.'[28]

The leaders of the SSD banked upon a loss of confidence among Gehlen's agents and believed that they had succeeded in making a decisive break-through into his espionage network in the zone; only a little propaganda assistance was needed, they thought, to persuade the mass of Gehlen's agents to desert. At an agitators' conference held by the Central Committee of the Socialist Unity Party on September 15th an SSD representative proclaimed that in a few weeks' time his authority would completely expose a Western secret service; this would reflect the greatest discredit, he said, on the imperialist 'warmongers'.

Although Geyer's unexpected defection had probably upset the SSD's timetable, it nevertheless attempted to destroy Gehlen's entire Eastern network in one operation. Those who contrived to escape arrest and take refuge in West Berlin suddenly found themselves being wooed by the SSD. Eastern couriers made mysterious appearances and slipped letters through letter-boxes. X/9592's fugitive agents received the following: 'Dear Sir, we know that you have been cast off by General Gehlen's organization. You will receive no further income. Your group has been blown and you will now be on the dole. That is the normal form of gratitude of the capitalistic West. With your capabilities it is not necessary for you to pay for the failure of others. Follow our advice: come to East Berlin, to one of the SSD agencies of which you already know. There you will be treated as a friend and directed elsewhere. You need fear no form of arrest. We guarantee you complete liberty, accommodation and a well-paid post.'[29]

To encourage potential defectors, on November 9th the SSD produced Geyer, the double agent, at a press conference; he was in a new role – that of the repentant Gehlen man. He had a seven-page script from which he read: 'As of today I have broken with my criminal activity and as a token of my sincerity I now hand over to the security authorities of the German People's Republic all the secret documents of Branch X/9592.' Professor Albert Norden, presiding, said: 'The People's Republic is generous when anyone admits their error and assists in the detection of crime.' Admittedly this invitation was closely followed by a threat. Colonel Hans Bormann, the SSD's counter-espionage expert and Geyer's watchdog at the press conference, declared that his authorities knew almost everything about the assignments, personnel and communications of the Gehlen Organization. SSD informers, the Colonel said, regularly gave 'signals' when the Org was planning some action.[30]

Whether this was true or mere bragging, the fact remains that, by working for the SSD, Geyer started an avalanche which ultimately swept away large sections of Gehlen's intelligence organization in East Germany. A few days later two members of Gehlen's Branch No 120a in East Germany defected and betrayed a forthcoming operation. During the night November 13th/14th, the two said, the head of their branch, ex-Major Werner Haase, proposed to lay a telephone cable up to the sector boundary in order to talk to one of his informers in the East; on the Eastern side of the Heidekampgraben, which formed the boundary at this point, was a summer-house, where the connexion was to be made. One of the Org's informers would be waiting there to take over the Western cable from Haase and connect it to one from East Germany.

On the night in question an SSD flying squad hid itself on the Western side of the Heidekampgraben. Gehlen's man appeared shortly after 9 PM and a few seconds later was bound and gagged. He was put on trial in December and sentenced to life imprisonment.[31]

Wollweber's experts left no stone unturned to induce Gehlen's people to defect. The *Tägliche Rundschau*, the official Soviet organ, said: 'During the Christmas holiday and the days preceding it a number of ex-agents of the Gehlen fascist espionage organization have applied to the State Secretariat for State Security. They are conscious of the guilt they have incurred in the eyes of the German people.' One after another they had to make public confession and to call upon their ex-colleagues still working for Gehlen to desert. At the end of December statements from thirty-one ex-agents of Gehlen and their dependants were published.[32]

Hardly any important members of the Org, however, answered the call. Wollweber's propagandists promptly devised a helpful subterfuge: they recalled agents whom they had infiltrated into Gehlen's agencies and presented them to the world press as repentant defectors. On April 27th, 1954, Gerhard Kapahnke, one of the SSD's double agents, appeared in East Berlin and he was followed a few weeks later by Gerhard

Prather, another SSD man. They brought with them sufficient material to enable the SSD to pursue its campaign against Gehlen's agents in East Germany. One blow now followed another.[33]

May 1954: a group of eight Gehlen agents sentenced in East Berlin. June: Trial of Schuppenhauer, one of the Org's agents, and his assistants. August: Arrest by the SSD of the most important group of Gehlen agents so far, including the high-level spy Karl Bandelow of the State Secretariat of Motor Traffic and Roads. September: Franz Neugebauer, a member of the Org, kidnapped from West Berlin by an SSD flying squad. On October 4th, 1954, the East German spy-chasers presented their first balance sheet: according to a statement by Norden, the State Secretary, they claimed to have arrested 547 agents of the Gehlen Org. The figure was, of course, inflated. (Norden had included everybody from the KgU 'diversionaries' to agents of the BfV.) Nevertheless the Org had suffered irreplaceable losses.[34]

In subsequent years Wollweber, who had meanwhile been appointed Minister of State Security, was able to crack many of Gehlen's strongholds. Early in 1955 the SSD captured certain informers in the headquarters of the Liberal-Democrat Party; in March they laid hands on Wilhelm van Ackern, head of Gehlen's Local Branch 904, and two other agents. On April 12th, 1955, Wollweber announced the arrest of 521 agents and in May a further 80 were said to have defected voluntarily to the SSD. The victims of the MfS offensive even included Gehlen's high-level source Elli Barczatis, private secretary to Grotewohl, the Minister-President. 'The Daisy' (her code-name) had been providing Pullach with official secrets ever since 1953. Now she was discovered, condemned to death, and guillotined.[35]

Such set-backs were bound to be depressing to a man who had just obtained official recognition of his secret service from Bonn, using the argument that no other organization had been as successful in infiltrating East Germany as the BND. In fact those BND circuits which were still intact were so threatened that Gehlen recalled his leading agents to West Germany; they included 'Brutus' and Kastner, the former Deputy Prime Minister of East Germany.

When Kastner heard from his contact Tarnay that he too was threatened, he waved the suggestion nonchalantly away. He only agreed after a personal invitation from Chancellor Adenauer, transmitted verbally by the BND, to come to the Federal Republic and assume a political post there. During the night September 5th/6th BND personnel conducted first Frau Kastner and then the old gentleman himself from East to West Berlin via the metro. They were received by BND representatives in

Tarnay's flat with flowers, champagne and a message of welcome from the Federal Chancellor.

Gehlen christened this enterprise 'Operation Autumn Storm' – an ominous title. The SSD storm had indeed swept away important parts of the BND machine.[36]

FRACTURE OF AN AXIS

IN the President's first-floor office in the headquarters at Pullach, a veteran of the Org presented himself to Reinhard Gehlen. The visitor, head of a Desk in the BND, wished to tell his Chief of his worries; he feared that the BND was gradually losing credibility. He sat down at a small occasional table and began: 'Mr President, I have noticed that in recent reports from the Russian Zone we have quoted as source "a collaborator in the Central Committee of the Socialist Unity Party".'

'So what?' said Gehlen. The head of the Desk replied: 'But we have no collaborator in the Central Committee.' 'Who can prove otherwise?' Gehlen chuckled. The desk officer: 'We cannot quote a source which does not exist; still less can we pretend in our reports to Bonn that we have our own man in the Socialist Unity Party's Central Committee.' Gehlen interrupted him: 'Of course we can. I have already said to you: Who can prove otherwise?' The desk officer hesitated for a moment and then voiced a cautious protest: 'I regard such procedure as irresponsible. In any case there is no need for it.' The President dismissed him coldly.[1]

This conversation between Gehlen and a member of his staff in the summer of 1958 shows that the BND's great days of espionage in the East were drawing to a close. Gehlen calls 'Wollweber's efforts to smear the BND in the eyes of the West and the neutrals' a 'vain attempt'. Nevertheless he is forced to admit that the Org's set-backs in East Germany and the sacrifice of agents, frequently through inefficiency, were factors in preventing the West German government from taking the Org into its service earlier, in 1953 in fact. Two years after its acceptance as the sole foreign intelligence service of the German Federal Republic the BND had practically no insight into the centres of political decision in East Germany. Step by step the East German SSD had destroyed Gehlen's intelligence network. It was hard for the BND to find fresh high-level sources in the East German administrative and Party machines. The theme propagated by the Socialist Unity Party that, with its entry into NATO, West Germany had turned its back on reunification and had joined the imperialist camp, had not been without effect on East German officialdom, whose consciousness of East German nationhood grew as the years went by.

In Eastern Europe and the Soviet Union too, the BND's opportunities of acquiring intelligence were dwindling. With the Russian withdrawal from the now neutralized Austria, few bases existed from which to infiltrate official and military institutions. In the Soviet Union itself the BND was reduced to one or two casual spies whose work was uncertain and reports infrequent.

Gehlen refused to admit that his organization had now become ineffective in the acquisition of Eastern intelligence. He allowed over-zealous subordinates to quote in their reports to the Chancellery Eastern sources which existed only in their own imagination; they threw up a cloak of concealment around the lacunae and bottlenecks of the BND. Pullach's reports became woollier and increasingly shrouded in mystery. Even published sources (repeats from Russian newspapers or broadcasts) were elevated to the status of information 'from reliable Eastern circles'.[2]

The BND's credibility also suffered from the malpractice of refusing ever to cancel or correct reports proved to be false. Even when dealing with their expert colleagues of the American or British secret services, the BND clung obstinately to every report even long after some had proved to be erroneous.

Towards the end of the 1960s the BND alarmed both the Internal Security Office of Hesse and the Frankfurt Police Presidency with the news that Ceausescu, the Rumanian 'head of government', would pay an incognito visit to the Main motor show. Both internal security officials and the police prepared to keep him under unobtrusive observation. Ceausescu never came. Yet the BND did not think it necessary to explain their error to the Hessian authorities or even to cancel their announcement of the visit ahead of time. In its haste, moreover, the BND had overlooked the fact that Ceausescu was not a head of government but merely the leader of a party.

Many BND agents developed their own specialized methods of collecting intelligence. The Pullach headquarters was well aware of these machinations as the following report shows: 'Ref: H v. O. The above-named frequently appears in the "Institute for Russian Research" and asks to examine Russian books and periodicals. In this connection he allowed it to be known that he was working for a German agency in Pullach, as proof of which he produced his driving licence. In the presence of members of the Institute he is said to have expressed himself as follows: "Somehow I must earn my bread and butter, my 2,000 marks a month, although I really know little more than that schnapps is made from alcohol and water." For information!'[3]

Gehlen was able to conceal the sinking efficiency of his organization for some time because the few high-level agents whom he still had in East Germany enabled him to score occasional successes. They were mostly negative successes, however, show-pieces of Pullach counter-espionage, concerned more with confusing the enemy than collecting intelligence. One of these high-level agents even enabled the BND to checkmate the East German military secret service for years. This was Siegfried Dombrowski, a Lieutenant-Colonel in the People's National Army.

Dombrowski was the son of a long-distance driver, born in 1916; he trained as a motor mechanic and became a member of the communist youth organization. He joined the anti-Nazi resistance, was trained at an agents' school in Moscow and then became a political officer in the East German Barrack Police. In September 1955 he was summoned to a mysterious agency in East Berlin which bore the innocent title of 'Ad-ministration for Co-ordination' [Verwaltung für Koordinierung – VfK]. It was in fact the directing agency for military espionage against the Federal Republic. Dombrowski assumed office in a barracks in Berlin-Grünau as Deputy Chief of this new espionage organization.[4]

Unfortunately Lieutenant-Colonel Dombrowski had a weakness: he was a *bon viveur* and he liked going to West Germany. During one of his excursions to the Taunus at Easter 1956 he made the acquaintance of a professional secret-service man working for the Federal Internal Security Office of the CIA.

This intermediary offered Dombrowski a monthly salary of 800 marks if he would agree to work for the 'Federal German Counter-Espionage Service'. Dombrowski accepted. Subsequently the CIA and BfV agreed to transfer their agent to Gehlen's BND and henceforth Dombrowski delivered his material solely to Pullach. His reports told the BND of the methods, personnel and duties of the VfK, its failures and the rivalries between VfK and SSD.[5]

When on March 18th, 1958, General Linke, the head of the VfK, met the Soviet military espionage chiefs led by Colonel-General Shtemenko in Moscow, the BND was a fly on the wall. A few days later the Pullach headquarters could read what Linke (in rather bad German) had written in his diary: 'As regards the material (on the West German forces) handed to the Army General by the Minister, General Shtemenko stated as follows: Content was good apart from one or two differences in figures for divisional strengths, which our friends put somewhat higher, and the figure for ships which is given as 100 by our friends and 47 by us ... The most obvious omission is a politico-military forecast of developments until 1960. The report on the last manoeuvres in November was good except for the attempted analysis which was not a success. There was no geographic or military description of installations.'[6]

In KGB headquarters, however, it was soon rumoured that there was a BND agent in the headquarters of the VfK; this came to the ears of Colonel Igonin of the Russian advisory staff in the VfK and he began to suspect that Lieutenant-Colonel Dombrowski was the man. He asked General Dimitrov of the KGB to institute inquiries against Dombrowski. Dimitrov received his report in June – and it said that the BND spy was not Dombrowski but Igonin!

This was the surprising result of a gambit by the counter-espionage experts in Pullach. They had quickly realized that Dombrowski was in danger. He provided them with specimens of Igonin's handwriting and the specialists in Pullach's technical section then prepared reports in the Colonel's writing which were fed to the KGB. General Dimitrov was convinced by the Pullach forgeries. He had Igonin arrested and carted off to Moscow.[7]

The BND was doubtful, however, how long this trick could remain undiscovered. In August 1958 Dombrowski was ordered to photostat as much secret material as he could and hold himself in readiness for swift recall. He came even quicker than the Pullach sceptics had expected. He fled to the Federal Republic at Christmas – the Russians had discovered who had been betraying the East German military intelligence secrets. The East German Ministry of Defence hastened to carry out the necessary self-criticism, demoting General Linke and reorganizing the VfK. The VfK's rivals in the SSD, however, now seized their chance; on February 26th Linke, two colonels and 67 other members of the VfK were placed under detention; 200 officers and men of the intelligence service were dismissed. It was five years before East German military intelligence could become active again.[8]

The BND's balance sheet, however, registered successes such as the Dombrowski affair with increasing infrequency. A BND veteran said resignedly: 'We now have a couple of sardines in a pond which was alive with sharks and pikes a few years ago.' The days of the great Gehlen agents in the East were at an end. Yet the President of the BND scarcely lifted a finger to extract his organization from its blind alley. His staff saw with consternation that his energy and drive were failing; he seemed more concerned with the preservation of his own interests than with the efficiency of the service.

Admittedly he had long since ceased to bother with organizational details; his forte was intuition, analysis and a lightning grasp of future developments. Those who knew Gehlen, however, had never before seen him so complacent over questions of organization. Only rarely would he receive Section Heads or desk officers who wished to tell him of their worries; they were generally intercepted by 'Alo' (Annelore), Gehlen's dragon of a private secretary; he would frequently unload on to her decisions on personnel or unwelcome discussions with subordinates. He disliked criticism – he had sufficient vexations already with the sixteen relatives whom he had brought into the BND and who were a permanent source of office gossip.[9]

Gehlen only displayed energy when it was necessary to defend some position – his own or that of the BND. He had close ties to certain Bundestag deputies of the Christian-Democrat/Christian-Social alliance, who represented his interests in the House. His primary interest seemed to be to consolidate the position of power which he had acquired for himself and his secret service in West Germany's governmental system. In fact no other secret service had anything even approaching the influence exerted by the BND in Konrad Adenauer's State. Although in theory he had to share power with his two weaker rivals, the BfV and the MAD, his ties with the government machine were in fact of a very special nature.

He was directly responsible to the Chancellor and was subject to no departmental control (as the BfV was to the Minister of the Interior, for example). He was, so to speak, the Chancellery's private intelligence service. Hans Globke, State Secretary of the Chancellery and Adenauer's *éminence grise*, was responsible for supervising the BND. He was particularly assiduous in dealing with the BND's personnel problems, and carried out inspections of the headquarters. His was usually the final decision whether major BND operations were feasible or not. An inexhaustible stream of information, indications and reports from Pullach flowed on to his desk; the BND had an express service for important events, frequently summarized in a couple of sentences; in addition there were weekly reports, situation reports, memoranda and trend analyses.

The teleprinter, three aircraft and a whole squad of couriers were permanently at readiness to carry messages to the Chancellery. The regular service was provided by the couriers, mostly retired officers who travelled by night – invariably in pairs; they occupied a second-class railway compartment, and were not allowed to sleep or leave their leather-covered steel boxes unwatched even for a visit to the lavatory.[10]

Adenauer was so impressed by Pullach's reports that he held them up as models for other, allegedly more negligent, authorities. Whenever the BfV failed, for instance, Adenauer would immediately send it the BND's apparently more exhaustive reports. The worst sufferer from Adenauer's predilection for the BND was the Foreign Office. Chancellor's minutes on BND reports were continually pointing out to Heinrich von Brentano, the Foreign Minister, that once again the secret-service people had been more effective than the diplomats. Usually the Foreign Office mandarins suppressed their wrath, even when they found that (in the words of a Foreign Office Eastern expert) the BND reports read 'like travel or gossip columns in a newspaper, gave few details but were decked out with "Secret" stamps and padded with cunningly camouflaged information'.

The writer Ulrich Blank commented: 'The Gehlen Org is accorded the privileges of the aristocrat; it prepares analyses and specialist reports normally the prerogative of senior ministerial bureaucrats.' Even more significantly the BND frequently supplanted established authorities in their own fields. When Adenauer prepared to travel abroad, he would be briefed on the country he was visiting, not by the Foreign Office but by the BND. On one occasion, for instance, the BND had to wrestle for months with the mysteries of Japanese internal politics because Adenauer was proposing to visit that country: reports on Japan continued to pile up in Pullach for years since no one remembered to call the operation off.[11]

Adenauer urged other politicians and ministries to work closely with the BND. When President Lübke was visiting Brazil, for instance, he was given a glowing picture of Latin-American military dictatorships by a BND agent. The Foreign Office called upon the BND to assist in its security arrangements – to protect German missions abroad against 'bugging' by foreign secret services and the infiltration of the foreign service by enemy agents.

With so assured a niche in the centre of West German power Gehlen was able calmly to expand his influence. He arranged the transfer to Federal authority of the allied 'Interrogation Agency', which interrogated every Eastern bloc refugee, and its material was henceforth channelled primarily into the West German secret service. He also engineered for the BND the right to present its budget *en bloc* and to include special secret votes in the budgets of other ministries. The BND was also given the right to investigate itself and to refute any charges against it.[12]

But the further the BND expanded, the more unstable the basis of its power became. The destruction of Gehlen's networks in the East had upset the entire organization; there was next to nothing to do for the 2,500 members of Gehlen's local branches, district agencies and sub-agencies, which had hitherto been concerned exclusively with intelligence in the East. The channels of communication from individual BND agencies to their informers in the East, which now led nowhere, lay about in confusion and became entangled with each other. Now came the pay-off for Gehlen's labyrinthine construction of his organization; not even the Chief himself now knew which agencies were functioning properly and which were merely inventing fake material in order to perpetuate their own existence.

The chaos in the organization roused a group of its officers to revolt against Gehlen's lethargy and autocratic ways. They submitted to him that an organization expert must be obtained to bring some order into the confusion; Gehlen should have a Vice-President, they said, to modernize and expand BND. Gehlen took note of their arguments but was so dilatory in giving a decision that the rumour went round that he was proposing to appoint as Vice-President Brigadier-General Wolfgang Langkau, the head of a special section known as the 'Strategic Service', already responsible direct to the President.

The reformers, however, would have none of Langkau, whom they regarded as an intriguer and far too similar to Gehlen. Not only did he look like his master but he had served with him in the same artillery regiment and he adopted that air of mystery which both of them seemed to regard as inseparable from intelligence work. Langkau clearly had a penchant for conspiratorial ways; he would frequently lock himself in his office and open only on a previously agreed knock; he was Gehlen's main contact man to the political parties but liked to meet politicians in dubious localities. Langkau's enemies scoffed that he thought himself so secret that he did not allow himself to know that he even existed. They were more worried by the fact, however, that he played BND politics with the outside world totally free from control and to all intents and purposes divorced from all other sections of the Org.[13]

When Gehlen refused to deny the rumour of Langkau's candidature, the reformers experimented with an open revolt. Several BND officials passed word to the President that, if Langkau became Vice-President, they would leave the BND and go over to the Bundeswehr. Gehlen accepted the reformers' candidate, whom he himself had also considered – Hans-Heinrich Worgitzky, Head of the BND agency in Hamburg. Worgitzky, born in 1907, had been a colonel on the General Staff and Intelligence Officer of Army Group Centre during the war; he had been a member of the Gehlen Org since December 1946 and from June 1951 head of General Agency N (Bremen) dealing with 'Zone intelligence'. He was one of the most popular men in the BND and was universally regarded as a good organizer.

Worgitzky was appointed first Vice-President of the BND on May 24th, 1957, and he immediately set about reforming it. He proposed to dismantle the swollen machine and rationalize the acquisition of intelligence; since he doubted whether the employment of informers was either timely or possible in areas under Soviet control, he proposed to send only highly qualified peripatetic sources to the East and make greater use of non-secret material from the radio, press and technical publications.[14]

Worgitzky and his men had realized that the BND's acquisition and evaluation system must keep pace with the intelligence revolution which had largely rendered the traditional espionage methods obsolete. The manifold methods of automated espionage were increasingly taking the place of the 'Daisys' and the 'Brutus's'; optical, acoustic and electronic contraptions, working from static or mobile stations, ships, aircraft or satellites, were now able to spot every car parked in Moscow, report the firing of every Russian rocket and monitor all radio traffic inside the Soviet Union without anyone ever setting foot on Russian territory.

The twilight of the conventional spy, however, inevitably hit the BND particularly hard since its strength had long lain in its agents in the East who had worked genuine miracles of intelligence-gathering – supported by the local resistance to which any totalitarian regime gives rise. The increasing sophistication of the Eastern security system, however, had almost totally cut the ground from under the feet of Gehlen's agents. Now the new long-range methods of espionage offered the BND some substitute for its lost agents. The secret service was given a pronounced scientific and technological twist.

The BND was ill-prepared for this process of change. Worgitzky and his people, however, quickly perceived that this technical revolution in espionage offered the BND considerable advantages. Technology could make the secret service semi-independent of agents, who frequently produced valueless information and sometimes even manufactured intelligence in order to fulfil their stint and guarantee themselves continued employment. The technical methods of intelligence collection could lead to more objective analyses. Worgitzky saw every reason to rationalize the BND on these lines.

This did not entail the dismissal of productive agents, however; the spy will still have his role to play in the secret service provided he can furnish what automated espionage cannot – information on the enemy's intentions. Technical intelligence methods can register potential or actual movements; only an agent in the right place can find out the plans and intentions of the enemy leaders. Nevertheless the secret agent had lost his habitual key position. In the BND he was now competing on the same level with telecommunications and electronic methods of acquisition. The BND set up a chain of aerial masts along the frontiers of the Soviet empire to intercept the radio and radio-telephone traffic of the other side. The BND was also a customer for the findings of American satellites.

Worgitzky also ordered increased use to be made of non-secret material in the formation of estimates – non-secret in that it was accessible to anyone. The object was to maintain the BND's store of knowledge at the highest possible level and also to provide standards of comparison for the material obtained by conspiratorial methods. For Worgitzky this was the decisive point – the ability to differentiate between the valuable and the valueless report. He ordered introduction of a sophisticated system of intelligence evaluation.

Every message received now had to be examined from two points of view: whether the source was reliable and whether the news was credible. Sources were classified as: A – 'reliable', B – 'generally reliable', C – 'fairly reliable', D – 'not invariably reliable', E – 'unreliable' and F – 'no estimate of reliability possible'. Contents of a message were graded as follows: 1 – 'confirmed from another source', 2 – 'probably accurate', 3 – 'possibly accurate', 4 – 'doubtful', 5 – 'improbable' and 6 – 'estimate not possible'.[15] Only after this classification could the next stage begin – dissection of the intelligence material. The message was broken down into individual parts corresponding to the various intelligence objectives; it was analysed, compared with other background intelligence and then, in secret service phraseology, 'laid on the table'.

Here too Worgitzky introduced modern technique into the BND. West Germany's first official computer was installed in Pullach: a data bank was to facilitate the process of intelligence dissection. An automated card index and electronic data processing enabled reference to be made at any time to information already received and comparison with fresh intelligence to be made. If a message withstood these tests it was incorporated into the overall picture of the situation. It now formed part of the so-called 'current situation', a process of intelligence production which enabled the BND to give the Federal government at any time information on the external political situation.[16]

With this in view Worgitzky followed the pattern of the US secret service and set up a report centre; working in parallel with the specialist evaluation section, this provided an immediate round-the-clock service dealing with every message entering the acquisition section. It was christened 'Indication Centre' because it received and recorded every indication pointing to the development of an international crisis. Special attention was paid to the rapidity of communications to ensure that any crisis warnings reached the government in the shortest possible time – further rationalization, further refinement. Crisis reports were dispatched by the Indication Centre to the Federal Chancellery at varying speeds, depending on the priority allotted to them – M ('deferred'), R ('normal'), P ('urgent'), O ('immediate'), Y ('danger') and finally Z ('blitz').[17]

Although a reformer, politically Worgitzky was an ultra-conservative and his introduction of technology and science into the BND had consequences which he can hardly have anticipated. Modernization of the machine postulated a new type of staff officer, the expert trained in social and natural science, the technician and mathematician; their outlook was hardly in tune with the officer mentality of the Greater Germany period which the BND had been at such pains to revive. Gehlen was quickly alive to this. When Worgitzky proposed to prune the organization of useless personnel and reduce it to a productive hard core, Gehlen resisted him. He wanted no further rationalization. Gifted though he was, Worgitzky was a sensitive man and he gradually allowed himself to be ousted by Gehlen, who was the tougher character; he was eventually restricted to fringe areas – the Middle East later became his involuntary hobby.

Gehlen had in fact already spotted a possibility of diverting attention from his Eastern intelligence difficulties and raising the prestige of the BND. Bonn was now demanding what Worgitzky had long been proposing – that the secret service extend its activities outside the Eastern bloc. At last the BND could shed its fixation about the Soviet enemy. Pullach's tame historians regard this assumption of a worldwide role as a decisive stage in the story of the BND. An official BND 'orientation aide-mémoire' says: 'The restriction to politico-military intelligence in Eastern Europe imposed until this time (1956) will be abandoned. The service is now extending its activity to intelligence on crisis areas throughout the world.'[18]

This new assignment could in fact have become a turning-point in BND history. The Gehlen Org had begun as an anti-Soviet intelligence service, governed by Stalin's aggressive European policy; investigation of the Soviet Union and its satellites had been its sole task, suppression of communism its ideological mainspring. Now the BND had an opportunity to become a normal secret service, investigating everywhere as required by the interests of the State. This, however, required an internal change of outlook for which the majority of the BND's personnel showed little inclination. The BND had grown up in the military tradition of so-called enemy intelligence; it was directed against specific enemies who were to be overcome, or at least paralysed. The modern, scientifically sophisticated secret service, however, has long since shed the 'enemy' mentality.

Rigidly military and anti-bolshevist, only a few of the old hands grasped the implications of the BND's new world mission. One of their spokeman, ex-Major-General Erich Dethleffsen, head of the Evaluation Section, said: 'The task of the BND is to obtain from other countries information which is kept secret by them, knowledge which is important to the leaders of our own country.' He went on: 'We should never forgo the creation of a widespread network, which may ultimately embrace all continents; owing to the increasing economic interdependence of all countries together with ideological and racial influences, developments even in the most remote areas may be of importance for our own policy.'[19]

Gehlen agreed with this concept, although he undoubtedly added the proviso that one of the most important objects was to open up fresh sources of Soviet intelligence in other countries. In any case the change of direction inaugurated by Worgitzky suited his book; as early as the end of the 1940s he had had a few agents spying outside the Eastern bloc.

The Org's first contacts had been to South America. A number of Nazis had fled there from Germany and some of them were in such influential positions that Gehlen was unwilling to dispense with their assistance. As contact men he used ex-SS and SD men who established communication with their old comrades in Argentina, Brazil and Chile. Gehlen's attention was then drawn to certain ex-SS officers in the Middle East, hired by Arab secret services. To them also he dispatched a contact man with the right background – the former Nazi Gauleiter, Hartmann Lauterbacher, and he recruited some of the old gang to work for the Gehlen Org.

In 1952 Gehlen achieved a major break-through in the Middle East.

General Neguib, Egypt's pro-German President, called in German military advisers and they included an emissary of Gehlen's who had been Rommel's Intelligence Officer with the Afrika Korps during the war when his tentacles had reached as far as Cairo. The assignment given him by Neguib was highly useful from the Org's point of view – together with Zaharia Mohieddin, the future Minister of the Interior, he was to reorganize the Egyptian secret service.

When, therefore, the BND was commissioned by Bonn to collect intelligence in non-Soviet areas, it had established connections upon which it could rely. It moved into countries of the Third World, primarily the Middle East, with an aid programme for intelligence. Indonesian military intelligence officers were trained by a BND mission; anti-American propoganda was rife and the Germans liberated their Indonesian colleagues from the clutches of the CIA. In 1965 the BND training team even became involved in a civil war; they delivered Russian rifles and Finnish ammunition to the Indonesian army.

The BND's reputation as a provider of intelligence aid even penetrated Africa. When one of central Africa's black potentates felt himself threatened by his enemies, he called in the BND to train his bodyguard. Others followed his example – King Ibn Saud, the Congo government, the Persian cabinet, the secret services of Tanzania and Afghanistan; all had a shopping list. The BND's senior executives frequently netted valuable presents for such services. Gehlen, for instance, was given a golden sword by Ibn Saud and the houses of the great men of Pullach were covered in Persian carpets. The BND leaders returned such compliments from the East with miniature radios and photographic equipment.

The BND's spies, however, appeared in Western countries too. A resident officer was maintained in the capital of every NATO country, primarily to keep an eye on his host country's contacts with the Soviet Union. The BND resident in Washington (of the rank of General) was interested primarily in the USA's military policy.[20]

Camouflaged though they were, the BND's budget figures appearing in the Federal accounts showed that Gehlen's organization was growing year by year. In 1956 the BND's total expenditure was 23 million marks; four years later, at 43·4 million marks, it had almost doubled; for 1971 the BND budget stands at 78·9 million! Once more Gehlen displayed his old ability – in many areas of the non-communist world BND operations were more profitable than they had ever been in Eastern Europe.[21]

The BND's new African friends gave it, almost for the asking, what the ex-colonial powers such as Britain, France and Belgium had had to employ a comprehensive network of agents to obtain – pictures of the situation in the politically emergent continent of Africa. In addition the BND was able to ensure that the heads of the secret services in these young African states adopted a rigid anti-communist policy; this stood Bonn's Hallstein doctrine in good stead for years. West German industry and trade also benefited; they were able to oust foreign competitors in these African countries – frequently in cooperation with Gehlen's resident officer.

As a result of its good relationships with both the Israeli and Egyptian secret services the BND was better informed than its Western counterparts on the potential and intentions of the contestants in the Jewish/Arab conflict. The BND had early information on many a *coup d'état* in Africa and many a political upheaval in Asia. The Third World also offered an opportunity of improving once more the BND's East European intelligence. Here and there personnel of the diplomatic missions of the Soviet Union and other Eastern bloc countries showed themselves not averse to a talk with the BND.

Even the Western secret services' post-war Black Friday, the building of the Berlin Wall, left the BND less naked than its NATO colleagues. The BND did not know details or the date for construction of the wall; for weeks, however, it had been forecasting 'total isolation of West Berlin' (report of August 9th, 1961). As early as January 13th, 1961, the Chancellery had been informed that East Berlin streets near the sector boundary were being diverted. A situation report of July 19th stated that the Socialist Unity Party was planning 'formation of security units and establishment of emergency plans for all central points in East Berlin'. On August 1st came a further forecast: 'Closure of sector boundaries in Berlin and interruption of traffic on the metro and underground.'[22] The BND, however, did not register the decisive indications of Ulbricht's coup – transport and storage of large quantities of building material and barbed wire; at the time the military men in Pullach were preoccupied with watching the Warsaw Pact military manoeuvres in East Germany.

The BND was well informed on internal developments in the capitals of NATO countries. Since it was still largely concerned with military matters (25 per cent of its staff had a military background), it dealt primarily with strategy and defence policy. So in the spring of 1962 information came in from NATO channels which gave the BND evaluators reason to think that Washington and Bonn were heading for a serious clash. President Kennedy's new administration, the sources reported, had brought into influential positions defence politicians and generals who were determined to exclude West Germany from any co-ownership of atomic weapons.

This inevitably constituted a challenge to West Germany's ambitious Defence Minister, Franz Josef Strauss, who was already visualizing West Germany, rearmed with nuclear weapons, as the arbiter and protector of Europe. At the end of 1960 Eisenhower's military planners had offered their NATO European partners one hundred medium-range rockets for their own use and since that time Strauss had been dreaming of playing a leading role in a European nuclear super-power. The BND's reports to the Chancellery heralded the end of these daydreams; indeed they forecast a conflict with Washington if the Federal Defence Ministry pursued plans which had become obsolete.[23]

Adenauer passed the BND's analyses to Strauss, who reacted violently. He was afraid that the Chancellor, who was little interested in military matters, would attach more weight to the BND's reports than to the theories of his Minister and might drop him in deference to the Americans. Strauss took the offensive, demanding a fundamental reform of the BND; it was intolerable, he said, that a secret service should both acquire and evaluate intelligence – evaluation of military intelligence was a prerogative of the Defence Ministry. He already had a friend waiting to take over from Gehlen in Pullach.[24]

At precisely this moment a force appeared at Strauss's side which Gehlen thought that he had neutralized for good and all – the military counter-espionage service, the MAD. Gehlen had been a co-founder of the MAD; he had staffed its senior posts with his own people. He had not perceived, however, that the MAD had begun to develop interests of its own and that these inevitably conflicted with the position of the BND. The senior MAD officers had never forgiven Gehlen for excluding them from all questions of foreign military intelligence – the MAD was permitted only to carry on counter-espionage inside the Federal Armed Forces.

The dissatisfaction of the MAD leaders sprang mainly from the fact that their organization had originally been conceived as a military intelligence service. The MAD had originated from the Security Group in the Blank Office which had been formed 'as a semi-substitute for the BND' after the collapse of the short-lived Oster/Heinz organization. The fact that the Security Group had been turned into the MAD, a security service confined to the Federal Armed Forces, was due to intervention in the Chancellery by Gehlen. Nevertheless the MAD leaders with their seven Groups (total strength some 2,000 men) were continually trying to evade the restrictions placed upon them by Gehlen. At the very least they wished their organization to have some say in military intelligence in East Germany.[25]

The MAD could also expect some circumspect support from Section II of the Staff of the Bundeswehr, to which it was subordinate. Section II was responsible, not only for the MAD, but also for military intelligence (the Bundeswehr sub-sections responsible for enemy intelligence were known as G2 and A2). These sub-sections had their own methods of acquiring intelligence on and beyond the frontiers of the Republic; in the Baltic, for instance, they had the survey ships A–51 *Oste* and A–52 *Trave*; the Navy had reconnaissance aircraft in the Baltic area and both the army and the air force maintained radio intercept units on the East German and Czechoslovak frontiers.

The head of Section II was also responsible for the Military Attachés in German missions abroad; inevitably, therefore, he was interested in raising both the quality and scope of his intelligence service. As long as Wessel, Gehlen's ex-deputy, was in charge of Section II it constituted no threat to the BND, though, when the internal BND quarrel over Lang-kau was raging, even Wessel had toyed with the idea of taking over some of the BND's personnel and turning the MAD into an intelligence service. His successor, Brigadier-General Ferber, who was an adherent of Strauss, had even grander ideas. Moreover the senior officers of MAD now felt that they were actually being encouraged by their Minister to demand wider powers. Ex-members of Gehlen's staff, including Selmayr, the head of the MAD, and Ferber, joined Strauss's anti-Gehlen front.[26]

Thus hard pressed, Gehlen put up defences all round and looked for allies. He was only too pleased to note that the editors of a Hamburg magazine were opening a campaign to warn the public against the ambitions of the energetic Strauss, which they considered a danger to democracy and the rule of law. This magazine was *Der Spiegel*.

Colonel Adolf Wicht, head of the BND office in Hamburg, had been in contact with the magazine for some time – and even he had not been the first. Early in the 1950s there had been talks between Worgitzky and the editors of *Der Spiegel*. In early summer 1954 the idea of a cover story on the Gehlen Org, then totally unknown, had been mooted. Gehlen agreed, subject to the condition that the story be written 'by a responsible senior executive of *Der Spiegel*'. Hans Detlev Becker, then managing editor of *Der Spiegel* (later senior editor and now director of the firm), had been an NCO during the war in the radio counter-espionage section of OKW; he was therefore interested in secret-service matters and took on the project himself. He interviewed Gehlen in one of the BND's 'safe houses' in Munich. For years the *Spiegel* story entitled 'The Chancellor's favourite General' was regarded as the best-informed description of the Gehlen Org.[27]

Subsequently Worgitzky visited the *Spiegel* offices two or three times a year; in 1956, shortly before his appointment to Pullach, he brought along his successor, Adolf Wicht, then a Lieutenant-Colonel in the Budeswehr and formerly head of a group in Gehlen's FHO. So on September 18th, 1962, when the silent battle between Gehlen and Strauss reached its climax, the man on the spot was Colonel Wicht. He arrived at the right moment; Conrad Ahlers, the deputy Chief Editor, was just finishing an article on Foertsch, the Inspector-General of the Bundeswehr, which exposed Strauss's anti-American military policy. The article was due to appear the following week but its publication was immediately postponed for a fortnight.

Ahlers wished to seize the opportunity of Wicht's appearance to have certain military passages in his article checked by the BND in case they violated security regulations. Wicht was prepared to submit them to Pullach. Ahlers drew up two lists with a total of thirteen points and Wicht collected these lists on October 1st. Becker noted: 'Lists of questions drawn up by Ahlers handed to Wicht with a request for answers by Thursday at the latest since, from the technical point of view, the article must be firm by Thursday.' Wicht sent the lists to Pullach, where a member of Worgitzky's staff whose code-name was Winterstein, had them checked by BND officers. The answers came back: No objection except for one point (which had already been deleted by Ahlers). Wicht so informed Becker on October 4th.[28]

No sooner had the article appeared four days later, however, than machinery was set in motion to eliminate the main critics of Strauss and his policy. The *Spiegel* editors heard that the Defence Ministry had applied to the Federal Public Prosecutor for proceedings to be initiated against the magazine on suspicion of high treason. The only person who knew nothing of all this was Colonel Wicht. When Becker next met him on October 16th, he noted as follows: 'In the office ... Herr Wicht spoke to me on these lines: "Well, everything has gone very well. The Foertsch article was very good and all is in order with Foertsch." I said that people in other quarters seemed to be of another opinion since I had heard that something in the article was being subjected to examination. My firm impression was that this was news to Herr Wicht. His reaction was one of surprise and he made soothing noises.'

Wicht inquired of Pullach and two days later presented himself to

Becker again. Becker noted: 'Interview with Wicht: As a result of my remark he had inquired and had established that in fact investigations are under way concerning secrecy violations in the Foertsch article. It has to do with secrets of the Fallex manoeuvres. He and his agency could assume no responsibility for these matters, only for the questions submitted to them.'[29]

Wicht's statement illustrates the position of impotence in which Strauss's manoeuvres had already placed the BND. The BND knew nothing of the underhand assault which was clearly becoming imminent. From the outset it had been excluded from the secret conclaves between the Public Prosecutor, the Bonn Security Group and the Defence Ministry; when those concerned met in Karlsruhe on October 22nd to discuss final details of the operation, no BND representative was invited – not even State Secretary Globke who exercised supervisory control.[30]

Instead of the BND the MAD officers were in the lead. Selmayr, the head of the MAD, and Ferber, head of Section II, urged drastic action. Captain (Navy) Koch of MAD headquarters, the office responsible for security in the Bundeswehr, joined the group of investigators; three MAD observer groups set out to shadow the editors of *Der Spiegel*. Next day the assault squads formed up against the magazine. On October 23rd the Investigating Judge of the Federal Court issued arrest and search warrants against Ahlers and Augstein, the managing director; simultaneously Inspector Schütz with five officials of the Security Group of the Federal Criminal police office moved to Hamburg, where they were received by the MAD.[31]

About 9 PM on October 26th Schütz, assisted by Colonel Schirmer of the MAD, went into action. The *Spiegel* offices in Hamburg and those of its branch in Bonn were occupied, files were confiscated and every room was searched – for days and weeks on end. On the seventh day the investigators seemed to have found what they were looking for. In Becker's desk they discovered the notes which he had made after his meetings with Wicht. Gehlen's enemies were now in no doubt: he was behind the *Spiegel*'s criticism of Strauss; Wicht had warned the editors of the surprise attack and enabled them to salt away the treasonable material.[32]

The '*Spiegel* Affair' had suddenly turned into a 'Gehlen Case'. The hunters let no grass grow under their feet: on November 2nd the alleged conspirators, Becker and Wicht, were arrested and a few days later Gehlen and his team were in the firing line. Gehlen's enemies were indefatigable in painting a horrifying picture of Gehlen, the traitor, for the old gentleman in the Palais Schaumburg. Their tales of conspiracy became more outrageous and more sinister. They soon had conjured up a worldwide plot by the CIA in Washington via Gehlen in Pullach and ending with Augstein in Hamburg, designed to overthrow Adenauer and Strauss.

The Chancellor was no longer prepared to tolerate the traitor Gehlen in the governmental machine. In vain Globke vouched for Gehlen (and became so overwrought in the process that he had to go on holiday to recuperate): Adenauer was through with Gehlen. He had already made a reference to the BND in the Bundestag on November 7th when attacking Wicht: 'Is it not horrifying when a Colonel of the Bundeswehr, having heard that proceedings had been initiated against Augstein and the editors of *Der Spiegel*, goes to them and warns them so that incriminating material can be got out of the way?' He was now determined to nail the instigators of this treachery.[33]

On November 12th the senior officers of the BND had to make the pilgrimage to Bonn – 'to place themselves at the disposal of the General Attorney of the Republic', the order said. Gehlen, Worgitzky, Winterstein and Wendland, the head of administration, had to present themselves at the Chancellery. They were led into separate rooms. On the same day Stammberger, the Federal Minister of Justice, and Kuhn, the Public Prosecutor in Karlsruhe, received a summons from the Chancellery ordering them to Bonn forthwith. When they appeared Adenauer was already awaiting them impatiently. He said: 'Herr Stammberger, you must arrest Herr Gehlen. He is in a room next door and is available there.'

Stammberger did not quite understand. 'Why should I arrest Herr Gehlen?' he asked. The Chancellor replied: 'General Gehlen informed Colonel Wicht of the preparatory measures being taken against *Der Spiegel* and Wicht betrayed them to *Der Spiegel*.' But Stammberger refused, saying: 'Chancellor, if we have no concrete proof, no federal judge will issue a warrant for arrest.' Kuhn, the Public Prosecutor, supported him. Adenauer said resignedly: 'I was once a State Attorney. In the old days it was quite different.'[34]

Nevertheless Kuhn declared himself ready to interrogate the four BND leaders at once and individually. Gehlen was questioned first. He was clearly disconcerted, stuttered his answers, and hardly seemed to know what he was saying – No, he had not been involved in the affair – he really did not know what it was all about. When Kuhn insisted, however, that there was reason to suppose that Wicht had warned the *Spiegel* editors, Gehlen was evasive. It was not, of course, impossible, he said, that BND officials outside the headquarters had acted on their own initiative and had been in collusion with *Der Spiegel.*

The others were none too pleased when they heard what Gehlen had said. Winterstein was indignant, saying: 'If the President said that, then the President is making a serious error.' Gehlen was questioned once more and retracted his statement. The four BND officers were allowed to go.[35]

Back in Pullach, however, Winterstein and other officers worked on their President to issue a statement on behalf of Wicht. Gehlen would not commit himself; he procrastinated. Then, on November 21st, appeared a report in the *Westfälische Rundschau* to the effect that Gehlen 'had stated that "Colonel Wicht's contacts with certain editorial offices, including those of *Der Spiegel*, were made with the agreement and approval of the BND".' Gehlen and the Chancellery made fruitless efforts in Pullach to discover who had instigated this report. Two days later the Chancellery fired back: '1. The President of the BND has neither made such statements himself nor caused such statements to be made. 2. The President of the BND has always been clear that the official enlightenment of the public on BND matters is exclusively the responsibility of the Federal government.'[36] The Chancellery's disavowal was correct. Gehlen had neither made such a statement himself nor caused it to be made. He lacked the moral courage. It was left to two other senior members of the BND's staff to clear Wicht's name.

Worgitzky, the Vice-President, and his assistant Winterstein were not prepared to sit idly by while the head of a German government called Wicht a 'traitor', as Adenauer had done. The two drafted a statement on behalf of Wicht. A senior editor, a member of the Social-Democrat party and a friend of both Worgitzky and Winterstein, undertook to pass it by telephone to a newspaper which he was sure would not be afraid to publish it.

In January 1963 Gehlen's enemies struck again. State attorneys and officials of the Security Group entered the BND headquarters in Pullach and questioned Gehlen's closest associates about the alleged conspiracy between Pullach and Hamburg. They asked everyone the same question: 'What contacts have you with *Der Spiegel?*' Worgitzky, the Vice-President, in particular had some trouble in clearing himself. An expense-account chit found in the *Spiegel* offices was adduced as evidence of conspiratorial contacts; it showed that in 1956 'Worgy' and Becker had gone to the plush mahogany-panelled Ehmke restaurant in Hamburg, where they had dined off lobster and partridge, washing it down with a bottle per man of Château-Laffite Rothschild. In traditional German manner it had been a Dutch treat.[37]

Even the surprise assault on Pullach, however, was fruitless. Strauss fell, Wicht was rehabilitated and later promoted Brigadier-General; the MAD did not achieve its object. Nevertheless the Strauss/*Spiegel* affair had deprived Gehlen and the BND of their internal political buttress. The Gehlen–Adenauer axis had been destroyed – for ever.

Gehlen could never forget the humiliation of November 12th, 1962. For him it was the beginning of an uninterrupted decline. The BND was heading into an uncertain future.

THE FELFE AFFAIR;
FALL OF THE 'GRAND OLD MAN'

I N April 1950 a retired Criminal Police officer named Heinz Felfe presented himself, in a great state of excitement, to Gustav Heinemann, the Federal Minister of the Interior, and told him an adventure story. He had an opportunity, so he said, of checkmating a Soviet espionage coup against the Federal Republic. Felfe's story was this:

He and a friend, another ex-Criminal Police officer named Hans Clemens, lived in the village of Lendringsen near Trier; they had been approached by the Russians with an offer to enter their espionage service, to recruit wartime friends and themselves to infiltrate the Gehlen Organization. Contact with the Russians, Felfe continued, had been established by Clemens' wife Gerda who lived, separated from her husband, in Dresden. In January Gerda had suddenly appeared in Lendringsen and had said to her husband: 'I have been sent by a Russian Colonel; I have been working for him for some time. We call him Max. He would like to talk to you. They would give you a chance of earning something.' Early in March, therefore, Clemens had gone to Dresden and there had met Max and other Soviet secret-service officers. They had welcomed him enthusiastically as a fighter against Western imperialism. Clemens reported: 'They kissed and embraced me.'[1]

Felfe, the story-teller, now wished to gain Heinemann's approval for a plan to use the Dresden contact for a secret-service counter-play; we should, he said, pass doctored material to the Russians in order to gain their confidence and so obtain some insight into the Red spy network in West Germany.

Heinemann was not particularly interested in secret-service matters; he listened to his visitor for some five minutes and then passed him on to a civil servant, Dr Sauer, who was in process of forming the Federal Internal Security Office (the BfV) at the time. Sauer too was unable to make head or tail of Felfe's report, and a personal check on Felfe confirmed him in his doubts. Felfe had been an Obersturmführer

[Lieutenant] in the SS Security Service (the SD); after the war he had been employed by the British SIS, but they had dismissed him because he was altogether too double-faced – he had sold information to other secret services as well. The BfV, nevertheless, thought it worthwhile to interrogate Felfe once more. Felfe repeated – for the record – what had happened to him and Clemens. The record was placed in a file, and the file in a safe.[2]

No one in the BfV, however, noticed that, some years later, Felfe, who had been approached by the Russians and was suspected of being a double agent, was carving out a remarkable career for himself in the BND. It never occurred to any of the sleuths that Heinz Felfe, the temporary civil servant, might perhaps have accepted Max's proposals and joined the band of communist agents. At the head of them all Gehlen, the master of the BND, refused to entertain any suspicion of Felfe. When he eventually realized the truth, it was too late – too late for the BND and too late for Gehlen.

The Felfe affair demonstrated that Gehlen's methods of leadership had become obsolete, indeed self-destructive; he refused to take account of the lessons and experience of modern management. He trusted his own intuition rather than the common sense of his immediate advisers; though never a good judge of character, he insisted that he knew his staff better than the responsible security officers and section heads. Gehlen's sole criterion for a staff officer had always been the number and quality of the sources which he could produce. Only people recommended by other BND members were engaged. A process of secret-service inbreeding had therefore taken place which was in line with Gehlen's concept of the BND as 'the elite of the elite' but acted as a soporific for any system of security controls and helped the enemy to infiltrate the BND.

Heinz Felfe had come into the headquarters of the Org on this 'old-boy network' conveyor-belt. His main sponsors had been ex-SS fellow-officers – primarily his friend Hans Clemens and the lawyer Erwin Tiebel, with whom Felfe had lodged in Lendringsen after the end of the war.

The three had been together in Dresden where each in his own way had been serving Adolf Hitler – Clemens as head of the SD out-station, Tiebel as an SD informer and Felfe as office manager in the Gauleiter's headquarters. In 1943 they were together again in the Swiss Desk of the RSHA. Then, in Lendringsen in 1950, all three were looking for a job. Clemens had meanwhile pledged himself to the Russian organizer, Max, but Felfe was hesitant to put his money on the Russians. Since Clemens was in any case due to join the Gehlen Organization, he promised to find Felfe a place there.[3]

In the spring of 1951 in the Bonn–Düsseldorf express Clemens met an old SS crony who gave him the vital tip: ex-SS-Oberführer [Colonel] Willi Krichbaum was in Bad Reichenhall as Gehlen's District Representative; he was looking for ex-SD and ex-Gestapo experts for the Gehlen Organization. When Clemens presented himself, Krichbaum knew at once what was up. 'What are you doing?' he asked. Clemens replied. 'Dealing in scraps.' 'I've got something for you,' Krichbaum said. On June 15th, 1951 Clemens joined the Org with an assignment similar to that given him by the Russian Max. Clemens said later: 'My task was to report ex-SD men who were without a job; they could be employed once more.'[4]

Clemens at once thought of Felfe but Felfe had already taken steps on his own. Early in September he had gone to Max and signed on with the Soviet secret service. Hardly had he returned home, however, than there was Comrade Krichbaum at the door. On November 15th Felfe joined the Gehlen Organization. Later he said: 'I did not feel comfortable but I could no longer retract. From now on I had to play it two ways.' Felfe allowed himself to be reassured by Clemens – in any case he could see no way out, since, had he been loyal to the Org, he would have had to denounce Clemens as a Russian spy. So he became a double agent – the decisive factor was the financial reward promised him by Max which later rose to 1,500 marks a month.[5]

Together with Clemens, Felfe wrote a postcard to Max saying 'Everything clicked'. Since one of the KGB's main aims was to find out the extent of the Org's knowledge of the Soviet espionage network, Moscow was only too pleased when Felfe was appointed to the 'Soviet Union' desk in Gehlen's counter-espionage department. He started in the Org's Local Branch at Karlsruhe but had soon made himself so useful that in 1953 he was ordered to the Pullach headquarters. Under the cover-name 'Friesen' he became a desk officer in the Russian desk of the counter-espionage department. Now he could really show his Russian masters what he was worth. Felfe said: 'I wanted to rank as top class with the Russians.'[6]

Clemens was spying in the out-stations and Tiebel, who had meanwhile also been recruited by Max, acted as courier. With their help Felfe set up a busy channel of intelligence to the Russians. In KGB headquarters in Karlshorst 'Paul' (Felfe's Russian code-name) soon became synonymous with secret-service efficiency. Between 2 and 3 PM the music coming through Felfe's radio set would be interrupted by the morse signal 'dit-dah-dah-dit' and whenever this happened Paul would be there to note down and decipher the KGB's wishes. Every call was answered. Felfe would then drive over to Karlshorst and at kilometre stone 107 near Helmstedt hand to a KGB representative the material requested, packed in containers. Clemens and Tiebel were meanwhile also on the road.

Felfe realized, of course, that he would only learn the BND's innermost secrets if he succeeded in obtaining a key position for himself in Pullach. Here the Russians helped him since in their eyes, in addition to enemy intelligence, one of Felfe's most important tasks was 'disinformation' – enemy deception.

In 1953 'Friesen' astounded his colleagues with the news that he had succeeded in setting up a circuit of informers in Moscow led by a Soviet Colonel. His pretended informer network produced valuable intelligence – selected by the KGB of course; some of it was false but some, from Russian government, Party and Army circles, was genuine. The KGB enabled Felfe ostensibly to expand his sources in the East. Soon he was feeding in to Pullach secrets from the Kremlin and genuine minutes of secret meetings of the East German government; he even knew details of forthcoming operations by the Soviet secret service. Much of Felfe's information reached the Chancellery in Bonn and influenced Konrad Adenauer's political views on the East.[7]

Gehlen's attention was drawn to this espionage genius, and in 1954 the two met for the first time. Felfe described his Chief as 'a fascinating personality' and Gehlen was enthusiastic over 'Fiffi' (Felfe's headquarters nickname), saying: 'That fellow Felfe is outstanding. He can produce what others cannot.' In 1958 Felfe was promoted head of the 'Soviet Union' desk in IIIf (counter-espionage); he was appointed temporary civil servant with the salary of a Senior Civil Service officer (Oberregierungsrat).[8]

Whenever exalted visitors arrived from abroad or from Bonn, Gehlen would take them to Felfe's office where they were permitted to admire a gigantic plan, prepared and kept up to date by Fiffi, of the KGB headquarters in Karlshorst. In its detail it was, in fact, astonishing. The multi-coloured plan showed every house, every bunker and every parking space in the Soviet restricted zone; no KGB office was unknown, no stick of furniture escaped Fiffi's eagle eye. He knew, for instance, which lavatory the KGB General Dimitrov used and where the Advisory Group of the East German Ministry of State Security held its meetings. Felfe's picture of Karlshorst became an almost mythical showpiece demonstrating the efficiency peculiar to the BND. When

Gehlen travelled abroad, he frequently took Felfe and his plan with him.

For anyone so high in favour, looting the BND's safes and personal files was an easy matter. Year by year Felfe handed over more and more material to Karlshorst – from January 1957 the BND's weekly reports giving the state of current intelligence operations, from 1958 the monthly reports on the monitoring of enemy agents' radio traffic in the Federal Republic, from March 1959 the BfV's monthly counter-espionage reports, from June 1959 the BfV's situation reports, which appeared every four weeks.

Felfe photographed card-index entries on members of the BND, lists of resident BND agents abroad, lists of informers' cover addresses, clues to people suspected of espionage, the BND's secret telephone directory, the Org's office instructions. He gave warning of the imminent arrest of Kirpichev, the KGB officer in Hamburg, and helped him to escape. He obtained the transcript of the interrogation of Stashinsky, the KGB defector, who had admitted murdering two exiled Ukrainian politicians on KGB orders; he fed material to Karlshorst enabling the KGB to lay the two murders at the door of the BND.[9]

Felfe felt himself secure – and yet suspicion had already arisen against Gehlen's over-smooth favourite. Later, admittedly, no one in the BND could say who had first voiced that suspicion. Initially, no doubt, it was mere personal antagonism and dislike of the go-getter Felfe, who had a habit of approaching colleagues in other branches and questioning them about their work.

Professional doubts also played their part; many expressed scepticism about the slick perfection which distinguished Felfe from other members of the staff. Even Fiffi's show-piece, the plan of Karlshorst, aroused misgivings; no secret service, the Felfe critics argued, could have such precise information about its enemy as to know his lavatory habits. It was remarkable, moreover, that Felfe, the Soviet expert, should be able to produce material which did not belong to his province. The fact that he was able to collect secret minutes of the East German Politburo or the East German State Security Service's plans for action led to jealousy of their prerogatives on the part of the 'East German' desk officers.

With so much mistrust and antipathy abroad only a minor incident was required to cause people to voice their suspicions – and it came. In 1958 Felfe bought a two-storied ten-room country house in Oberaudorf, Upper Bavaria, for a sum of 100,000 marks. His colleagues asked themselves how a man whose monthly salary was 1,700 marks, had the money to acquire such a house. From this moment Felfe's enemies were convinced that he was not on the level.

Certain desk officers, led by Gehlen's own brother-in-law, voiced their doubts, but he slapped them down: 'You are simply envious of Felfe for the results he produces. The man is all right.' Today Gehlen maintains that his support of Felfe was only a stratagem; he was already suspicious of Felfe, he says, but wished to 'muffle' the others' doubts in order not to jeopardize investigations which had long been under way. The anti-Felfe faction, however, would not rest. Their spokesmen insisted that they must be allowed to put their views in writing. Gehlen allowed 'Alo', his private secretary, to record their statements; the notes were kept in Gehlen's private office.[10]

Despite these warnings Gehlen continued to entrust Felfe with the most delicate assignments. In November 1958 he placed him in charge of 'Operation Panoptikum', the object of which was to discover something which Felfe had every reason to keep secret – the extent of Soviet penetration into the BND.

Ever since the mid-1950s Pullach had known that the KGB was trying to 'convert' members of the BND. In 1955 Albert, an ex-Field Security Police official and a member of the BND's Local Branch in Frankfurt, had been exposed as a Soviet agent; Albert committed suicide shortly afterwards while in detention in Bruchsal. Two other members of the BND named Jagusch and Balthasar had also been convicted of spying for the Russians. The object of Operation Panoptikum was to nip any further KGB assaults in the bud. A BND informer was ostensibly to allow himself to be converted by the Russians, set up an imaginary network of informers, feed doctored material to the Russians and so discover the KGB's channels of infiltration into Pullach.[11]

Felfe alerted Karlshorst and the Russians were immediately a jump ahead of Pullach. The KGB told Felfe to propose ex-SS-Standartenführer Friedrich Panzinger for the role of the BND stool-pigeon; he had been head of a group in Gestapo headquarters and, while a prisoner of war in Russia, had allowed himself to be used against his former comrades because he was afraid that, if he did not, the Russians would bring him to trial for his participation in war crimes in German-occupied Russia. He had been released by the Russians in 1955 with a broad hint that, should he misbehave himself, the question of his war crimes would be resurrected.

Panzinger was accepted for 'Panoptikum' by the BND and for months Felfe threw dust in the eyes of the Pullach headquarters. Not until the summer of 1959 did Panzinger's former BND friends learn of his sinister role in Russia and they severed all contact with him. Panzinger was now cornered; on June 21st he wrote: 'The future looks black here and I feel a stranger to everyone. I am so miserable. Who will rid me of this life?' When, a few weeks later, the Munich Public Prosecutor opened proceedings against him for Nazi crimes, he committed suicide.

Having thus lost his stooge, Felfe now looked for another BND man to play the KGB's role. Before he could find one, however, the Security Section's investigations had made such progress that responsibility for the operation was removed from him. There had been so much talk about Felfe that even Gehlen could no longer object to an unobtrusive inquiry. Ten years later he was even prepared to present himself as chief anti-Felfe investigator; in his memoirs he says proudly: 'Under my personal direction a small group of selected members of the staff pursued the investigation.' By the autumn of 1961 grounds for suspicion had become so numerous that the case was bordering on certainty, although final proof was still lacking.[12]

The BND's critics later maintained that Pullach itself was never responsible for the exposure of Felfe; the clue had been provided, they say, by a KGB defector named Anatol Golytzin when under interrogation in Washington but he had not divulged the name. Such suppositions disregard one simple fact: Golytzin defected to the West on December 15th, 1961 – five weeks after Felfe's arrest.[13]

Felfe could not now move a step without being watched. Weeks passed until finally, on the afternoon of October 27th, conclusive proof came: the BND's cryptanalysts deciphered a KGB radio message referring indubitably to Felfe. The rest was routine: Felfe was further shadowed in order to discover his accomplices. Gehlen left the final scene to his confidant, General Langkau, head of the 'Strategic Service' section. On November 6th he summoned Felfe into his office on some pretext. He had already pronounced sentence when the door was burst open by three officials of the Bonn Security Group. One of them said: 'Herr Felfe, you are under arrest.' His accomplices, Clemens and Tiebel, were also arrested a short time later.[14]

The initiated registered with dismay the extent of the damage wrought by Felfe. His treachery had cost the BND its last bases in the Soviet sphere of influence. Ninety-four informers, including forty-six senior members, had been blown, together with codes, communications, dead-letter boxes and courier channels – all carefully registered on 300 Minox films totalling 15,661 photographs, 20 tapes and innumerable radio messages passed to his Soviet masters by Felfe. The psychological effects were even worse than the material losses. Gehlen's agents in the

East were now a prey to fear; no informer now knew whether he had not himself been blown or whether he could still trust any of his contacts. Even Gehlen himself later admitted: 'It was a severe set-back,' although he comforted himself with a teleprinter message sent to Pullach by the French secret service: 'Congratulations, we have not yet found our Felfe.'

An inquiry was immediately initiated and this unearthed Felfe's system of contacts inside the BND; every member of the organization had to state for the record what contact he had had with the spy. Gehlen offered an amnesty, promising freedom from punishment to any of Felfe's accomplices who severed their ties with the KGB. Fifteen microfilms found in Felfe's country house provided further information on the double agent's methods and contacts. Felfe himself filled in any gaps for his former colleagues.[15]

There could be no further doubt: Reinhard Gehlen's life's work was in ruins. Moreover it was Gehlen's personal tragedy that he had himself contributed to the downfall of his organization; his methods of leadership and personnel policy had clearly eased Felfe's task. Yet, with the obduracy of the ageing autocrat, Gehlen refused to accept any responsibility for the Felfe case. He blamed his subordinates, ordered the destruction of the written warnings against Felfe from members of his staff and continued loudly to proclaim his own innocence.

Gehlen knew what faced him when the Felfe trial opened before the Federal Court in Karlsruhe. He reorganized parts of his machine, placed those agents in the East who had been blown by Felfe but not yet arrested, in cold storage and ordered most of the former SS men to leave the BND. In this he was assisted primarily by an ex-SS man whose cover-name was Ackermann, who collected incriminating material against his former comrades. This, of course, proved to be a costly manoeuvre since many of the SS men had lucrative contracts and demanded large 'golden handshakes' (in some cases as high as 100,000 marks). Such measures, however, could not protect the BND from the storm of public criticism which broke when the Felfe case came before the Federal Court in July 1963.[16]

The few sessions to which the public were admitted were enough to produce so bleak a picture of the moral climate of the BND that it made a mockery of everything hitherto believed about the mysterious General Gehlen and his secret service. Felfe and his co-defendants, Clemens and Tiebel, revealed themselves as such intransigent Nazis that *Die Welt* concluded that 'owing to a catastrophic personnel policy' the BND had provided 'a comfortable retreat for both major and minor Nazis'. Ritzel, the Social-Democrat deputy, spoke of 'an unparalleled scandal'; the Free Democrats demanded strict screening of all medium-level and junior BND personnel.

The *New York Times* correspondent cabled to his editor: 'During these days a Karlsruhe courtroom has witnessed the destruction of a legend and a good name which has been carefully preserved for the last fifteen years, the legend of the superior capabilities of the Federal Intelligence Service and the reputation of General Gehlen.' Weber, the Federal judge who presided over the court, could not refrain from mentioning, when giving the grounds for his sentence (Felfe was given fourteen years' hard labour), that he had received many letters whose authors maintained that 'a lot was rotten' in the BND.

The weekly *Christ und Welt* commented: 'The Felfe trial should not be without consequences for the Federal Intelligence Service.' This was justified indignation on the part of the press, but Gehlen wrote it off as the 'sensationalism of the mass media'. Their interest, he says, was concentrated 'not on the traitor and his deeds but on the alleged "faulty personnel policy" of the service' and 'drawing a subjective superficial analogy', they described the BND as 'a nest of ex-Nazis'. So once again the fault was not Gehlen's but that of a subjective and superficial judgement by the press. Nevertheless word was already going round in Bonn that the Federal government proposed to retire Gehlen prematurely on October 1st, when the Chancellery's State Secretary, Hans Globke, once more leapt to the defence of his intelligence expert, declaring that 'measures had been taken to ensure that there could be no repetition of such a case in the BND'.[17]

Gehlen could now feel secure. However, instead of instituting a fundamental reform of the BND and making the service more attractive to the younger generation by discreet publicity, he drew the opposite conclusion – he raised an even thicker curtain between the secret service and the public. Numerous unjustified attacks by the press, radio and television merely reinforced his evangelical conviction that he alone knew what was good for the BND and the Republic. Ever since the '*Spiegel* affair' had destroyed his relationship with Adenauer, Gehlen had wanted to escape from Chancellery control and become his own master.

Gehlen had never really been happy with the BND's subordination to the Chancellor nor with the fact that Adenauer had passed immediate supervisory authority to his State Secretary, Globke. Gehlen had originally urged that the BND should be subordinate to a Security Council on the lines of the American 'National Security Council'; with its divergent votes and opinions supervision exercised by such a council could hardly have been very strict. His views had not prevailed, however, and the compromise solution had been 'subordination to the Chancellor'. Argument had arisen, however, as to whether the BND was on a level with or subordinate to the Chancellery Office, whether it was merely an official agency or a senior Federal Authority. Gehlen now wished his secret service to be declared a supreme independent Federal authority (somewhat comparable to the Federal Press Office) and himself to be appointed State Secretary.[18]

His path was made easier by the ending of the Adenauer era. In October 1963 there moved into the Palais Schaumburg three men who had little conception of the significance, power or malice of a secret service. Ludwig Erhard, the Chancellor, Ludwig Westrick, head of the Chancellery Office, and Karl Hohmann, the senior civil servant, all came from the Ministry of Economics, whose experts had long doubted whether a secret service was really necessary at all; the professional economists had found many of the BND's economic reports amusing rather than informative.

The head of Section III in the Chancellery, responsible for the BND, was Hohmann but he could barely bring himself to take the secret service seriously, saying: 'After all they do no more than journalists. They investigate sometimes well and sometimes badly, just like journalists.' Owing to the poor quality of the BND's reports and his own almost superstitious horror of spies, the Chancellor developed an aversion to the BND. He even forced the BND's small liaison staff in the Chancellery attics to evacuate the building, saying: 'I will not live under the same roof as these people.'

Gehlen was hardly ever given an opportunity to brief his Chancellor. Westrick, too, cared little about the BND. Initially, as an economist, Westrick had felt bound to concern himself with the BND because of its high rate of expenditure (there was a serious clash between Pullach and Bonn on the subject at the end of 1963), but his interest soon flagged. The extent of Gehlen's generosity with the tax-payer's money was well illustrated by the construction of a German printing works in Elizabethville, capital of the former Belgian Congo. Gehlen accepted a proposal by a visitor from black Africa for the construction of a printing works there to distribute pro-German literature. When the building was half finished this gentleman presented himself to some of the innumerable visitors from Pullach and asked for payment – he owned the freehold. Hardly had the BND paid this than he reappeared to say that a fee was now required for the official building permit. Once more Pullach had to raid the till. Total costs eventually reached two million marks. At this point the Congo government nationalized the BND's propaganda enterprise.

Although Gehlen's dream of promotion to State Secretary was never fulfilled, the increasingly obvious relaxation of supervision by the Chancellery Office suited his plans. He barely had to fear any intervention from Bonn; he was an autocrat.[19]

This was a specially serious matter since the BND's presidential chair was no longer occupied by the energetic Reinhard Gehlen with his sure touch, but by a tired man of 61, isolated from the majority of his staff, thinking only in terms of influence and his personal power, burnt out after forty years of uninterrupted toil and badly in need of a rest. Such a man was hardly suited to exercise sole control over an organization of 5,000 men. The extent to which he allowed the service to degenerate is illustrated by an affair which did considerable damage to German interests in a sensitive area of the world political scene.

In late autumn 1964 Gerhard Bauch, the BND's representative in Cairo, issued a warning against a German gentleman rider and owner of a stud-farm named Wolfgang Lotz; he suspected, Bauch reported, that Lotz was spying for a foreign power and working against German interests. Bauch accordingly requested a search in the BND's card index to see whether Lotz was really a German citizen, as he maintained. Bauch, born in 1923, now a civil servant, was experienced in Middle East affairs; moreover he was the adopted son of Hans-Heinrich Worgitzky, Vice-President of the BND, and was rated as one of the BND's most successful intelligence officers. He could therefore be sure that a thorough check would be made in answer to his question.

Bauch occupied a key position in Cairo. The BND's representative there had the task of developing the already friendly relations between the BND and the Egyptian secret service, completing the BND's monitoring system encircling the Soviet bloc by constructing a base on the Nile, and opening new channels of information into central Africa. He had gone to Cairo with Gehlen's agreement, camouflaged as the representative of a West German industrial grouping. Before his departure Gehlen had presented him with a silver salver inscribed 'Be wise as the serpent and harmless as the dove.' Bauch was frequently to be seen quite openly in the company of Egyptian secret-service men.

Bauch had no wish to have his plan spoilt by Lotz. Although he had an uneasy feeling, the Pullach headquarters gave him no reassurance. Three times he asked about Lotz, but no answer ever arrived. Eventually Bauch became so uneasy that in November 1964 he went to Pullach to find out for himself. Even to Worgitzky, who was fully *au fait* with BND work in the Middle East, the name Lotz meant nothing. A check through the relevant BND desks was equally fruitless.[20]

In fact Lotz was an Israeli agent – trained and equipped by the BND. Even today the case is still one of the BND's secrets – their tame historians deny all connection between the BND and the Lotz case. According to them Bauch never inquired about Lotz in Pullach and he was dismissed from the service precisely because of this omission. Papers among the property of deceased high-level BND functionaries, however, tell another story.

Late in 1959 the Israeli secret service had turned to Pullach with a request for assistance in the infiltration of an agent into Egypt. Gehlen agreed and commissioned Langkau, who favoured a pronounced pro-Israeli policy, to work out the details. The Israelis sent Major Zeev Lotz, who originated from Mannheim; early in 1960 he appeared as an East German refugee in the West Berlin reception camp at Marienfelde and was passed on to Munich by BND personnel. In a BND 'safe house' in the Giselastrasse he was then trained in the rudiments of agent's work; his knowledge of German table manners was improved and he was provided with German papers. Finally the BND took him along to Pullach Camp firing range.

Disguised as a horse dealer and ex-Captain in Rommel's Afrika Korps, Lotz set out for Cairo in January 1961. Gehlen treated the affair as top secret; apart from Langkau no senior officer in Pullach knew that Gehlen was officially assisting the enemies of Cairo. Gehlen held his tongue when Lotz deserted the conventional espionage field and started to terrorize the German rocket technicians on the Nile by sending them parcels of explosives. He also held his tongue when it had long since become clear that the Israeli spy was acting against the wishes of Bonn – in fact against the immediate interests of the BND.[21]

Bauch only learnt the truth about the Israeli after Lotz had been arrested by the Egyptian police on February 22nd, 1965. Under interrogation Lotz incriminated the BND representative as an accomplice to such effect that Bauch found himself facing the interrogation arc-lights of the Cairo police. The whole BND organization in Egypt was paralysed at one blow.

Worgitzky flew to Cairo three times to arrange Bauch's release from arrest and ensure that he was not placed in the dock alongside Lotz. On March 17th Bauch was permitted to leave Egypt. He had had enough of the BND and its methods – he resigned. The BND, however, remained loyal to Lotz; when, on his premature release from Egyptian arrest, he stopped off at Munich airport with his wife, he was welcomed by BND officials at the foot of the gangway of the Lufthansa aircraft from Cairo, shepherded past passport and customs controls and royally entertained until the El Al plane left for Israel.[22]

Once more Gehlen shuffled responsibility for this set-back on to a subordinate; he let it be known that in the Lotz/Bauch case Worgitzky, the Vice-President, had been at fault. Worgitzky never recovered from Gehlen's evasive manoeuvre. For months Gehlen had been squeezing him out of all administrative responsibility in the BND and he now ceased to try.

As time went on Gehlen's mistrust of Worgitzky became so profound that he even had his deputy's telephone tapped. A few months later 'Worgy' suffered a heart attack. It was followed by a long illness and he never returned to his Pullach office. He died on December 13th 1969; all the members of his immediate staff, including Gerhard Wessel, the new President of the BND, were present at his funeral; only one man, as usual, was missing – Gehlen.[23]

The Bauch/Lotz case was not the only one to cast doubt on Gehlen's qualities of leadership. Richard Christmann, the representative in Tunis, for instance, found his secret reports to Pullach in the hands of the German Ambassador; on Pullach's recommendation, moreover, he was approached by so many journalists that the most junior policeman in Tunis soon knew who the BND representative was. Gehlen apparently saw nothing peculiar in Christmann's embarrassments, since in his memoirs he described an incident involving his man in Tunis which he ascribes to the stupidity of the German Ambassador: 'On one occasion, for instance, a German Ambassador asked one of his foreign colleagues about a certain piece of information passed to him by the Foreign Office; it originated from us [from Christmann of course] and dealt with certain highly secret activities by the gentleman concerned. Having once been a member of the intelligence service of the country concerned, the man of course indignantly disputed the accuracy of the information, whereupon the Ambassador requested the Foreign Office not to pester him with such nonsense in future.'

Ulrich Klitschke, an East German refugee, could also tell a remarkable story of the peculiar use to which the BND put its agents. He had been an officer in the National People's Army, had been trained in Moscow and on his defection in 1958 had been registered into the interrogation camp, 'Camp King' (Oberursel). He had then been approached by Pullach and at Easter 1964 had been dispatched to Prague to meet another East German, although the BND must have known that he was on the East German list of suspects. He was promptly arrested and handed over to the SSD.[24]

Naturally it is not possible to ascribe any and every set-back to Gehlen. The fact remains, however, that the mandarin-like airs of the ageing President produced an atmosphere conducive to negligence, reduction of output and a system of favouritism hitherto inconceivable. He who had once been so indefatigable an office-worker now stayed away with increasing frequency; he was often on holiday, generally taking his dormobile to a piece of ground on Lake Constance owned by his driver's sister (swimming and sailing are his hobbies). He hardly dealt with his files. His secretary would send him off at the weekend with a suitcase-full of files but usually it came back on Monday unopened.

'Reinerl', as his wife called him, became more and more preoccupied with technical gadgets at home. In his study, on the wall of which hung a death-mask of Frederick the Great and an enlarged photograph of Canaris, he seldom received visitors. The legendary cigar-case inscribed 'Secret Service' (even his belts carried the same inscription) was now no longer in use.

The more he cut himself off from the outside world, the greater the confidence he placed in a small circle of people to whom he felt himself drawn by shared memories and experiences. Alo, his secretary for years, was one of them, as was Langkau, his friend from regimental days in Silesia; the circle also included many figures from the aristocracy, Silesia and the officer corps, not forgetting the sixteen relatives whom he had rewarded with senior BND posts (some on security grounds).

These relatives were not all such peculiar characters as some of Gehlen's critics thought. One of his brothers-in-law, now a Brigadier-General, was quite prepared (during the Felfe affair, for instance) to criticize his eminent relation. Gehlen's son was one of the most promising experts in BND electronics. Even Hans Gehlen, the BND's senior medical officer, known as 'Schlömmel', was passable, although there were divergent views on his medical abilities.

Another of Gehlen's relatives, a printer with no intelligence experience, also made himself conspicuous, and had to leave his resident post in Latin America. Of all these relatives, however, the most colourful figure was Johannes Gehlen, the President's brother, known as 'Don Giovanni'. He was a physicist and an economist; although entirely without intelligence training, he was appointed BND representative in Rome, where he ranked as a senior civil servant [Oberregierungsrat, later Leitender Regierungsdirektor]. As his secretary in Rome Gehlen gave his brother another member of the family, his wife's niece. The BND justified 'Don Giovanni's' appointment by the good relations which he was said to have with the Vatican; in fact his reports to Pullach were received with much reserve.

For years he plagued the BND with all sorts of peculiar conjectures; twice, for instance, he wrongly predicted a papal election. He was regarded as a *bon viveur* who preferred to amuse himself on the Via Veneto rather than pursue secret investigations. A BND man recalls: 'Eventually it was too much even for old Gehlen. He quarrelled with his brother after he had got us into great difficulties with the Italian secret service.' Even Wessel, Gehlen's successor, holds up his hands in horror at the mention of 'Don Giovanni'.[25] Such experiences, however, and even his successor's criticism, do not prevent Gehlen from flatly denying that there was ever any nepotism or favouritism in the BND. Any member of the staff, he says, had to 'prove himself like anyone else and his subsequent career was dependent upon his achievements' – his own relatives, however, were excepted.

With such disregard of the principles of leadership and career structure many men were promoted to senior and middle-level posts who would hardly have been so successful in any other agency. Ageing officers, friends of Gehlen and old secret-service hands chased after lucrative posts abroad, for which they were not qualified. One BND representative in Asia was an ex-SS-Sturmbannführer and commander of an SD Einsatzkommando [murder squad]; he could not visit Pullach because the Munich Public Prosecutor had an arrest warrant out against him. An ailing Colonel successfully applied for a series of posts in the Middle East; the BND's medical officer invariably passed him fit for tropical service although he was quite unable to keep regular hours in the heat.

The material reasons leading to this competition for posts abroad frequently became obvious on the relief or retirement of a representative. There was then a savage struggle for every stick of furniture and every carpet in the official residence.

In the light of such malpractices it is astounding that the BND did not founder in a morass of inefficiency. In certain sectors of the intelligence field it still showed all its old brilliance; in Latin America and the Middle East it was still regarded as the best-informed secret service. The BND's Middle East experts, for instance, forecast the breakdown of German–Arab relations long before Bonn had accorded diplomatic recognition to Israel.

The high spot of BND intelligence work was perhaps the fact that early in June 1967 it foretold the outbreak of the Six-Day War in the Middle East almost to the hour. When Dean Rusk, the US Secretary of State, declared in the National Security Council that Israel would not strike, he was interrupted by Richard Helms, the head of the CIA, who commented that he had reliable information to the effect that the Israelis would attack in the next few days. Rusk replied: 'That is quite out of the question. Our Ambassador in Tel Aviv assured me only yesterday that everything was normal.' To which Helms replied: 'I am sorry, but I adhere to my opinion. The Israelis will strike and their object will be to end the war in their favour with extreme rapidity.'

The President asked the source of Helms' information. Helms said: 'I have it from an allied secret service. The report is absolutely reliable.' Johnson asked: 'Have the Israelis given you a hint?' Helms replied: 'Mr President, I cannot answer your question. I merely state once more: there will shortly be war in the Middle East. And the Israelis will start it.' Helms' report came from the BND.[26]

The fact that the BND could still score certain successes was primarily due to the devotion of long-standing members of the staff who attempted to safeguard the existence and efficiency of the BND despite Gehlen's abdication of responsibility. The less Gehlen functioned, the more determined the senior staff members became to hold the position – for the sake not only of the BND but of themselves. Unfortunately the old hands seldom gave the slowly advancing younger generation a chance to substitute new ideas for the old habits. They largely ignored their juniors, partly due to lack of time, partly to egoism. The more perspicacious heads of section such as Winterstein (Foreign Political Intelligence) and Dethleffsen (Evaluation) rode through the crisis caused by Gehlen's leadership by adhering to established routine; other old hands used their seniority to keep the youngsters from High School confined to junior posts.

The younger members would probably have resigned, had they not been circumspectly assisted by a man who increasingly came to be regarded as a sort of substitute for Gehlen. This was Major-General Horst Wendland, born in Berlin in 1912 and a regular artillery officer like Gehlen; in 1944 he had been head of the Organization Section in Army Headquarters and had been on Gehlen's staff since 1946. He was in charge of the Administration and Organization Section of the BND and was regarded as a management genius.

On Worgitzky's departure Wendland had taken his place, though without being appointed Vice-President – Gehlen had known how to prevent that. In practice, however, he was the Vice-President and, more important, he was the only hope of the BND's younger generation. 'Papa Wendland', as he was known in Pullach, had long since become the focus of leadership in the BND. He was the man who listened to the complaints of rebellious members of the staff; he was the man who worked out fresh organizational directives; he was the man who travelled abroad visiting allied services, who maintained contact with Bonn and considered reforming the entire organization.[27]

Of the many who liked him for his realism and habit of under-statement few realized that basically Wendland was a sick man; he suffered from fits of depression. He had served the autocrat Gehlen for too long, had too frequently merely obeyed orders. He was too weak to stand up to Gehlen, though he had long since realized that the only future for the BND lay in Gehlen's departure. Moreover he had to un-dertake all the work and all the official journeys which Gehlen, on his continual holidays, either neglected or was not prepared to do.

Chance then came to Wendland's assistance: in December 1966 the political scenery in Bonn changed. Chancellor Erhard resigned and the period of Kurt Georg Kiesinger's Great Coalition began. The new Chan-cellor found that Erhard had left an unsolved problem: who would one day be Gehlen's successor? Gehlen would reach the age limit in spring 1967 and the moment would have been ripe to look for a successor forthwith. But Kiesinger shelved the problem and solved it for the moment in his habitual manner: in the spring Gehlen was given a year's extension.[28]

Kiesinger's State Secretary in the Chancellery was Captain (retd) Werner Knieper; he was too experienced in organization not to realize that the state of affairs in Pullach necessitated an early changing of the guard at top level. Knieper found a supporter in the Ministry of Defence, who was determined to give West Germany a functioning secret service once more; this was the State Secretary, Professor Karl Carstens.

Carstens thought it dangerous to leave the BND to itself. His view was that the Chancellery Office must once more exercise real super-vision over the BND and that the Chancellor should make more use of the advantages the BND offered him. Carstens had another special reason for wanting an efficient BND. As State Secretary in the Foreign Office he had appreciated the BND's reports (apart from those on the Eastern bloc). But the Foreign Office was now in the hands of the Social-Democrats; the obvious course, therefore, was to ensure that the BND provided a source of intelligence independent of the Social-Demo-crats.

From the Ministry of Defence Carstens watched the first moves in the struggle over the succession to Gehlen, ready at any time to intervene in the discussions. Meanwhile the Chancellery Office had decided to relieve the ageing President of the BND. Neither the Chancellor nor Knieper were prepared to extend Gehlen's term again.

Gehlen, now sixty-six, knew that he had reached the end. For some time he himself had had doubts whether he ought to remain any longer at the head of the BND; thinking back over this period, he now says that this was the time when he made up his mind finally to allow himself to be retired. He soon learnt from the Chancellery Office that there was only one thing left for him to do – nominate his successor. In the late summer of 1967 Gehlen proposed two candidates, Wendland and Gerhard Wessel, his old companion from FHO and the Org.[29]

Wendland was the natural successor; the majority of the Pullach staff supported him and wanted him to take the job on. Gehlen, however, clung to Wessel; he could not forget that he had once written in Wessel's confidential report: 'An outstandingly efficient staff officer of above-average ability ... Personality suitable for command positions.' Gehlen accordingly decided in favour neither of Wendland nor Wessel. He proposed both, although in Pullach he spread the story that he had voted for Wendland. Kiesinger had to choose.

But the easy-going Chancellor hesitated; he had no wish to decide. Three times he summoned Wessel, who was on leave in Germany, and three times he called the interview off. Carstens now entered the lists on the side of Wessel.

Gerhard Wessel, fifty-four years old at this time, was a Holsteiner, son of a pastor. He seemed an almost ideal successor to Gehlen. He had worked with Gehlen for ten years and had been a co-founder of the Org; he had once been Gehlen's successor in FHO and now he was ready once more to inherit the BND from Gehlen. Echoing the West German press, Die Welt later headed its announcement of his appointment with 'The pupil relieves his master'. This was not only an historical inaccuracy (Wessel had been in intelligence long before Gehlen); the aphorism ignored the considerable differences between the two men.[30]

In contrast to Gehlen, the secret-service king who 'for thirteen years successfully competed with Greta Garbo in his ambition to remain undetected',[31] Wessel's concept of espionage was much more prosaic. The felt hat and dark glasses, avoidance of photographers and conspiratorial 'secret-agent' airs seemed to him to be obsolete trappings which gave an already suspicious public a false picture of the modern methods used by a secret service. Fifteen years of politico-military duty in the Defence Ministry and as German Representative on the

NATO Military Committee had taught Wessel that a secret service can only justifiably exist if it is fully integrated into the governmental planning and decision-making process. Gehlen had always been trying to safeguard the BND against any over-strict control from the Chancellery Office. Wessel took no part in manoeuvrings for power.

The Defence Ministry and Chancellery experts considered such a man eminently suitable to head the BND. Kiesinger realized this too. On October 15th he received Lieutenant-General Wessel. The Chancellor took an immediate liking to the intelligent elegant officer; an historic friendship and understanding was formed. Later Wendland was also summoned, but the Chancellor was not impressed by the reserved introverted organizational expert. The decision was made: Gerhard Wessel was to be the new President of the BND.[32]

A few months later Carstens moved into the Palais Schaumburg as the new State Secretary. He immediately took interest in the BND. Fundamental reform of the BND was required and new ideas and techniques had to be accepted in Pullach. Early in 1968, with Kiesinger's agreement, Carstens ordered an inquiry into the BND, to be conducted by a three-man commission. The chairman was a State Secretary, Reinhold Mercker, formerly head of Section I in the Chancellery Office which had also dealt with BND affairs. Mercker's co-inquisitors were Alfred Raab, a senior civil servant of the Foreign Ministry and a friend of Carstens, and Paul Zerbel, a retired General of the Bundeswehr.

Carstens' three detectives combed Pullach Camp for weeks; they interrogated BND officials of all grades and rummaged in the Sections' files. Then came the turn of the BND out-stations; every man questioned was given a stern warning to tell the truth without regard for his superiors. Interviews frequently turned into brutal interrogations. Mercker, Raab and Zerbel then recorded their findings in a secret report which even today is still political dynamite in Bonn. Only three copies of the Mercker report exist. It is like a Pandora's box: a mere hint that it might be opened is enough to reduce to silence even the most vocal admirer of former BND brilliance.

In this report is set out in detail the full extent of the mismanagement current in the BND: the nepotism of the Gehlen clan, the President's defective leadership, the predominance of inexperienced officers both old and new, misappropriation of funds to serve the personal ambitions of the BND veterans, the casual treatment of the younger BND officials, the aversion to publicity and mystery-mongering of the higher levels.[33] The report summarized the BND in so many words as 'a corrupt institution'.

Carstens refused Gehlen's request to be allowed to read the report. Gehlen was determined to discover, however, the approximate trend of the 'BND moral picture' as the report was nicknamed; to this end he was even prepared to summon subordinates he had never seen before and interrogate them on the questions they had been asked and the answers they had given. Meanwhile the Chancellery was preparing Wessel to reform the BND. He promised fundamental change. On April 30th, 1968, Carstens summoned the senior officers of the BND into the dining-hall of the Evaluation block in Pullach to complete the changing of the guard. Lieutenant-General (on the reserve) Reinhard Gehlen, fresh from his investiture with the Grand Cross of the Federal Republic's Order of Merit with star and sash, appeared and said not a word.

Carstens, of course, praised Gehlen's 'outstanding services' and expressed the gratitude and thanks of the Federal government. Nevertheless his criticism of Gehlen's organization was unmistakable. He saw in the change of President 'an opportunity to introduce a new manner of working, a manner perhaps somewhat less burdened with secrecy, which will to some extent substitute cooperation between partners for obsolete hierarchical structures'. 'The profession of espionage,' Carstens continued, 'will thus, in my view, achieve that advancement in status which has long been its due since it will be openly integrated into our society and accept those structural principles effective in the modern world.'[34] In plain language these words amounted to an order to Wessel at last to bring the secret service into harmony with society.

CRISIS IN THE BND

AT 9.0 AM the commanding officer arrived, in a well-cut suit, one hand in his trouser pocket. He sauntered up to the guardroom at the entrance to Pullach camp and nonchalantly waved his pass. The guard on duty, however, was not taken in by his master's casual manner. He clicked his heels, saluted and asked for the pass, he scrutinized it for a moment or two and then handed it back. He knew only too well that the new President of the BND insisted on strict observance of the security regulations.

The President walked on, but instead of going to his own office, he turned into one of the BND office blocks and a few minutes later appeared in front of the desk officers, who could barely conceal their astonishment. He toured the offices, peered into cupboards and thumbed through files; wherever he saw signs of slovenliness he made a note; he listed those who were not at their desks. He made careful notes of everything he saw during these unannounced morning visits. He dictated orders to bring abuses to an end; he summoned desk officers to his own office to discuss changes with them; he questioned the experts, inviting suggestions.

Every measure he took and every gesture he made was designed to indicate that Gerhard Wessel, Lieutenant-General (retd) and Gehlen's successor as President of the BND, was determined to turn the BND into an efficient secret service once more. The new President planned what he called a 'reconstruction' or 'caesura', saying: 'We must keep things constantly on the move and abandon obsolete methods if we are to do our job in future.'[1]

Wessel realized from the outset that it would not be easy for him to assert himself in face of the ponderous machine with its elderly personnel and rigid overgrown structure; the BND had lost much of its intelligence system in the East and many of its bases abroad; it was suffering from lack of new blood and from inflated expenditure. Even more serious, however, was the fact that the Pullach team was split; the new President was acceptable only to a few.

The secret-service community, reared in an atmosphere of exclusiveness and isolation, rebelled against the appointment of an outsider as head of the BND. Wessel had admittedly belonged to the Org until 1952 but since then he had not been regarded as a member of the Order, particularly seeing that, when in the Ministry of Defence, he had been responsible for building up the MAD which had increasingly proved itself to be a rival of the BND. The men of Pullach had not forgotten that on several occasions the MAD had attempted to snatch responsibilities from the BND. Even these mortal sins against the Pullach fraternity, however, could have been forgiven if the majority of BND staff had not been united in support of another candidate as successor to Gehlen. Their choice was Major-General Horst Wendland, Head of Organization and acting Vice-President of the BND.

Wessel repeatedly let it be known that he held Wendland partially responsible for the abuses exposed in the Mercker Report, but Wendland's supporters continued to demand that he should have a greater say in affairs. Even Gehlen, the ex-President who frequently came into the camp, thought it advisable to lend his support to the Wendland faction; he was only too ready to say that he had really wanted Wendland as his successor. Gehlen still retained three rooms in the camp where he was assembling material for an official history of the BND; Wessel ensured that he vacated them and forbade members of the BND to have any further communication with him.

Wendland too still hoped that one day Wessel would accept him as Vice-President. Having served in key secret-service positions for twenty years, he regarded himself as indispensable. In the months before Gehlen's fall he had seemed to many in Pullach to be the real President of the BND. Moreover he could not forget the day in Pullach when he had addressed Guido Hertel, chairman of the Federal Accounts Commission, together with members of the BND Sub-Committee of the Bundestag Budgetary Committee, on the BND's financial position. Hertel had been enthusiastic; he had drawn Gehlen aside and said: 'You have an outstanding administrative lawyer.' Gehlen had replied superciliously: 'He is neither a lawyer nor an administrator. He is a General-Staff officer – and a General Staff officer can do anything.'[2]

Wendland too thought that under President Wessel he could do anything. Talking to an officer of the Evaluation Section after his first conversation with Wessel, Wendland had said: 'Now we will construct a secret service which will have cleaned itself up.' He thought that the new President was genuinely ready to work closely with him for the good of the service. Not until late summer 1968 did he realize that he had no future in the BND. His health was so bad that he was forced for the first time to indicate to Wessel that he wished to resign. Wessel advised him to go to a doctor and take a special cure. Wendland went on leave, but he never recovered his old drive and eventually resigned.

As the weeks passed Wendland's friends watched with increasing consternation as he deteriorated. He had always been reserved and absorbed in his work; now he was visibly suffering from depression and occasional lapses of memory; he seemed tired and curiously absent-minded.

On the morning of October 8th, 1968, in his house in Feldafing, Wendland said goodbye as usual to his wife Ilse and his four children; then he drove to Pullach Camp. He called for some papers in his office and made some notes. About 11.50 AM he put a Belgian 9 mm pistol to his right temple and shot himself. His secretary found him dead at his desk at 12.07 PM. Many of his friends took the fact that he had shot himself in his office, rather than outside the camp, to be a last demonstration against his rival Wessel.[3]

Wessel took it calmly. He reported forthwith to Chancellor Kiesinger in the Palais Schaumburg when the news of Wendland's death arrived. The Chancellor and Carstens, his State Secretary, nervously asked Wessel to explain how it had been possible for a man subject to 'severe reactive depressions' (in the words of the medical opinion) to occupy important positions in the BND for years. Wessel promised to investigate. For the moment, in so far as the demise of Wendland was concerned, he contented himself with saying: 'When I arrived [in Pullach], the problem was already there.'[4]

As chance would have it Wendland's death was followed by a whole series of mysterious suicides. On the very same day, October 8th only three hours after Wendland's suicide, Rear-Admiral (retd) Hermann Lüdke used a shotgun on himself in the Eifel; on October 15th Hans-Heinrich Schenk, a senior civil servant in the Ministry of Economics, hanged himself in Köln; on the next day Edeltraud Grapentin, a reader in the Federal Press Office, took an overdose of sleeping tablets; on October 18th Lieutenant-Colonel Johannes Grimm, duty officer in the Defence Staff Operations Section, killed himself; on October 21st Gerhard Böhm, a senior civil servant in the Ministry of Defence, disappeared and was later found dead.

The general public immediately suspected 'an espionage affair of European proportions', in the words of the Paris *Figaro*. In fact Admiral

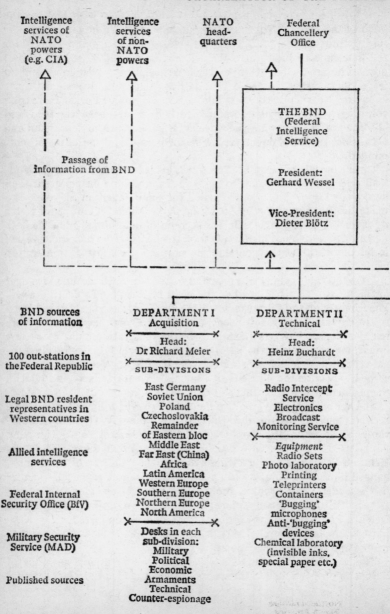

Intelligence services of NATO powers (e.g. CIA)

Intelligence services of non-NATO powers

NATO headquarters

Federal Chancellery Office

THE BND
(Federal Intelligence Service)

President:
Gerhard Wessel

Vice-President:
Dieter Blötz

Passage of information from BND

BND sources of information

100 out-stations in the Federal Republic

Legal BND resident representatives in Western countries

Allied intelligence services

Federal Internal Security Office (BfV)

Military Security Service (MAD)

Published sources

DEPARTMENT I
Acquisition

Head:
Dr Richard Meier

SUB-DIVISIONS

East Germany
Soviet Union
Poland
Czechoslovakia
Remainder
of Eastern bloc
Middle East
Far East (China)
Africa
Latin America
Western Europe
Southern Europe
Northern Europe
North America

Desks in each sub-division:
Military
Political
Economic
Armaments
Technical
Counter-espionage

DEPARTMENT II
Technical

Head:
Heinz Buchardt

SUB-DIVISIONS

Radio Intercept
Service
Electronics
Broadcast
Monitoring Service

Equipment
Radio Sets
Photo laboratory
Printing
Teleprinters
Containers
'Bugging'
microphones
Anti-'bugging'
devices
Chemical laboratory
(invisible inks,
special paper etc.)

INTELLIGENCE SERVICES (BND)

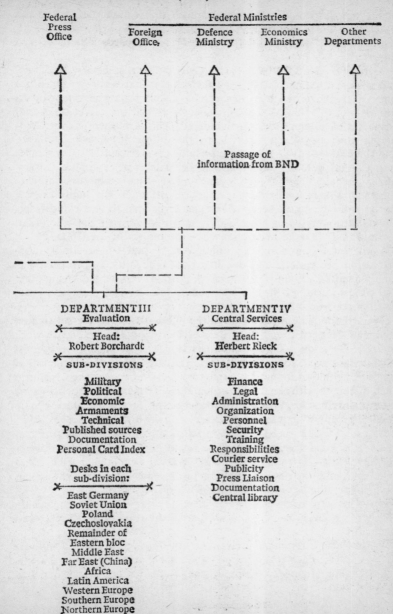

Federal
Press
Office

Federal Ministries

| Foreign Office | Defence Ministry | Economics Ministry | Other Departments |

Passage of
information from BND

DEPARTMENT III
Evaluation

Head:
Robert Borchardt

SUB-DIVISIONS

Military
Political
Economic
Armaments
Technical
Published sources
Documentation
Personal Card Index

Desks in each
sub-division:

East Germany
Soviet Union
Poland
Czechoslovakia
Remainder of
Eastern bloc
Middle East
Far East (China)
Africa
Latin America
Western Europe
Southern Europe
Northern Europe
North America

DEPARTMENT IV
Central Services

Head:
Herbert Rieck

SUB-DIVISIONS

Finance
Legal
Administration
Organization
Personnel
Security
Training
Responsibilities
Courier service
Publicity
Press Liaison
Documentation
Central library

Lüdke was suspected of spying and both the criminal police and the MAD were encountering great difficulties in their investigations. All six dead men were therefore labelled as a sinister coterie of Red spies.[5]

As head of the BND Wessel was given his first, somewhat dramatic, experience of the nervousness with which the Germans react whenever 'one of the government's most discussed but least understood institutions', as the *New York Times* once described the secret service, is suspected of failure. Kiesinger thundered: 'This is monstrous'; the *Hamburger Morgenpost* was incensed by these 'incomprehensible failures' and the *Bild* asked: 'Is the counter-espionage service asleep?' A Bundestag Commission of Inquiry had to delve into these supposed cases of espionage; a committee of State Secretaries had to discuss improvements in the counter-espionage service. Although the inquiries produced nothing and the series of suicides turned out to be a coincidence, the public outcry was a signal to Wessel to put his own house in order. He initiated what he had promised – the reform of the BND.

Immediately on assuming office Wessel had called for a modernization programme and this had been ready shortly before Wendland's death. Its main object, according to Wessel, was: 'Streamlining and concentration of the Service upon its primary task – acquisition of intelligence from abroad.'[6]

From the impenetrable jungle of the old departments Wessel created four new sections designed to deal exclusively with intelligence work abroad – Section I (Acquisition), Section II (Technical), Section III (Evaluation) and Section IV (Central Services). This entailed the fall of that stronghold of internal snooping which had brought the BND into such disrepute with the public – the old Department III, responsible for internal intelligence. Wessel also abolished the 'Strategic Service' run by Gehlen's crony Wolfgang Langkau, which many BND critics regarded as a tool of the Christian Democrats; Langkau resigned. Precise instructions from Wessel were designed to ensure that the BND would never shadow West Germans again. The BND was no longer allowed to process even those products of counter-espionage known in the jargon as 'fringe findings' on West Germans suspected of spying. Wessel ordered genuine 'fringe findings' to be passed to the BfV, the responsible counter-espionage agency, and untrustworthy reports to be destroyed forthwith.

Wessel also attempted to clear the undergrowth of cliques and private interests which had grown up in the Gehlen era. Many of Gehlen's relatives found themselves retired; many of Gehlen's aristocratic friends had to resign; many of the old hands had to relinquish their sinecures and content themselves with secondary jobs. Wessel dispatched supervisors to the out-stations to eliminate questionable practices in the collection of intelligence. They were to ensure that it would no longer be possible for over-astute members of the staff to listen to reports on the foreign radio and pass them on as their own discoveries, or for the staff of an out-station to rewrite an agent's report as a series of individual items in order to give the impression of higher output.

But now the BND was called to account for the fact that the image of it projected by Gehlen had for so long been either false or non-existent. The majority of West Germans regarded the BND as a collection of James Bond types who tapped telephones, opened letters, snooped after innocent German citizens and were flies on the wall in the offices of the Kremlin potentates. All this had left the BND leaders unmoved, however, either because they were barely in contact with public opinion or because the legend of the watchful and efficient secret service had been carefully propagated by a bodyguard of journalists. Gehlen had turned the BND into an exalted and exclusive Order whose bonds were esprit de corps and the sense of membership of an elite. Its guiding principle was that brand of mystery-mongering which Gehlen considered to be the hallmark of a true secret service.

Methods of recruitment and engagement had been calculated to give the newly-joined member of the BND the impression that he had entered another world. No one was engaged without a recommendation from a member of the BND; applications were objects of suspicion and according to Gehlen they should be put 'straight into the wastepaper basket'. The BND man led a secluded life, unlike that of any other profession. He had to assume a cover-name at once; he could tell only the immediate members of his family what his calling was. If he met a colleague in the street he had to pass him without a sign of recognition. He had to report to his superiors the personal details of any acquaintance he made; even his charwoman was an object of investigation by Pullach.[7]

Gehlen's personnel policy had increased this isolation from the community at large. He had not recruited from all walks of society but primarily from those personal or professional groupings which he regarded as the BND's natural manpower reserve – the Third Reich's secret-service experts, the aristocracy, the armed forces, the police and émigrés from the East. In West Germany's consumer society, however, these groups played mainly a minority role. But they confirmed the BND in habits of thought and behaviour which were gradually disappearing in the rest of society – the crusading anti-communist mentality, the supremacy of the military viewpoint, the obsession with law and order.

Thus divorced from the mass of the community, many BND men had taken refuge in a select closed-circle mentality. The conviction had grown that only secret-service men were prepared to do their unpleasant duty in the service of the state, with no thanks from the public – in fact at risk of being regarded as morally dubious. Between the secret service and society there opened a gulf more menacing in West Germany than in other democratic states. It is in any case hard to find a common denominator between a secret service and democracy; a democratic society increasingly tends to demand public control and absence of secrecy; a secret service, however, must be secret simply because its task is to protect the secrets of its own country and discover those of others.

So long as the structure of society was authoritarian it did not feel the secret service to be a foreign body. The most successful secret services in history had always been the instruments of an aggressive social system which required for its expansion secret prior knowledge of the enemy it intended to attack; the hordes of Mongol agents, the spies of Frederick the Great and Napoleon, Hitler's and Stalin's armies of informers demonstrate the point. The introduction of liberal societies in the West, however, changed the role of the secret services. The greater the freedom of action accorded to the individual citizen, the narrower the field of activity allowed to the secret service. It moved out to the fringe of democratic society, an object of suspicion to a public unable to forget the traumatic experience of arbitrary action by the Gestapo and snooping by the SD.

The reintroduction of a secret service after the 1945 catastrophe seemed to this society to be a mortal sin on the part of the new German democracy. In the security field the unsolved organizational problems were a source of confusion rather than reassurance; there was the Internal Security Office (the BfV) which, in addition to legitimate counter-espionage, carried on a somewhat dubious surveillance of political extremists; there was a Foreign Intelligence Service which, despite its title, shadowed citizens who had incurred official displeasure; there were parliamentary controllers who were allowed to know only what the secret service wished to tell them; there were competing secret services coordinated by no central authority.

The obscurity of this situation only increased the unease felt by the ordinary citizen about the secret services; it also contributed to his ignorance. There were many politicians who could not distinguish between the BfV and the BND; there were thousands of West Germans who did not know that the BND was not entitled to arrest or even interrogate a single citizen. And all the time the BND had been actually cultivating this ignorance on the part of the public, in which horror of snoopers combined with an almost superstitious admiration for General Gehlen's legendary army of spies. When, however, the technological revolution arrived to change the work of the men of Pullach, then this picture of an organization composed of agents in felt hats and dark glasses became a serious disadvantage to the BND.

Agents and informers had long since ceased to be the main figures on the espionage stage; James Bond had died long before he became a hero of the screen. The increasing perfection of counter-espionage systems through the use of television cameras and intercept apparatus, together with the increasing complexity both of the science of war and of society, had left the traditional spy almost without employment. Year by year the proportion of information gathered by spying decreased. Taking the CIA as an example, the provenance of secret-service information today is: 20 per cent from secret sources (agents, electronic espionage); 25 per cent from published material (radio, press and television, published documents, specialist literature); a further 25 per cent from routine reports by official agencies (Foreign and Defence Ministries); 30 per cent from the reports of military attachés and other military representatives in international organizations such as NATO.[8]

In practice this implied that the place of the secret agent was taken over by the scientist and the technician. The processing of material, its analysis and incorporation into the overall picture of the situation, required experts who could work according to scientific criteria parallel to those of their counterparts in universities, institutes and laboratories. A further factor was the expansion of secret-service work into the technical field which again demanded academically qualified specialist personnel. Progress in electronics, in long-distance and micro-photography, satellites and computers, new code-breaking systems – all these opened up new vistas for the secret service and made it increasingly dependent on the work of intellectuals.

The requirement for scientists, however, caught the BND unprepared. It had hardly done anything to make the secret service attractive to West Germany's growing generation of academics. What was there to induce a young scientist to join a badly-paid controversial agency, dominated by soldiers and with a reputation for snooping?

Universities and their students reacted violently against the BND's attempts to recruit new men. Michael Freund, professor of political science in Kiel University, refused to assist career officers from the BND; when, late in 1968, a certain Colonel Löffelholz tried to obtain addresses of students who might be interested in secret-service work, other professors and students rose in wrath. Their indignation was perhaps not unjustified. In at least one case Löffelholz had dispatched a young student to a target area outside Europe, commissioning him to send to Munich reports on the economic infrastructure in the under-developed country concerned; his monthly salary was to be 400 marks. What Löffelholz did not tell his recruit to the espionage trade, how-ever, was that in the country concerned any attempt to photograph a barracks carried the death penalty. Professor Eschenburg of Tübingen encountered a storm of protest from his students when it was rumoured that he was proposing to help BND recruitment. Ulrich Dübber, the radio commentator, thereupon ridiculed the BND's 'new image', saying that the organization consisted of 'officials with a lifetime in secret-service work, industrious and honest, married with two children, living in a council house with no prospect of a move for years'.[9]

Wessel found himself in a hopeless situation: under civil-service rules the older generation could not be phased out quickly and no new blood was coming forward. Faced with this maze of shortcomings Wessel and his reformers could see only one solution: to throw the BND open to the community. New methods of recruitment were introduced: appli-cations were now welcomed in Pullach. Wessel painted an improved picture of the BND: 'The members of the BND are not spies in the sense of being agents or informers who work for dishonourable motives and are rightly detested by the public'; service in the BND was de-scribed as 'legitimate and in no sense morally equivocal'.[10]

Wessel also insisted on the abandonment of obsolete conspiratorial ways. The dark glasses typical of the Gehlen agent disappeared, as did aversion to publicity on the part of many of the BND's senior officers. BND headquarters took its place in the telephone directory; the rele-vant specialists were instructed to maintain closer contact with the public at large. Wessel himself was conspicuous in breaking with the past; he kept open house for a limited circle of society; he went to so many parties that Herbert Wehner, one of the Social-Democrat leaders always prone to satirical comment on matters concerning the BND, called him 'the cocktail General'.

Under pressure from the government, Wessel also relaxed the rigid attitude which Gehlen had always adopted to problems of East/West exchanges of agents. Gehlen had always feared that any over-generous system of exchanges would inevitably lower to an unacceptable level the threshold of risk for Eastern agents.

The difference between Gehlen and Wessel was particularly marked in the case of Heinz Felfe, the Soviet spy sentenced for treason. While under detention awaiting trial Felfe had smuggled out a note to 'Alfred', his Russian conducting officer, saying 'Get me out of here.' The Russian secret service immediately prepared an exchange deal, in which they received involuntary assistance from the American CIA.

On September 3rd, 1961 the CIA had dispatched two Heidelberg students named Peter Sonntag and Walter Naumann on a mission to the Soviet Union described by the BND professionals as an 'amateur game'. Sonntag and Naumann were to photograph troop movements, radar installations and power-stations in Russia. The two amateur spies were known to the Russian counter-espionage even before leaving Heidelberg; the KGB, however, allowed them to click away with their cameras for a month. On September 27th, while on the return journey, the pair were arrested at Czernowitz in the Ukraine and on November 22nd, 1961, they were placed on trial in Moscow.

Gehlen immediately suspected that the Russians would try to use Sonntag and Naumann in exchange for Felfe, who had been arrested shortly before. Colonel Terekov, President of the Supreme Court Martial in Moscow, sentenced Sonntag and Naumann to twelve years' imprisonment.

Eighteen months later the KGB tried to do exactly what Gehlen had feared. No sooner had Felfe been sentenced to fourteen years' imprisonment by the Federal Court on July 22nd, 1963, than Moscow offered for exchange the two mini-spies, Sonntag and Naumann.

Gehlen, however, refused to agree to so unequal an exchange. In his view Felfe still knew too much; in secret-service jargon he was a 'dormant crater' (as opposed to a 'dead crater' – an agent who had been dropped and was of no further importance from the intelligence point of view). Moreover he feared, as did the BfV, that any move towards releasing Felfe would strengthen the hand of his rival in the East: if the release of a star agent like Felfe could be bought, all the KGB's spies would feel certain that their Moscow headquarters would not leave them in the lurch even when in prison. The Soviet offer was refused.

The KGB then started again. In the summer of 1968 it requested the East Berlin Ministry of State Security to transfer to Rummelsburg prison in East Berlin and hold ready for exchange with Felfe a group consisting of BND agents sentenced in East Germany, members of the Social-Democrat 'Eastern Bureau' and certain political prisoners. The 'Grotewohl express' (prison slang for a prison train fitted out with four-man cells) accordingly set forth from four prisons and from MfS labour-camps carrying eighteen political prisoners to the MfS model prison in Rummelsburg.

There the KGB and MfS instituted a clandestine war of nerves. The eighteen prisoners were given no official reason for their move. By tapping out messages on the heating pipes, however, their gaolers gave them to understand that their names were on a list for exchange; whether they were actually released, however, depended entirely on the government in Bonn and it had so far refused all offers from the East. In letters to their relatives the prisoners accordingly urged them to intercede in Bonn. Simultaneously KGB agents spread word in Bonn that, should the Kiesinger government pardon Felfe, eighteen political prisoners would be released to the West from East Berlin.

Finally Günter Wetzel, State Secretary in the West German Ministry for All-German Questions, received a formal offer of exchange from East Berlin. The Ministry had already arranged a number of deals; in October 1964, for instance, the Federal government had made available 32 million marks for the purchase in the West of consumer goods and foodstuffs such as coffee and butter in exchange for 800 prisoners from East Germany. Now, in the winter of 1968, the Eastern request was not for money but for Felfe. The official offer was on a three-to-one basis: in addition to the students, Sonntag and Naumann, the KGB offered up a third academic from Heidelberg, Volker Schaffhauser, who had been sentenced in Leningrad in May 1967 to four years' forced labour for espionage. As additional bait for the release of Felfe Wolfgang Vogel, the Berlin lawyer representing the interests of the German People's Republic, offered the eighteen political prisoners to Jürgen Stange, his West Berlin counterpart.

Herbert Wehner, Minister for All-German Questions, informed Chancellor Kiesinger of the offer. Wessel, however, like his predecessor, initially had doubts; Felfe knew too many of Pullach's secrets and his return would be a moral victory for the other side. Hubert Schrübbers, President of the BfV, supported Wessel. Kiesinger was unwilling to make up his mind.

At this point one of the KGB's German allies started to take an interest in the eighteen prisoners in Rummelsburg. This was Major-General Markus Wolf, head of the Acquisition Section in the Intelligence Office of the East German Ministry of State Security, and he ordered the transfer of the eighteen prisoners from Rummelsburg to the prison in Karl-Marx-Stadt (Chemnitz). For prisoners in East Germany this particular establishment has a good name since a section is set aside for prisoners due for release. The eighteen were accorded long-forgotten privileges; food was of hotel standard and they were allowed to buy civilian clothes with their earnings in Eastern marks. Via the grapevine, however, Wolf let the prisoners know that Bonn was jeopardizing their release. His agents in Bonn also spread the word that if the Federal government did not soon agree to the exchange of Felfe, the eighteen men would be returned to their former cells.

Faced with this pressure, in January 1969 Wehner urged Chancellor Kiesinger to accept the East's offer, thereby reinforcing the absurd suspicions against him (Wehner) harboured by the rabid anti-communists of the CIA. Wessel now gave up opposing the exchange and agreed to it. He had no wish to carry the odium of sending eighteen men back behind bars. In contrast to his predecessor, moreover, Wessel felt no personal antipathy to Felfe; Gehlen had never forgiven his former favourite for his treachery.

On February 13th an MfS Colonel read out a court order to the eighteen prisoners in Karl-Marx-Stadt prison – early release for good behaviour. On the same day Dr Wilhelm Stärk, governor of Straubing prison, informed the prisoner Felfe that he was free to leave.

On the following day the exchange mart in human beings opened at the Wartha-Herleshausen frontier crossing. From behind Eisenach along the secondary road leading to Wartha came a convoy of three vehicles: a Mercedes (registration number IS 86–71), a Russian-type bus and a BMW 1800. Near Pferdsdorf, where the Wartha road bends sharply south, the column halted. The driver of the BMW got out and waved the bus across the road and then back into a clearing in the wood. In the Mercedes were the two lawyers, Wolfgang Vogel from East Berlin and Jürgen Stange from West Berlin, ready to complete the deal.

After some twenty minutes another bus with a local registration (GI for Giessen in West Germany) appeared from the direction of Wartha. It stopped alongside the parked car. An MfS official got out of the BMW, took some papers from the West German bus-driver, read them by the light of a torch and handed them back. Then he opened the rear door of the Eastern bus and ordered: 'Get out.' The fifteen men and three women left the vehicle, suitcases in hand, and climbed into the West German bus.

The Mercedes drove on down the road, the bus following. About a mile before reaching Wartha the BMW pulled out to the left, overtook both bus and Mercedes, and stopped at the barrier. A few minutes later the barrier was raised. The Mercedes and the bus moved across the demarcation line and 900 yards farther on, in Herleshausen, the West German barrier went up. A frontier policeman saluted the bus.

At the same time, in the guardroom of the West German frontier post at Herleshausen, a civil servant from the Federal Ministry of Justice confronted Felfe, the ex-prisoner, and read him a court order: his term of imprisonment for treason had been suspended; in the event of mis-behaviour he would be required to serve the remainder of his sentence; under Article II of the Basic Law of the German Federal Republic he was free to choose his place of residence.

An official of the frontier service opened the door of the hut. Outside, Vogel, the East German lawyer, took Felfe by the arm, led him to the Mercedes and drove back to Wartha. The 'Felfe Affair' was over.

Wessel later found himself being accused by his critics of having given way too quickly in the affair of the Felfe exchange. For the BND's old hands this was merely further proof of their conviction that Wessel was jeopardizing the secret service with his attempted reforms, which they regarded as irresponsible demolition of Gehlen's machine and its camouflage system, once so efficient. Five senior BND officials resigned in protest. From his retirement Langkau added fuel to the anti-Wessel fire. The six old hands often visited Gehlen together; he had meanwhile built a second house on a plot overlooking Lake Starnberg and here, protected by a burglar alarm and an ex-policeman masquerading as a gardener, he would sit with his visitors and mull over the evil of the times. Many of the 'Grand Old Man's' pronouncements, embellished while on their way to Pullach, became known in BND headquarters.

The headquarters contained many opponents of Wessel who saw their positions threatened. They included the 'hydrocephaloids' of the bureaucracy, who had proliferated unchecked under cover of the strict secrecy, and there were also the 'frothblowers', old hands who had been sidetracked into jobs 'where they were theoretically in charge of evalu-ation of incoming intelligence material, but where so little arrived that some "froth" had to be squeezed out of it to provide the necessary bulk in the secret files'.[11] The 'hydrocephaloids' and the 'frothblowers' combined with other officials opposed to the abandonment of internal intelligence either for ideological reasons or because they were intelli-gence perfectionists. On the other side Wessel's cautious attempts to reduce the BND's fixation on Russia as the enemy offended the cold-war warriors, who already thought that the Great Coalition's Eastern policy was going too far.

Whatever the bonds between them, they stood shoulder to shoulder in opposing Wessel's reforms. It was soon common knowledge that the

President's determination to change things had not penetrated to all parts of the BND. There was a sudden reduction in the rate of destruction of internal intelligence material ordered by Wessel, but no one seemed to know who had cancelled the order. From the out-stations cases were reported giving rise to the suspicion that internal intelligence was still being collected there.

In the autumn of 1968, for instance, the Christian-Democrat newspaper *Bayernkurier* published a BND report on Egon Bahr, who had been press spokesman in West Berlin and was then serving in the Foreign Office with ambassadorial status. He was a friend of Brandt's and in 1967 Kiesinger had commissioned Gehlen to inquire into Bahr's contacts in East Germany and other Eastern bloc states between 1963 and 1967. Gehlen had accepted but Wessel was now summoned to Bonn and compelled to order an investigation.[12]

To make matters worse, in the spring of 1970 Wessel had to submit to interrogation by a man deeply suspicious of the BND ever since the 'Spiegel affair' – Franz Josef Strauss. Strauss had heard that, in connexion with a murder in Munich, the BND suspected him of arms smuggling and Wessel was summoned to an interview. He was completely taken aback by Strauss's questions, checked with his staff in Pullach, and then assured Strauss that the BND had never instituted inquiries against him. In fact Wessel was wrong; when Strauss was Defence Minister, the BND had had an informer, an officer, on his staff. Wessel did not know this and so was not telling an untruth when he assured Strauss that he was a victim of rumour. Unfortunately, as Strauss learnt later, Wessel had been given false information by his own people. This was known in BND jargon as 'evading' questions from head office.

For the first time it seemed doubtful whether Gerhard Wessel was a strong enough man to shake up the ossified structure of the BND. Many thought him too weak, too ready to compromise. Doubts about Wessel's capacity for leadership were already taking root when, in October 1969, the change of regime in Bonn plunged the BND into a new crisis of confidence. The advent of the Socialist-Liberal coalition changed the traditional relationship between Bonn and Pullach.

The Socialists, the leading partners in the alliance, shared society's built-in mistrust of the secret service. They had had bitter experiences with Bismarck's and Hitler's secret police; they were plagued with ideological prejudice and were inexperienced in the exercise of power. The Party had long debated whether secret services had any right to exist at all.

T–K

Ever since Pullach had existed the BND and the Social-Democrat Party had been at odds. In 1955 the Social-Democrats had warned against over-enthusiastic acceptance of the Gehlen Org into the Federal service; in 1958 they had demanded Gehlen's dismissal for alleged BND activities in French armaments works; for its part the BND had been impervious to any socialist influence and had relied entirely upon the Gehlen–Adenauer axis.[13] Hardly a single prominent Social-Democrat did not suspect that he was himself being shadowed by the BND. Erich Ollenhauer had been under surveillance; Heinemann was a target for observation; Wehner had been pilloried as an enemy of the state; when Brandt was Burgomaster of Berlin a BND informer had noted every glass of whisky he had ordered while on a visit to the Hotel Bristol in Paris. Many Social-Democrats bore a grudge against the ex-officers of Pullach for their rigid attitude to the socialist past – forgetting that, on their own side, there were men who took delight in emphasizing their opponents' Nazi past, while brushing aside as sheer calumny any reference to their own activities in the jungle of communist conspiracies.

After the construction of the Berlin Wall the socialist leaders had begun to have their doubts whether the BND was adequately informed on the East. Social-Democrats began increasingly to suspect that the BND was serving up cold-war myths instead of factual reports. Wienand, the socialist Bundestag deputy, lamented that Pullach produced 'a picture of enemy powers consonant only with the wishful thinking of the [Christian-Democrat] government'.[14]

Willy Brandt in particular could not forget August 13th, 1961. He was then Burgomaster of Berlin and on the day after the building of the Berlin Wall he received a BND report dated August 11th saying that no East German initiative was likely that weekend. Weeks earlier the BND had forecast that measures would be taken to divide the city but it did not know their scope or timing. The BND reports which Brandt had seen as Foreign Minister had done nothing to allay his doubts. He had told a senior visitor from the BND that all this was 'not funny'; the BND was undoubtedly required for military intelligence but as far as the political field was concerned it had all too often reported wrongly, late, or not at all.[15]

This negative view of the BND was certainly not justified during the period of the Czech crisis in 1968; in that instance the work of the BND had been outstanding – but here it was, of course, dealing primarily with military intelligence. As early as May the BND had forecast the move of Warsaw Pact forces into Czechoslovakia, at a time when the US secret service still did not believe in such 'fraternal assistance'. At the latest by the end of June the BND was convinced that: 'The Soviet government considers the toleration limit to have been exceeded. Military intervention is increasingly entering the realm of probability.' Llewellyn Thompson, the American Ambassador in Moscow, indignantly described this as 'a German fabrication'.

Only gradually were the Americans prepared to admit that the BND had been right. On August 15th other Western secret services reported that an invasion of Czechoslovakia was imminent. Three days later Western intelligence recorded that twenty Eastern bloc divisions had 'gone to ground' on the Czechoslovak frontiers: vehicles and uniformed personnel had vanished from the streets and railways, the cities and villages into the woods – a sure sign, to any secret service, that an attack was imminent. Date and timing of the invasion, however, were still unknown.

Shortly after 9 PM on Tuesday August 20th the radio monitoring sets in BND headquarters ceased to record; for two hours there was total wireless silence in the Eastern operations room. The experts were in no doubt: the twenty divisions were moving across the Czechoslovak frontier that night. At 11.11 PM the BND radar operators reported activity in the airspace above Prague – the first Soviet squadrons were landing. A few minutes later the telephone rang in one of the BND's out-stations in Bavaria. Someone gave the alarm signal: 'The Russians are coming.' He was located in Prague.[16]

After becoming Chancellor, Brandt held up to ridicule a BND report showing that Leo Bauer, his adviser, who had been condemned to death in Moscow in 1952 and later pardoned, had been a communist in the past. 'Leo,' Brandt said, 'now at last I know that you have been a communist.' Newspaper editors suddenly began to receive copies of the BND's 'High-level Intelligence Guide' (not to be confused with the secret report to the Chancellery Office), thirty copies of which were sent regularly to Bonn 'for personal information'. Officials in Pullach suspected that they were being passed on by the Chancellery. President Heinemann told journalists officially that the BND reports were 'unfortunately not exciting'. Heinemann was also the originator of the joke that the BND could save at least half its budget if only it would order a few additional copies of the *Neue Zürcher Zeitung*. He did not realize that owing to the high quality of its foreign reporting, many of the BND's specialists did in fact use this newspaper as a source of information when their own intelligence was inadequate.

The fact was that Brandt's team was disillusioned by what seemed to them inadequate political reports and appreciations on the Eastern bloc.

Instead of concrete information the men of Pullach served up to their masters in Bonn disquisitions such as this extract from the 'High-level Intelligence Guide': 'With the start of the Soviet-American rocket talks, with the preparations for the European Security Conference and with the continuation of negotiations in Peking the impression continues to gain ground that, under cover of a policy of peaceful coexistence, the Soviet Union is trying to further its own aims: a temporary balance of nuclear power and preservation of the European status quo.'[17]

Bahr, the Chancellery State Secretary, classified such secret-service productions flatly as 'poppycock'. Eventually Brandt's team lost all desire to read the BND's analyses; instead they pitched their requirements for information from East Germany so high that the Head of the Acquisition Section lamented: 'After all, I haven't got a man crouching under Ulbricht's desk!'

Chancellor Brandt was astute enough to take immediate steps to reduce this antipathy to the BND. In the new Chancellery Minister, Professor Horst Ehmke, he had found a man determined to solve the BND problem in a more rational manner – and to do so in collaboration with Wessel.

After an abortive attempt to bring all the agencies concerned, the BND, the BfV and the MAD, under one coordinating authority, Ehmke turned his attention to the reform of the service for which he was actually responsible – the BND. He submitted the Pullach headquarters to a test. Almost every Tuesday, after the Chancellor's conference, he would summon Wessel and discuss with him the strengths and weaknesses of the secret service. Whenever Wessel was evasive, the Minister pressed him brusquely and perspicaciously. He inquired about possibilities and capabilities. He wanted to read reports from the Central Committee of the Socialist Unity Party. He demanded fundamental analyses on the Ulbricht regime. He expected to be told how far the BND was informed on internal happenings within the Kremlin. He was continually calling for facts and yet more facts. The ill-assorted pair would part exhausted. Eventually, however, Ehmke decided that he could work with Wessel, that Wessel had the will to push through the reforms begun in 1968 and, moreover, that he constituted some guarantee for the continuity of the service. According to the *Süddeutsche Zeitung* Ehmke had left Wessel in office 'as a non-political, somewhat pliable, though conservative, figurehead'. Ehmke himself said that the 'weakness of the President' made it impossible for him to leave Wessel in sole control of the BND; he must be given a Vice-President and new section heads.

Ehmke was determined to counterbalance the conservative President with a phalanx of trusted Social-Democrat supporters. The choice of the section heads presented little difficulty but the appointment of the Vice-President proved to be an agonizing operation. There were various possibilities: a civilian intelligence expert to support Wessel, who thought primarily in military terms, and to relieve the President of representative duties in the Chancellery and with 'friendly services' abroad. Alternatively a manager from the economic department, industry or the press could have been appointed Vice-President to reduce the BND's over-luxuriant bureaucracy and modernize the intelligence service. Yet a third type was possible – a political administrator with only limited knowledge of espionage or organization but selected primarily 'to win for the BND the confidence of those circles of our society which still have reservations regarding this institution or are still, rightly or wrongly, suspicious of it'.[18]

The search for a Number Two unexpectedly gave rise to positional warfare in Pullach about the Number One – Wessel. The old secret-service hands thought that their President was on the Minister's knock-down list. Colour was lent to this idea by the rumour that Ehmke was treating the thin-skinned Wessel very roughly and that Wessel had not the courage to rebut Ehmke's criticisms of the BND. The story went round that Ehmke had dressed-down the head of the secret service like Hitler addressing his Generals.[19]

In this situation the staff of the BND sought support from another socialist minister whom they regarded as Ehmke's rival – the Defence Minister, Helmut Schmidt. The BND's ex-officers prophesied a NATO catastrophe; seventy per cent of all NATO's military information on the Eastern bloc came from the BND; if Wessel was sacked, NATO military intelligence would be paralysed for a long time to come; if Wessel went, almost all senior ex-officers, including ten Generals and some fifty Colonels, would go too.

Faced with uncertainty in his own secret service and suspicion on the part of his allies, Ehmke felt that he must act. He asked his Party friends for suggestions and Heinz Ruhnau, a Hamburg senator, suggested first Hans Detlev Becker, director of *Der Spiegel*, and finally, among others, Dieter Blötz, provincial manager of the Hamburg Social-Democrat Party.[20]

Early in March 1970 Ehmke summoned Wessel to the Palais Schaumburg and told him what he had decided: to appoint Blötz Vice-President and dismiss two sections heads. Wessel agreed. In order to avoid agitation among his staff, however, he treated these changes as a 'Top

Secret' matter. The majority of those in Pullach did not know what Ehmke had said to him.

On March 28th, however, the *Hamburger Morgenpost*, a newspaper close to the Social-Democratic Party, discovered who Wessel's deputy was to be and a week later the left-wing liberal *Die Zeit* put a shot across his bows, saying: 'Party officials have no place in the higher levels of the BND.' The *Zeit* went on to criticize Blötz: 'He is no expert in the acquisition of intelligence – well and good. But must he not therefore be an experienced administrator? Nothing is known on this point. But at least, then, he must be an outstanding organizer? Only the Hamburg Socialist Party can testify on this point.'[21]

In the 'tricky moment' of the staff conference in the Evaluation Section's building even Wessel was able to tell his section heads and desk officers little about his future deputy – he had never seen him. There was no entry on Blötz in the BND's personal card-index.

Wessel found himself in a ridiculous position. During the Wendland controversy he had insisted that the BND be kept free of party-political influences – and now he was faced with a primarily socialist-orientated team. He had wished to select his Vice-President himself – but Blötz had been found by Ehmke. He wished to have solely specialists in the higher ranks of the BND – and not one of Ehmke's candidates had ever been in intelligence before. Nevertheless he did not protest; he did not resign. Clearly he was banking on the hope that Ehmke's people would help to solve the most difficult problem faced by any secret service (and particularly that of West Germany, when serving a left-wing government): to convince its customers of the quality of its products.

Though every secret service assembles reports, evaluates them and forwards them to its government, these products are quite often regarded with suspicion by its customers. Sometimes reports are false; on occasions, however, they run counter to the wishes and prejudices of those in power. Wessel had every reason to fear that it would be difficult to harmonize the BND's intelligence on the Eastern bloc with the hopes placed in their Eastern policy by the Socialist-Liberal coalition. There would be no harm, therefore, in having socialist supporters in high places in the BND to shield it against censure from Bonn.

Wessel's agreement gave rise to a storm of indignation in Pullach, in particular from the section heads whose dismissal had been decided upon and who first learnt of the change from the press. Winterstein, head of the Acquisition Section, rumbled: 'Why did the President not have the courage to tell me this himself?' The greatest offence was created by the choice of Vice-President; the BND's old hands grumbled that Wessel should have forestalled Ehmke and made his own proposal for Vice-President – from his own staff. Instead he had had his deputy forced down his throat. In answer Wessel insisted that he would ensure that the BND remained a vital regulator for the Eastern policy of the Social-Democrat/Free Democrat coalition.[22]

On April 7th Ehmke invited those concerned to meet in the Chancellery so that he could introduce Wessel to his new staff. For the first time Wessel could take stock of his new 'top-level team' – Blötz, the Vice-President, Meier, head of Section I (Acquisition) and Rieck, head of Section IV (Central Services, Administration, Organization, Personnel).

Finally on May 5th, 1970, the new era officially opened. In the dining-hall of the Evaluation building 200 staff members assembled in serried ranks for the installation of their new masters. Wessel's speech was a circumspect plea for reform of the BND: 'The pattern of this organization cannot be changed overnight. We are not called upon to reconstruct this service but to revise it. Urgent though this task is, it must be approached with caution to ensure that, in these years of transition, the factual, realistic and objective quality of this service's reporting, free from internal and party-political influences, is not jeopardized.'

To the general surprise Ehmke presented himself to the offended secret-service men as their guardian and patron. It was his task, he said, 'not to leave the BND to itself but to assist and support it, to help it attain the status which is its due in the light of its importance'. His audience had not expected this; they had anticipated a ministerial drubbing. Instead the Minister demanded 'increased efficiency' from the BND. The service, Ehmke said, must 'concentrate on its true role and be freed from unnecessary and futile work. The task of the service is to gain foreign intelligence, to acquire for the Federal government knowledge of importance – and to do so at high pressure.'[23]

Thus encouraged by Bonn, the new team made a promising start. Ehmke and his master Brandt had no further need to fear that, in pursuing their Eastern policy, they would find their own secret service standing in their way. The BND began to gain good marks in Bonn. It gave early warning, for instance, of every interference with the free movement of traffic to West Berlin imposed by the East German regime whenever West German functions were held in the city – in January, November and December 1970, late January and early March 1971. In the summer of 1970 the BND produced valuable briefing material for Willy Brandt's talks with East Berlin. The BND had an up-to-date picture of the situation; every report proved it. Summer 1970: East Berlin still insisting on its demand for recognition; refusal of further inter-German arrangements; demand for unqualified recognition under international law. September 1970: despite the signature of the Moscow Agreement, no spectacular détente or concessions regarding Berlin. November 1970: the East German object in the internal German talks on Berlin is to undermine the responsibility of the Four Powers and validate its own position; the Socialist Unity Party determined not to allow discussions between experts to appear as an approach towards an inter-German dialogue. December 1970: the Socialist Unity Party's aim in its policy towards Bonn. 'No rapprochement but separation *vis-à vis* the Federal Republic.'

Even more valuable were the warnings gathered by the BND from the Allied secret services to the effect that Washington, London and Paris would only agree to arrangements made by the Federal government with Moscow, Warsaw and East Berlin provided that the balance in Central Europe was not adversely affected. The Bonn diplomats lapped up the BND reports and Wessel was continually stressing the good relationship between Bonn and Pullach. Ehmke, too, publicly expressed pleasure with the work of the BND. Early in 1970 the BND top echelons already knew that arrangements between Washington and Peking had progressed further than the Sino-American ambassadorial discussions in Warsaw allowed the public to think.

The Polish disturbances of December 1970, however, showed that Wessel and his new team had not altogether succeeded in raising the efficiency of the BND. The mood of the Polish people, which eventually led to rioting, was inevitably a subject of close scrutiny by the Federal government and the BND, particularly since Bonn was just setting out to conclude a treaty of reconciliation with Poland. Chancellor Brandt was due to fly to Warsaw on December 6th for the signature of this treaty. He went without being prepared by the BND for the upheaval which shook Poland a fortnight later and ended in the fall of his co-signatory.

The BND of course knew that the economic situation in Poland was serious, that opposition was building up in the Communist Party, in the armed forces and in the trades unions, but it had in no way prepared the Federal government for the possibility of rioting. Brandt would hardly have gone to Warsaw on December 6th if the BND had given him warning. Back in Bonn he lamented: 'What do we have our information services for? Why did no one tell me anything?'[24]

This story went round in Pullach and the barometer of morale in BND headquarters fell once more. Dissatisfaction was rife and it was rumoured that Wessel's reforms had failed. Primarily in the Acquisition Section, but also in others, the staff ganged up against the new top level. Whatever their motives, the critics could still point to depressing shortcomings in the BND.

The fact is that Pullach is still dominated by the long-established ageing officers, even in those intelligence and evaluation sections which are not concerned with foreign troop movements. Moreover – and this was previously unthinkable – discontented members of staff now talk quite openly about office secrets because they think that only by broadcasting their difficulties can they achieve the necessary BND reforms.

Finally the BND is a haven for a type of man found in no other West German authority: officers who feel themselves indispensable and remain voluntarily at their posts after retirement. Since the BND makes good the shortfall between their previous salary and their pension, these ostensibly indispensable officers are known as 'shortfallers'. When they have received their extension they normally go off on a prolonged cure. Since, before extension, the official medical officer must testify to the intellectual and physical vigour of the candidates, some of whom are over seventy, the members of the BND wonder whether the doctors are incompetent or, alternatively, subjected to pressure. Naturally only the most senior officers are considered as potential 'shortfallers' – and the most conspicuous of them all was Gehlen himself. When he retired on May 1st, 1968, his full salary was paid until December 31st of that year; in addition he was allowed to set up on Lake Starnberg a subsidiary of the BND run by his old-established secretary 'Alo', who was given Senior Civil Service Grade for this purpose.

The most important post for which Wessel had to find an incumbent he allotted admittedly not to a 'shortfaller', but to a Brigadier-General who thought solely in military terms; this was the post of 'Inspector'. In America's secret service the Inspector is the most exacting taskmaster in the whole organization. He exercises a continuous and punctilious control of output, working on a system described as 'barbaric' by those who know it. Many members of the BND think that the introduction of the CIA system is vital for the BND. One BND man of six years' standing who is a protagonist of reform, put it thus: 'The Inspector must be able to appear unannounced at any time of the day or night in the offices of the most important agencies in our firm. His object is not to check whether every member of the staff is sitting at his desk; from the point of view of results that is unimportant. Instead, taking an outstation as an example, the Inspector should make a minute check of the volume of incoming reports and then examine them for value. This would soon show where there was negligence or mismanagement, where reports were simply recordings from foreign broadcasts "dolled up" and presented as information from some "high-level" source.' But the BND's Inspector was not like that. He inspected the kitchens, he visited the out-stations, he passed on good wishes and thanks from the President, he asked whether people had any special requirements. The BND reformer's comment was: 'With such control of output the BND can continue to sleep happily – unchanged and punctilious.'[25]

The critics were not content merely to uncover abuses such as this and demand their elimination. They also sniped at the new top level, concentrating on the weakest member, Vice-President Blötz (who was known in the office as the 'flame-thrower' because he was so quick to come to the help of cigarette-smokers with his lighter). He did not succeed in making his mark in his new surroundings; his critics in fact thought him so incompetent that they withheld important information from him.

The malcontents were also opposed to Meier, the new head of the Acquisition Section; they considered that he knew more about counter-espionage than intelligence. Under his direction the BND concentrated on East German intelligence and this aroused the opposition of experienced secret-service men since it entailed the neglect of other areas of tension in South America, Asia and the Middle East. In addition, the critics objected, the abandonment of operations in the 'Third World' would impede work against East Germany; East German diplomatic missions in neutral countries were frequently profitable targets for Western secret services.

The background to the critics' arguments was in fact a suspicion that the Socialists and the Chancellery wished gradually to paralyse the secret service and do away with all reporting from the East. Some credence was even given in Pullach to the rumour that Wessel had handed to the Chancellery lists, showing real names and cover-names, of all BND informers who were critical of the government's Eastern policy or had previously assisted in keeping leading Social-Democrat politicians under observation. One BND man said indignantly: 'Our most closely-guarded secrets are now openly lying around on desks in Bonn.'[26]

BND officials who had spent twenty-five years in underground conflict with the Soviet Union could not bring themselves to believe that the Russians now genuinely wanted a relaxation of tension in Europe. They also feared that an over-violent swing Eastwards by Bonn would scare away old friends. They accordingly allowed stories to filter through alleging that the BND was gradually losing credibility with its foreign friends. The secret services of Germany's NATO allies were said now to regard BND reports on the East as unreliable, since they originated from 'Brandt's News-Desk' (the British nickname for the BND) and were over-coloured by wishful thinking stemming from Bonn's policy of détente; the US secret service was said to have largely discontinued exchange of information with the BND since reports from the 'Non-intelligence Service' (the CIA's nickname) had been found to be barely fit for use.

These speculations were, however, far from reality. Ehmke had in fact briefed the BND to raise its reporting on the East to a new peak of efficiency; the West German government's new Eastern policy necessitated precise knowledge of internal developments in the socialist countries. Ehmke had said: 'I want East Germany and more East Germany and more East Germany.' The new men, however, went about their business so ineptly that it was easy for their internal opponents to present their attempts at reform in a very different light.[27]

The great source of complaint was the series of precipitate radio messages dispatched from Pullach to a number of BND resident representatives ordering them to prepare to close their offices and report themselves to Pullach. There an ultimatum awaited them: either to content themselves with a 'golden handshake' which might reach as high as 30,000 marks, or to take over some other BND post – less lucrative owing to the absence of an expense account. When engaging these men the BND had held out considerable prospects to them and in many cases their recall implied a serious reduction in living standards. Moreover their masters failed to produce a plausible explanation for the decision, such as increase in efficiency and concentration on essentials. The victims therefore looked upon this as capitulation by the BND and alerted public opinion; some of them even took the BND to law in the Munich courts for breach of contract.

The opponents of the new BND leadership even tried to bring the former president, Gehlen, into the game. Some of those who had been dismissed visited Gehlen and asked him for his views on their cases; he promised to be available as a witness. At once the rumour went round in Pullach that the old gentleman on Lake Starnberg was disillusioned with Wessel and would emerge from retreat to prevent injury to the service. Then it became known what Gehlen proposed. The ex-president was writing a book which would amount to a showdown with the Social-Democrats and a devastating criticism of Ehmke's conduct of the BND's affairs. Gehlen's primary purpose was to exploit the halo surrounding his name in order to warn the German people and the Western

266 THE GENERAL WAS A SPY

world against the Eastern policy being pursued by the Social-Democrat/Free Democrat coalition. With such rumours in circulation, undisguised factions formed in Pullach Camp.

Certain of the medium-level officials formed a group to discuss further proposals for reform which they ultimately summarized in a seventeen-point programme. Among the main suggestions were the following: '1 The Chancellery and the BND leaders to cease continuously talking about reform and finally to do something. 2 The BND not to be further dismantled but personnel to be strictly limited to really capable people. 3 The BND's career structure to be brought into line with that of other authorities, in other words an increase in senior and top-level posts producing increased attraction for new blood. 4 The BND age limit to be reduced from sixty-five to sixty, again to attract new blood.'

These demands show both how little the BND leaders had done to make their reform plans known and also how little account their opponents took of the obstacle to any reform constituted by the civil-service rules. Nevertheless the critics remained mistrustful and Ehmke's over-forceful interventions in BND affairs only served to increase the unrest in headquarters. This being so, Wessel's efforts at reform could hardly count on support from many of his staff. Many of his critics doubted whether the President really had the will to impose any reform, saying: 'Things are organized, reorganized and over-organized. But nothing comes of it.'

A fundamental reform of the BND must be initiated, however, if it is to fulfil the function which alone justifies its existence. The main points in the reform programme should be: establishment of geographical priorities for collection of intelligence by the BND; abandonment of intelligence-gathering in countries outside these priorities; published material to be evaluated only in so far as this is necessary for the analysis of intelligence from secret sources; no evaluation of published material for purposes of general reporting; reduction of the workload on BND personnel by transfer of routine evaluation of published material to Records and Research institutes not belonging to the BND; improvement of the evaluation system; enhanced recruitment prospects for the BND through an improved pay structure, increased use of technical methods and limitation of general reporting to areas and subjects not dealt with by West German diplomatic representatives; reduction of military personnel in the BND to those required for military intelligence and their replacement by technical specialists.

Admittedly reform can only be partial unless the legislators in Bonn eliminate the fundamental obstacle threatening to prevent any major change in the BND – the necessity for strict adherence to civil-service regulations. The obligation to employ almost all BND officials up to retirement age militates against any influx of fresh personnel. It is therefore for consideration whether the BND should not adopt the two-grade pension system in force in the US secret service; this allows notice to be given to officials at the age of fifty, thus giving them the opportunity of starting on a second career. This might restore to the BND the internal flexibility which it so urgently needs.

Such a programme might help to raise the BND from its present low level of efficiency. Twenty-five years of victory and defeat, of hope and resignation have shown that, despite the many unattractive aspects of the trade, the BND can be a useful instrument of West German policy. So long as the insulated social systems of the East close their doors to a world eager for détente, so long as the Federal government, in the clear interests of West Germany, must seek to discover other countries' secrets in order to protect itself against surprises, the BND is still necessary. It remains a key to the success of any Federal government.

It can, of course, work no miracles; the time of the Gehlen myth is past. Bedell Smith, when head of the CIA, once said sarcastically: 'They expect you to be on a communing level with God and Joe Stalin . . . They expect you to be able to say that a war will start next Tuesday at 5.32 PM.'[28] The world has long since realized that that is not the way of a secret service. Nevertheless the BND *can* produce what it was designed to produce: decisive assistance to Bonn – in the interests of West German security and the security of the entire Western world.

APPENDICES

APPENDIX A

THE CHEQUERED HISTORY OF GERMAN ESPIONAGE

THE origins of the FHO can be traced back to the late 18th century, to the time of the French Revolution when the feudalist pattern of military organization had been swept away and the capabilities of national armed forces had risen to an explosive degree. This was the period when, for the first time, leaders of an army required more precise information of their enemy's war potential.

In the early nineteenth century working groups were set up in the emergent General Staffs to collect and analyse information on enemy armies. In Prussia's Great General Staff also (as opposed to the 'little' General Staffs of formations) three sections emerged in the course of time, each responsible for military intelligence in a certain part of Europe. No. 1 (or Russian) Section dealt with the East and South-East including Russia, No. 2 (or German) Section with the central and southern German States and No 3 (or French) Section with West and South-West Europe, including France. In Bismarck's days the German Section disappeared from the troika and turned into the Deployment or Operations Section; the two remaining Sections, however, despite changes in organization, were still investigating foreign armies in East and West in 1945. They were the ancestors of Gehlen's 'Foreign Armies East'.[1,2]

From the outset the problem was how to penetrate the military secrets of a potential enemy, yet without concrete data no estimate of other countries' armies could be formed. The collection of this material, which of course was mostly secret, should have been the business of some espionage organization, but as yet no such thing existed. Intelligence was largely the chance product of individual agents belonging to no organization but linked in varying ways to whoever might be their masters at the time.

At this point someone remembered a plan put forward in 1795 by the Prussian Colonel von Massenbach: 'To every embassy should be allotted an officer of the Quartermaster-General's staff who has served for sev-

eral years in that body; let there be military/diplomatic ambassadors.'
The foreign army analysts seized upon the plan. The Military Attaché
had been born.

In 1830 the Prussian General Staff dispatched the first military
attaché to an embassy (Paris); further appointments followed in mid-
century. The attaché's special reports broadened the General Staff's
knowledge of enemy strength potential and the first soundly-based
enemy appreciations appeared. The attachés, however, were unable to
satisfy the General Staff's appetite for intelligence; moreover officially
they were not allowed to spy and they had to humour their heads of
mission who were frequently prickly and regarded the military as out-
siders and competitors.[3]

Since, however, published material (books and the Press) were inadequate to enable an estimate of the strengths and weaknesses of an
army to be made, the Military Attachés began to engage spies. Early in
the 1860s there appeared in Paris, Turin, Vienna, Pest and Linz secret
emissaries of the Military Attachés who kept War Ministries, barracks
and troop units under observation.

Nevertheless in the (for Germany) decisive year 1866 the Great General Staff was very badly informed about Prussia's opponents. Graf von
Waldersee (late Field Marshal) said that intelligence officers produced
'almost exclusively uncertain and inferior material'. The General Staff
had no overall picture of Austrian armaments and knew nothing of the
Austro-Hungarian army's concentration against Prussia.[4]

Before the Prussian army marched off to war against Austria, however, a civilian registered as unfit for service showed how enemy intelligence should be run. This was Dr Wilhelm Stieber, a police officer, son
of a civil servant in Merseburg, born on May 3rd, 1818. He had first been
a law-court official, then an attorney; he was a protagonist of democratic liberties, had spent ten years as chief of the Berlin criminal police
but had been compulsorily retired for over-forceful methods of interrogation; he finally became head of a private detective agency and had
worked for the Russian State Police; from autumn 1863 Bismarck had
been entrusting him with secret missions abroad. He was regarded as a
genius in the art of deduction in criminal cases. This Prussian Sherlock
Holmes, moreover, had numerous international connexions which had
made him a much-sought-after consultant for those in high places.[5]

Following the abortive attempt by the student Blind to assassinate
Bismarck on May 7th, 1866, Stieber was brought back into government
service. Bismarck commissioned him to set up a secret state police for
the protection of the Minister-President and of the King. Since war with

Austria was imminent, Stieber's secret police started with a military bias; a royal cabinet decree of June 23rd, 1866, empowered him to head 'a political police force [later entitled Secret Field Police] for the fulfilment of high-level police functions in the King's headquarters'.

The cabinet decree launched Stieber into the centre of the military intelligence organization, for paragraph 5 of his commission read: 'Support to the military authorities in the collection of intelligence on enemy armies.' Stieber mobilized his numerous agents abroad and for the first time the General Staff received concrete intelligence on the Austrian Army's concentration.[6]

At the end of the war Stieber expanded his secret service still further. On August 1st, 1866, he occupied a couple of rooms in the Foreign Office and his secret police was given a new title – Central Intelligence Bureau. Stieber's agents hunted out opponents of Bismarck among the supporters of the House of Hannover; they tracked down the authors of anti-Prussian newspaper articles both at home and abroad – but they also collected military and political information. The Central Intelligence Bureau maintained small circuits of agents in Paris, London and Vienna, and they kept their ears open for anything Stieber thought important.[7]

Stieber's success and the failure of military intelligence impelled Helmuth von Moltke, the Chief of the Prussian General Staff, to set up his own secret service. On February 11th, 1867, the first military secret service in modern German history was formed – the Intelligence Bureau of the Great General Staff. It had an annual budget of 2,000 thaler and comprised two permanently-employed agents and one headquarters officer, Major von Brandt, whom even his friend Waldersee considered 'a bon viveur rather than a soldier and lacking basic military knowledge'. It could therefore hardly compete with Stieber's band of agents.[8]

During the Franco-Prussian war Stieber's Secret Field Police consisted of 31 police officers and 157 soldiers. To them were connected numerous intelligence circuits which Stieber had set up in France and Switzerland. Admittedly Stieber had nothing like the 36,000 spies which legend ascribed to him; nevertheless he had agents and informers in every major town in France.[9]

Whenever the General Staff's intelligence officers wished to be informed about the enemy's situation, they were forced to turn to Stieber's 'Secret Field Police'. This they did with decreasing enthusiasm, however, since Stieber's agents were not solely occupied in collecting information about the enemy; they were also spying on the Prussian Generals – at the behest of Bismarck. In September 1870 came an open clash. Stieber was interfering with the prerogatives of the Military Administration and was called to order by the General Staff. The Chancellor supported Stieber and refused to accept any criticism from the military.[10]

The General Staff drew its conclusions and set about systematically expanding its Intelligence Bureau. The secret service, they resolved, should be an exclusive preserve of the military. Times were favourable to them. After the war Stieber and his Secret Field Police withdrew and devoted themselves entirely to the work of the Central Intelligence Bureau. Moreover, although industrialization was beginning, society was still semi-feudal and, in the jingoistic mood of the Germans at the time, revolved around the military.

In 1872 Brandt, the secret service chief, was replaced by a more energetic officer who expanded the organization. Initially he confined collection of secret intelligence to Germany's most important enemies, France and Russia; he recruited agents abroad and obtained an annual budget of 100,000 marks from the Foreign Office's secret funds. By 1889 the Intelligence Bureau had agents in Paris, Brussels, Luxemburg, Belfort and Nancy and no fewer than seventy-five informers in Russia.[11]

Expansion of the military secret service, however, met increasing resistance from the Foreign Office, which looked askance at the soldiers' intelligence ambitions. The Foreign Office itself maintained a form of intelligence service, though admittedly not as a definite organization; it was merely in secret contact with voluntary informers who kept it posted on developments of interest abroad. In addition Prussian/German diplomatic missions had a number of local agents. The resistance of the Foreign Office, however, was not politically motivated; it was merely the reaction of the diplomat caste defending their interests and prerogatives against a rival. Stieber, on the other hand, had a definite idea: through the Central Intelligence Bureau he wished to make the Foreign Office the authority solely responsible for a political and police foreign intelligence service. He was unable, however, to gain Bismarck's ear. A severe attack of gout forced Stieber to leave the Foreign Service and in 1882 he died.[12]

With the departure of Stieber the soldiers were increasingly able to enforce their demands. The mouth of the military secret service opened even wider when Graf Waldersee, who had political ambitions, became Chief of the General Staff. He urged Military Attachés to keep a critical eye on the work of their heads of mission and to report everything of political and military importance to him, by-passing the diplomatic authorities. Simultaneously he ordered full steam ahead for the expansion of the secret service; it was given a new chief, Major Waenker von Dankenschweil, and a new title under which it became known to history – IIIb, coined because, as an independent section, the secret service came under *Oberquartiermeister III* [Deputy Chief of Staff III].[13]

Waldersee thereupon demanded more money from the secret Foreign Office funds – one million marks! On January 19th, 1891, the Prussian Minister of War wrote to Leo von Caprivi, the new Chancellor, saying that the head of the military secret service needed more money 'to find contacts for the acquisition of documents and obtain correspondents for war'. Then followed the vital sentence: 'Only a military organization can guarantee security and achieve something.' The soldiers could not have staked a clearer claim to predominance in the field of German secret intelligence.

The wily officials of the Wilhelmstrasse did succeed in cutting down the military demand for a million marks and persuading the War Ministry that it could do with an annual budget of 250,000. Nevertheless the negotiations between the War Ministry, the Foreign Office and the Reich Chancellery showed that pride of place in secret intelligence matters was now firmly established in military hands.[14]

Chancellor Caprivi was not particularly interested in secret-service questions; he disliked any air of mystery and did not grasp the decisive role which a foreign intelligence service can play in government decisions. His support of the Foreign Office in their opposition to the military advance in the intelligence field was therefore somewhat half-hearted. Moreover the diplomats themselves showed signs of weary resignation; when Krüger, a police official who had succeeded Stieber in the Foreign Office, was retired in 1890, no secret-service officer was appointed in his place. The Central Intelligence Bureau had already been disbanded.[15]

A decision had therefore been taken which was to govern the development of the German secret service for half a century: secret intelligence became the province of the General Staff; secret-service officers thought in military terms alone. IIIb, the secret military intelligence service, had been born on the eve of the new era of arms races and world wars; it knew no world other than that of politico-military power and rivalry, measurable in divisions, artillery, concentration plans and manpower potential. The development of military power was all that counted; uppermost in secret-service thinking were military blocs, economic warfare and birth statistics. Germany came to believe that espionage was invariably an affair of military intelligence about the enemy. Political espionage withered away.

So the belief grew up in Germany that espionage and military intelligence were one and the same thing. In their writings General Staff Officers propounded the theory that the whole business of espionage was 'of military origin' – a questionable thesis, not borne out by history. Perhaps Moses had sent out the first agents in history when he dispatched the twelve leaders of the tribes of Israel to spy out the land of Canaan; perhaps Hannibal was using spies when he sent emissaries to northern Italy to persuade the Gauls to support Carthage. In every case, however, the primary motive had been political – to obtain a clearer view of the world outside and gather information which would help the leaders of the State to take their decisions. The civilian, but military-minded leaders of Wilhelmian Germany ignored this fact. They basically abandoned control of the secret service to the military and so deprived themselves of an instrument which might have enabled them to understand the world better than they did.

So the IIIb machine expanded, barely controlled by civilian authority and with little hindrance from the Naval Intelligence Service which had meanwhile been formed. Yet the secret service still lacked a solid organizational basis; in practice it consisted merely of a small headquarters in Berlin and some agents abroad. This was not enough. Both its own country and its own army, the General Staff thought, must come within the secret-service's purview; listening posts were required on the frontier to observe the other side's border zone. The spur was provided by the deteriorating international situation – German officers were no longer allowed to travel to France or Russia.

From 1890 onward IIIb stationed retired officers in the frontier Military Districts with the special task of collecting information. They recruited agents on either side of the frontier. They also kept in close touch with the frontier police, who were urged to assist in the collection of intelligence. As a result a new plan was developed – formation of intelligence posts manned by IIIb and the frontier police combined.[16]

A brisk stream of information was soon flowing into these intelligence posts and life in the headquarters became busier. A single General Staff officer could no longer deal with the incoming material by himself and in 1897 two additional officers joined the section. IIIb now learnt an art at which it became adept after a few years – the business of counter-espionage.

IIIb quickly found out how to gain contact with an enemy secret service by the use of doctored ('play-back') material and thereby gain an insight into its intentions. Sometimes the Section admittedly had to pay dearly for the opening of contact. For instance IIIb sold the (genuine) mobilization plan of 16 Army Corps to the French secret service for 6,000 francs, though without its vital appendices. However the Germans had succeeded in gaining contact with the 'bureau de renseignements' in Paris and so for years knew what it was interested in. The head of the German secret service met his French opposite number on several occasions in Luxemburg, Liège and Brussels.

On the other side of the coin, IIIb's knowledge was broadened by a policy of secret-service alliances. Major Waenker von Dankenschweil forged links to the secret services of Germany's allies, thus initiating that collaboration with friendly services which the BND so successfully pursues today. In 1889 he gained touch with the Austro-Hungarian 'Evidenz' bureau, which was always well informed; later he agreed an intelligence exchange with the British secret service – from which, however, the British profited more than the Germans.[17]

As international crises succeeded each other with increasing rapidity after the turn of the century, however, it became evident that IIIb's intelligence posts were not up to their job. District officers were frequently untrained, and knew neither foreign armies nor languages; they lacked the flexibility to react quickly and positively in times of tension.

Moltke's officers then had an idea: instead of the incompetent District Officers, serving young General Staff officers should be appointed who would know about foreign armies and be intelligent enough to direct their agents to the right places in times of tension. In peacetime they would be attached to the headquarters of corps located near the frontiers and in war would take over intelligence duties in the relevant corps headquarters. This was the plan which Moltke submitted to Karl Wilhelm von Einem, the Prussian War Minister on March 6th, 1906. A new creature had appeared in the secret-service world – the Intelligence or Ic officer.* In June 1906 the first intelligence officer of the Prussian Army was appointed, a General Staff Lieutenant. It was for him to prove that Moltke's concept was sound.[18]

The officer's name was Walter Nicolai and he was destined, in the space of a few years, to build up for IIIb a position of political power such as no military secret service had ever before possessed. Nicolai, born in 1873, came of a family of North German pastors, though his father was an officer. After attending a church school and joining the cadet corps, he entered the army as a twenty-year-old 2nd Lieutenant.

* In the German army Ia = Operations, Ib = Supply and Ic = Intelligence.

After three years at the Staff College he was appointed to the General Staff in 1904. He had grown up in the traditionalist protestant Prussian world in which it seemed natural that the officer should govern the fate of the nation. Loyal to his sovereign, ultra-conservative and ostensibly the typical non-political soldier, he was in fact the embodiment of the politically-minded officer corps of the imperial period.

Nicolai was interested in Russia and the Russians. He had learnt Russian while at the Staff College and his first General Staff assignment, survey work in the Vistula valley near the fortress of Graudenz, had put him on the trail of Russian spies. When Moltke ordered him to become the first intelligence officer at the headquarters of I Army Corps in Königsberg, he was only too eager to set up a circuit of agents in Russia.[19]

On July 1st, 1906, Nicolai took over the Königsberg intelligence post and expanded it into a headquarters for his planned informer organization in Russia. He built up contacts to the Jewish population living in the Russian frontier zone, among whom in his own words 'many were prepared to carry out espionage assignments and act as intermediaries to officials and officers in senior positions'. Nicolai was able to locate numerous informers in the neighbourhood of Russian barracks and along the vital railway lines which the enemy must use for the deployment of his troops.[20]

Nicolai was so successful that from the summer of 1907 practically all Army Corps were given intelligence officers, to whom the more efficient District Officers were attached as deputies. This opened a new phase of official jockeying for position; a lively quarrel arose between the War Ministry IIIb and the Corps headquarters as to whose subordinates the intelligence officers were – the General Staff's or Corps headquarters. The battle carried on even into the Third Reich.

The introduction of intelligence officers marked the beginning of an increased expansion of IIIb, since the gathering clouds of the First World War forced the secret service into ever more furious activity. Lieutenant-Colonel Erich Ludendorff, head of Section 2 of the Great General Staff, was primarily responsible for the rise in tempo. He took an unusual interest in secret-service matters. Without a secret service he could visualize neither total war nor the authoritarian regime of his dreams.

Ludendorff helped the secret service to obtain additional staff; he raised IIIb's annual budget to 450,000 marks; he used his influence to engineer Major Nicolai's nomination as head of the secret service in the spring of 1913. Two congenial spirits had thus come together and their bond was that arrogant superiority complex of the military caste which looked down on civilian politicians and was soon destined to seize the reins of power from a weak political leadership.[21]

When the much-heralded test came in 1914, however, the secret service was still barely able to satisfy the Intelligence Section's appetite for information. IIIb did in fact report both the Russian and French concentrations in good time, but detailed information on enemy operational intentions was still lacking.[22]

The Intelligence Section's estimate of enemy intentions was therefore largely based on supposition. It knew nothing of the moves of the French Fourth and Fifth Armies during the early days of the war; it did not believe that the British Expeditionary Force would undertake any major operations away from its disembarkation points. In the Battle of the Marne in September 1914 the German lack of information nearly resulted in catastrophe for the army in the West; after the surprise counter-attack by the French left wing Hentsch, the head of the Intelligence Section, who had been armed with extraordinary plenary powers by Moltke, advised withdrawal, primarily because he had had secret-service reports to the effect that fresh British forces had landed on the Belgian coast and even that the arrival of a Russian expeditionary force was imminent. Both reports later proved false.[23]

From this point onwards many in the Intelligence Section refused to place any further confidence in IIIb's reports. Antipathy and misunderstanding between the two Sections (IIIb had meanwhile become a General Staff Section) grew, since it was all too often obvious that some message had been false or that a report had been wrongly evaluated. The sharp distinction drawn between the collection of intelligence and its evaluation proved disastrous, since the one Section did not know what the other was doing. Even after Nicolai had raised the quality of secret-service information, the Intelligence Section remained suspicious.

Nicolai was only too well aware that intelligence officers with armies and corps were in no position to direct agents in rear of the enemy or recruit additional informers. They were so occupied with immediate front-line intelligence that they had no time for the longer-range work. Nicolai therefore sub-divided his organization; the intelligence officers were now only to deal with 'front-line intelligence' and intelligence posts were formed in the army rear areas to collect information from the enemy's hinterland.

In addition Nicolai formed a new office, the 'Intelligence Officer Berlin' (Nachrichtenoffizier Berlin – NOB), whose task was to make good the serious lack of information on Russia. This office set up sub-stations in Stockholm, Flensburg, Budapest, Piraeus and Galatz to collect information on events in Russia and forward it to Berlin. The NOB for the first time developed a procedure at which Gehlen's organization subsequently became expert – prisoner interrogation.[24]

NOB's interest and influence became wider and wider. It applied itself to the development of a system of secret codes; it set up a false papers office where fake passports were prepared and genuine foreign passports collected; it set up laboratories in which scientists discovered methods of manufacturing secret inks. No IIIb agent now left Germany without being provided with technical gadgets produced by 'NOB Wis', NOB's technical section.[25]

Nicolai had considerable difficulty in holding his growing espionage empire together. He became more and more deeply involved in the minefield of disputes over spheres of authority: he fought with the Military Attachés and the Naval Secret Service; he was suspicious of his own subordinate agencies such as the NOB, which he thought were becoming over-powerful; he wrestled with headquarters of Armies which were trying to bring his intelligence officers under their control. He was even unable to preserve the Intelligence Officer's title. The German word 'Nachrichten' can be used to mean both 'Intelligence' and 'Signals' and when the Signals Service was formed in 1917, its officers were also called 'Nachrichten' officers. Gradually Nicolai's officers came to be referred to as 'Ic Officers' and the Intelligence Section acquired a new name – the 'Foreign Armies' section.

Nevertheless by January 1917 Nicolai felt strong enough to give his department a definitive organization. He divided his headquarters into Sections – Section I (Secret War Intelligence), Section II (German and foreign press) and Section III (Counter-espionage). Two further sections dealt with intelligence in the eastern and western theatres of war and one last section with intelligence originating from Germany.[26]

Nicolai had barely finished his reorganization before Ludendorff summoned him to fresh endeavours. Since August 29th, 1916, Ludendorff had been Quartermaster-General and immediate adviser to Hindenburg, the new Chief of the General Staff. Ludendorff was determined to make use of Nicolai's secret service to assist his politico-military strategy of holding on until victory was won.

Step by step Ludendorff had seized the reins of power. Under pressure from him the decision in favour of unrestricted U-boat warfare against the United States had been taken; Theobald von Bethmann-Hollweg, the weak Chancellor, had been overthrown and an even weaker successor had been elected. In Bethmann-Hollweg's words, the Kaiser and the Reichstag 'had surrendered political power to the military authority'.

Now came Walter Nicolai's great moment. Ludendorff gave him the opportunity to realize what he had always wanted, consciously or unconsciously — extension of the military secret service into the political field. The head of IIIb had never been satisfied with a purely military role; he regarded his secret service as something more — the General Staff's propagandist, the stern inculcator of the will to military victory, the watchdog and the archetype of what was then termed patriotic self-discipline.

Moreover he already had the power to penetrate with his intelligence machine into all those fields which Germany's weary political authorities had already abandoned. He had representatives in the Military Division formed in the Foreign Office on the outbreak of war. The secret service controlled counter-espionage, which it ran in collaboration with the police and the Secret Field Police. It was in charge of the War Press Office and the senior censorship authorities; not a line could be printed in the German press about military affairs without the approval of Nicolai's officers and officials.

Ever since 1915 Nicolai had in addition an internal intelligence service which maintained informers in firms, institutions and private circles. It had admittedly only been responsible initially for the collection of information about foreign countries outside Germany. Its responsibilities had quickly changed however; the deterioration of the war situation had led Nicolai to demand, in addition, information about the position inside Germany.[27]

Many of the senior officers of IIIb had already begun to feel that it was the secret service's responsibility to regiment the entire people. An intelligence officer of IIIb West put it thus: 'Only when everyone feels in his bones that unnecessary talking, writing or questioning may endanger the security of his country, his comrades and himself can the way definitely be barred to an enemy intelligence service. The Japanese example has shown that it is possible to inculcate this into a nation.' Such was Nicolai's programme — but with a vital difference: instead of a foreign intelligence service the enemy was the internal German opponent.

An instruction from Hindenburg dated May 8th, 1917, authorized Nicolai: '(a) to inform the High Command of the Army about internal political developments in so far as they are of importance for the conduct of the war; (b) to take overall charge of military information necessary for the conduct of the war at home, in occupied territory and within the army in the field.' Put simply this meant: 'Maintenance of the war spirit among the German people.' With his wonted zeal Nicolai set about propagating his military masters' watchword: 'Hold on to the end.'

Nicolai set up a propaganda office 'to act as initiator and intermediary between the individual authorities dealing with propaganda (the War Press Office, Field Press offices, the Quartermaster-General's department, etc)'; he introduced 'patriotic instruction' for the troops; his officers canvassed for the sixth War Loan. Then he formed a political intelligence organization within the army; he set up an overall censorship office for war reporting. Among his instructions was: 'The cooperation of army chaplains is desired (these are said to be the main vehicles for propaganda in Britain).'[28]

Wherever Nicolai saw morale threatened, wherever he sensed a desire for peace, he went into attack. He was behind the formation of the Fatherland Party with its chauvinistic and reactionary programme of conquest; he roused public opinion against the moderate Social Democrat leaders; he mobilized popular nationalistic indignation whenever the impotent Reichstag dared to make peace proposals incompatible with total victory. No press conference took place at which Nicolai did not call for the sternest propaganda in favour of the war effort.

In vain the officers of the 'Foreign Armies' section voiced the opinion that the secret service would do better to devote itself to improving enemy intelligence. Nicolai had found his true profession. As the months went by his shadow lay darker over the editorial offices of Germany; his left-wing opponents christened him the 'Father of Lies'. The left-wing pacifist *Weltbühne* thought that his name was linked with 'every development in systematic obscurantism, political chicanery and the ever-changing lie, until the entire monstrous edifice began to totter and finally collapsed'.[29]

Never before had a secret service degenerated into an instrument of propaganda as did that of the Great General Staff. Its ultimate collapse in November 1918 came quicker than even its most pessimistic officers had feared. Nicolai was recalled; most of the secret files of Army Headquarters and the General Staff at home were burnt, and IIIb was disbanded. For a long time the secret service was discredited as a symbol and a horrifying example of the misuse of an intelligence organization for political purposes.[30]

Post-war Germany's red revolutionaries, who had been both the targets and the victims of the secret service's investigations, were determined to sweep away everything reminiscent of the secret service and secret police. Never again, the marxist republicans swore, should secret minions spy on the people on behalf of the class enemy. A Socialist Party brochure of 1911 had already said: 'Away with the secret political police, this shameful sink of the basest corruption.' The political police in nearly all the German *Länder* were disbanded and their officials transferred elsewhere. The Social Democrat moderates, however, who succeeded the revolutionaries of the extreme left in the Police Presidents' offices, quickly re-created their own political police. The backwash of revolution and the continuous threat of further *putschs* both from Right and Left forced the republicans to try to obtain prior knowledge of every move by extremists.

Admittedly the new leaders did not dare to give their secret security force the title of political police – that was far too tainted. They accordingly concealed their political police from the public by incorporating it into agencies which did not 'smell' of a political police force. Prussia's new secret police, for instance, started as an appendage to Section I of the Berlin Police Presidency, which had nothing to do with such activities. It developed into Special Section Ia, later the clearing-house for the political police of all German *Länder*.[31]

Officially a political secret service was as unacceptable as a secret police – it was an offence to democratic morals. Once more, therefore, Germany's politicians let slip an opportunity to create an effective political intelligence organization. The Weimar Republic had no foreign intelligence service. The political authority having failed, however, the military again seized the initiative.

The military secret-service experts were soon under way once more. In the autumn of 1919 an 'Intelligence and Reconnaissance Service' was introduced into the remnants of the army, the so-called Provisional Reichswehr and the Free Corps; it was run by the least tainted officers of IIIb. It was to shield the troops against the political upheavals of the time and insulate them from the left-wing revolutionaries. In practice, of course, this meant that the purposes of the army's new secret service were political as well as military.

On November 24th, 1919, Reichswehr Group Headquarters No 1 issued the following order: 'Abwehr [Counter-intelligence] offices are to be set up in all headquarters of Military Districts and Reichswehr brigades. They have the following tasks: 1. (*a*) Frontier intelligence service; (b) Countering enemy espionage; 2. Internal intelligence service; 3. Observation of our own forces.' Group Headquarters No 2 was even more explicit: the duties of the intelligence service included 'observance of political life in general, particularly of extremist left-wing parties'.[32]

The chiefs of the new secret service, however, took fright at any repetition of Nicolai's political experiment. They realized that their intelligence service could only continue to exist if they stressed its purely defensive character; its sole task was supposedly the protection of the troops — against spies and revolutionaries. It was accordingly entitled 'Abwehr' (Defence), not least with an eye on the Allied victors who had banned the maintenance of any offensive German secret service in the Treaty of Versailles.

Thus circumspectly camouflaged, the military secret service could once more officially appear in the open. In the summer of 1920 three General Staff officers, seven re-employed retired officers and a few clerks, all under command of Major Gempp, Nicolai's former deputy, occupied the third floor of No 80 The Tirpitzufer, Berlin, the former Reich Navy Office and future Reichswehr Ministry. The Abwehr was divided into Eastern and Western Desks. It was, of course, concerned only with counter-espionage and counter-sabotage. Gempp's organization was attached to the 'Army Statistical Section' of the Troop Office, as the 'Foreign Armies' Section was now called. For the first time collectors and evaluators of intelligence were brought together in one Section.[33]

In the mid-1920s, when the Abwehr was reorganized, these two parted company once more. Gempp set up three sub-groups. No 1 Intelligence, No 2 Codes and Radio Monitoring and No 3 Counter-Espionage. At the same time the Abwehr posts in the seven Military Districts established secret communications abroad. This suited Colonel Kurt von Schleicher, who had his eye on the Chancellorship and was beginning at this time to build up his position within the Reichswehr Ministry. In 1926 he removed this politico-military organization from the Troop Office and constituted it an independent inter-service section, taking charge of it himself. He was also determined to bring the secret service under his control.[34]

Major Schwantes, Gempp's successor, was only too ready to help Schleicher on his way, particularly since the latter held out to him the prospect of a spectacular expansion of his service — combination of the Army Abwehr and the Naval Secret Service under his (Schwantes') command. In effect on March 30th, 1928, Groener, the Reichswehr Minister, did order formation of an Abwehr Section formed from the Army and Navy secret services; one year later the expanded Abwehr moved a further step up the ladder: alongside the Armed Forces and Legal Sections it was incorporated into Schleicher's new 'Minister's Office', later the most important agency in the Reichswehr Ministry.[35]

This move initiated an explosive development which was to set the military secret service once more on the path of string-pulling and power politics. The prime movers in this were the naval officers who had meanwhile joined the Abwehr. The majority of them came from the nationalist camp still loyal to the Kaiser and many of them were more hostile to the Republic than to a foreign enemy. In June 1932 one of them even assumed command of the Abwehr. This was Captain (Navy) Conrad Patzig; he developed the Abwehr into a full-blown intelligence service. It now employed agents, informers and officers to penetrate the secrets of potential enemies abroad.[36]

Foreign espionage in Germany was at the time a thriving business and, to deal with it, the Abwehr had to work with the police, for it had no executive authority and was therefore unable to arrest a spy. The police, however, were only moderately effective. In particular the police sleuths had no central organization; there was no headquarters for the 'Central State Police' offices in the German *Länder*. In fact the police were helpless in face of the assaults of the French, Polish and British secret services, also in face of communist Russia's industrial espionage which alone employed over 3,000 informers in German concerns.[37]

Then came Adolf Hitler's 'national revolution', bringing into the Police Presidencies men who, according to their lights, were determined to put an end to half-measures. They visualized a police system permitting the existence neither of a spy nor a political opponent. Hermann Göring, Prussia's Nazi Minister of the Interior, divorced Section Ia from the Berlin Police Presidency and constituted it an independent Prussian police authority, giving it the title Secret State Police Office [Geheimes Staatspolizeiamt]. Some unknown post office official, faced with the necessity of designing a stamp for the new agency, invented an abbreviation – Gestapa. Popular slang turned it into that sinister word which, for twelve long years, struck horror and fear into millions – Gestapo.

The Gestapo was soon totally separate from the official administration and became a power in its own right. Even physical expression was given to this fact; it moved from the Berlin Police Presidency into a former art school at No 8 Prinz-Albrecht-Strasse. There the political policemen and the spy-chasers divided their duties. The political police, in the strict sense of the word, formed Division [Hauptabteilung] II, the counter-espionage police Division III. Gestapo headquarters maintained offices in every government district and later head offices at the headquarters of a government President [Oberpräsident] or *Land* government. The Frontier Commissariats, hitherto under Provincial Police headquarters, were subordinated to the Gestapo, which later organized its own frontier police.

No German police force had ever exercised such detailed control. A complicated system of lists and card indexes registered every opponent of the regime and every potential spy; a sophisticated investigation system ensured that no fugitive could escape the Gestapo's all-seeing eye. Authority over the concentration camps and the torture-houses of the Nazi *Gleichschaltung* machine provided it with an additional weapon. Pending 'expulsion' the Gestapo could confine undesirable aliens in a concentration camp.[38]

The counter-espionage experts of Abwehr III, like many soldiers, were prone to authoritarian solutions and were impressed by the nationalistic slogans of the new regime. They looked on with satisfaction as the cold-blooded perfectionists of the counter-espionage police went to work in the Prinz-Albrecht-Strasse. This was how they had always visualized counter-espionage – stern, clear-headed, silent. They were prepared to disregard the political accompaniments, the loss of freedom of the individual and the terror of the SA marching columns. They were interested only in the efficiency of the new machine.

Only later did a few officers suspect that the Gestapo system represented something more than a new governmental system's natural requirement for security. Behind the Gestapo stood all the diabolism of a totalitarian movement, recognizing no norms and no standards. Patzig, the head of the Abwehr, had been among the first to realize this – and his realization dated from a summer's day in 1934 when he had met the incarnation of Nazi evil, the Lucifer of the police state, Reinhard Heydrich, the new chief of the Gestapo office.

Patzig's revulsion was all the greater in that SS-Oberführer [Colonel] Heydrich had once worn naval officer's uniform. He was born in Halle in 1904, the son of an opera singer, had joined the Navy in 1922 and reached the rank of Lieutenant, serving in the training cruiser *Berlin* and the Fleet Flagship *Schleswig-Holstein*. In April 1931 a naval court of honour had cashiered him 'for unworthy behaviour' because of a breach of promise of marriage. Since then he had always displayed hatred and arrogance towards any naval officer – as Patzig was soon to discover.

On his expulsion from the Navy Heydrich had been unemployed until, on June 14th, 1931, he arrived at a poultry farm in Waltrudering belonging to Heinrich Himmler. Heydrich at once realized that Himmler's SS, the 'Schutz-Staffel', was destined to be the *corps d'élite* of the Nazi Reich. In a matter of twenty minutes Heydrich had sketched out on a sheet of paper for the pedantic theatrically-minded Reichsführer-SS the outlines of an SS security service. It was destined to be the military Abwehr's most savage opponent. Himmler christened Heydrich's brainchild the 'Security Service of the Reichsführer-SS' [Sicherheitsdienst – SD] and appointed its creator as its first head.[39]

Subsequently Heydrich constructed a model close-knit system of surveillance to shadow every sphere of the nation's life and guarantee the total dominance of the Nazi Party under the aegis of the SS and a police force trained and formed by the SS. This new police force differed from its predecessors, however, in one vital point. Under previous systems the police had been satisfied to catch enemies of the state in *flagrante delicto*; they intervened when a positive threat could be foreseen. Heydrich's police, however, were designed to track down the enemy before he had even had any thought of opposition, let alone taken any action.

Step by step Heydrich implemented his programme. By the end of April 1934 he had become head of the Gestapo (Himmler had meanwhile been appointed Inspector of the Gestapo). Then, using the preponderance of Prussia, he imposed unification of all provincial police forces into a Reich police force – under SS command. In June 1936 Himmler was nominated 'Chief of the German Police' and at the same time Heydrich took over the newly-formed 'Security Police Department' [Hauptamt Sicherheitspolizei] combining the Gestapo and Criminal Police. The SS now controlled Germany's entire police force. As Chief of the Security Police and SD Heydrich, in the space of a few years, had gathered into his hands all the important threads of the police state.[40]

In such a system what place was there for the Abwehr? Patzig had asked himself this question in the summer of 1934 and had answered it in the negative. Nevertheless he believed that, with the help of the military he could halt, or at least delay, the invasion of police institutions by the SS. However, Werner von Blomberg, the Reichswehr Minister, and his advisers were already afraid that the Abwehr might be too late in adapting itself to the new era. At the head of the Abwehr must be a man who could speak the Nazis' language and Patzig knew such a man – Captain (Navy) Wilhelm Canaris, Fortress Commandant of Swinemünde.[41]

Canaris was regarded as one of the best diplomatic brains in the Navy. During the 1920s he had made a name for himself in extremist right-wing conspiratorial circles as an anti-republican. Moreover he could boast friendship with Heydrich, who had served under him as a cadet and played the violin with his wife Erika. Canaris was ready to take over the job of Head of the Abwehr.

Canaris was the son of a Duisburg industrial manager. He had joined the Navy in 1905 and had trained in cruisers; after the Battle of the Falkland Islands he had been taken prisoner but had escaped. He had been sent to Spain by the Naval Secret Service, had captained a U-boat in the Mediterranean, had fought with the Free Corps and been involved in the Rosa Luxemburg/Karl Liebknecht murders. He had then been a desk officer in Naval Headquarters and had commanded a ship in the Baltic. At the age of forty-seven he was resigned to the thought that his career was at an end when the great call came.

When, therefore, in January 1935 Captain Canaris summoned the heads of all Abwehr stations to his first conference on the Tirpitzufer, the impression he made was that of an old gentleman. One of his audience noted: 'A small, apparently worn-out sea captain with white hair, bushy eyebrows and tired eyes.' He appeared curiously disinterested, nervous and somewhat unpredictable; organization was not his strong point and he cared little about systems. But he showed at once that he would be an unyielding, though flexible, defender of the Abwehr. His policy was: closest possible collaboration with the Gestapo but no concessions to Heydrich and no abandonment of territory in the secret service and counter-espionage fields.

His good relations with Heydrich enabled Canaris to protect the Abwehr from almost all the regime's importunities. They played croquet together and there were musical evenings in Canaris' house. His influence on Heydrich was such that the Abwehr was in no serious danger from the Gestapo. When a new head of the counter-espionage police, SS-Oberführer Werner Best, was appointed, Canaris negotiated with him an agreement regulating the spheres of responsibility of Abwehr and Gestapo.[42]

The agreement was signed on December 21st, 1936. It laid down that the Abwehr should deal with espionage abroad and investigation into espionage by foreign powers; the Gestapo, on the other hand, was responsible for 'investigation of culpable actions under para. 163 of the Penal Code (treason) and the necessary follow-up action'. Canaris had therefore conceded to the Gestapo a certain technical predominance in the investigation field but had obtained agreement to priority for the Abwehr's military requirements.[43]

Having thus set the stage, Canaris was now able to expand his Abwehr into a powerful organization, eventually numbering over 3,000 officers. The secret intelligence service (Abwehr I) under Lieutenant-

Colonel Hans Piekenbrock extended its tentacles into practically every country in Europe; the counter-espionage section was constituted as Abwehr III under Canaris' friend Richard Protze. In every part of the world the Abwehr recruited agents and informers to provide it with news of every military development.

During 1937 Canaris contrived to expand his organization still further. The Foreign Section of the Reich War Ministry under Captain (Navy) Leopold Bürckner, the central agency for Germany's Military, Naval and Air Attachés, was subordinated to the Head of the Abwehr. With his headquarters Group 'Ausland/Abwehr' [Military Intelligence – literally Foreign Defence] Rear-Admiral Canaris was entitled to consider himself even more powerful than his predecessor Nicolai.[44]

Though Canaris was basically willing to conform, the increasingly obvious extremism of the Nazi regime turned his thoughts in a totally different direction. Above all Hitler's foreign policy of brinkmanship caused him to lend an increasingly willing ear to the anti-Hitlerites of the Abwehr centred on Lietenant-Colonel Hans Oster. Oster was head of the Abwehr Central Section and so, in a sense, Canaris' chief of staff; he had formed a political intelligence service with contacts in numerous ministries and Party agencies. It was assembling proof of the regime's deeds and misdeeds to provide grounds, one day, for the removal of the Nazi leaders.

Oster's information convinced Canaris that Hitler must be eliminated if Germany was not to be plunged into the catastrophe of a new world war. At the height of the Sudeten crisis in the autumn of 1938 Canaris was ready to have Hitler arrested. Even after the outbreak of the Second World War he still wanted to overthrow Hitler, but soon resigned himself to events.[45]

Canaris had also turned against the Hitler regime for another reason, in this case connected with preservation of the Abwehr's existence. He had soon been forced to recognize that his armistice with the Gestapo was illusory, for alongside the Gestapo that other SS organization, of which Heydrich was both the founder and the head, came increasingly to the fore – the SD.

The SD's initial *raison d'être* had been investigation and discovery of hostile elements within the ranks of the Nazi Party. In 1933, after the hungry years of the famous 'struggle period', the Party had threatened to dissolve in the scramble for posts and pickings and at that time the SD had been the only centrally-directed organization upon which the Party leadership could rely. Although less than one hundred strong, it had set up a system of surveillance and acquired intelligence ambitions.[46]

As Chief of the Security Police and the SD, Heydrich could see what part the SD should play in his plans for the seizure of power. The Gestapo was still manned primarily by the traditional type of official who had simply switched his ideology. Heydrich, however, required men sufficiently pliable morally to undertake any — literally any — assignment and these he found in the SD. They were the young sons of the bourgeoisie uprooted by the economic crisis, thinking only in terms of efficiency, adherents basically of dynamism without doctrine, of a technology of tyranny, asking no reasons why.[47]

In June 1934 the SD was promoted to the position of sole intelligence service of the Nazi Party; it was expanded and its system of surveillance improved. It was also given a headquarters: the 'Security Department' [Sicherheitshauptamt] located at No 102 The Wilhelmstrasse, Berlin. From SD Headquarters, with its coordinating and other departments, communications ran to seven SD 'Regions' [Oberabschnitte], each divided into two or three 'Districts' [Unterabschnitte]. The intelligence octopus extended its tentacles into every sphere of German society.

For the technicians of the Führer dictatorship the SD soon became 'the flexible instrument, the people's sense of touch and feel in all opposition circles and all spheres of life'. The description was that of a young manufacturer's son from Saarbrücken named Walter Schellenberg. At the elbow of his master Heydrich he was dreaming a dream full of menace for the Abwehr: he was determined to create that great politico-military super-secret service which the Germans had never managed to achieve.[48]

Schellenberg possessed both the dynamism and lack of principle necessary to embark on a plan of this sort. He quickly rose to be Heydrich's closest adviser and he put forward bold plans for an expansion of the SD. He did not accept that the SD should be solely an internal political intelligence service. He wanted more — in his eyes the SD should also become a foreign intelligence service, the overriding authority in the conspiratorial underground of Nazi internal and external policy.

As early as the end of 1938 SS-Sturmbannführer [Major] Schellenberg, at the time in charge of the Private Office in SD headquarters, was planning a 'Reich Security Service'. He wished to combine SD and Gestapo into a 'Reich Security Department' with security districts throughout the country and to amalgamate SD, Gestapo and Criminal Police into a 'State Protection Corps'.

But Heydrich's and Schellenberg's lord and master, Himmler, the

Reichsführer-SS, lacked the courage to implement the grandiose plans of the SD expansionists. On September 27th, 1939 a 'Reich Security Department' [Reichssicherheitshauptamt – RSHA] was in fact formed, combining Gestapo and SD, but it remained a paper exercise; the SD was still only a Party organization without executive powers. Typically, Schellenberg thereupon deserted the SD and took charge of the counter-espionage police. He continued to await his moment.[49]

The activities of the SD, however, were enough to bring it into sharp conflict with the Abwehr, for the SD had long since begun to make inroads into the Abwehr's preserve – foreign intelligence.

The SD's secret foreign intelligence service was in fact more or less a product of chance, arising from the fact that the SD pursued anti-Nazis even across the Reich frontiers. In January 1935, for instance, the SD Untersturmführer (2nd Lieutenant) Alfred Naujocks was ordered to destroy the clandestine transmitter located near Prague which was the mouthpiece of the Nazi renegade, Otto Strasser. On the night of January 23rd Naujocks and another SD man set fire to the transmitter and shot its operator, Formis.

This was the beginning of the SD's work abroad. Subsequently the SD recruited from among Germans resident abroad informers prepared to work for the Wilhelmstrasse. Military information was also naturally obtained. The SD based its case on a Wehrmacht/Gestapo agreement of January 17th, 1935, which included among the 'Tasks of the Security Service' of the Reichsführer-SS 'Intelligence cooperation (or executive action) in the field of . . . the Frontier Intelligence Service'.[50]

The SD was continually expanding this frontier intelligence service. Foreign intelligence was systematically assembled in the SD posts near the frontiers and certain SD officers obtained information from acquaintances living abroad. SD expansionism, however, called in question the Abwehr's position in matters of foreign intelligence as laid down in the Canaris–Best agreement. The SD began to operate in foreign countries on its own and interfered with the work of the Abwehr.

Nowhere were the effects of the Abwehr/SD duel more damaging than in the field of espionage against Soviet Russia. The SD was fired with the spirit of the totalitarian anti-communist crusade compounded with anti-Semitism and it thought that it was the sole repository of the gospel of truth; its dilettante efforts drove a coach and four through the last intelligence openings available to the Abwehr from the era of Russo-German military collaboration.

Russia had always been the thorniest problem facing German espionage. Few countries had better knowledge of the conspiratorial machinations of the other's secret service than did Germany and Russia. Wilhelm Steiber, the Prussian, had once been the preceptor of the Czarist secret police; the German secret service had infiltrated Lenin into war-weary Russia in 1917; Russian secret-service officers had directed the revolutionary efforts of the German communists after the First World War. The two sides knew each other and put up their defences, the Russians frequently more effectively than the Germans. Russia became Target No 1 for the German secret service – the Soviet Union still is today.[51]

Piekenbrock, the head of Abwehr I, later recalled' 'Russia is the most difficult country for a foreign intelligence service to penetrate. The reason is that the country is extremely isolated, entry and exit being difficult; moreover few foreigners are to be seen in Russia and few Russian nationals to be found in Europe. Foreigners in Russia can therefore be kept under strict observation and cannot travel around unobtrusively. As a result they are able to see practically nothing.' The German secret service, whether Abwehr or IIIb, had always found infiltration into Russia to be a matter of extreme difficulty.[52]

The Germans entered the First World War inadequately informed about the Russian Army. Not until the Czarist regime had collapsed and war-weariness had overtaken the Russian people was it possible for the German secret service to penetrate the Russian army. Then intelligence officers such as Lieutenant Bauermeister and Captain Hey made their way into the Russian positions while fighting on the eastern front was still in progress, fraternized with the enemy and arranged local cessations of hostilities on their own initiative. They worked their way through the Russian trenches without being challenged by any Russian soldier. Enemy intelligence had never been so easy. Such exploits formed the first contacts leading to the post-Versailles cooperation between the Reichswehr and the Red Army. During the 1920s the two armies had helped each other. German arms firms installed themselves in the Soviet Union, German officers instructed the Red Army and Soviet officers attended German staff courses. No secret service could have produced more; German and Soviet military leaders knew each other better than their predecessors, even in the heyday of the alliance between the Prussian and Russian monarchs. When Blomberg visited Russia in 1928, he said: 'The consequential reinforcement of the Red Army is in the interests of Germany.'[53]

But Hitler, the rabid anti-bolshevist, put a quick end to this form of alliance. An iron curtain descended between the two countries. Once more the German secret service was cut off from all its Russian sources. Attempts had again to be made to infiltrate into Russia by conspiratorial methods.

The more unsuccessful the Abwehr's operations in the East, however, the more eager the SD became to annex the prerogative of collecting Russian intelligence. The SD faithfuls were obsessed with the crazy notion that Soviet communism was merely another manifestation of world Jewry's thirst for power and that the overthrow of the Soviet regime would accordingly be a service to Aryan mankind. So the SD rejected the Abwehr's traditional picture of Russia; they dreamed of an impotent, even a dismembered, Russia – a target for the SD's secret service.

The SD leaders allied themselves with Russian émigrés who sensed in Heydrich's and Schellenberg's machine a force which might one day bring them back to Russia. A typical representative of this émigré society was Michael Achmeteli, a Georgian agricultural expert, employed as a reader in Breslau University; he joined the camp of the SS who expected him to provide the expertise for their anti-Russian fantasies in the East.

The SS forced the 'East European Institute' of Breslau University to relinquish its library and other scientific apparatus. Armed with these, the SD set up for Professor Achmeteli a research institute, known from its location as the 'Wannsee Institute'. Achmeteli recruited other eastern experts and émigrés, men such as SS-Untersturmführer Emil Augsburg, his senior assistant responsible for questions of nationality groups in Russia, Dr Swetschin, the cartographer, and Dr Speer, the librarian. They assembled material on Russia, built up a card-index of personalities, prepared maps and built up a detailed picture of conditions in Soviet Russia.

Although he was suspected of working also for the Soviet Secret Police, one of the SD's main contacts was Nikolai Skoblin, an ex-Czarist General living in exile in Paris. Late in 1936 Heydrich learnt from him that an opposition group was forming in the Soviet Union whose object was to overthrow Stalin by force. The leader of the group was said to be Marshal Tukhachevsky, Deputy Commissar for War of the Soviet Union and an old friend of the Reichswehr. Heydrich had a fantastic idea: suppose it were possible to feed this information to Stalin, giving it verisimilitude by means of one or two forged documents. It might then be possible to destroy the entire Russian Army leadership and liquidate the men in whom Germany's conservative soldiers were placing their hopes of re-establishing the alliance between the two armies.

The SD looked out some old correspondence between Reichswehr and Red Army generals and dressed it up in 1937 terminology well enough to give Moscow to think that Soviet officers had been intriguing with the Germans against Stalin. This material was then fed to the Soviets. On June 11th, 1937, the world was told that Tukhachevsky and seven generals had been executed for treason – it was the beginning of the most fearful 'purge' which any army has ever undergone. Shortly thereafter Lieutenant-Colonel Karl Spalcke, a Russian expert in the 'Foreign Armies' Section, heard that Heydrich was boasting of having overthrown Tukhachevsky. His comment was: 'Pure bragging by Heydrich.' He suspected that Tukhachevsky had been liquidated for internal Russian reasons; if Heydrich had had any part in the affair it was as involuntary assistant to the Soviet Secret Police and their stool-pigeon Skoblin.[54]

A dangerous abyss opened in front of the military intelligence experts. How could they work if one secret service blocked the intelligence openings of another? The months which followed brought no abatement in the rivalry between Abwehr and SD, and the more fiercely they fought each other the more miserable the intelligence output inevitably became.

The first sufferers from this situation were the twenty-three officers, eleven NCOs, forty-nine men and six employees of the General Staff Section 'Foreign Armies East' [Fremde Heere Ost – FHO], formed in autumn 1938 on the break-up of the 'Foreign Armies' Section. Their task was to prepare situation maps of the Soviet Union, Poland, Scandinavia, the Balkans and the Far East and to keep them up to date, to establish the strength and war organization of potential enemies, to form a picture of the enemy's military personnel and assemble information on his fortifications and communications.[55]

Theoretically both the staff and material available to FHO were adequate. Head of the Section was Lieutenant-Colonel Eberhard Kinzel, an eastern expert who, in the Weimar Republic period, had been escorting officer to itinerant Soviet generals in Germany and from 1933 to 1936 had been Assistant Military Attaché in Warsaw.[56] The main sources of information were the Military Attachés, the intercept companies which monitored the military traffic of foreign armies on manoeuvres, Soviet military literature and, above all, the Abwehr's secret service. The latter poured an impressive stream of reports on Russia into the FHO's safes. Kinzel's officers, however, were too astute not to realize quite soon that much of the Abwehr's material was of questionable quality. Goth, one of the desk officers, wrote to the Abwehr: 'Our knowledge of Soviet Russian weapons and armaments is extraordinarily sketchy.'[57]

When Germany and Russia became immediate neighbours after the Polish war, the Abwehr was able to improve its Russian intelligence to some degree. Moreover its investigating squads had discovered much comprehensive material about the Red Army in the captured files of the Polish General Staff. They included reports on the types of bombs and offensive tactics used by the Soviet Air Force, reports on the morale of Soviet officers, details of Soviet artillery, studies on Soviet war organization. For the first time the FHO experts obtained some insight into the secret Soviet military world. The Abwehr was overjoyed, promising its FHO comrades on July 4th, 1940, 'most comprehensive material'.[58]

FHO accordingly learnt full details of the Soviet T26 tank ('the glass of the observation slit is no different from ordinary plate-glass'). There was a report on 'Offensive methods of the Red Air Force'; a secret-service appreciation gave Hitler's officers the comforting news that 'as a result of the terror anti-Stalin sentiment among senior officers is on the increase. The middle level (Lieutenant to Major) are careerists without self-assurance or initiative; the main supporters of the regime are the NCOs and men; confidence in their superiors has been undermined; much talk as to whether people are "antis or not".'

Following Hitler's series of victorious campaigns many of Greater Germany's satellites opened their secret-service files to the Germans. The Finns showed the Abwehr every Soviet weapon which fell into their hands during the winter war against Russia in 1939–40; the Italian Military Attaché in Reval produced a report on Soviet artillery which led to a drastic revision of FHO's thinking; in October 1940 the Rumanian secret service reported its 'Conclusions from the Russo-Finnish war'–'in general the Russians lacked basic knowledge of the tactical employment of weapons.'[59]

Nevertheless Kinzel's Section in fact knew little of what was going on in Russia. When asked to estimate strength and organization of Russian formations in preparation for the campaign against the Soviet Union, he had to admit to large-scale gaps in his knowledge. On January 15th, 1941, FHO estimated that, in the event of successful mobilization, the Red Army could produce a maximum of four million men. In fact it already had nearly five million under arms. FHO thought that the 'main Soviet concentration' would be in the area 'Chernowitz–Lemberg, around Bialystok and in the Baltic states'. This too was wrong. The heaviest Soviet troop concentration was hundreds of miles away – in the south, in the districts of Kiev and Odessa.

Even worse were FHO's erroneous estimates of the enemy's strategic intentions. A month before the opening of the eastern campaign Kinzel estimated that 'in the event of attack from the west it is improbable that the main weight of the Soviet forces would be withdrawn into the interior of the country'. His reasons: 'Major dependence on the armaments and war industries of the Ukraine, Moscow and Leningrad ... Ponderous nature of the military command ... Lack of capability for rapid manoeuvre ... coordinated strategy impossible.'[60]

Seldom has a General Staff made so light-hearted an underestimate of its enemy. The actual course of operations, however, plunged Kinzel into a fatalistic mood from which he found it impossible to escape. For weeks he heard nothing but criticism from Halder, the Chief of the General Staff, who had himself once thought that Soviet Russia was like a window-pane – 'One has only to put one's fist through it and the whole thing will smash to pieces.' Halder became more vocal in his vexation the more it proved that false reports from the Abwehr and inaccurate appreciations from FHO were leading his strategy dangerously astray.[61]

In the spring of 1942 Colonel Kinzel was relieved by Reinhard Gehlen. A briefcase full of erroneous reports on the Russian offensive was among the first papers which Gehlen read on taking over the Section. It was enough to cause him to insist on a fundamental reorganization of FHO.

APPENDIX B

THE AFFAIR OF THE CIA TUNNEL

By Hermann Zolling

THE Americans had long nurtured the suspicion that the British Intelligence Service (the old MI6, now SIS) was penetrated by Soviet agents and run by communist-inspired intellectuals from Oxford and Cambridge. They were not alone. Gehlen too had reservations about the British service, although sometimes the BND and SIS had cooperated on the medium, and in one specific case, the lower levels.

Gehlen's suspicions were reinforced by a spectacular intelligence incident which made headlines throughout the world's press on April 25th, 1956. At about 7 PM on the evening of the previous day a number of West Berlin journalists were called to the telephone. Representatives of the news agencies, radio stations and newspapers were invited to assemble one hour later (8 PM) in the cinema of the Russian officers' mess in Karlshorst. This was a quite unprecedented request. Those who went were given a surprise of the first order and got the story of the year.

In the plush hall in Karlshorst Colonel I. A. Kozyuba, the reigning Russian Military Commandant, welcomed his guests from the West. Then he revealed the reason for this unusual invitation. Under a certain field, Kozyuba said, the American secret service had dug a tunnel leading from West into East Berlin in order to tap the East German telephone system and to intercept conversations. The journalists would now be given the opportunity to drive to the site in convoy and inspect the tunnel in detail.

A column of vehicles thereupon roared off, led by Russian Military Police on motor-cycles with a jeep-full of Russian Field Gendarmerie behind them; they were followed by a car carrying Kozyuba and a string of vehicles with the Western correspondents. All rushed off at breakneck speed through darkening East Berlin. The cavalcade finally halted in the suburb of Alt-Glienicke, some 500 yards from the West Berlin quarter of Rudow, in front of an area brilliantly illuminated by searchlights manned by Russian army engineers. Freshly dug clods of earth surrounded a large hole from which appeared the head of Colonel Kozyuba. He invited the journalists inside: 'Come along, gentlemen, come closer; climb down to me.'

A ladder led down into the hole, where there was electric light. Colonel Kozyuba was geniality itself. He welcomed each of his guests from West Berlin with a grin and said: 'Look around – almost German workmanship but not done by Germans.' What the journalists saw was quite fantastic. Some of the West Berlin visitors felt that the Colonel and his officers were barely concealing a sportsmanlike admiration.

There stood large electronic assemblies bearing the name-plate 'Siemens', connected to outsize tape-recorders; there were also boxes labelled 'Westinghouse', from which wires led to three large cables. A Russian officer explained in perfect German the purpose of all this technical display. A tunnel had been dug from the Western side, he said, by the American secret service; it was 300 yards long and fifteen feet deep; the object was to tap the 300 official and military circuits which at this point ran through three cables six feet underground. The subterranean technique seemed perfect.

With its cement floor and white-painted reinforced concrete walls the intercept chamber looked like a laboratory. Fresh air was supplied through a ventilation system; on a table in front of the intercept apparatus lay a vacuum cleaner with which it was kept free of dust. A coffee machine stood in an alcove. The Russian also showed his guests an alarm system by which the Americans could be recalled from the area beneath the territory of the German Peoples' Republic.

Into the US sector ran a tunnel 300 yards long and six feet high, supported by steel girders and lit by neon lights. The subterranean boundary between East and West was some thirty yards from the intercept chamber and there, in front of a sandbag barrier, stood a Soviet sentry. A placard in German and Russian characters said: 'Warning! Here begins the US sector of Berlin. Entry strictly forbidden.' Those who stared across the sandbags into the darkness could see a small streak of light in the distance; it came through the slits of a steel door behind which snatches of American conversation could be clearly heard. At the forward end, where the Americans had installed their sophisticated intercept apparatus, were further placards in Russian and German forbidding entry. They were signed 'The Commandant' and the US secret service had obviously thought that, should the installation be accidentally discovered by East German post-office mechanics or Russian soldiers, this would be enough to scare away intruders.

The Russian intelligence experts and military engineers who had discovered the shaft and opened up the enemy intercept station, however, had not done so accidentally. Treachery was abroad. When Colonel Kozyuba said 'almost German workmanship but not done by Germans', he knew – or was telling – only part of the truth. The conception, the planning, the construction and finally the betrayal of the tunnel was a product of the system of alliances between the Western secret services.

In 1954 a member of the Gehlen Org met an old friend in Berlin who was working for the East Berlin postal authorities as a long-distance communications engineer. This post-office official disliked both the East German regime and the Russian occupation; it was part of his job to know full details of the post-office cable system in East Berlin, and he also had access to plans showing the precise run of the cables. Gehlen's man soon persuaded his friend to tell him the exact location of the telephone circuits leading to Moscow from Berlin and Zossen, the Russian Army Headquarters for East Germany. Gehlen's section 'Foreign Armies East' had once been stationed in Zossen.

A special Org working party studied the cable plans and discovered the point at which the cables ran closest to the Western sectors; fortunately for Gehlen it was in Alt-Glienicke, opposite Rudow in the US sector – the Org obviously had better prospects of obtaining support for the project of tapping the cables from the Americans than from the British or French.

Gehlen personally approached Allen Dulles, head of the CIA, about the project; he was immediately attracted by the idea, which was of course fascinating to any professional secret-service man. The Americans quickly developed a plan for reaching the enemy cables – by means of an underground passage.

Early in 1955 US Army engineers began major earth-moving operations on the edge of a field near Rudow. The Americans spread the story that they were building a radar station to observe air traffic on the near-by East Berlin airport of Schönefeld. Work proceeded behind a high impenetrable fence; the urgency was such that trucks removing earth from the tunnel worked throughout the night. A stone building and aerials were soon in position; round-the-clock truck traffic continued and finally it began to deliver tall cases. On the return journey from Rudow to the US barracks in Lichterfelde-West the cases were filled with earth, the few US soldiers who had to spread this earth in Lichterfelde found it surprising but made no attempt to find an explanation.

Specialists of the US Signal Corps were now in action, working their way fifteen feet underground from the 'radar station' and approaching a cross-roads in Alt-Glienicke, East Berlin. In the late summer of 1955 the tunnel was complete. Army trucks delivered cases of highly sensitive electronic gear. Long-distance communications experts rolled the instruments forward to the line of the cables. Now began the most difficult part of the work.

It was vital that no one using one of the 300 circuits must be given any inkling that the line was being tapped. Using a generator on their own side, the CIA technicians ensured that the lead to be connected carried a current precisely adapted to that of the cable being tapped; the object was to ensure that, far from interrupting any conversation in progress, the users should not even notice any reduction in clarity of speech. Had this happened, any secret-service man or long-distance communications expert on the other side would immediately have suspected that the line was being tapped. This stage took several weeks but was finally successful.

The CIA could now intercept and listen-in to any conversation with official agencies in Moscow from the East German government in East Berlin, the Russian Embassy on Unter den Linden or Russian Army Headquarters in Zossen. The East German official circuits between Berlin and Saxony (to Dresden and Leipzig) also passed through this junction and so through the CIA's intercept machines. Although technical direction lay entirely in the hands of the CIA, Gehlen's Org benefited from the results. The tale spread by some spy-romancers that CIA and BND personnel sat peacefully side by side and selected the conversations in which they were particularly interested, is quite untrue. In fact the Americans only passed to the Org what it must or should be allowed to know. The Americans naturally kept to themselves the highest-grade information from the subterranean listening post. Nevertheless, despite all the secrecy with which the CIA and BND had surrounded the enterprise, it was no longer secret. The Russians at first maintained that two of their Signal Corps NCOs had suddenly noticed reductions in current in the telephone network and had discovered where the cables had been tapped – Colonel Kozyuba preened himself, saying 'We have some smart NCOs.' The truth, however, was quite different.

Until 1955 a man named Horst Eitner had been working for the Gehlen Org as an agent in Berlin – spying on the East Germans and the Russians. The Org's security experts, however, suddenly formed the impression that Eitner was 'playing it both ways', in other words was a double agent working for the Russian secret service as well. The Org could not produce proof but nevertheless severed contact with Eitner on some official pretext. What Gehlen's security people, however, did not know was that Eitner had knowledge, at least in its broad lines, of the great state secret – the tapping of the Soviet telephone cables by the CIA, although he did not know the location of the secret tunnel, the technical details or the magnitude of the effort made.

In April 1955 one George Blake joined the Berlin office of MI6 in the Olympia Stadium, taking over the post of Deputy Director of 'Technical Operations'. One of the first agents recruited by Blake was Horst Eitner who, having been in the Gehlen Org, was indisputably a professional among the purveyors of intelligence in Berlin. The files of the British court which eventually sentenced Blake could probably tell us how the most important intelligence secret of the time came to change hands. The fact remains, however, that the day came when Eitner told Blake that the CIA was tapping telephone cables in the East.

Whether Eitner really knew what Blake was doing or whether the Russians were using Eitner against Blake – all this is still hidden in the obscurity of secret-service trafficking. In April 1956, on a hint from Eitner, Blake urged the Russian secret service to check their telephone cables. The fact was that Blake had been a double agent for nine years, working for both MI6 and the Russian KGB. On April 22nd, 1956, nine months after the start of interception, the alarm sirens suddenly blew in the tunnel between Rudow and Alt-Glienicke. The CIA interceptors fled from their posts; the coffee machine went on cooking until it boiled over. What had happened?

The sentries in the 'radar station' had suddenly spotted Soviet military vehicles from which officers disembarked, carrying special equipment looking like portable direction-finders. They were in fact instruments for the location of the tapping-in point. Within a few minutes the Russians had discovered the spot below which the CIA listeners were sitting. Soviet engineers shovelled away until they came to a steel cover on which was written – again in Russian and German characters – 'Stop! Not to be opened. By order of the Commandant.' Naturally no one took any notice. The CIA listeners had to sprint their 300 yards and slam the steel door at the other end behind them. Over a period of six weeks the Russians displayed the tunnel to a total of 15,000 East Berliners. Many of them had difficulty in concealing their amusement at the way the Russians had been bamboozled by the US technicians.

The Russians did something else calculated to make them a laughing-stock and contribute to a sporting recognition that the Americans had brought off a secret-service coup. In a note published in all newspapers the C-in-C of the Soviet forces in East Germany described for the benefit of the Chief of Staff US Troops in Europe how efficiently the CIA group had worked:

On April 22nd of this year members of the Signal Corps of the Group of Soviet Forces in Germany discovered a tunnel in the area of Alt-Glienicke which had been dug from American positions to the long-distance cables of the Soviet forces and those of the German Democratic Republic running across the territory of the Republic.

As investigations showed, the American secret service had constructed a tunnel, 300 yards long, in the sovereign territory of the German Democratic Republic and cables had been laid from the American sector of Berlin to tap the cables of the Soviet forces.

On the doors the American organizations responsible for this undertaking had affixed misleading notices in the Russian and German languages. In one of the sections, thirty yards long and on the territory of the German Democratic Republic, were three American telephonic conductor distributors with leads connected to three cables used by the Soviet forces. In this section was also a variety of equipment designed for the interception of telephone conversations, in particular nine amplifiers, one magnetophone, measurement and other equipment.

The tunnel ends on the territory of the German Democratic Republic in a specially constructed chamber, provided with anti-humidity devices, electric light and permanent metal roofing, at the spot where the Soviet underground cables run. The construction of the tunnel and its equipment, on which large sums of money were expended, are of a permanent nature and intended for prolonged usage.

This tunnel, these subterranean works and the apparatus located therein show clearly that the organizers of this undertaking were acting with intent to carry on criminal espionage in that they had arranged for continuous interception of telephone conversations on the long-distance lines of the Group of Soviet Forces in Germany and those of the German Democratic Republic.

In connexion with the above-mentioned, the staff of Soviet Forces in Germany protests to the staff of US Forces in Europe against these illegal and inadmissible actions on the part of American military authorities and insists that those responsible be brought to justice and that such activities cease in future.

Major-General Uncles, Chief of Staff US Forces in Europe, acknowledged receipt of the protest note but at the same time stated that he had passed the case to Washington. The Russians never received a reply – not even five years later when, in a further note of August 18th, 1961, the Kremlin reminded the Americans of the 'vast tunnel equipped with special apparatus and appliances for the interception and recording of conversations conducted over the lines mentioned'. The United States said nothing.

In October 1960 Horst Eitner was arrested on suspicion of being a double agent. In April 1961 Blake, who had meanwhile been transferred to the MI6 office in Beirut, was recalled to London, arrested and sentenced to 42 years' imprisonment as a self-confessed Russian spy.

Senior BND officials claimed that they had discovered from Eitner that Blake was a double agent and had so informed SIS headquarters in London. This, they said, had enabled SIS to recall Blake to London on some pretext and put him on trial.

Blake's trial took place at the Old Bailey in London, mostly with the public excluded; on one occasion even the heavy wooden shutters of the courtroom were closed for 53 minutes. This may well have been the moment when Blake admitted what he later stated in public – that he had betrayed the CIA's Berlin tunnel to the Russians. In 1966, in some manner still not totally explained, Blake escaped from prison in London to Moscow where he was awarded the Order of Lenin and the Order of the Red Banner. In an interview with the Soviet official newspaper *Izvestia* he boasted proudly of his betrayal of the tunnel, saying that this had happened when the planning first started in 1953. 'In this way,' he said, 'the operation was doomed to failure even before the drawings had been prepared.' (This was mere bragging. Blake was not posted to Berlin until April 1955 and in any case technical planning started, not in 1953, but a year later.)

It is far more probable that in 1956 Blake merely passed on Eitner's warning to the Russians. When Eitner was arrested, to save his own skin he presumably denounced Blake to the BND as a double agent. The probability that this was so is increased by the facts that Eitner was kept in detention for over a year, that he was not sentenced in West Berlin until after the Blake trial (at which he made a brief appearance as a witness) and that he received only three years' imprisonment, a relatively mild sentence for a Russian agent of his calibre. It may be taken as certain that the Russians had discovered the tunnel several weeks before their invitation to Western journalists to visit it and that they had meanwhile been hoodwinking their CIA audience with fake telephone conversations.

As with many other incidents in the espionage and secret-service trade, in addition to the spectacular aspect of its premature failure after great expense, the construction of this tunnel had its comic sequel. One day a farmer from Alt-Glienicke presented himself to a West Berlin court and explained that he was the owner of the field under which the Americans had dug. He now demanded compensation from the United States: his field had sunk along the line of the tunnel and he was afraid that his plough would sink in along the whole 300 yards. His field was therefore now divided, not only into eastern and western halves by the sector boundary, but also northern and southern halves by the tunnel. The Americans should pay, he said, for undermining his ground. The court rejected his plea; it is not known whether the Russians or East German army engineers have meanwhile filled the shaft in again.

NOTES

NOTES

Journalists or historians who attempt to describe and analyse the work of a secret service are invariably faced with the question of how to obtain the source material which alone can provide reliable information on secret-service activity. Original sources have been available only in rare cases since, over the years, secret services have developed sophisticated methods of preserving their records from the public gaze. The authors of this book have had the good fortune to receive information and material which has enabled them to write the first (they think) objective account of the Federal Intelligence Service. Innumerable sources have assisted the authors in their work, confident that their personal safety would be guaranteed against any possible investigations by BND officials, and the authors have assured their informants that any degree of privacy desired would be respected. Nevertheless they have thought it right to produce these notes, without which no book on such a subject can retain credibility. Almost all facts and statements in this book can be proved, including those based on hitherto secret sources. A small residue can only be described in vague terms or not at all – the reason will be obvious to any observant reader.

PROLOGUE

1. *Welt am Sonntag*, March 14th, 1971; Deutsche Presse-Agennir, Report No 145 id. March 15th, 1971; *Tagesspiegel*, March 16th, 1971; *Z DF-Magazin*, March 17th, 1971; *Presse*, March 15th, 1971.

2. *Kölner Stadtanzeiger*, March 19th, 1971; *National-Zeitung* (evening edition), March 17th, 1971; *Neue Bildpost*, March 28th, 1971.

3. *Der Spiegel*, Nos 11–25 of 1971.

4. *Der Spiegel*, No 14 of 1969, pp. 106 et seq.

5. *Der Spiegel*, No 16 of 1970, p. 34.

6. Verbally to the authors from Horst Ehmke and Dieter Blötz.

7. Unsigned memorandum on an intelligence conference in the Reichswehr Ministry, January 11th, 1935, National Archives, Washington, Microfilm T-77/808.

8. Harry Howe Ransom: *The Intelligence Establishment*, p. 6.

9. German Bundestag: Shorthand record, 2nd electoral period, 150th sitting, p. 7981D, June 20th, 1956; Günter Bachmann: 'Das Bundeskanzleramt' in *Die Staatskanzlei*, p. 178; Federal

Budget for budget year 1971, p. 153. The Confidential Parliamentary Panel initially (1956) consisted of the three parliamentary floor leaders of the Bundestag; in 1964 it was increased to six members, since 1969 it has consisted of nine members: the Christian-Democrat/Christian-Social deputies Baier, Jäger and Benda, the Socialist Party members Schäfer, Hermsdorf and Wienand, the Free Democrats Ollesch, Schmidt and Kirst. Its authority has meanwhile been extended; initially it was planned only as controlling authority for the BND, but since 1968 it has also been responsible for the Internal Security Office (BfV) and the Military Counter-espionage Service (MAD).

10. *Daily Express*, August 10th, 1954.

11. Information from BND circles, December 15th, 1970; see also *Die Zeit*, April 26th, 1968, pp. 9–10, Federal budget.

12. *Der Spiegel*, No 31 of 1967, p. 26 and No 18 of 1969, p. 54; *Stern*, January 26th, 1969; SIS budget 1971/72; interview with Kirkpatrick, Deputy Director of CIA, in 'Pueblo – A Question of Intelligence', NBC Television broadcast of August 25th, 1969.

13. Memoirs of a BND member in *Capital*, No 7 of 1968, p. 72

14. Information from BND circles; Albrecht Charisius and Julius Mader: *Nicht länger geheim*, pp. 402–3.

15. *Die Welt*, December 4th and 7th, 1968; *Die Zeit*, December 20th, 1968; *Frankfurter Rundschau*, December 4th, 6th and 7th, 1968.

16. Statement by Franz Pankraz, a BND radio operator arrested in East Germany; *Neue Justiz*, No 9 of 1966.

17. Information from BND circles.

18. Ransom, op. cit., p. 7.

19 Thomas M. Walde: *Intelligence im westdeutschen Regierungssytem*, pp. 96, 135.

20. Information from BND circles.

CHAPTER ONE:

MAN IN THE SHADOWS

1. E. H. Cookridge: 'The Spy of the Century' in *Daily Telegraph Magazine*, March 7th, 1969.

2. Alain Guérin: *Le Général Gris*, p. 569; Andrew Tully: *Central Intelligence Agency*, p. 158; Louis Hagen: *The Secret War for Europe*, p. 33.

3. *Weltwoche*, 1955; *Welt am Sonntag*, November 13th, 1955; Parliamentary Political Press Service, August 9th, 1954; Julius Mader: *Die graue Hand*, pp. 68 et seq.

4. The Soviet historian Lev Bezymenski for instance, in his book on Operation Barbarossa.

5. Information from BND circles.

6. Report (not published) dated September 6th, 1954 by Volkmar, a *Spiegel* correspondent, in *Der Spiegel* archives.

7. Voluntas: 'Ich sprach mit Gehlen' in *Revue*, October 20th, 1963; *Der Spiegel*, No 39 of 1954, p. 12.

8. Reinhard Gehlen's personal file in *Der Spiegel* archives.

9. *Newsweek*, July 25th, 1955, p. 22.

10. Klaus-Jürgen Müller: *Das Heer und Hitler*, p. 24.

11. Herbert Urban: 'General a.D. Reinhard Gehlen'. p. 1, in *Der Spiegel* archives.

12. *Die Zeit*, April 26th, 1968.

13. Urban, op. cit., p. 2; Mader, op. cit., pp. 8, 11.

14. Urban, op. cit., p. 1; Speech in Munich on April 30th, 1968 by Head of Chancellery Office on the occasion of change of President of BND, p. 1; Reinhard Gehlen's personal file in *Der Spiegel* archives.

15. Gehlen's personal file; German Army List 1923–1932; Hans Möller-Witten: 'General Gehlen', in *Der Spiegel* archives.

16. Gehlen's personal file.

17. Ibid.

18. Nikolaus von Vormann: *Der Feldzug 1939 in Polen*, p. 113; Burkhart Müller-Hillebrand: *Die Blitzfeldzüge*, p. 64; Gehlen's personal file.

19. Gehlen's personal file; Burkhart Müller-Hillebrand: *Das Heer bis zum Kriegsbeginn*, p. 172; Colonel-General Halder: *Kriegstagebuch* [War Diary], Vol I, pp. 193, 211.

20. Halder, op. cit., pp. 175, 179, 193; Möller-Witten, op. cit., p. 2.

21. Manning chart of Operations Section of Army Headquarters — National Archives Washington, Microfilm T-78/499.

22. Gehlen's personal file – entries for February 19th, 1941, and April 1st, 1942.

23. Halder, op. cit., Vol II, pp. 153, 170, 243, 262, 312; *Die Zeit*, April 26th, 1968.

24. Halder, op. cit., Vol II, pp. 262, 252; Gehlen's personal file.

25. Halder, op. cit., Vol III, pp. 367, 422.

26. Gehlen's personal file.

27. Ibid.

28. Jürgen Thorwald: 'Der Mann im Dunkeln' in *Welt am Sonntag*, November 20th, 1955; *Abendzeitung*, July 20th, 1967; Halder, op. cit., Vol II, p. 147.

CHAPTER TWO:

MIRACLE ON THE EASTERN FRONT

1. Jürgen Thorwald: *Wen sie verderben wollen*, p. 54; Summary appreciation of enemy situation by FHO, April 4th, 1942, National Archives (NA) Washington, microfilm T-78/467.

2. Minute from Evaluation Group of FHO to Group II — appreciation of enemy situation, May 1st, 1942, NA T-78/467.

3. War staffing table of FHO, November 1st, 1939, NA microfilm T-78/499.

4. Gerhard Wessel's personal file in *Der Spiegel* archives; Wessel's confidential report, March 15th, 1944; information from head of a Group in

FHO, May 21st, 1970.

5. Thorwald, op. cit., p. 44; Heinz Herre's personal file in *Der Spiegel* archives.

6. Herre's personal file; Thorwald, op. cit., pp. 44, 45.

7. Chart of distribution of duties in FHO, undated, NA T-78/499.

8. Ibid.

9. Ibid.

10. Comments signed by Gehlen on evaluation of troop locations, September 1st, 1943, pp. 1, 2, 3, NA T-78/480; FHO (IIc) Evidence for evaluation of fighting strength of Russian rifle formations, November 29th, 1943, NA T-78/486.

11. Comments on evaluation (Note 10 above), pp. 5, 7.

12. Chart of distribution of duties (Note 7 above).

13. Ibid.

14. From head of a group in FHO, May 21st, 1970.

15. 'Cooperation with Intelligence Sections of other agencies involved in the collection of intelligence', note by FHO, NA T-78.

16. Operation instruction for detachment commanders issued by Deputy Chief of Staff IV, Army General Staff, NA T-78/458.

17. Ibid.

18. Hermann Baun's personal file, in Der Spiegel archives.

19. Ausland/Abwehr order Abw. I, No 89/41 Secret, dated June 10th, 1941, NA T-78/458.

20. Operation instruction for intelligence Officers and Detachment Commanders.

21. Sector Staff East Prussia – minute ref. operations of Abwehr on Russian territory, May 21st, 1941; addendum to minute dated June 3rd, 1941, ref. recognition signs for saboteurs, NA T-78/482; Oscar Reile: Geheime Ostfront, pp. 3, 6, 9.

22. Minute by Sector Staff East Prussia, May 21st, 1941, NA T-78/482.

23. From ex-head of a Group of FHO, May 21st, 1970.

24. Gert Buchheit: Der deutsche Geheimdienst, p. 261. War staffing chart of FHO, 1943, NA T-78/499.

25. Information from Gerhard Wessel, June 3rd, 1971.

26. 'Operation Scherhorn', monograph by Colonel Hans-Heinrich Worgitzky, spring 1945, NA T-78/479; Cookridge: 'The Spy of the Century' in Daily Telegraph Magazine, March 7th, 1969, p. 19.

27. Herbert Rittlinger: Ultima Thule, pp. 189, 191; Ladislas Farago: Burn After Reading, pp. 114 et seq.

28. Cookridge, op. cit., p. 19.

29. Reile, op. cit., pp. 408 et seq.; Buchheit, op. cit., p. 263.

30. War staffing table of FHO 1942, NA T-78/499; Adolf Wicht's personal file in Der Spiegel archives.

31. FHO Group III directive, August 1943, NA T-78/480.

32. Ibid.

33. Comments on evaluation of troop locations, September 1st, 1943, pp. 32, 1, 31.

34. Minute by Gehlen on radio intelligence situation on eastern front, May 30th, 1944, p. 1; 'Lessons of evaluation of results of air reconnaissance for appreciation of enemy situation' (drafted by Gehlen), December 1943, p. 3, NA T-78/483.

35. OKW War Diary, Vol II, 2, pp. 1283, 1305, 1306.

36. 'Lessons on evaluation of air reconnaissance . . .' (Note 34 above), pp. 14 et seq., 20 et seq.; Paul Carell: Verbrannte Erde. p. 388.

37. Comments on evaluation of troop locations (Note 33 above), p. 4.

38. Note by IId for Desk IIc, FHO, December 28th, 1944, p. 1, NA T-78/499.

39. Extract from minutes of 19th session of Commission in the case of Party purge of General Danilovich Cherniashovsky, October 15th, 1936, NA T-78/499.

40. Captured documents – minutes of restricted Party meeting of No 1 Rifle Company, February 10th, 1944, NA T-78/487.

41. FHO report on 38 Army, pp. 8, 10, NA T-78/483; summary report by 3 Panzer Army on interrogation of deserters and prisoners, No 9, January 22nd, 1944, p. 2, NA T-78/487.

42. Summary report from 3 Panzer Army, No 13, March 25th, 1944, NA T-78/487.

43. Register of available notes, studies, evaluations, aides-mémoire, handbooks and regulations (16 pages),

January 20th, 1944, NA T-78/497.

44. Letter from Gehlen, July 13th, 1943, NA T-78/480.

45. Letter from Gehlen to Ritter von Schramm, March 14th, 1945, NA T-78/493.

CHAPTER THREE:
UNDER THE SHADOW OF THE SS

1. Hitler order, February 12th, 1944, National Archives (NA) Washington, microfilm T-78/497.

2. Peter Hoffmann; *Widerstand, Staatsstreich, Attentat*, pp. 345 et seq.; Paul Leverkuehn: *Der geheime Nachrichtendienst der Wehrmacht im Kriege*, pp. 192 et seq.

3. Herbert Rittlinger: *Ultima Thule*, pp. 205 et seq.; Gert Buchheit: *Der deutsche Geheimdienst*, p. 429.

4. Letter from Keitel to Himmler, April 11th, 1944, NA T-78/497.

5. Ibid. Order by Chief of Security Police and SD on formation of Amt Mil, May 23rd, 1944, NA T-78/497.

6. Agreements between Chief of OKW and Reichsführer-SS, May 14th, 1944, p. 2; manuscript note (probably by Wessel), undated, in headquarters papers of FHO, NA T-78/497.

7. Review of organization of FHO and subordinate agencies, NA T-78; 'Cooperation with Intelligence Sections of agencies concerned in the collection of intelligence', NA T-78. Both documents date from spring 1945.

8. Record of statement by Gehlen to Rehabilitation Chamber of Provincial Court in Karlsruhe, February 1st, 1951, pp. 1, 2; letter from Gehlen to Gräfin Rittberg, May 20th, 1957, in the Rittbergs' private papers.

9. Wolfgang Wehner: *Geheim*, pp. 62, 100; Jürgen Thorwald: 'Der Mann im Dunkeln' in *Welt am Sonntag*, November 27th, 1955.

10. Thorwald, op. cit., November 27th and December 18th, 1955.

11. Information from former head of a group in FHO, May 21st, 1970.

12. Klaus-Jürgen Müller: *Das Heer und Hitler*, p. 41.

13. Information from ex-head of a group in FHO, May 21st, 1970.

14. Statement by Gehlen to Rehabilitation Chamber (see Note 8 above); Heinz Herre's diary, entry for January 15th, 1943, in *Institut für Zeitgeschichte*, Munich.

15. Herre's diary, p. 2.

16. Wilfried Strik-Strikfeldt: *Against Hitler and Stalin*, pp. 65 et seq.; Alexander Dallin: *German Rule in Russia*, pp. 520, 521, 572 et seq.; Herre's diary, p. 5; Sven Steenberg: *Vlassov*, pp. 54–56.

17. Jürgen Thorwald: *Wen sie verderben wollen*, p. 56; Herre's diary, pp. 1–3.

18. Herre's diary, entry for November 18th, 1942, p. 3; *Die Zeit*, April 26th, 1968.

19. 'Urgent questions of partisan warfare and recruitment of auxiliaries', quoted from Dallin, op. cit., pp. 545 et seq.

20. Strik-Strikfeldt, op. cit., p. 42; Steenberg, op. cit., p. 42.

21. Steenberg, op. cit., pp. 41–43; Dallin, op. cit., pp. 523, 553 et seq.; Strik-Strikfeldt, op. cit., p. 78.

22. Dallin, op. cit., pp. 559 et seq.

23. Ibid, p. 560.

24. Ibid, pp. 580 et seq.

25. Ibid, pp. 570 et seq.; Strik-Strikfeldt, op. cit., p. 136.

26. Steenberg, op. cit., p. 42; Thorwald, op. cit., p. 225; Dallin, op. cit., p. 580.

27. Heinz Höhne: *The Order of the Death's Head*, p. 506; Thorwald, op. cit., p. 236; Dallin, op. cit., pp. 582 et seq.; Steenberg, op. cit., p. 126.

28. Letter from Gehlen to Roenne, March 16th, 1943, in Ladislas Farago's papers.

29. Statement on oath by Helga Gienanth, August 25th, 1950; letter from Wilhelm von Gwinner to Welfare Centre for political victims of Nazi System in Pforzheim, July 17th, 1946; statement by Carl Vigo von Moltke, July 22nd, 1950; Rittberg's private papers; Hoffmann, op. cit., p. 451.

30. Statement on oath by Gehlen, November 13th, 1950; Rittberg's private papers.

31. Strik-Strikfeldt, op. cit. pp. 201–2; statement by ex-head of a group in FHO, May 21st, 1970. Reinhard Gehlen: *Der Dienst*, p. 58.

32. Statement by Gehlen (see Note 30); Rittberg's private papers; statement by former head of FHO Group, May 21st, 1970.

33. Strik-Strikfeldt, op. cit., p. 202.

34. Höhne, op. cit., p. 488; Walter Schellenberg: *Memoirs*, p. 308.

35. Schellenberg: *Memoiren*, p. 241 (not in English translation); 'Experiences of operations in the Soviet Union' by an ex-SS-Obersturmbannführer who wishes to remain anonymous, in private papers.

36. Telegram from RSHA VI C2 to FHO, July 7th, 1943 and telegram from FHO in reply, July 10th, 1943, NA T-78/485.

37. 'Experiences of operations' (see Note 35 above), Chap. 4, p. 3, Chap. 5, pp. 4 et seq., 12 et seq., Chap. 4, pp. 3 et seq.

38. Dallin, op. cit., pp. 596 et seq.; Thorwald, op. cit., pp. 433 et seq.

39. Personal files of Herre and Wessel in *Der Spiegel* archives.

40. Army General Staff Operations Section order, November 12th, 1944, NA T-78/497.

41. Cf. Thorwald: 'Der Mann im Dunkeln' in *Welt am Sonntag*, November 27th, 1955; note by Gehlen on measures to activate front-line intelligence, February 25th, 1945, NA T-78/496.

42. Ibid.

43. 'Political Information, Research Service East,' pp. 14 et seq., NA T-175/222.

44. Review signed by Gehlen on partisan situation for period January 1st–31st, 1945, NA T-78/497.

45. List of institutes in files of the Wannsee Institute, NA T-175/222.

46. Schellenberg, op. cit., p. 12 (not in English translation); letter from FHO Ib, March 26th, 1945, NA T-78/487; teleprint Gehlen to RSHA/Mil.F, March 27th, 1945, NA T-78/488.

47. Note by Gehlen, February 24th, 1945, NA T-78/488.

48. Army General Staff Operations Section order, November 12th, 1944, NA T-78/497; order from Army General Staff Operations Section, FHO and Training Section 1 to Army Groups and Armies, February 6th, 1945, NA T-78/496.

49. Reinhard Gehlen's personal file in *Der Spiegel* archives.

50. Appreciation of overall enemy situation AM January 20th, 1945, drafted by Gehlen, NA T-78/496.

51. Heinz Guderian: *Panzer Leader*, p. 383.

52. Letter from Gehlen to Winter, January 4th, 1945; Gehlen's letter for Athenstaedt, January 4th, 1945; letter from Winter to Gehlen, January 23rd, 1945, NA T-78/496.

53. Overall appreciation of enemy situation on German eastern front, signed by Gehlen, January 1945, NA T-78/503.

54. Guderian, op. cit., p. 387.

55. Cornelius Ryan: *The Last Battle*, pp. 226–7 (pp. 173–4 in British edition); Guderian, op. cit., p. 428; Jürgen Thorwald: *Die grosse Flucht*, p. 320.

56. Gehlen's personal files. Reinhard Gehlen: *Der Dienst*, p. 117.

CHAPTER FOUR:
CHANGE OF ALLEGIANCE

1. Speech in Munich on April 30th, 1968, by State Secretary Carstens, head of Federal Chancellery Office on the occasion of the change in President of the Federal Intelligence Service. p. 2; Halder's diary, Vol III, p. 432.

2. Memorandum dated February 9th, 1944, signed by Gehlen, 'The Resistance Movement in former Poland', p. 2, National Archives (NA) Washington, microfilm T-78/497.

3. Oscar Reile: *Geheime Ostfront*, p. 195; Julius Mader: *Die graue Hand*, pp. 47–8.

4. Sworn statement by Max Schwerdtfeger, August 15th, 1950, in Rittberg's private papers.

5. Speech by Carstens (Note 1), p. 2. Reinhard Gehlen: *Der Dienst*, p. 122.

6. Alain Guérin: *Le Général Gris*, p. 14.

7. Information from former head of FHO group, May 21st, 1970.

8. Order by Gehlen 'Ref.: Preparation for road movement', February 19th, 1945, NA T-78/496; letter FHO IV to FHO IIc, April 4th, 1945, NA T-78/485.

9. Hermann Baun's diary, entry for April 4th, 1945, privately owned; Erich Murawski: *Der deutsche Wehrmachtsbericht*, p. 551.

10. Baun's diary, April 4th, 1945. Gehlen, op. cit., p. 124.

11. Information from former head of FHO group, May 21st, 1970.

12. Cornelius Ryan: *The Last Battle*, p. 413 (not in British edition); note by Captain Remé of Records Section, OKW Operations Staff, May 20th, 1945, NA T-77/863.

13. Information from former head of FHO group, May 21st, 1970; additional information from Gerhard Wessel, June

3rd, 1971; Louis Hagen: *The Secret War for Europe*, p. 34; Mader, op. cit., p. 55. Gehlen, op. cit., p. 130.

14. From Kreidl to the authors.

15. Gehlen, op. cit., p. 132.

16. Gehlen, op. cit., pp. 133, 134.

17. Wilfried Strik-Strikfeldt: *Against Hitler and Stalin*, p. 257. Gehlen, op. cit., p. 136.

18. Order of Head of Allied Mission for control of OKW, May 13th, 1945, NA T-77/863.

19. Note by Borchers on interview with Russian Commission, May 19th, 1945, NA T-77/863.

20. Note by Borchers on interview with Russian Commission on counter-espionage and intelligence questions, May 20th, 1945, ibid; note by Scheibe, May 17th, 1945, NA T-77/863.

21. Information from Edwin L. Sibert, February 1970.

22. *Who's Who in America* 1950/51, p. 2514.

23. Allen Dulles and Gero von Gaevernitz: *The Secret Surrender* pp. 36–42; Chester Wilmot: *The Struggle for Europe*, p. 587; Sir K. Strong; *Intelligence at the Top*, pp. 178–9.

24. Information from Edwin L. Sibert; Wehner, op. cit., p. 105.

25. Ibid.

26. Thomas M. Walde: *Intelligence im westdeutschen Regierungssystem*, p. 56; Guérin, op. cit., pp. 297 et seq.; Cookridge, op. cit., p. 7.

27. Information from Sibert; Walde, op. cit., p. 56.

28. Charles W. Thayer: *Diplomat*, pp. 167 et seq.

29. Ransom, op. cit., pp. 65 et seq.

30. Ibid, p. 77.

31. Louis J. Halle: *The Cold war as History*, pp. 38–41.

32. Cookridge, op. cit., March 14th, 1969, p. 7.

33. Gehlen, op. cit., p. 140; Information from a former member of FHO, December 1970.

34. Ransom, op. cit., p. 78; Cookridge, op. cit., p. 7.

35. Baun's diary, entry for September 19th, 1945.

36. Baun's diary, entries from October 10th to November 28th, 1945.

37. Ibid, entries from December 10th, 1945, to end March 1946.

38. Wehner, op. cit., p. 106.

39. Gehlen, op. cit., p. 146: Baun's diary, entries from end June 1946 to July 12th, 1946.

40. BND aide-mémoire on history of Federal Intelligence Service, April 1968, p. 2, in Der Spiegel archives.

41. Baun's diary, entry for early August 1946; Cookridge, op. cit., March 14th, 1969, p. 7; Guérin, op. cit., pp. 189 et seq.

42. Baun's diary – entry of August 1946.

43. 'Das Opel-Jagdhaus' [The Opel hunting lodge], report of March 1971 by Wiesbaden office of Der Spiegel, in Der Spiegel archives; Hermann Baun: 'Erfahrungen beim Aufbau', p. 9, privately owned.

44. Baun's diary 1946/47; information from former head of FHO Group, May 21st, 1970.

45. Baun's diary 1946/47; Baun: 'Erfahrungen beim Aufbau', p. 10.

46. Information from a retired Colonel of the Bundeswehr who prefers to remain anonymous, March 10th, 1971; Albrecht Charisius and Julius Mader: Nicht länger geheim, p. 138.

47. Adolf Wicht: 'Auszug aus meinem Tagebuch der Kriegsgefangenschaft', May 12th, 1970, privately owned.

48. Review of material received by Desk IIb during month of October, dated November 1944, NA T-78/497.

49. Realpolitik Tagesdienst, No 171, July 28th, 1954; letter from Friedrich Hecker, September 4th, 1953, in Der Spiegel archives.

50. Information from BND circles.

51. Der Spiegel, No 9 of 1956, p. 31; information from Heinz Herre, autumn 1970; Sefton Delmer: Black Boomerang, pp. 275, 283; information from former head of FHO Group, May 21st, 1970.

52. Munzinger Archiv: Heinz Günter Guderian, February 24th, 1968; Josef Moll, March 8th, 1969; Ernst Ferber, July 25th, 1970.

53. Der Spiegel, No 39 of 1954, p. 18; Mader: Die graue Hand, p. 6; memoirs of a BND man in Capital, No 7 of 1968, p. 72.

54. Statement on oath, in private ownership.

55. Hagen, op. cit., p. 40; memoirs of a BND man in Capital, No 7 of 1968, p. 73.

56. 'Training', memorandum from the Gehlen Organization, in private ownership.

57. Walde, op. cit., p. 58.

58. Baun's diary, entry for January 14th, 1947; Gehlen, op. cit., p. 159.

59. Neues Deutschland, September 28th, 1954.

60. Wilhelm Jungk: Die Aktion Hermes, pp. 22–27, in private ownership.

61. Ibid.

62. Ibid.

63. Report dated March 11th, 1950, from one of the Org's informers 'Ref.: German ex-prisoner of war escaped from the Soviet Union, Kurt Rosen,' in private ownership.

64. Jungk, op. cit.

65. Ibid.

66. Ibid.

67. Ibid.

68. Report C by one of the Org's informers, May 28th, 1949, in private ownership.

69. Information from Herre, autumn 1970; Der Spiegel, No 39 of 1954, p. 18.

70. Information from BND circles.

CHAPTER FIVE:
AGENTS, AGENTS, AGENTS

1. Louis J. Halle: *The Cold War as History*, p. 84.

2. Konstantin Pritzel: *Die Wirtschaftsintegration Mitteldeutschlands*, p. 30.

3. Information from BND circles.

4. Ibid.

5. Ibid.

6. Ibid.

7. Ibid.

8. Ibid; Thomas M. Forster: *NVA*, p. 39.

9. Wilhelm Jungk: 'Die Aktion Hermes', pp. 35–42, in private ownership.

10. Ibid.

11. Information from BND circles.

12. *Saturday Evening Post*, October 9th and 16th, 1954.

13. Information from Heinz Herre, autumn 1970.

14. Report C by one of the Org's informers, May 28th, 1949, in private ownership.

15. Report B by one of the Org's informers, May 28th, 1949, in private ownership.

16. Wolfgang Höher: *Agent 2996 enthüllt*, pp. 17, 20, 21; *Neue Justiz*, No 1 of 1954, p. 27.

17. *Neue Justiz*, No 1 of 1954, p. 27; No 9 of 1966, p. 261.

18. *Neue Justiz*, No 13 of 1963, pp. 386 et seq.; *Frankfurter Allgemeine Zeitung*, June 19th, 1963.

19. *Süddeutsche Zeitung*, November 10th, 1954; *Frankfurter Allgemeine Zeitung*, August 31st, 1954; *Neue Justiz*, supplement to No 22 of 1954, pp. 44 et seq.; *Neues Deutschland*, September 7th, 1954.

20. Julius Mader: *Die graue Hand*, p. 175.

21. Mader, op. cit., pp. 170 et seq., 172.

22. 'Fall Brutus', memorandum by Gehlen Organization, 1954, Part II, on personality of Walter Gramsch, in *Der Spiegel* archives.

23. 'Fall Brutus', Part II, p. 2.

24. Horst Günter Tolmein: *Der Aufstand beginnt 17.50 Uhr*, Part IV, p. 6; David J. Dallin: *Soviet Espionage*, pp. 126–7.

25. Tolmein, op. cit., pp. 9, 10, 11; Dallin, op. cit., pp. 127–8, 131; *Hamburger Abendblatt*, July 25th, 1953.

26. Dallin, op. cit., pp. 370, 131; 'Fall Brutus', Part VI on Wollweber, p. 1.

27. Wolfgang Wehner: *Geheim*, pp. 195–6; Dallin, op. cit., p. 371; Tolmein, op. cit., p. 13.

28. 'Fall Brutus', Part VI, p. 5.

29. Charles Wighton: *The World's Greatest Spies*, pp. 101–2; Tolhein, op. cit., pp. 13–14.

30. Conversation with an ex-member of the Org in Hamburg, October 17th, 1970.

31. 'Fall Brutus', Part VI on Wollweber, pp. 1–3.

32. Wehner, op. cit., pp. 197 et seq.

33. Interpress No 470 of 1956; information from a refugee administrator of the Liberal-Democrat Party, June 12th, 1970.

34. Information from Liberal-Democrat administrator.

35. Conversation between Johannes R. Becher and one of the authors, 1953.

36. Information from Liberal-Democrat administrator.

37. Ibid; sworn statements by Herta Field, May 22nd, 1954, Günter Tomasczewski, October 1st, 1967, and Otto Thränert, December 9th, 1955, in private ownership.

38. Interpress No 470 of 1956.

39. Information from ex-BND official, October 10th, 1970.
40. Mader, op. cit., pp. 182 et seq.
41. Ibid, p. 137.
42. Ibid, p. 167.

43. Conversation between one of the authors and 'Hunter', September 10th, 1969.
44. *Neues Deutschland*, December 23rd, 1953.

CHAPTER SIX:
THE ORG: ITS MEN, ORGANIZATION AND METHODS

1. Alain Guérin: *Le Général Gris*, p. 292.
2. Thomas M. Walde: *Intelligence im westdeutschen Regierungssystem*, p. 82.
3. Information from BND circles.
4. Wolfgang Höher: *Agent 2996 enthüllt*, pp. 17, 19.
5. Walde, op. cit., p. 82; Höher, op. cit., p. 18; Guérin, op. cit., pp. 210, 211, 216, 219; Hans-Heinrich Worgitzky's personal file in *Der Spiegel* archives; information from BND circles.
6. Walde, op. cit., p. 83; Guérin, op. cit., pp. 210, 222, 224; information from BND circles.
7. *Die Welt*, November 17th, 1953; Guérin, op. cit., p. 210.
8. Memoirs of a BND man in *Capital*, No 7 of 1968, p. 72; Julius Mader: *Die graue Hand*, p. 126; Höher, op. cit., pp. 18, 22.
9. Walde, op. cit., pp. 82 et seq.; Bernd Ruland: *Krieg auf leisen Sohlen*, pp. 214 et seq.; information from BND circles.
10. Information from BND circles.
11. Org training instruction dated June 27th, 1953, in private ownership.
12. *Der Spiegel*, No 39 of 1954, p. 18; memoirs of a BND man in *Capital*, No 7 in 1968.
13. Walde, op. cit., p. 87; Mader, op. cit., p. 135.
14. Report by informer 'Sch', September 7th, 1948; report by an Org informer to Agency 60, August 5th, 1953; report by an Org informer ref: 'Intelligence Potentialities of P.L.', March 29th, 1950, in private ownership.
15. Org training instruction.
16. Report by an Org informer, July 27th, 1954; report by an Org informer to Agency 60, August 5th, 1953; report by an Org informer, December 5th, 1962, in private ownership.
17. Report by an Org informer to Agency 70, October 29th, 1953; letter from an informer to the BND's Munich office, April 4th, 1956, in private ownership.
18. Letter from an informer to Agency 60, September 16th, 1953; letter from an informer to the BND's Munich office, February 10th, 1963, in private ownership.
19. Information and documents from BND circles.
20. Conversation with a former BND official.
21. 'Principles of compilation of a report', Org instruction (undated), in private ownership.
22. Org training instruction, June 27th, 1953.
23. Conversation with a former BND official.
24. 'Supplementary questions on report of 12.4.49', letter from the Org, April 14th, 1949, in private ownership.
25. Org instruction, 'Principles of compilation of a report.'
26. Organizer's report, December 14th, 1952, in private ownership.

27. Conversation with a former BND official.

28. Activity report by one of the Org's Munich agencies, May 16th–September 15th, 1950, in private ownership.

29. Washington Platt: *Strategic Intelligence Production*, p. 28.

CHAPTER SEVEN:
ADVANCE TO MOSCOW

1. Julius Mader: *Die graue Hand*, p. 102; *Tägliche Rundschau*, August 1st, 1954.

2. Activity reports by one of the Org's Munich agencies for period 16.5.50 to 15.6.50, p. 2, in private ownership.

3. Org questionnaire 1950, in private ownership.

4. Activity report by one of the Org's Munich agencies, May/June 1950; informer's report 'Ref.: Nikolai Wassily, G,' January 20th, 1950, in private ownership.

5. Ibid; informer's report 'Ref.: W.B.', January 22nd, 1951, in private ownership.

6. *Neues Deutschland*, September 28th, 1954; report on meeting arranged with two informers in Berlin, May 27th, 1949, in private ownership.

7. Informer's report 'Ref.: P.G.'s contacts in Poland', April 26th, 1950; Mader, op. cit., pp. 102, 103, 117, 133.

8. Information from a former BND official.

9. Informer's report 'Ref.: Reinforced Czech frontier control on the Bavarian–Czechoslovak frontier', October 25th, 1950, in private ownership.

10. Informer's reports 'Ref.: Information on Czech arms expert', March 18th, March 25th and April 8th, 1950, in private ownership.

11. Report by informer 'Sch', August 8th, 1948, in private ownership.

12. Mader, op. cit., p. 103.

13. Informer's report to Agency 70, December 11th, 1953, private ownership.

14. 'The Austrian as informer', Org memorandum of summer 1949, in private ownership.

15. Ibid.

16. Informer's report to Agency 60, August 5th, 1953.

17. Report by a Russian member of the Org staff, November 14th, 1952; informer's report to Agency 60, October 1953, in private ownership.

18. Informer's reports to Agency 60, July 20th, October 11th, 1953, in private ownership.

19. Informer's reports to Agency 60, October 19th, 27th, 28th, 29th, November 13th, 15th, December 3rd, 1953, in private ownership.

20. Defection aide-mémoire No 1 'Preliminaries to the recruitment of Soviet sources' (undated), in private ownership.

21. Informer's report to Agency 70, 'Ref.: Approach through black-market dealings', October 26th, 1953; informer's report, 'Ref.: Deals with Soviets', October 26th, 1953, in private ownership.

22. Ibid; informer's report to Agency LRL 'Ref.: Informer's direct or indirect contacts to members of Soviet forces or occupation authorities', November 30th, 1953, in private ownership.

23. Organizer's report, December 14th, 1952; informer's report to Agency 60, July 28th, 1953, both in private ownership.

24. Informer's report to a BND Munich agency, December 28th, 1959, in private ownership.

25. Information from BND circles.

26. *Neues Deutschland*, September 28th, 1954.

27. 'The Russian emigration' memorandum by a Local Branch of the Org (undated), in private ownership.

28. 'Air defence mobilization plan in the Soviet Union,' report by 'K', June 29th, 1949.

29. 'The Russian emigration', pp. 20, 22.

30. Information from BND circles.

31. ibid.

32. Conversation with former staff member of the Org. January 12th, 1971;

DEFA television film 'Rottenknechte' [Rank and file], January 1971; *Neues Deutschland*, January 14th, 1971.

33. 'Clandestine operations in the Baltic', report by a participant, in private ownership.

34. 'Rottenknechte', sound track, Part IV, Federal Press office.

35. 'Clandestine Operations in the Baltic'.

36. 'Rottenknechte', Part IV.

37. Informer's report to Agency 70, October 29th, 1953; informer's report to a BND agency, March 9th, 1960, in private ownership.

CHAPTER EIGHT:
IN PURSUIT OF 'ENEMIES OF THE STATE'

1. Information from a former BND official.

2. Hermann Baun: 'Richtlinien für die Weiterentwicklung der Organisation', p. 11, in private ownership.

3. Wolfgang Wehner: *Geheim*, pp. 116 et seq.

4. Ibid, pp. 129–31.

5. Ibid, pp. 142–4.

6. Information from BND circles; supplementary information from Milan Ilinic, May 11th, 1971.

7. Informer's report to Pullach, March 12th, 1962; report by informer 'Sch' – 'Fef.: K, Vladimir (Volodya), June 12th, 1949; report by informer 'K.B.' – 'Ref.: S, Gudrun alias Sonya Vinogradova', in private ownership.

8. Informer's report 'Ref.: 'Report on Marshal Sokolovsky's sister', September 26th, 1940; informer's report 'Ref.: Nina Kikodse', November 8th, 1949, in private ownership.

9. Informer's report 'Ref.: Lists of CIC informers in the hands of the Bavarian communist party', April 29th, 1950, in private ownership.

10. Jürgen Thorwald: 'Der Mann im Dunkeln' in *Welt am Sonntag*, December 18th, 1955.

11. 'Experiences during operations in the Soviet Union', Chap. V, p. 18 and Chap. III, p. 8, in private ownership.

12. Ibid; unsigned report 'Operation Zeppelin actions', in private ownership.

13. Information from an ex-member of Operation Zeppelin.

14. Louis Hagen: *The Secret War for Europe*, p. 57; Helmuth Grosscurth: *Tagebücher eines Abwehroffiziers*, p. 581; Alain Guérin: *Le Général Gris*, pp. 208 et seq., 220.

15. Guérin, op. cit., pp. 210, 213, 216, 224; Jacques Delarue: *History of the Gestapo*, pp. 228–9.

16. 'The Russian emigration', memorandum by a local branch of the Org (undated), in private ownership (p. 14); report by informer 'B', 'Ref: Alarich Bross', September 28th, 1950; informer's report 'Ref.: Hans Brachmüller', February 24th, 1951, in private ownership.

17. Thomas M. Walde: *Intelligence im westdeutschen Regierungssystem*, p. 90; Oscar Reile: *Geheime Ostfront*, p. 13; Paul Seabury: *The Wilhelmstrasse*, pp. 70, 182.

18. Informer's reports to BND 'Ref.: E.S., December 4th, 1962, and May 8th, 1963, in private ownership.

19. Informer's report 'Ref.: Maria I.', November 25th, 1960, in private ownership.

20. Informer's report 'Ref.: Interpreter School in Heidelberg', February 12th, 1960, in private ownership.

21. Informer's report 'Ref.: K, Valentina', August 23rd, 1952, in private ownership.

22. Conversation with a former member of the Org.

23 Informer's report, summer 1954, in private ownership.

24. Information from a former BND official.

25. Mader: *Die graue Hand*, p. 190.

26. Informer's report to BND 'Ref.: Dr (Phil) F.K.', January 7th, 1963, in private ownership.

27. Informer's report 'Ref.: NM', June 20th, 1963, in private ownership.

28. Mader, op. cit., p. 142.

29. Ibid, pp. 190, 192; Guérin, op. cit., p. 213.

30. Conversation with a former member of the Org.

CHAPTER NINE:

CAPTURE OF THE CHANCELLERY

1. Orientation aide-mémoire on history of the BND, April 1968, p. 2. *Der Spiegel* archives.

2. *Daily Express*, August 10th, 1954.

3. Conversation with former BND official; parliamentary commission, stenographic report, 4th session, September 15th, 1948, p. 59.

4. Information from BND circles.

5. Personal file on Max Waibel in *Der Spiegel* archives.

6. Informer's report to the Org 'Ref.: Polish espionage in Baden-Baden' (undated), in private ownership.

7. Information from BND circles; speech in Munich on April 30th, 1968, by Head of Chancellery Office on the occasion of change of President of the BND, p. 3, in *Der Spiegel* archives.

8. Thomas M. Walde: *Intelligence im westdeutschen Regierungssystem*, p. 45; Johannes Erasmus: *Der geheime Nachrichtendienst*, p. 83.

9. Personal file on Hans Globke, in *Der Spiegel* archives.

10. Note by an ex-Major-General of the Abwehr who wishes to remain anonymous.

11. Hans Ulrich Evers: *Privatspäre und Ämter für Verfassungsschutz* p. 80.

12. Walde, op. cit., p. 46; Hans Schäfer: 'Verfassungsschutz im demokratischen Rechtsstaat' in *Verfassungsschutz*, p. 45.

13. Walde, op. cit., p. 46; Evers, op. cit., p. 81; Bundesgesetzblatt (Official Gazette), 1950, p. 682.

14. Walde, op. cit., p. 47.

15. Louis Hagen: *The Secret War for Europe*, pp. 67 et seq.; Otto John: *Zweimal kam ich heim*, pp. 169–212.

16. John, op. cit., pp. 206 et seq.

17. John, op. cit., p. 219; Walde, op. cit., p. 50; Sefton Delmer: *Black Boomerang*, p. 274.

18. *Frankfurter Allgemeine Zeitung*, August 11th, 1954; Hagen, op. cit., pp. 73–4.

19. John, op. cit., p. 233; Hagen, op. cit., p. 75.

20. Walde, op. cit. p. 69; Hans Joa-

chim Schwagerl and Rolf Walther: *Der Schutz der Verfassung*, pp. 66 et seq., 161 et seq.; John, op. cit., pp. 227, 250; Hans Detlev Becker: 'Verfassungsschutz und Spionageabwehr' in *Verfassungsschutz*, p. 143.

21. John, op. cit., p. 243; *Der Spiegel*, No 31 of 1954, p. 8; conversation with Otto John, May 20th, 1970.

22. *Süddeutsche Zeitung*, December 11th, 1956; *Frankfurter Rundschau*, December 11th, 1956.

23. *Der Spiegel*, No 31 of 1954, p. 8; *Süddeutsche Zeitung*, May 27th, 1955.

24. Arnulf Baring: *Aussenpolitik in Adenauers Kanzlerdemokratie*, p. 23; Walde, op. cit., p. 63.

25. Walde, op. cit., p. 63; information from Gerhard Graf von Schwerin, May 18th, 1971; Peter Hoffmann: *Widerstand, Staatsstreich, Attentat*, pp. 345 et seq.

26. Information from Schwerin; Hoffmann, op. cit., pp. 121–5; Walde, op. cit., p. 65.

27. Information from a former member of the BND; Gert Buchheit: *Der deutsche Geheimdienst*, p. 325; Margaret Boveri: *Verrat im XX Jahrhundert*, Vol II, p. 111; *Der Spiegel*, No 47 of 1953, pp. 10 et seq., No 31 of 1954, pp. 8 et seq.

28. Albrecht Charisius and Julius Mader: *Nicht länger geheim*, p. 138; interview with a former member of the Org.

29. *Der Spiegel*, No 47 of 1953, pp. 10 et seq., No 31 of 1954, pp. 8 et seq.; Walde, op. cit., p. 65; *Daily Express*, August 10th, 1954.

30. Walde, op. cit., pp. 67–8

31. *Frankfurter Allgemeine Zeitung*, July 16th, 1963.

32. *Newsweek*, September 12th, 1955; Andrew Tully: *Central Intelligence Agency*, pp. 158–9.

33. German Bundestag shorthand record, 2nd electoral period, 37th session, July 8th, 1954, p. 1734B; Walde, op. cit., pp. 71–2.

34. Hagen, op. cit., pp. 84 et seq.; John, op. cit., p. 278.

35. *Deutsche Woche*, September 1st, 1954.

36. *Deutsche Zeitung*, July 27th, 1955; Walde, op. cit., p. 61.

37. ibid; *Der Spiegel*, No 30 of 1955, p. 7.

38. *Frankgurter Rundschau*, April 25th, 1956.

39. Walde, op. cit., pp. 62, 74.

40. Federal budget for financial year 1956, pp. 786–7.

CHAPTER TEN:
COMMUNIST COUNTERBLAST

1. *Der Staatssicherheitsdienst*, Vol I, pp. 36, 11.

2. Erich Wollenberg: *Der Apparat*, pp. 9, 10, 11.

3. Wilhelm Zaisser's personal and political file, OKP 009, in *Der Spiegel* archives.

4. Wollenberg, op. cit., pp. 13, 29; *Der Staatssicherheitsdienst*, Vol II, p. 10.

5. Wollenberg, op. cit., p. 29; *Der*

Staatssicherheitsdienst, Vol II, p. 8; Munzinger Archiv, Wilhelm Zaisser, April 26th, 1958.

6. Thomas Forster: *NVA*, p. 237; Gert Buchheit: *Der deutsche Geheimdienst*, p. 114; Peter Strassner: *Verräter*, p. 225; Hans Bernd Gisevius: *Bis zum bittern Ende*, Vol I, p. 278 (not in English translation).

7. *Ostprobleme*, April 24th, 1951; *Der*

Staatssicherheitsdienst, Vol II, p. 8; Wollenberg, op. cit., p. 11.

8. Information from the Federal Internal Security Office; Richard Gerken: *Spione unter uns*, pp. 33–5; Arthur Dubin: 'Kommunistische Agentenzentrale Ost-Berlin' in *Amerika-Dienst*, January 12th, 1962.

9. 'Das Mfs'. monograph by an unknown author in *Der Spiegel* archives, p. 34; *Der Staatssicherheitsdienst*, Vol I, pp. 15, 16. SBZ Archives; *Der Staatssicherdienst*, November 20th, 1953, p. 338.

10. Official gazette of the German Democratic Republic, issue 15 of 1950, p. 95; *Der Staatssicherheitsdienst*, Vol I, p. 17; David Dallin: *Soviet Espionage*, pp. 365–6.

11. *Der Staatssicherheitsdienst*, Vol I, p. 63.

12. SBZ Archives, June 25th, 1956. The organizational structure given here is in fact a further development described by Bernard Sagolla in *Die Rote Gestapo*, p. 13.

13. *Der Staatssicherheitsdienst*, Vol I, pp. 25, 31.

14. Ibid, pp. 34, 49, 55.

15. Forster, op. cit., p. 237; Information from Document Centre, Berlin; Sagolla, op. cit., p. 23.

16. Personal files on Heinrich von zur Mühlen and Rainer Hildebrandt in *Der Spiegel* archives; Wolfgang Höher: *Agent 2996 enthüllt*, p. 40.

17. Note by Section IIb of KgU – in KgU files.

18. Letter from Dr Heinrich von zur Mühlen to Federal Ministry for All-German Questions, September 13th, 1951, in KgU files.

19. Scharlau's personal dossier, in KgU files.

20. Letter from von zur Mühlen, p. 6.

21. *Neues Deutschland*, July 26th, 1952; *Dokumentation der Zeit*, No 32 of 1952, pp. 1430–2.

22. Peter Deriabin and Frank Gibney: *The Secret World*, pp. 199, 200.

23. *Rheinischer Merkur*, December 11th, 1953.

24. *Der Staatssicherheitsdienst*, Vol I, pp. 18, 19; Vol II, p. 14.

25. *Die Welt*, November 10th, 1953; *Frankfurter Allgemeine Zeitung*, November 10th, 1953; *Der Spiegel*, No 47 of 1953, pp. 15 et seq.

26. *Der Spiegel*, No 47 of 1953, p. 18.

27. *Stuttgarter Zeitung*, December 30th, 1953; *Frankfurter Allgemeine Zeitung*, November 20th, 1953.

28. *Tägliche Rundschau* and *Neues Deutschland*, November 17th, 1953.

29. *Der Spiegel*, No 47 of 1953, p. 18.

30. *The Times*, November 10th, 1953; *Deutsche Zeitung*, November 14th, 1953; *Süddeutsche Zeitung*, November 10th, 1953.

31. *Frankfurter Allgemeine Zeitung*, November 19th, 1953; *Tägliche Rundschau*, November 17th, December 14th, 22nd, 1953.

32. *Tägliche Rundschau*, December 30th, 1953.

33. *Die Welt*, August 6th, 1954; *Frankfurter Allgemeine Zeitung*, August 6th, 1954; *Neues Deutschland*, August 6th, 1954.

34. *Neue Justiz*, supplement to No 22 of 1954, pp. 3 et seq.; *Tägliche Rundschau*, November 2nd, 1954; *Neue Zürcher Zeitung*, June 25th, 1954; *Der Fortschritt*, October 28th, 1954; *New York Herald Tribune*, October 5th, 1954; *Frankfurter Rundschau*, October 5th, 1954.

35. *Neues Deutschland*, February 22nd, 1955; *Neue Justiz*, No 13 of 1955, pp. 396 et seq.; 'Democratic German Report', May 13th, 1955; Wolfgang Wehner: *Geheim*, p. 204.

36. Information from a refugee administrator of the Liberal-Democrat Party, June 12th, 1970.

CHAPTER ELEVEN:
FRACTURE OF AN AXIS

1. Diary of head of a BND Desk, summer 1958, in private ownership.

2. Information from BND circles.

3. Reports by a BND informer of February 28th and July 2nd, 1962, 'Ref.: H. v O.', in private ownership.

4. Personal file on Siegfried Dombrowski, in *Der Spiegel* archives.

5. 'Exposé on the case of Siegfried Dombrowski, formerly deputy head of the Administration for Coordination of the German Democratic Republic', pp. 3, 4 (note by an unknown author), in *Der Spiegel* archives.

6. Manuscript note by General Linke, March 18th, 1958, in *Der Spiegel* archives.

7. 'Exposé Dombrowski' (see Note 5 above).

8. Ibid, pp. 1, 5.

9. Conversations with BND officials, August 1970.

10. Ibid.

11. *Stern*, No 40 of 1967, p. 182, *Westfälische Rundschau*, August 7th, 1963.

12. Thomas M. Walde: *Intelligence im westdeutschen Regierungssystem*, pp. 79, 83, 162, 163; Hans Joachim Schwagerl and Rolf Walther: *Der Schutz der Verfassung*, p. 80.

13. Conversations with BND officials.

14. Personal file on Hans-Heinrich Worgitzky, in *Der Spiegel* archives.

15. Summarized in 'Nachrichtendienstliche Führungsorientierung', November 20th, 1969, p. 13.

16 Walde, op. cit., pp. 26, 27.

17. Ibid, p. 29.

18. BND orientation aide-mémoire on history of Federal Intelligence Service, April 1968, p. 2, in *Der Spiegel* archives.

19. Erich Dethleffsen: 'Die Aufgabe eines Auslandsnachrichtendienstes' in *Aussenpolitik*, November 1969, p. 656.

20. Conversations with BND officials.

21. Federal budget: for financial year 1956, p. 790; for financial year 1960, p. 197; for financial year 1971, p. 129.

22. Overall situation before construction of the Wall (August 13th, 1961); 'Die Berliner Mauer', memoranda by a BND agency, May 1970.

23. *Der Spiegel*, No 41 of 1962, pp. 42, 43.

24. Walde, op. cit., p. 198.

25. Ibid, pp. 117 et seq.

26. Ibid, pp. 125 et seq.

27. Hans Detlev Becker: 'Zur Vorgeschichte der Spiegel-Affäre', p. 3, *Der Spiegel*, No 39 of 1954.

28. Becker, op. cit., p. 5; Conrad Ahlers: 'Der Hintergrund der Affäre' in *Der Spiegel*, No 22 of 1965, pp. 4 et seq.

29. Becker, op. cit., p. 7.

30. Jürgen Seifert: *Die Spiegel-Affäre*, Vol 1, p. 582.

31. Seifert, op. cit., p. 157; Louis Hagen: *The Secret War for Europe*, p. 255.

32. Becker, op. cit., pp. 5–8.

33. German Bundestag stenographic record, 4th electoral period, 45th session, p. 1982C.

34. *Der Spiegel*, No 22 of 1965, pp. 4–6.

35. Information from BND circles.

36. *Westfälische Rundschau*, November 21st/22nd, 1962; *Frankfurter Allgemeine Zeitung*, November 24th, 1962.

37. Conversation with a BND official.

CHAPTER TWELVE:

THE FELFE AFFAIR; FALL OF THE 'GRAND OLD MAN'

1. Louis Hagen: *The Secret War for Europe*, p. 57; *Der Spiegel*, No 30 of 1963, p. 22; 'Moscow calling Heinz Felfe' (henceforth referred to as 'Moscow calling'), account drafted in the BND for later publication in book form, p. 24.

2. *Frankfurter Rundschau*, July 13th, 1963; *Der Spiegel*, No 30 of 1963, p. 21.

3. 'Moscow calling', pp. 11, 18; *Der Spiegel*, No 30 of 1963, p. 21; personal files on Heinz Felfe, Johannes Clemens and Erwin Tiebel, in *Der Spiegel* archives.

4. *Frankfurter Allgemeine Zeitung*, July 10th, 1963; *Der Spiegel*, No 30 of 1963, p. 23; 'Moscow calling', pp. 41, 42.

5. *Frankfurter Allgemeine Zeitung*, July 10th, 1963; *Der Spiegel*, No 30 of 1963, p. 23; 'Moscow calling', pp. 47 et seq.

6. 'Moscow calling', pp. 47 et seq. Felfe, alias Friesen, first appears in East German publications in Wolfgang Höher: *Agent 2996 enthüllt*, pp. 18, 19. *Tägliche Rundschau*, August 31st, 1954.

7. 'Moscow calling', p. 76; Hendrik van Bergh: *ABC der Spione*, p. 174.

8. 'Moscow calling', p. 94; *Der Spiegel*, No 9 of 1969, p. 76.

9. *Hamburger Abendblatt*, July 10th, 1963; *Der Spiegel*, No 30 of 1963, p. 23; *Die Welt*, July 10th, 1963; *Tagesspiegel*, July 10th, 1963; 'Moscow calling', p. 120.

10. *Frankfurter Allgemeine Zeitung*, July 10th, 1963; 'Moscow calling', p. 161; *Der Spiegel*, No 9 of 1969, p. 23.

11. 'Moscow calling', pp. 105, 111; *Frankfurter Allgemeine Zeitung*, July 10th, 1963.

12. Heinz Höhne: *Codeword: Direktor*, p. xix (footnote); *Abendzeitung*, August 12th, 1959; letter from Friedrich Panzinger to a friend, July 19th, 1963, in *Der Spiegel* archives.

13. *The Times*, July 13th, 1963; *Neue Zürcher Zeitung*, July 19th, 1963; David Wise and Thomas B. Ross: *The Espionage Establishment*, p. 116; E. H. Cookridge: *The Third Man*, p. 128.

14. *Tagesspiegel*, July 5th, 1963; 'Moscow calling', pp. 166–7.

15. *Der Spiegel*, No 9 of 1969, p. 76.

16. Information from BND circles.

17. *Die Welt*, July 24th, 1963; *Nürnberger Nachrichten*, July 12th, 1963; *Stuttgarter Zeitung*, July 12th, 1963; *Frankfurter Allgemeine Zeitung*, July 15th, 1963.

18. Thomas M. Walde: *Intelligence im westdeutschen Regierungssystem*, pp. 129, 130, 76.

19. Walde, op. cit., p. 152; Johannes Gross: *Die Deutschen*, p. 108; *Stern*, No 31 of 1964, p. 80.

20. Diary of a deceased BND official, in private ownership.

21. *Frankfurter Allgemeine Zeitung*, August 12th, 1965; *Neue Zürcher Zeitung*, March 6th, 1965; Steve Eytan: *Das Auge Davids*, p. 118; *Stern*, No 32 (pp. 24 et seq.), 34–6 of 1970.

22. *Süddeutsche Zeitung*, March 8th, 1965; *Frankfurter Allgemeine Zeitung*, March 30th, 1965; *Die Welt*, March 30th, 1965; information from BND circles.

23. *Der Spiegel*, No 52 of 1969, p. 144.

24. Conversation with Richard Christmann on April 1st, 1969; Christmann resigned from the BND on June 15th, 1961, and severed all connexion with Pullach; he was nevertheless arrested in

Algeria in 1965 on suspicion of being a BND agent; Personal report on Ulrich Klitschke, November 14th, 1968, in *Der Spiegel* archives.

25. Information from BND circles.

26. 'Middle East crisis 1967', summary by a BND agency, in *Der Spiegel* archives.

27. Personal file on Horst Wendland, in *Der Spiegel* archives.

28. Walde, op. cit., p. 149.

29. Ibid, pp. 149, 150.

30. Personal file on Gerhard Wessel, in *Der Spiegel* archives.

31. *Industriekurier*, November 9th, 1968.

32. *Süddeutsche Zeitung*, October 12th, 1968.

33. Information from BND circles.

34. *Süddeutsche Zeitung*, May 2nd, 1968; speech in Munich on April 30th, 1968, by Head of Chancellery Office on the occasion of change of President of the BND, p. 4.

CHAPTER THIRTEEN:
CRISIS IN THE BND

1. Speech by Gerhard Wessel in Pullach, May 5th, 1970; Chancellery Office.

2. Information from BND circles.

3. *Die Welt*, October 10th, 1968; *Stuttgarter Zeitung*, October 11th, 1968; *Der Spiegel*, No 42 of 1968, pp. 73, 74.

4. *Der Spiegel*, No 45 of 1968, p. 28.

5. *Weltwoche*, November 8th, 1968; *Der Spiegel*, No 45 of 1968, pp. 27–32.

6. *Der Spiegel*, No 45 of 1968, pp. 27, 31, 32; Wessel's speech, May 5th, 1970.

8. Harry Howe Ransom: *The Intelligence Establishment*, p. 19.

9. *Die Welt*, December 4th and 7th, 1968; *Hamburger Abendblatt*, December 9th, 1968; *Der Spiegel*, No 50 of 1968, p. 62 and No 51, p. 52; *Die Zeit*, December 20th, 1968.

10. Jörg Lolland: 'Wie wird man Spion?' in German television broadcast, February 3rd, 1970.

11. *Münchner Merkur*, January 17th, 1968.

12. *Bayernkurier*, November 23rd, 1968; *West am Sonntag*, November 24th, 1968.

13. German Bundestag shorthand record, 2nd electoral period, 99th session, p. 5545; Thomas M. Walde: *Intelligence im westdeutschen Regierungssystem*, p. 210.

14. *Frankfurter Allgemeine Zeitung*, November 8th, 1966.

15. Information from a BND official.

16. *Der Spiegel*, No 36 of 1968, pp. 82–6; No 15 of 1969, pp. 101 et seq.

17. 'High-level Intelligence Guide', November 20th, 1969, p. 2.

18. Speech by Horst Ehmke in Pullach, May 5th, 1970; Chancellery Office.

19. Information from BND circles.

20. *Exclusiv-Dienst*, No 7 of 1970, February 17th, 1970.

21. *Hamburger Morgenpost*, March 28th, 1970; *Die Zeit*, April 3rd, 1970; *Christ und Welt*, April 10th, 1970.

22. Information from BND circles.

23. Speeches by Gerhard Wessel and Horst Ehmke (p. 3), May 5th, 1970.

24. Information from BND circles.

25. Ibid.

26. Ibid.

27. *Welt am Sonntag*, December 20th, 1970.

28. Ransom, op. cit., p. 44.

APPENDIX A:

THE CHEQUERED HISTORY OF GERMAN ESPIONAGE

1. Walter Görlitz: *The German General Staff*, pp. 50 et seq.

2. Ulrich Liss: *Westfront 1939/40*, pp. 14 et seq.

3. Manfred Kehrig: *Die Wiedereinrichtung des deutschen militärischen Attachédienstes nach dem ersten Weltkrieg*, pp. 3, 4, 5, 8, 9.

4. Alfred Graf von Waldersee: *Denkwürdigkeiten*, pp. 24, 53, 54.

5. Wilhelm Strieber: *Denkwürdigkeiten*, pp. 1 et seq., 9 et seq., 191 et seq., 216 et seq.; Walter Horn: 'Abwehrspionage in der Ära Bismarck's' in *Die Weltkriegsspionage*, p. 560.

6. Stieber, op. cit., pp. 222 et seq.; Horn, op. cit., p. 560; Friedrich Gempp: *Geheimer Nachrichtendienst und Spionageabwehr des Heeres*, Vol I, p. 1.

7. Steiber, op. cit., pp. 239 et seq.

8. Gempp, op. cit., Vol I, pp. 2, 3, 4; Waldersee, op. cit., p. 10.

9. Stieber, op. cit., p. 253; *American People's Encyclopaedia*, Vol VII, p. 301.

10. Waldersee, op. cit., Vol I, p. 95.

11. Stieber, op. cit., pp. 303 et seq.; Gempp, op. cit., Vol I, p. 12.

12. Gempp, op. cit., Vol I, p. 17.

13. Kehrig, op. cit., p. 5; Gempp, op. cit., Vol I, p. 21.

14. Gempp, op. cit., Vol I, pp. 281, 28, 29, 32.

15. Gempp, op. cit., p. 260.

16. Ibid, pp. 37 et seq. 263, 41.

17. Ibid, pp. 283, 285.

18. Ibid, pp. 74, 75, 76, 77.

19. Walter Nicolai: *Geheime Mächte*, pp. 15, 16, 17; Munzinger Archiv: 'Walter Nicolai', July 22nd, 1948.

20. Gempp, op. cit., Vol I, p. 77; Nicolai, op. cit., p. 20.

21. Gempp, op. cit., Vol I, pp. 78, 79, 86a, 90, 103.

22. Ulrich Liss: 'Der Nachrichtendienst in den Grenzschlachten im Westen im August 1914' in *Wehrwissenschaftliche Rundschau*, March 1962, p. 142.

23. Sir Basil Liddell Hart: *Strategy*, pp. 175–6; Sir Kenneth Strong: *Men of Intelligence*, pp. 11 et seq.

24. Gempp, op. cit., Vol VII, pp. 62, 101, 102, 103, 113, 121, 122, 152, 154, 159.

25. Ibid, Vol X, p. 71; Vol VII, pp. 127–30.

26. Ibid, Vol. X, pp. 3, 4.

27. Ibid, Vol X, p. 4; Vol VII, pp. 30 et seq., 119.

28. Ibid, Vol VII, pp. 73 et seq.; Vol X, pp. 47, 48, 49.

29. Gerhard Ritter: *Staatskunst und Kriegshandwerk*, Vol IV, pp. 162, 457, 473, 544; *Weltbühne*, July 29th, 1920, pp. 137, 140

30. Walter Nicolai: *Nachrichtendienst, Presse und Volksstimmung im Weltkrieg*, p. 147; Gempp, op. cit., Vol VIII, p. 166.

31. Eugen Ernst: *Polizeispitzeleien und Ausnahmegesetzen;* Hans Buchheim: 'The SS – Instrument of Domination' in *Anatomy of the SS State*, pp. 144–5.

32. Albrecht Charisius and Julius Mader: *Nicht länger geheim*, p. 78.

33. Ibid, p. 80; Paul Leverkuehn: *Der geheime Nachrichtendienst der Wehrmacht im Kriege*, p. 9; Will Grosse: 'Geheimdienst, Fahneneid und Hakenkreuz' in *Echo der Woche*, February 24th, 1950.

34. Kehrig, op. cit., pp. 38 et seq.; Liss: *Westfront*, pp. 16 et seq.; Buchheit: *Der deutsche Geheimdienst*, pp. 33, 34.

35. Buchheit, op. cit., pp. 36, 38, 40.

36. Leverkuehn, op. cit. p. 10; Buchheit, op. cit., p. 40.

37. Buchheim, op. cit., p. 145; Heinz Höhne: *Codeword: Direktor*, p. 18.

38. Shlomo Aronson: *Heydrich und die Anfänge des SD und der Gestapo*, pp. 95 et seq., 255–318.

39. Aronson, op. cit., pp. 25–58.

40. Heinz Höhne: *The Order of the Death's Head*, pp. 161 et seq.

41. Aide-mémoire on interview with Admiral (retd) Conrad Patzig, January 18th/19th, 1966, pp. 4–5, Military History Research Unit, Document Centre, Freiburg.

42. Buchheit, op. cit., pp. 52–63; Höhne: *The Order of the Death's Head*, p. 229.

43. Werner Best: *Die deutsche Abwehrpolizei bis 1945*, pp. 19 et seq.

44. Leverkuehn, op. cit., p. 11.

45. Karl Heinz Abshagen: *Canaris*, pp. 155 et seq.

46. Buchheim, op. cit., pp. 166 et seq.

47. Aronson, op. cit., pp. 82 et seq.

48. Hans Buchheim: *SS und Polizei im NS-Staat*, pp. 62–3; note by Schellenberg April 4th, 1939 – National Archives Washington, microfilm T-175/239.

49. Walter Schellenberg: *The Schellenberg Memoirs*, pp. 24–8; Aronson, op. cit., pp. 281 et seq.; memorandum by Schellenberg February 24th, 1939 'Reorganization of the Security Service of the Reichsführer-SS'. National Archives, microfilm T-175/239; Buchheim: *Die SS*, p. 76.

50. 'Abwehr/Gestapo division of duties', extracts from undated memorandum (approx 1935) in National Archives microfilm T-175/403; Werner Best: 'Wilhelm Canaris', p. 6, in Best's private papers.

51. Stieber, op. cit., pp. 217 et seq.; Gempp, op. cit., Vol X, p. 109; Erich Wollenberg: *Der Apparat*, p. 10.

52. Lev Bezymenski: *Operation Barbarossa*, p. 245.

53. Gempp, op cit., Vol X, pp. 110 et seq.; Francis L. Carsten: *Reichswehr und Politik*, pp. 306 et seq.

54. Julius Mader: *Die graue Hand*, pp. 158 et seq., 200; F. A. Krummacher and Helmut Lange: *Krieg und Frieden*, p. 338 et seq.; 'Das Wannseeinstitut', note by ex-member, in *Der Spiegel* archives.

55. Liss: *Westfront*, p. 17; War staffing table of FHO, November 1st, 1939, National Archives, Washington, microfilm T-78.

56. Eberhard Kinzel's personal file in *Der Spiegel* archives; Kehrig, op. cit., p. 225.

57. Letter from Goth, May 4th, 1940, National Archives T-78/488.

58. Buchheit, op. cit., p. 254.

59. Messages and reports in FHO files, summer 1940 – National Archives T-78/488.

60. Halder's diary, Vol I, p. 290; Bezymenski, op. cit., pp. 248–9, 246; Georgi K. Zhukov: *Memoirs*, p. 216; appreciation of enemy situation June 1941 – National Archives T-78/479.

61. Bezymenski, op. cit., p. 253.

BIBLIOGRAPHY

BIBLIOGRAPHY

I. *Unpublished Sources*

Baun, Hermann: Diaries. In private ownership.

Best, Werner: 'Wilhelm Canaris.' Notes dated April 10th, 1949, in Best's private papers.

Best, Werner: 'Die deutsche Abwehrpolizei bis 1945', in Best's private papers.

'Fall Brutus', memorandum by the Gehlen Org, 1954.

Files of the KgU ('Anti-inhumanity Combat Group').

Files of OKH (High Command of the German Army). Microfilms Group T-78 in National Archives, Washington.

Files of OKW (High Command of the German Armed Forces). Microfilms Group T-77 in National Archives, Washington.

Files of the Personal Staff of the Reichsführer-SS and Chief of the German Police (Himmler). Microfilms Group T-175 in National Archives, Washington.

Gemp, Friedrich: 'Geheimer Nachrichtendienst und Spionageabwehr des Heeres', Thesis for Reich War Ministry Intelligence Division or OKW Ausland/Abwehr, 1939–43. Microfilms ML 68 and T-77/1440 in National Archives, Washington.

Herre, Heinz Danko: Diary. In Institut für Zeitgeschichte, Munich.

Informers' reports from various agencies of the Gehlen Organization and the BND, in private ownership.

Jungk, Wilhelm: *Die Aktion Hermes,* in Jungk's private papers.

Möller-Witten, Hanns: 'General Gehlen', in *Der Spiegel* archives.

'Moskau ruft Heinz Felfe', unpublished book by the BND.

Papers from the BND and Federal Chancellery office.

Rittlinger, Herbert: 'Ultima Thule', unpublished manuscript.

Tolmein, Horst Günter: 'Der Aufstand beginnt 17.50 Uhr', in *Der Spiegel* archives.

Walde, Thomas, M.: 'Intelligence im westdeutschen Regierungssystem', unpublished manuscript, Hamburg 1970.

Wicht, Adolf: 'Auszug aus meinem Tagebuch der Kriegsgefangenschaft,' in Wicht's private papers.

II. *Published Sources*

Abshagen, Karl Heinz: *Canaris*, Union Deutsche Verlagsgesellschaft, Stuttgart, 1950; *Canaris*, translated A. H. Brodrick, Hutchinsons, London, 1956.

Aronson, Shlomo: *Heydrich und die Anfänge des SD und der Gestapo (1931–35)*, Dissertation of Faculty of Philosophy in the Free University of Berlin, 1967.

Bachmann, Günter: 'Das Bundeskanzleramt' in *Die Staatskanzlei–Aufgaben, Organisation und Arbeitsweise auf vergleichender Grundlage*, Berlin, 1967.

Baring, Arnulf: *Aussenpolitik in Adenauers Kanzlerdemokratie*, Oldenbourg, Munich, 1969.

Bergh, Hendrik van: *A B C der Spione*, Ilmgau, Pfaffenhofen/Ilm, 1965.

Bezymenski, Lev: *Sonderakte Barbarossa*, Deutsche Verlagsanstalt, Stuttgart, 1968.

Boveri, Margaret: *Der Verrat im XX Jahrhundert*, Vol II, Rowohlt, Hamburg, 1957.

Buchheim, Hans: *SS und Polizei im NS-Staat*, Selbstverlag der Studiengesellschaft für Zeitprobleme, Duisdorf bei Bonn, 1964.

Buchheim, Hans: 'Die SS, Herrschaftsinstrument', and 'Befehl und Gehorsam' in *Anatomie des SS-Staates*, Vol I, Walter, Olten, 1965; 'The SS, Instrument of Domination' and 'Command and Compliance', translated Richard Barry, in *Anatomy of the SS State*, Collins, London, 1968.

Buchheit, Gert: *Der deutsche Geheimdienst*, List, Munich, 1966.

Buchheit, Gert: *Die anonyme Macht*, Athenäum, Frankfurt, 1969.

Carell, Paul: *Verbrannte Erde*, Ullstein, Berlin, 1966.

Carsten, Francis L.: *Reichswehr und Politik 1918–1933*, Kiepenheuer & Witsch, Köln, 1965.

Cookridge, E. H.: 'The Spy of the Century' in *Daily Telegraph Magazine*, Nos 230–32, March 7th–12th, 1969.

Cookridge, E. H.: *The Third Man*, Arthur Barker, London, 1968.

Dallin, Alexander: *German Rule in Russia*, Macmillan, London, 1957.

Dallin, David J.: *Soviet Espionage*, Yale University Press, New Haven; Geoffrey Cumberledge, OUP, London, 1956.

Deane, John R.: *Ein seltsames Bündnis*, Neue Welt, Vienna, 1946.

Delarue, Jacques: *Histoire de la Gestapo*, Fagard, Paris, 1962: *History of the Gestapo*, translated Mervyn Savill, Macdonald, London, 1964.

Delmer, Sefton: *Black Boomerang*, Secker & Warburg, London, 1962.

Deriabin, Peter & Gibney, Frank: *The Secret World*, Doubleday, New York & Arthur Barker, London, 1959.

Dethleffsen, Erich: 'Die Aufgabe eines Auslandsnachrichtendienstes' in *Aussenpolitik*, November 1969, pp. 655–60.

Dönhoff, Marion Gräfin: 'Der Mann ohne Gesicht' in *Zeit*, No 17, April 26th, 1968.

Dulles, Allen, and Gaevernitz, Gero von: *The Secret Surrender*, Weidenfeld & Nicolson, London, 1967.

Erasmus, Johannes: *Der Geheime Nachrichtendienst*, Musterschmidt Verlag, Göttingen, 1952.

Evers, Hans-Ulrich: *Privatsphäre und Ämter für Verfassungsschutz*, Walter de Gruyter, Berlin, 1960.

Eytan, Steve: *Das Auge Davids*, Molden, Vienna, 1970.

Farago, Ladislas: *Burn After Reading*, Walker & Co, New York, 1962.

Federal (West German) Budget for financial years 1956–71.

Forster, Thomas M.: *NVA. Die Armee der Sowjetzone*, Markus, Köln, 1964.

Gehlen, Reinhard: *Der Dienst*, von Hase & Koehler, Mainz & Wiesbaden, 1971 (English language edition, *The Gehlen Memoirs*, Collins, London, 1972).

Gerken, Richard: *Spione unter uns*, Ludwig Auer, Donauwörth, 1965.

Gisevius, Hans Bernd: *Bis zum bitteren Ende*, Vol I, Classen & Goverts, Hamburg, 1947; *To the Bitter End*, translated Richard and Clara Winston, Jonathan Cape, London, 1948.

Görlitz, Walter: *Der deutsche Generalstab*, Verlag der Frankfurter Hefte, Frankfurt, 1953; *The German General Staff*, translated Brian Battershaw, Hollis & Carter, London, 1953.

Görlitz, Walter: *Kleine Geschichte des deutschen Generalstabes*, Haude & Spenersche Verlagsbuchhandlung, Berlin, 1967.

Gramont, Sanche de: *Der geheime Krieg*, Paul Neff, Vienna, 1963.

Groscurth, Helmuth: *Tagebücher eines Abwehroffiziers 1938–40*, Deutsche Verlagsanstalt, Stuttgart, 1970.

Gross, Johannes: *Die Deutschen*, Heinrich Scheffler, Frankfurt, 1967.

Grosse, Will: 'Geheimdienst, Fahneneid und Hakenkreuz' in *Echo der Woche*, February 7th–June 9th, 1950.

Guderian, Heinz: *Erinnerungen eines Soldaten*, Vowinckel, Heidelberg, 1951; *Panzer Leader*, translated Constantine Fitzgibbon, Michael Joseph, London, 1952.

Guérin, Alain: *Le Général Gris*, Julliard, Paris, 1968.

Hagen, Louis: *The Secret War for Europe*, Macdonald, London, 1968.

Hagen, Walter (Hoettl, Willi): *Die geheime Front*, Nibelungen Verlag, Linz, 1950; *The Secret Front*, translated R. H. Stevens, Weidenfeld & Nicolson, London, 1953.

Halder, Franz: *Kriegstagebuch 1939–42*, three Vols, W. Kohlhammer, Stuttgart, 1962–4.

Halle, Louis J.: *The Cold War as History*, Chatto & Windus, London, 1967.

Höher, Wolfgang: *Agent 2996 enthüllt*, Kongress Verlag, Berlin, 1954.

Höhne, Heinz: *Der Orden unter dem Totenkopf*, Sigbert Mohn, Gütersloh, 1967; *The Order of the Death's Head*, translated Richard Barry, Secker & Warburg, London, 1969 and Pan Books, 1972.

Höhne, Heinz: *Kennwort: Didektor*, S. Fischer, Frankfurt, 1970; *Codeword: Direktor*, translated Richard Barry, Secker & Warburg, London, 1971.

Hoffmann, Peter: *Widerstand, Staatsstreich, Attentat,* Piper Verlag, Munich, 1969.

John, Otto: *Zweimal kam ich heim,* Econ Verlag, Düsseldorf, 1969 (English language edition, *Twice Through the Lines,* Macmillan, London, 1972.

Kehrig, Manfred: 'Die Wiedereinrichtung des deutschen militärischen Attachédienstes nach dem Ersten Weltkrieg' in *Wehrwissenschaftliche Forschungen,* Section *Militärgeschichtliche Studien,* Vol II, Harald Boldt, Boppard, 1966.

Kriegstagebuch des Oberkommandos der Wehrmacht [OKW War Diary], edited by Andreas Hillgruber, Vol II, Bernard & Graefe, Frankfurt, 1963.

Krummacher, F. A. & Lange, Helmut: *Krieg und Frieden,* Bechtle, Munich, 1970.

Leverkuehn, Paul: *Der geheime Nachrichtendienst der Wehrmacht im Kriege,* Athenäum Verlag, Frankfurt, 1964.

Liddell Hart, Sir B. H.: *Strategy,* Faber & Faber, London, 1967.

Liss, Ulrich: *Westfront 1939/40,* Kurt Vowinckel, Neckargemünd, 1959.

Liss, Ulrich: 'Der Nachrichtendienst in den Grenzschlachten im Westen im August 1914' in *Wehrwissenschaftliche Rundschau,* March 1962, pp. 140–60.

Mader, Julius: *Die graue Hand,* Kongress-Verlag, Berlin, 1960.

Mader, Julius & Charisius, Albrecht: *Nicht länger geheim,* Deutscher Militär-Verlag, Berlin, 1969.

Müller, Klaus-Jürgen: *Das Heer und Hitler,* Deutscher Verlagsanstalt, Stuttgart, 1969.

Müller-Hillebrand, Burkhart: *Das Heer 1933–45,* Vol I (*Das Heer bis zum Kriegsbeginn*) Mittler & Sohn, Darmstadt, 1954; Vol 2 (*Die Blitzfeldzüge*) 1956; Vol 3 (*Der Zweifrontenkrieg*), 1969.

Murawski, Erich: *Der deutsche Wehrmachtsbericht 1939–1945,* Harald Boldt, Boppard, 1962.

Nicolai, Walter: *Nachrichtendienst, Presse and Volksstimmung im Weltkrieg,* Mittler & Sohn, Berlin, 1920.

Nicolai, Walter: *Geheime Mächte,* Koehler Verlag, Leipzig, 1925.

Platt, Washington: *Strategic Intelligence Production,* Frederick A. Praeger, New York, 1962.

Pritzel, Konstantin: *Die Wirtschaftsintegration Mitteldeutschlands,* Wissenschaft und Politik, Köln, 1969.

Ransom, Harry Howe: *The Intelligence Establishment,* Harvard University Press, Cambridge, Massachusetts, 1970.

Reile, Oscar: *Geheime Ostfront,* Welsermühl, Munich, 1963.

Ritter, Gerhard: *Staatskunst und Kriegshandwerk,* Vol IV, Oldenbourg, Munich, 1968.

Ruland, Bernd: *Krieg auf leisen Sohlen,* Goverts, Stuttgart, 1971.

Ryan, Cornelius: *The Last Battle,* Simon & Schuster, New York; Collins, London, 1966.

Sagolla, Bernard: *Die Rote Gestapo*, published by the KgU, Berlin, 1952.

Seabury, Paul: *The Wilhelmstrasse*, University of California Press, Berkeley & Los Angeles, 1954.

Seifert, Jürgen & Grosser, Alfred: *Die Staatsmacht und ihre Kontrolle. Die Spiegel-Affäre*, Walter, Olten, 1966.

Schellenberg, Walter: *Memoiren*, Politik und Wirtschaft, Köln, 1956; *The Schellenberg Memoirs*, translated Louis Hagen, André Deutsch, London, 1961.

Schlierbach, Helmut: 'Die politische Polizei in Preussen' in *Universitas-Archiv*, Vol 96, *Rechtswissenschaftliche Abteilung*, Vol 23, Lechte, Emsdetten, 1938.

Schwagerl, Joachim & Walther, Rolf: *Der Schutz der Verfassung*, Carl Heymann, Köln, 1968.

Der Staatssicherheitsdienst – Vol 1 issued by Federal Ministry for All-German Questions, Bonn & Berlin, 1962, Vol 2 issued by Investigating Commission of Liberal Lawyers, Berlin, no date.

Steenberg, Sven: *Vlassov*, Wissenschaft und Politik, Köln, 1968.

Stieber, Wilhelm: *Denkwürdigkeiten des Geheimen Regierungsrathes*, Julius Engelmann, Berlin, 1884.

Strassner, Peter: *Verräter, Das Nationalkomitee 'Freies Deutschland'* – *Keimzelle der sog. DDR*, Schild, Munich, 1960.

Strik-Strikfeldt, Wilfried: *Gegen Hitler und Stalin*, von Hase & Koehler, Mainz, 1970; *Against Hitler and Stalin*, translated David Footman, Macmillan, London, 1970.

Strong, Sir Kenneth: *Men of Intelligence*, Cassell, London, 1970.

Strong, Sir Kenneth: *Intelligence at the Top*, Cassell, London, 1968.

Thayer, Charles W.: *Diplomat*, Harper Bros., New York, 1959.

Thorwald Jürgen: *Wen sie verderben wollen*, Steingrüben Verlag, Stuttgart, 1952.

Thorwald, Jürgen: 'Der Mann im Dunkeln' in *Welt am Sonntag*, November 13th, 1955, to January 1st, 1956.

Thorwald, Jürgen: *Die grosse Flucht*, Steingrüben Verlag, Stuttgart, no date.

Tully, Andrew: *Central Intelligence Agency*, Arthur Barker, London, 1962.

Verfassungsschutz – *Beiträge aus Wissenschaft und Praxis*, issued by Federal Ministry of Interior, Heymann, Köln, 1966.

Vormann, Nikolaus von: *Der Feldzug 1939 in Polen*, Prinz-Eugen, Weissenburg, 1958.

Waldersee, Alfred Graf von: *Denkwürdigkeiten des General-Feldmarschalls*, Deutsche Verlagsanstalt, Stuttgart, 1922.

Wehner, Wolfgang: *Geheim*, Süddeutscher Verlag, Munich, 1960.

Wighton, Charles: *The World's Greatest Spies*, Odhams Press, London, 1962.

Wilmot, Chester: *The Struggle for Europe*, Collins, London, 1952.

Wise, David, and Ross, Thomas B.: *The Espionage Establishment*, Random House, New York, 1967.

Wollenberg, Erich: *Der Apparat*, Ruhrländische Druckerei, Essen, 1950.

Zhukov, Georgi K.: *Erinnerungen und Gedanken*, Deutsche Verlagsanstalt, Stuttgart, 1969.

INDEX

INDEX

General War Stories

History and Biography

General Titles and World Affairs

These and other PAN Books are obtainable from all booksellers and newsagents. If you have any difficulty please send purchase price plus 7p postage to PO Box 11, Falmouth, Cornwall.

While every effort is made to keep prices low, it is sometimes necessary to increase prices at short notice. PAN Books reserve the right to show new retail prices on covers which may differ from those advertised in the text or elsewhere.